The Good Writer's Guide

(tell your story)

Program Author

Gretchen Bernabei

 NATIONAL GEOGRAPHIC

 Hampton-Brown

Acknowledgments

Within this collection of strategies resides the work of hundreds of teachers and students from all over the world, products of the work of their teachers and their teachers. While it is impossible to thank every one of these by name, there are special individuals who have directly contributed to the philosophies and practices in this program.

Thank you to Cathy McFeaters, Cynthia Peña, Laura Lott, Laura Gunn, Amy Stengal, Dottie Hall, Tracy Winstead, Jeff Anderson, and Jayne Hover, public school teachers who have shared countless conversations with me about experiments and discoveries in our classrooms, exchanging ideas and results with gusto and delight.

Thank you to Linda Stubbs whose experiments and discoveries with the target lesson have provided us all with a perfect-fit strategy for some students who despair of ever fitting.

Thank you most of all to Barry Lane, who has not only shared classroom tools like snapshots and thoughtshots, but has devoted his adult life to modeling and supporting, from the easiest part—adding resources to our students' arsenals or tool belts; through the work—building daily in our students the muscles with which to hoist up these tools and wield them expertly; and into the magic—breathing into our lessons the spirit of curiosity, passion, humor, and greatest of all, compassion.

Finally, thank you to the wonderful and memorable students who have been willing to speak, listen, write, and play with ideas. A list of student contributors appears on pages 548–549.

Appreciation

The Publisher gratefully acknowledges that ideas for the following lessons in this book have previously appeared in other works by Gretchen Bernabei and/or Barry Lane:

- Truths, Idea Organizers, and Kernel Essays (pages 218–225), Ba-Da-Bings! (pages 232–233), and Throwaway Writing (pages 256–257) are based on ideas in **Reviving the Essay** © 2005 by Gretchen Bernabei and published by Discover Writing Press.

- Get Into an Argument and Ways You Know Things (pages 226–231) are based on ideas in **Why We Must Run with Scissors** © 2001 by Gretchen Bernabei and Barry Lane and published by Discover Writing Press.

- Snapshots and Thoughtshots (pages 244–245), and Zero In on a Moment (pages 252–253) are based on ideas in **The Reviser's Toolbox** © 1999 by Barry Lane and published by Discover Writing Press.

Gretchen Bernabei and Barry Lane present open-enrollment seminars nationwide, and are available for inservice workshops with students and teachers. For more information, contact:

Discover Writing Press
1-800-613-8055
www.discoverwriting.com

Cover photo by Liz Garza Williams.

Acknowledgments continue on page 550.

National Geographic School Publishing
Hampton-Brown
P.O. Box 223220
Carmel, California 93922
800-333-3510
www.NGSP.com

Printed in the United States of America

Hardcover:
ISBN 10: 0-7362-3399-7
ISBN 13: 978-0-7362-3399-6

Softcover:
ISBN 10: 0-7362-3375-X
ISBN 13: 978-0-7362-3375-0

08 09 10 11 12 13 14 15 9 8 7 6 5 4 3 2

Contents

Trade Secrets of a Writer

featuring **Gary Soto**

The Writing Process

What Makes Good Writing Good?

featuring **Julius Lester**

Troubleshooting Tips

*featuring **Marian Haddad***

What You Can Do . . .

The Many Writers You Are

featuring **David Yoo**

Writing for Real 276

A Matter of Facts

featuring **Barbara Kingsolver**

Research and Writing

Author Essay

In Love with the Details: Researching The Poisonwood Bible
by Barbara Kingsolver

Gather Information

Organize And Digest Information

Present Information

Trade Secrets of a Writer

featuring **Gary Soto**

"**I** kick-started my latest novel in my mind with a few scenes sketched on paper, and with floating notes and pictures in my head. I wasn't certain of the direction."

The Writing Process

Writing is like anything else—if you want it to be good, you have to work on it. And there's a process involved: some things you do first; some things you do later.

Writers don't just sit down and write a book in a few hours. They follow a process to make their writing the best it can be. The writing process usually involves five stages: prewriting, drafting, revising, editing and proofreading, and publishing. These stages are explained in more detail on page 15. On pages 13–14, Gary Soto describes his process for planning and drafting *Mercy on These Teenage Chimps*, his novel about a pair of teenage guys who look like chimpanzees.

Pulling Strings:
How I Wrote *Mercy on These Teenage Chimps*

I knew that I needed to use the boys' problem to create drama and, aside from their chimp looks, I had to have a story with twists and turns—think plot—to make the reader turn the pages. Here's what I imagined: Joey, an athletic boy who is

5 a star wrestler and able to climb great heights with ease, is attracted to a girl at the annual sports awards ceremony. He becomes dreamy-eyed. His twitching ears and chimp grin are a dead giveaway. *But how could I get her attention?* Joey wonders.

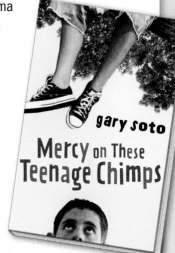

10 As the novelist, I pull strings. I make characters come and go, change scenes, slow or quicken the story's pace, add dialogue, get rid of dialogue, and so on. And this is what I did to write about the awards ceremony. I pulled my strings and watched Joey demonstrate his courage. He gets his chance when the balloon the

15 girl is holding floats to the rafters. Quickly, Joey scampers up the side of the wall and retrieves it. The boy is gifted! But on the way down, he is scolded by Coach. Insulted and hurt when Coach calls him a monkey, Joey storms out of the gymnasium. He mutters that since he's a so-called monkey, he will live in a tree!

20 And that's where he goes—to a tree in front of his house.

Though I never make lengthy notes to plan out my stories, I felt confident that this story had its own thrust once the novel was set up in my mind. I knew that Joey would sulk in the tree and swear never to come down, though, of course, he does. He climbs the tree on Friday and descends on

25 Sunday in time for a bath and school on Monday.

How I Wrote *Mercy on These Teenage Chimps*, continued

And who brings him down? His friend, Ronnie, who is loyal beyond words. Ronnie realizes that the only thing that can make Joey climb down is the girl who rocked him on his heels in the first place. Ronnie's mission in the novel is to fetch her.

30 I didn't monkey around writing these quickly paced chapters, twelve in all. I had a natural chimp grin on my face——I enjoyed getting to know these two furry buddies of mine. I enjoyed the writing experience. I recall the 33 days it took to write this novel and the private checklist I kept:

1) write no more than four hours a day;

35 2) keep a dictionary at my side;

3) report what I'd written each day to my wife (a second reader is very helpful), and

4) abide by the rules of strong creative writing—— descriptive scenery is high on my list.

40 By the way, I first featured these characters, Ronnie and Joey, in an unpublished short story from 1976. As with some of our friends, we can lose touch with fictional characters, but then they can come back more mature, more interesting, and ready to tell their stories.

Stages of the Writing Process

Here's a closer look at the stages of the writing process, which you can read about in this chapter. Not all writers follow this process in exactly the same way, but most writers practice some version of it.

▶ *PREWRITING:* Get Ready to Write

Prewriting is what you do before you write. You choose a topic, think about what to say, and develop a plan. Plan your writing in any way that works for you—notes, an outline, or even drawings.

▶ *DRAFTING:* Get It Down on Paper

The next step might be the hardest—getting that first draft down. But it can also be the most exciting. Remember, your first draft doesn't have to be perfect. You can go back and make changes later, so relax and let yourself enjoy the work.

▶ *REVISING:* Get It to Sing

After you finish your draft, put it aside for a while. Then you can come back to it with a fresh perspective. You might end up making major changes! You might reorganize an essay or add new ideas. Try showing your work to someone else, too, and ask for feedback.

▶ *EDITING AND PROOFREADING:* Get It Right

Once you've made the big changes, work on perfecting the details. You might correct your sentences or fix mistakes in grammar, spelling, or punctuation.

▶ *PUBLISHING:* Get It Out There

Do you want other people to read your work? Then publish it! Writers can share their work in newspapers, magazines, and books. More and more writers choose to publish on the Internet, too. And sharing your writing with your family, friends, and classmates is another form of publishing.

hbgoodwriters.com

Find addresses of publishers who may be interested in publishing your work.

Get Ready to Write

If you were invited to a costume party, who would you go as? Viking warrior? Pop-music diva? Popular action star? There are many choices. You would pick one and then start planning your costume. Prewriting is like that. Choose an idea and plan the best way to impress your readers.

How Do Writers Get Started?

"**F**or me, the joy of being a writer is to take things I see and hear and then rearrange them. I like to tamper with reality and create new possibilities."

There are so many things to write about, how do you get started? Try these tips:

- Collect a lot of ideas—pictures, quotes and notes, objects that matter to you. Go to this "idea file" and you'll always find something to write about.

- Think about why you're writing and who will read your work.

- Choose the kind of writing that fits what you want to say. Maybe it's a story, a letter, a speech, or a bumper sticker.

- Plan how you will organize your ideas.

FOCUS POINT Page 17 shows a clam-shell ornament belonging to Gary Soto. The memory of a similar ornament from his childhood inspired Soto's poem "Waterwheel." What objects from your childhood bring up strong memories for you?

WATERWHEEL

I sat with slivers of foxtails in each sock
And a stick that stirred rainwater,
Gush of a cloud that passed over our house.
I was five, and it was five in the afternoon,
Spring I guess. The mailman had come and gone
On his bicycle, his pants gnashed in the oily chain.
The diesels had stopped. The whistle at Sun-Maid Raisin
Had cleared the air. Men the color of sparrows
And swinging their lunch pails like lanterns.
I was coming alive. Sure, I was cold,
And my shoes were curled. Sure, my hair was wet
And I was beginning to shiver. But I was waiting
For Arnold, a boy up the alley. He promised
Me the Chinese garden in a clam shell —
Waterwheel, bridge, and a woman with a fan,
Quiet beauty on a street stomped all night by machinery.
I waited with rain on my eyelashes.
Fortune was mine. After all, hadn't I raced my bicycle
Under a moving diesel? Hadn't I pushed myself
Hand over fist on the telephone wire?
I waited for the Chinese garden
And its waterwheel to turn in the long life of rain.

Collect Ideas

Where can you get ideas for your writing? Look around you. What you see, hear, and read will give you ideas. You can get ideas from inside, too—from your feelings and imagination. Once you start looking for inspiration, you'll find it everywhere.

Ways to Come Up with Ideas

Rev up your idea engine. Think about:

- funny, strange, or confusing situations in your life
- the music you love
- places, objects, or events that mean a lot to you
- your top ten favorite memories
- your favorite people
- your favorite fictional or historical characters
- an imagined or overheard line of dialogue
- times when you felt really sad, nervous, or thrilled
- why you've kept things like tickets, letters, photographs, or souvenirs
- important truths you've learned in your life
- quotations you feel strongly about

Top Ten Memories

1. The day my baby sister was born
2. My fishing trip with Uncle Julio
3. Going to the prom with Emily
4. Passing my driver's test

"To love someone deeply gives you strength. Being deeply loved by someone gives you courage."
—Lao Tzu

Where to Keep Your Ideas

Start an idea file to keep your ideas together in one place. Just about any kind of container will do.

- Put your ideas inside a cereal box or in a basket.

- Keep a journal of your thoughts and feelings.

- Fill a file folder with interesting articles, stories, and photos.

- Make a section in your Writer's Notebook just for collecting your ideas.

- Keep a special Writing Ideas file on your computer.

- Send voice-mail idea messages to yourself.

On-the-Go Inspiration

When you don't have your idea collection with you, try asking yourself questions like these:

- What would a perfect day be like for me?

- What would my best friend's perfect day be like?

- What would a perfect day be like for Juliet in *Romeo and Juliet*?

- What's the most important value I want to teach my children?

- If I could travel anywhere in the world, where would I go?

- Where would my sister like to travel?

- What's one action I would go back and undo if I could?

- What action would Scout from *To Kill a Mockingbird* undo?

Choose Your Topic

You can use your idea collection to come up with a topic—the subject you want to write about. Make sure you narrow your topic so that it is not too general, or broad, for the kind of writing you'll do.

A specific, or smaller, topic is easier to write about and is much more interesting for your readers. Take a look at how one writer narrowed the topic "Friendship" for a three-paragraph essay.

Friendship

This topic would take pages and pages to cover. Why?

Broad

My best friend

This is better, but still too broad. How many things are there to say about a best friend?

The day I almost lost my friendship with Carlos

This topic is interesting because it's specific. Would it be easy to tell what happened in three paragraphs?

Narrow

Your Topic is Too Broad When . . .

- you type key words into a search engine and get dozens of hits

- you search a library database and find hundreds of books

- there are so many main ideas, you don't know where to start

Choose Your Audience

After choosing a good topic, you need to think about your audience—the people who will read your writing. When you know your audience, you can choose the appropriate style and tone for your writing.

Audience	Tone	Language
your best friend or someone your own age	very informal	Hey, Karen— What's up? You ready for Frank's party on Thursday?
an older relative	somewhat informal	Hi, Uncle Terry, Do you have any Hawaiian shirts I could borrow? I need one for a party Thursday. Thanks.
your teacher	somewhat formal	Dear Mrs. Smith, I wonder if it might be possible for me to turn my paper in on Monday instead of Friday. I have an important after-school event on Thursday night.
someone you don't know	very formal	Dear Tropical Paradise Staff: Do you carry Hawaiian shirts in size Large? I'm looking for something under $25.00. I'd appreciate any information you could give me. Thank you.

Who is the audience for each of these e-mails?

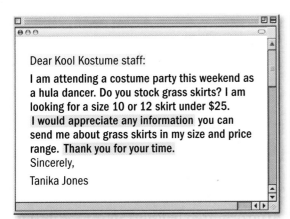

Dear Kool Kostume staff:

I am attending a costume party this weekend as a hula dancer. Do you stock grass skirts? I am looking for a size 10 or 12 skirt under $25. I would appreciate any information you can send me about grass skirts in my size and price range. Thank you for your time.

Sincerely,

Tanika Jones

The writer uses a **formal greeting** and language that gives her message **a polite, businesslike tone**.

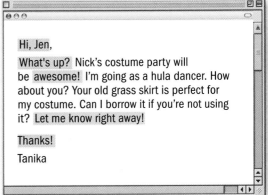

Hi, Jen,

What's up? Nick's costume party will be awesome! I'm going as a hula dancer. How about you? Your old grass skirt is perfect for my costume. Can I borrow it if you're not using it? Let me know right away!

Thanks!

Tanika

The writer uses an **informal greeting** and **casual, friendly language**. Her words show **strong emotion or feelings**.

Choose Your Purpose

What do you want your audience to know or to do? That'll be your **purpose**, or reason for writing. Choose your words and tone to fit your purpose.

What is the writer's purpose in the e-mail below? What is the writer's purpose in the journal entry?

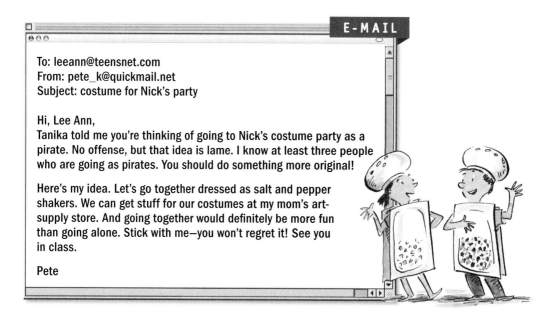

E-MAIL

To: leeann@teensnet.com
From: pete_k@quickmail.net
Subject: costume for Nick's party

Hi, Lee Ann,
Tanika told me you're thinking of going to Nick's costume party as a pirate. No offense, but that idea is lame. I know at least three people who are going as pirates. You should do something more original!

Here's my idea. Let's go together dressed as salt and pepper shakers. We can get stuff for our costumes at my mom's art-supply store. And going together would definitely be more fun than going alone. Stick with me—you won't regret it! See you in class.

Pete

JOURNAL ENTRY

Tuesday, 10/13

I am such an idiot! All I wanted was to get Lee Ann to go to Nick's costume party with me. So yesterday I e-mailed her and said her pirate costume idea was lame and she should go with me instead. I told her my idea was way better than hers. Stupid move. I totally insulted her! This morning in Spanish class, she wouldn't even look at me. Forget about going to the party with her—now I'll be lucky if she even talks to me again!

Pete wrote the e-mail to persuade Lee Ann to change her costume and go with him to the party. He wrote in his journal to express his feelings about what he had done. What was his purpose for writing this letter to his friend Gabe?

October 16, 2007

Dear Gabe,

You know that girl Lee Ann that I've had a crush on ever since seventh grade? I finally asked her out. And if there's ever a TV show called *Worst Dating Bloopers of All Time*, I'll be the star.

You see, I asked Lee Ann to go with me to Nick's costume party. She wanted to be a pirate, but I figured we could go as salt and pepper shakers instead. I tried to convince her by saying that pirate costumes were lame and unoriginal. She was so mad

Are Your Audience and Purpose Connected?

Yes. One way to get clear on your purpose is to think about how you want your audience to react to what you have to say.

If You Want Your Audience to . . .	Your Purpose Is . . .	For Quick Topic Ideas, List . . .
• learn something new • understand something better	to inform or explain	• ten things people can learn from you • ten things you can do really well
• laugh • feel a deep emotion • enjoy reading your work	to entertain	• ten situations that made you laugh • five opening sentences that would get a reader hooked on a book
• believe something • do something • take action on an important issue	to persuade	• ten different ways to complete this sentence: *If people would just _____, then we wouldn't have to worry about _____.* • five of your strongest opinions
• know how you feel • know what you think	to express	• your best or worst memories • ten things about yourself you wish you understood better

How to Write for a Specific Purpose

You can change how and what you write to fit your purpose.
Look at the examples on these pages.

To Express

Write a journal entry to tell about your personal thoughts and feelings.

> November 15, 2006
> My Sweet 16 party was so much fun!
> I was especially glad that Carmella
> and Lucy could make it. They bought
> me tickets to see my favorite band in
> concert! I'm so excited.

Journal Entry

Share your feelings with a friend in a personal note.

> *Thank You*
> Dear Carmella and Lucy, Thank you
> so much for the concert tickets you
> gave me for my birthday! I can't wait
> to go. This was the best gift ever!
> Love,
> Joanna

Thank-You Card

To Inform or Explain

You might give directions to explain how to do something.

> Directions to My House
> (from School)
> 1. When you leave the parking lot, turn right onto Hurffville Road.
> 2. Go through two traffic lights.
> 3. Make a right onto Greentree Road.
> 4. Make a left onto Haines Drive.
> 5. My house is number 20, on the right.

Directions

Or, you could write a paragraph to give readers important information.

> My house is all the way
> at the end of the street.
> It's a red house with a
> brown roof and brown trim.
> There's a big vacant lot
> right before my house. A
> brown station wagon and
> a black pickup truck are
> parked in the driveway.

Paragraph

To Persuade

In an advertisement, you can use persuasive words and phrases to convince someone to buy something.

Ad

In an editorial, give your opinion and use persuasive words to get people to change the way things are.

THE PRICE OF A GOOD PARTY

I think it's ridiculous how much money people spend on parties. From little kids' birthday parties to after-prom get-togethers, parties are getting more and more costly. People try to outdo each other by buying expensive presents, flashy party clothes, and fancy decorations. I enjoy parties, but the point of a party is to socialize with people, not to try to impress them.

Editorial

To Entertain

You could write a funny essay to make your readers laugh.

The Worst Party Ever

The birthday cake lay on the ground where I had dropped it. Then the doorbell rang, and I stepped right in the cake on my way to answer it. Now my foot was covered with chocolate icing! I greeted my friend anyway, but my foot slipped and kicked her in the shin. When we both looked down to see if she was OK, we bumped heads—ouch! "Welcome to my party," I said. And that was only the beginning!

Essay

You could write a suspenseful short story to keep readers on the edge of their seat.

An Uninvited Guest

Kendra and Damon stared wide-eyed at the movie on TV. Something terrible was about to happen to the main character. Right at that moment, they heard a loud, insistent knocking. Their hearts beating wildly, they both jumped up from their seats. "Did you invite someone over?" asked Kendra. "Nope," said Damon. "I don't know who that could be so late at night." Then they heard the doorbell chime loudly, again and again.

Short Story

Choose Your Form

Writing is like going on a trip. Your topic, audience, and purpose are your map. Your form, or the type of writing you'll do, is the vehicle that gets you where you want to go.

Just as a car would be better than a bicycle for a very long trip, some forms of writing are more appropriate than others to fit your audience, topic, and purpose. Start your writing roadmap by recording your topic, audience, and purpose in an FATP chart.

FATP Chart

Form: _____

Audience: _classmates_ _____

Topic: _the day I almost lost my_
friendship with Carlos

Purpose: _to explain how friendships_
can be damaged

Then go shopping for a form and choose one that goes with your audience and purpose.

Good Writers

Writing Forms | Writing Advice | Writing Topics

Advice column	Fable	News story
Biography	Flyer	Personal narrative
Book review	Haiku	Play
Business letter	Invitation	Poem
Cartoon	Journal entry	Recipe
Character sketch	Letter to the editor	Research report
Comic strip	Magazine article	Résumé
Directions	Movie review	Screenplay
Editorial	Myth	Song lyrics
E-mail		
Essay		

FORMS

Organize Your Ideas

You know your topic, and you've chosen a form. You have your audience well in mind, and you've set a purpose for writing.

FATP Chart

Form: _personal narrative_

Audience: _classmates_

Topic: _the day I almost lost my friendship with Carlos_

Purpose: _to explain how friendships can be damaged_

Your next step is to organize your ideas. Start by choosing an appropriate text structure for your writing.

Text Structures — If You Want to . . .	Organize by . . .
• explain a central idea by discussing related ideas • discuss a topic that does not fit the other text structures below	**Logical Order**
• present events in order • show the steps in a process or procedure	**Chronological Order**
• describe a scene	**Spatial Order**
• explain how two or more people, places, things, or ideas are alike or different	**Comparison and Contrast**
• explain causes and effects in science or nature • give reasons for certain actions or conditions • explain the results of an event or action	**Causes and Effects**
• show how a real-life person or story character tries to reach a goal	**Goals and Outcomes**
• show how a person or story character solves a problem • explain why something is a problem and present ways to solve the problem	**Problems and Solutions**
• explain your opinion about an important issue • persuade people to take action or agree with you	**Position Statement and Supporting Arguments**

Organize Your Ideas, continued

Some text structures fit your form, audience, topic, and purpose better than others. For example, spatial order isn't the best choice for an editorial, but it's a great way to organize a description. Choose a structure that will help your writing accomplish what you want it to do.

Choosing a Text Structure

To write a composition based on the following FATP chart, how would you organize the ideas?

FATP Chart

Form: _personal narrative_

Audience: _classmates_

Topic: _the day I almost lost my friendship with Carlos_

Purpose: _to explain how friendships can be damaged_

Here are two possibilities:

1. Maybe you want to show how you and your friend are nothing alike. You could use a comparison-and-contrast structure to emphasize your differences.

Comparison and Contrast

Carlos	Me
never studies, but gets A's	work hard just to get B's and C's
cool and confident	shy, good listener
girls crowd around him	girls treat me like a brother

Carlos and Me

We may be best friends, but Carlos and I are nothing alike. Carlos never cracks open a book, but somehow manages to get straight A's. As for me, I struggle just to scrape by with B's and C's. Carlos is cool and confident—always the life of the party.

2. Maybe your point is that, over the years, your friendship has had many highs and lows. Then you might choose to present your ideas in chronological order.

Ideas in Chronological Order

2002	2003	2004	2005
Carlos and I met in 8th-grade algebra class. We started hanging out all the time.	Carlos tutored me every day after school so that I would do better in geometry.	Carlos and I both tried out for the lead in the school play. He got the part.	Carlos lied to me when I asked if he was seeing Julie, my ex-girlfriend.

Carlos and Me

My friendship with Carlos goes back a long way and, over the years, it's had its highs and lows. We met in algebra class in eighth grade and started hanging out all the time. Carlos can be very kind and helpful. In ninth grade he tutored me every day after school so I would do better in geometry. However, our friendship has had its rocky spots, too. Things were tense between us when we competed for the lead in the school play and he got the part. And last year I found out that he was seeing my ex-girlfriend Julie behind my back.

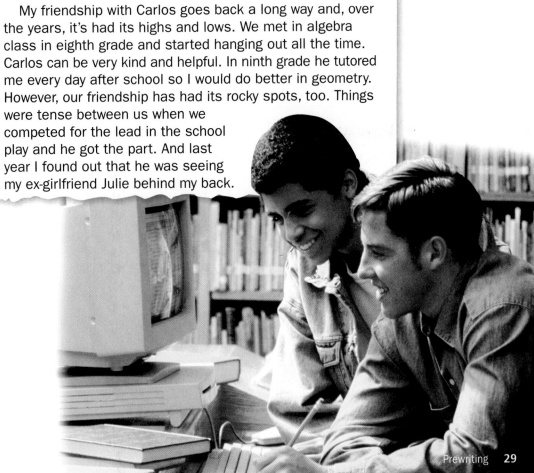

Graphic Organizers for Text Structures

Logical Order

Logical order makes the most sense when you want to group ideas that have something in common, or you want to organize them by importance.

Topic and Main Idea Diagram

A diagram like this can help you plan the focus for each paragraph in an essay.

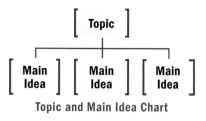

Topic and Main Idea Chart

Main Idea and Detail Diagrams

For each paragraph in the essay, try one of these diagrams to plan the details you'll include.

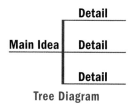

Tree Diagram

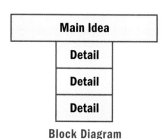

Block Diagram

Category Chart

Try sorting information into groups or categories.

Carlos and Me

Helped me	Caused me problems
helped me pass math class	was rude to my parents
convinced me to try out for the football team	never shows up on time
lent me money to buy concert tickets	went to the concert with someone else

Category Chart

Hypothesis-and-Results Chart

You could use a chart like this to explain the results of a survey.

Question: What percentage of teens at Washington High School sometimes lie to their best friends?	Hypothesis: Most teenagers at Washington High lie to their best friends occasionally.
	Data: 50 teens surveyed 30 have lied about minor things (60%) 5 have lied about something important (10%) 15 always tell their best friends the truth (30%)
Conclusions: 70% of teens sometimes lie to their best friends.	Observations: Most teens will not lie to their best friends about something important.

Hypothesis-and-Results Chart

Outline

You can also use an outline to help you organize your ideas logically. List the main ideas and supporting details using roman numerals, letters, and numbers.

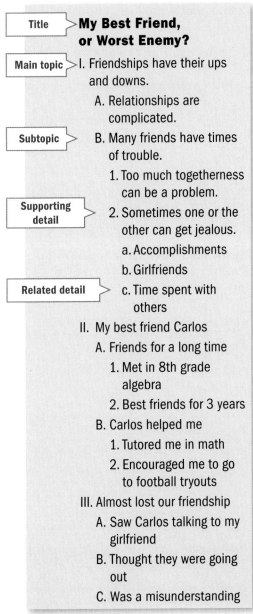

| Title | **My Best Friend, or Worst Enemy?** |

Main topic — I. Friendships have their ups and downs.

    A. Relationships are complicated.

Subtopic —   B. Many friends have times of trouble.

      1. Too much togetherness can be a problem.

Supporting detail —   2. Sometimes one or the other can get jealous.

        a. Accomplishments

        b. Girlfriends

Related detail —   c. Time spent with others

  II. My best friend Carlos

    A. Friends for a long time

      1. Met in 8th grade algebra

      2. Best friends for 3 years

    B. Carlos helped me

      1. Tutored me in math

      2. Encouraged me to go to football tryouts

  III. Almost lost our friendship

    A. Saw Carlos talking to my girlfriend

    B. Thought they were going out

    C. Was a misunderstanding

Outline

Order-of-Importance Diagrams

Sometimes you'll want to organize your ideas by how important they are.

1. You can organize from most important to least important.

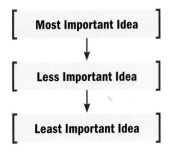

2. Or, you can organize from least important to most important.

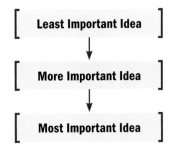

Graphic Organizers for Text Structures

Chronological Order

To tell about events in the order in which they happen or to explain the steps in a process, use chronological order.

Sequence Chain

A diagram like this one can help you plan plot events for stories.

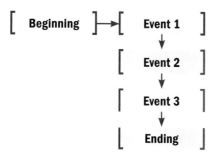

[**Beginning**]→[**Event 1**]
                        ↓
                [**Event 2**]
                        ↓
                [**Event 3**]
                        ↓
                [**Ending**]

Sequence Chain

Flow Chart

Use a flow chart to explain how to do something or how something works.

Making a 3-D Theatrical Mask

Step 1
A cast of the actor's face is made.

↓

Step 2
The cast is then used to shape the features of the mask.

↓

Step 3
This new character's "face" is then used to make a mold for the final mask.

↓

Step 4
Latex rubber is poured into the mold to create the mask.

↓

Step 5
The mask is then painted and attached to the actor with a special glue.

Flow Chart

Time Line

Use a time line to help you keep track of when important events happened.

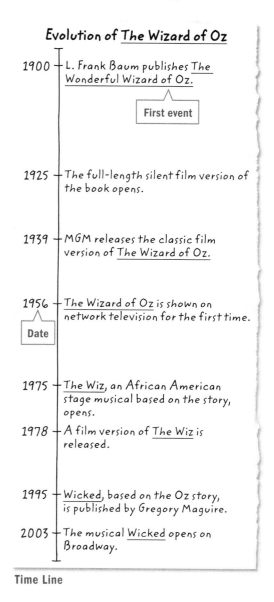

Evolution of The Wizard of Oz

1900 — L. Frank Baum publishes The Wonderful Wizard of Oz.

First event

1925 — The full-length silent film version of the book opens.

1939 — MGM releases the classic film version of The Wizard of Oz.

1956 — The Wizard of Oz is shown on network television for the first time.

Date

1975 — The Wiz, an African American stage musical based on the story, opens.

1978 — A film version of The Wiz is released.

1995 — Wicked, based on the Oz story, is published by Gregory Maguire.

2003 — The musical Wicked opens on Broadway.

Time Line

Spatial Order

For a description, try using spatial order to tell what you see—from left to right, from near to far, or from top to bottom, for example.

Picture Diagram
Try labeling a picture—or drawing one—to show how you'll organize details for a description.

Picture Diagram

beat-up hat

plaster nose

rope belt

hay stuffing

busted shoes

Circle Diagram
Whether you want to describe an area from the inside to the outside or vice versa, try using a circle diagram to show your plan.

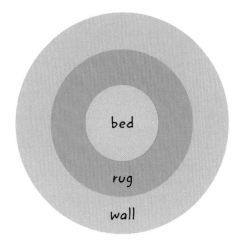

bed

rug

wall

Circle Diagram

Showing Causes and Effects

When you write about causes and effects, you explain what happens and why.

Cause-and-Effect Chart

Sometimes a cause leads to a single effect. You might want to show each cause and its effect in a chart.

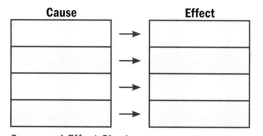

Cause-and-Effect Chart

Cause-and-Effect Diagrams

Maybe what you want to explain has a single cause and multiple effects, or a single effect and multiple causes.

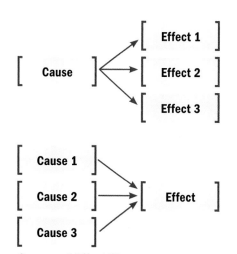

Cause-and-Effect Diagrams

Cause-and-Effect Chain

Sometimes causes and effects form a chain of linked events. One event causes the next event to happen.

Cause-and-Effect Chain

Showing Comparisons

Plan what you'll say about how people, places, or things are alike or different. It'll be easy to see the comparisons if you show your ideas side by side.

T-chart

Use a T-chart to help you compare and contrast specific characteristics of a topic.

What you compare

Buying a Costume — **Making a Costume**

limits your choices — gives you many choices

requires little work or skill — may require skills, such as sewing or painting

can be done quickly — takes a long time

T-chart

Characteristics

Venn Diagram

A Venn diagram uses overlapping circles to compare and contrast.

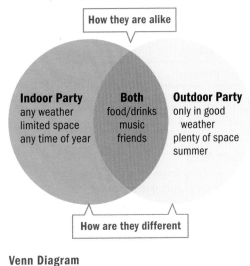

How they are alike

Indoor Party
any weather
limited space
any time of year

Both
food/drinks
music
friends

Outdoor Party
only in good
weather
plenty of space
summer

How are they different

Venn Diagram

Showing Goals and Outcomes

Whether you want to share your own personal accomplishments or create a story about a fictional character, try organizing your ideas by goal and outcome.

Goal	Actions	Obstacles	Outcome
I wanted to get the lead role in the school play.	I found out the date and time of the audition. I prepared a monologue. I attended the audition and performed the monologue.	I had a cold on the day of the audition. I kept coughing during my monologue. My best friend tried out for the lead, too.	My friend got the lead role. I got a minor part.

Goal-and-Outcome Chart

What stands in the way?

Graphic Organizers for Text Structures

Showing Problems and Solutions

Both fiction and nonfiction often present problems and solutions. In your writing, organize the ideas by first telling why something is a problem and then how the problem is or can be solved.

Problem-and-Solution Chart

A chart like this one works best for nonfiction in which there are several problems, each with its own solution.

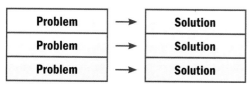

Problem	→	Solution
Problem	→	Solution
Problem	→	Solution

Problem-and-Solution Chart

Story Map

Use a story map to show your characters' problems, or conflicts, and how they work to solve the problems.

Title: Finding a Place
Author: Jasmine Porter

Characters: Cathy, Cathy's German host family, Anke, other students
Setting: Munich, Germany

Problem: Cathy feels lonely.
↓

Event 1: Cathy signs up for a study-abroad program and goes to Germany.
Event 2: She has trouble fitting in because she doesn't speak German.
Event 3: She meets and befriends a German student named Anke.
↓

Solution: Anke helps Cathy improve her German and meet more people.

Story Map

Essay Map

For an essay, complete a map to help you organize and explain your ideas.

The Problem
Few students are submitting works for publication in the literary magazine The Scribbler
↓

Why It Needs to Be Solved
The Scribbler can't survive without any work to publish.
↓

The Solution
Many students may not know about The Scribbler, so we need to make the magazine more visible.
↓

How the Solution Works
The staff will
• add a page about The Scribbler to the Fowler High School Web site.
• put a notice in the school newspaper.
• ask English teachers to let students submit work to The Scribbler for extra credit.
↓

Conclusion
If more students know about the literary magazine, there'll be an increase in the number of submissions.

Problem-and-Solution Essay Map

Showing Your Position

When you write to persuade, you want to convince people to agree with you. So, to be sure you've included all the important and persuasive details, use a chart or a diagram to plan what you'll say.

Opinion Chart
You can use an opinion chart to organize the reasons and supporting evidence for your opinion.

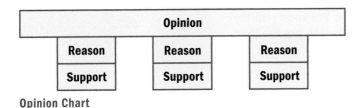

Opinion Chart

Position-and-Support Diagram
Sometimes people will disagree with you. When this happens, you need to plan how to respond to their objections with rebuttals.

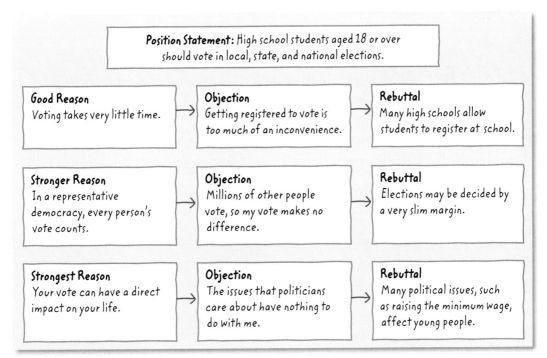

Position-and-Support Diagram

Get It Down on Paper

Remember the first time you dived off a diving board? You were probably pretty scared, and you knew it wasn't going to look like on TV. But you went ahead and did it anyway. Drafting is like that. You just dive in and put your ideas down. You know your first draft isn't going to be perfect, but you take the risk and trust the process.

How Do You Face a Blank Page?

Gary Soto explains how he fills in a blank page:

"**A** blank page is like a blank face—you fill it in. And, like faces, the moods of the writing may change. You'll have laughter on one page, and two pages later boiling anger. Or you may have faces that are downright ugly! Or way, way pretty!"

Here are some ideas to help you face a blank page:

• Gather all the tools you'll need—pencils, paper, notes, graphic organizers, and other resources. If you are going to write on a computer, schedule time to work on it.

• Find a good place to write—a place that works for you!

• Then just start writing. Remember, your draft doesn't have to be perfect! Just get your ideas down on paper.

FOCUS POINT Look at the start of a first draft for an essay on page 39. What makes it a good start? Should the writer worry about spelling and grammar errors now?

My Best Friend—or My Worst Enemy?

Jeff Kominsky

All friendships have their ups and downs. Not just between girls either. Guys have complex relationships too. We just don't like to admit it.

I've known my best friend Carlos since eighth grade. He tutered me in math. He made me try out for football. He is the guy I can always count on. But no friendship free from problems.

Last month I went to ask Kelly if she wanted to walk home with me. Kellys my girlfriend. I entered the hallway where her locker is and what did I see? She and Carlos were laughing together.

Carlos and I have been rivals at times. Take the school play last year. I wanted the lead role. I asked Carlos if he was going to try out. He didn't seem interested. Then later he decides he wants a part after all. Some friend.

Drafting Checklist

In a good draft:

- ☑ The title often shows the main idea of the essay.
- ☑ The writing includes the main points from beginning to end.
- ☑ The message is clear and the writing sticks to the topic.

- ☑ Writers quickly set down their ideas, without worrying about spelling or grammar errors.

  If you're working on a computer, color squiggles identify possible errors. If you're writing by hand, add your own squiggles to show words to check later.

Drafting Q & A

No two people create a draft in exactly the same way, but like good athletes, writers always want to improve their game. On the next few pages are some frequently asked questions and answers about drafting. Which ideas sound familiar? Which seem like techniques you'd like to try?

Getting Started

Q: What do I need to get started?

A: After you find a quiet, comfortable place where you won't be interrupted, gather all your tools. You'll need paper and pencil or a computer, of course. Also, have your prewriting materials close by. Your **FATP** chart will help you stay focused on your **F**orm, **A**udience, **T**opic, and **P**urpose. Your notes or graphic organizer will keep you on track paragraph by paragraph.

Q: What's the right way to start a draft?

A: Writers are like snowflakes: no two are exactly alike. While there's no single "right" way to start, here are a few approaches:

- Some writers get all their ideas down in one quick burst. They don't pause between paragraphs or agonize over choosing the perfect word.

- Other writers work more slowly. They spend a lot of time crafting the opening paragraph before they develop the body of the essay.

- Some writers even work out of sequence, writing the body of their draft first, and then going back to add the introduction.

Do whatever works best for you.

How Do You Get Started on Your First Draft?

"If I can't think of anything to say, freewriting usually gets me going in the right direction. I'll just sit and write anything that comes to mind for ten or fifteen minutes—as fast as I can. It's like doodling with words."

—Karen

"I like to draw pictures of something that has to do with my main topic. If I'm describing something, the picture I draw helps me see it."

—Matthew

"I write on the computer. If I'm at home, I'll instant-message a buddy and swap some ideas about my topic. The other thing I do is explore my topic on the Internet."

—Gilberto

"Before I start a draft, I loosen up by doing stretching exercises while I let my mind wander over the topic. Often a good idea comes to me, and I can use it to get started."

—Sylvia

Drafting Q & A, continued

Staying on Track

Q: Sometimes while I'm writing I get distracted or lose my train of thought. How can I stay on track?

A: You can try working with a writing partner—someone you trust. You can ask your partner to read your work, or you can read your work aloud and ask your friend for feedback.

Another approach is to write a "kernel essay" first, before you begin your real essay. A kernel essay shows just the main points of your essay, without any details. It can help keep your writing on track. See how this writer used the ideas from her kernel essay in her composition.

Kernel Essay

My Ocean Rescue

| I was at the beach. | → | I realized I didn't know where my little sister was. | → | I looked around and yelled her name. | → | I spotted her in the water and ran to get her. | → | I was so relieved that she was all right! |

Essay

    I was at the beach, absorbed in my book, when I looked up. Suddenly my heart stopped. Where was Elisa, my little sister? I was supposed to be watching her. I had seen her just a minute ago, but now she was nowhere in sight.

Q: Sometimes I run out of things to say right away. How can I keep myself going?

A: Don't stop even when your writing seems to be flowing very slowly. Write about not having anything to say, if you have to!

How Do You Keep Your Draft on Track?

" I need quiet when I write. I look for a private space where I can put all my notes up on the wall. I keep them all in front of me and look at them when I need to. "

—Eva

" I usually write for five or ten minutes and reread what I've written. If I like it, I go back and write for ten more minutes. If not, I take a short break. Then I decide how I want to fix it. Maybe I need to add more details. Maybe I need to cut out a chunk. "

—Marcus

" I just let myself get distracted sometimes—but I try to control my distractions so that I will finish. Sometimes I just need to empty my head of my writing so that I can go back to it feeling fresh. "

—Melanie

" If you're writing a short story, get it down on paper in two or three days. That way, the continuity will be more natural, and by 'continuity' I mean if you have a girl wearing white pants on page 1, you can't have her wearing blue jeans on page 6, unless she went home and changed them. Inconsistencies jar the reader. Get the story written. You can go back and polish later. "

—Gary Soto

Drafting Q & A, continued

Knowing When You're Done

Q: How do I know when I'm done with the draft and it's time for the next step?

A: You are done when your ideas are all down on paper (or in your hard drive) and they feel complete. Ask yourself:

- Would my opening paragraph grab a reader's attention?

- Does my writing say what I want it to say? Am I getting my message across? Do I need to cut or add anything?

- Does the ending seem tacked on, or does it flow smoothly from the rest of the piece?

The Truth About Drafting

FICTION: You should write a draft all in one sitting.
FACT: Sometimes you can write a short draft in one sitting, but most drafts take more time than that.

FICTION: You should use a pencil and lined notebook paper for a draft.
FACT: Emily Dickinson, the author of hundreds of poems, wrote her drafts on odd scraps of paper. Other writers might use felt-tip pens and even crayons on unlined paper, or compose their drafts on the computer.

FICTION: You should never, ever write a draft without doing prewriting first.
FACT: Sometimes the best way to decide what you want to say is to write a draft first. Then you can use that draft to plan out a more polished piece.

FICTION: You always start a draft at the top of a page and write down to the bottom until the page is filled. Then you go on to the next page.
FACT: Each writer has a unique way of working on a draft. Some writers write paragraphs on index cards and then arrange the cards in the right order. Others might fill just the middle of each page so they can go back and add notes or new ideas as they think of them.

FICTION: As you write a draft, you have to stick to your plan.
FACT: It's a good idea to stick to your basic plan, but be flexible. As you write, new and better ideas might pop into your head. Don't be afraid to change your plan if you need to.

What's One Truth You Want to Share About Drafting?

" Writers don't have to fill up the page. They just have to fully express the ideas they have well enough for the reader to comprehend."

—Greg

" You can be doing something like singing in the shower or eating ice cream and then it hits you. And you get a new excitement to add to the draft."

—Monica

" You *can* change your plan while you're drafting. I, for one, change my mind a lot while I'm drafting."

—Sam

" Not all writers use regular notebook paper for drafting. Some use journals that are pink with flower-scented paper, or type on their laptops. It shouldn't matter how or where you write, just that you do!"

—Angela

Drafting from Beginning to End

You're ready to start your draft, and you know it doesn't need to be perfect the first time around. But, like a fun party, your writing needs a good beginning, middle, and end. It sounds simple, but it doesn't happen by itself—you need a plan.

A plan for an essay, for example, might work like this:

BEGINNING	MIDDLE			END
Introductory paragraph	**First paragraph**	**Second paragraph**	**Third paragraph**	**Concluding paragraph**
Captures the reader's interest and introduces the topic.	States your first point and includes evidence to support it.	States your second point and includes evidence to support it.	States your third point and includes evidence to support it.	Summarizes your points and gives your final thoughts.

For a story about something that happened to you, your plan might work like this:

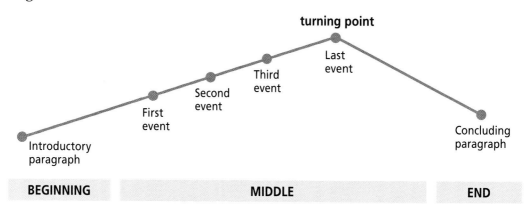

No matter what you're writing, remember the "**Big Three**":

1. **Beginning**: Get the reader's attention and establish the controlling idea of your paper.

2. **Middle**: Develop your ideas.

3. **End**: Bring your work to a close with a memorable conclusion.

How to Hook the Reader in the Beginning

Your first paragraph is like a party invitation. It should capture your readers' interest right away, getting them hooked on your topic and motivating them to read on. Try these techniques:

- Ask a question: *What good is advice if you don't give it away?*

- Recount an anecdote or personal story. In the beginning paragraph below, readers might wonder what happened when the writer didn't follow his grandfather's advice.

> My grandfather always told me, "Never give advice to a friend you want to keep." Unfortunately, I didn't listen to his wise words.

- Reveal a shocking or intriguing fact: *Most people are more open to advice from a stranger than from a friend.*

- Introduce a thought-provoking quotation.

- Present a snippet of conversation: *If I were you, I'd leave.*

- Describe a memorable visual image:

> Great grandma's skin was already a prune, or a cracked windshield. When she laughed her great gap-toothed laugh, she got wrinkles on her wrinkles.

- Define a key word or concept in your own words: *Good advice is advice that doesn't feel like a putdown.*

- Share an insight:

> ### Prom Dreams
>
> Sometimes it takes a crisis to learn who your real friends are. I learned this the hard way on the night of my junior prom. Like most of my friends, I was expecting prom night to be a magical evening out of a fairy tale. Little did I realize that I was about to get a serious reality check.

Drafting from Beginning to End, continued

How to Follow Through in the Middle

Okay, you've got the reader interested and motivated. Now you've got to deliver. Use the middle part of your draft to follow through on the ideas you introduce in the beginning. Include details that will keep your reader interested.

Prom Dreams

Sometimes it takes a crisis to find out who your real friends are. I learned this the hard way on the night of my junior prom. Like most of my friends, I was expecting prom night to be a magical evening out of a fairy tale. Little did I realize that I was about to get a serious reality check.

It all started when my date, Ricky, called me an hour before he was supposed to pick me up. My wonderful Prince Charming sounded more like a frog! "I think I've come down with the flu," Ricky croaked. "I'm running a 103-degree fever... I'm sorry, but there's no way I can go tonight."

"I hope you get well soon," I mumbled and hung up the phone. I hate to admit it, but I wasn't really all that concerned about Ricky's health at the moment. I was too busy feeling sorry for myself. After all, I was the one who would be stuck going solo to my junior prom.

From then on, the evening only got worse. Everything that could go wrong, did.

BEGINNING

Captures the reader's interest and introduces the **main idea** of the writing.

MIDDLE

Describes the main events with interesting **details**.

How to Wrap It Up at the End

When your guests leave the party, you want them to remember what a good time they had. That's why some people give party favors to their guests. Similarly, when you write, leave your readers with something to remember. One technique is to tell what you learned from an experience.

> Although my prom wasn't the perfect, magical experience I had anticipated, I learned a lot that night. I learned that I'm not afraid to stand alone in a crowd full of happy couples. I discovered that sometimes the best times in life aren't the perfect, planned evenings—they're the nights when nothing goes the way you planned. Finally, I learned that no matter how crazy life gets, my best friend Danisha can still get me to laugh about it.

END
Summarizes the events and offers a final **lesson or reflection**.

Here are some more techniques for a memorable finish:

- Summarize your main points.

- Tell how a problem was resolved: *After all my fretting, I got together with a few kids who were going as a group, and I had a great time.*

- Refer to an image that symbolizes the theme of your writing.

- Ask your reader to take action about an issue.

- End on a strong emotional note: *Anyway, I'll have to get over it. I can't let my life be ruined by a spoiled junior prom.*

- End with a quotation or question.

> I am stronger and wiser for my spoiled-prom experience. In spite of that, one question nags me: Would I still prefer that Ricky had shown up that night as planned? If I had had the choice, would I have traded wisdom for happiness?

Get It to Sing

You're going to a party and you know what you're going to wear. But you want to look your best, so you take the time to consider your appearance: *Is this just the right shade of lipstick? Would a blue shirt go better with those pants?* Revising is like that: you know what you want to say in your writing, but you want to be sure you're saying it most effectively.

What Is Revising?

When you revise your draft, you improve your writing by

- elaborating on your ideas to add interesting details, to show your thoughts and feelings, or to add support for your main points

- working on the progression, or flow, of your ideas

- replacing dull words with ones that are more specific or more colorful

- varying your sentences, and achieving a good pace and rhythm to your writing.

Revising starts with good feedback. As an experienced writer, Gary Soto recognizes the importance of getting feedback from readers. He comments:

> "**A**fter thirty-plus years of writing, I know that I should have others look over my work. To applaud it in praise? To tell me how good I am? No, to scratch out poorly crafted sentences with a red pencil!"

FOCUS POINT Read the model below. The notes point out some features that make this writing effective. What else do you see that you would like to emulate in your own writing?

from Taking Sides
by Gary Soto

When he had arrived in the new neighborhood, Lincoln had liked the peacefulness of sprinklers hissing on green lawns and the sycamores that lined the street. He liked the splashes of flowers and neatly piled firewood. He liked the hedges where jays built scrawny nests and bickered when cats slithered too close. The people seemed distant, but that was fine with him. It was better than the loud cars that raced up and down his old block. It was better than littered streets and graffiti-covered walls that called out "*Con safos*" and "F-14."

> Specific details; colorful nouns and verbs

Now, three months later, Lincoln was having second thoughts. He missed his old school and its mural of brown, black, and yellow kids linking arms in friendship. He had liked Franklin Junior High, tough as it was, with its fights in the hallways and in the noisy cafeteria. He had liked to walk among brown faces and stand with the Vietnamese and Korean kids. He missed his friends, especially his number-one man, Tony Contreras, whom he had known forever, even before first grade when Tony accidentally knocked out Lincoln's front baby teeth going down the slide. And he missed Vicky. They had parted on bad terms, but Lincoln felt that if he could speak with her everything would turn out OK.

> Ideas flow logically from past to present.

> Varied sentence length creates rhythm.

Gather Ideas: Put a Listener on It

How can you figure out what's good about your draft and what needs to be fixed? Try it out on some listeners. They can give you great feedback to help you improve your draft. Try one or more of these techniques.

Read Your Paper Aloud to Yourself

The most important listener is you. As you read your paper aloud to yourself, listen to it as if it had been written by someone else. Do you hear anything confusing or awkward? Can you think of ways to make things sound better?

My Best Friend—or My Worst Enemy?
Jeff Kominsky

All friendships have their ups and downs. Not just between girls either. Guys have complex relationships too. We just don't like to admit it.

I've known my best friend Carlos since eighth grade. He tutored me in math. He made me try out for football. He is the guy I can always count on. But no friendship free from problems.

Last month I went to ask Kelly if she wanted to walk home with me. Kellys my girlfriend. I entered the hallway where her locker is and what did I see? She and Carlos were laughing together.

The writer thinks:

" My short sentences sound kind of choppy together. I'll see if I can combine some."

Read Your Paper Aloud to a Partner

First, ask for a "sketch" of your work. If your partner can "see" your ideas in his or her mind, you'll know that your writing is clear, easy to follow, and complete. Then ask your partner to write three questions about your draft. Thinking about the answers will help you know what needs to be revised and how.

Carlos and I have been rivals at times. Take the school play last year. I wanted the lead role. I asked Carlos if he was going to try out. He didn't seem interested. Then later he auditions for a part after all. Some friend.

1. Why did Carlos change his mind?
2. Did you get the lead role?
3. Wait—why were you mad at Carlos? I don't get it.

The writer thinks:

" I didn't really explain what happened. I'll add more details about the auditions. "

Read Your Paper Aloud to Different People

Share your work with at least one adult and one peer. When you read, ask your listeners for feedback using some of these ideas.

10 Good Ways to Ask for Feedback

1. What's the one part that you remember best?

2. What one word confused or surprised you? Why?

3. What's one truth about people that's revealed by my story?

4. Which part could you see most clearly?

5. Write three things you could tell about the narrator (things that other people might not notice).

6. Name two things this piece made you wonder.

7. Does this make you think of something that happened to you? What?

8. What's one thing you wish you could picture more clearly?

9. Which part of my story held you in suspense?

10. Are there any parts where the story doesn't "flow" quite right?

Gather Ideas: Put Readers on It, Too

Let some people read your draft. You can get great feedback from readers, too.

- Have family members and friends read your draft. What did they like most? How can they tell *you* wrote it?

- Post your writing on your school's website or your blog. Ask for comments.

- Share your writing during a peer conference. As your classmates share ideas, take notes. You might not follow them all. That's okay, but do think about why your reader suggested the change.

How to Conduct a Peer Conference

GETTING FEEDBACK	GIVING FEEDBACK
• Don't explain your ideas beforehand. Let your paper speak for itself.	• As you read, look for the writer's main idea and supporting points. Decide whether the flow of ideas makes sense.
• Ask for your reader's overall opinion. What were the strongest and weakest parts? Were any parts confusing?	• Start by giving your overall opinion. Did you understand the writer's ideas? What parts of the paper did you like most or least? Why?
• Ask for specific suggestions. What parts could be cut out or expanded? Do the ideas flow in a logical order?	• Next, give more-specific suggestions. What parts need more detail? What parts could be cut out? Do any parts of the paper need to be reorganized?
	• Be polite, but be honest. Don't say the paper's fine if it needs improvement. Help the writer find ways to improve the paper.
	• Don't focus just on problems.

Make Your Changes

Consider all of the feedback you've gotten and mark up your paper or add sticky notes to show what you want to revise.

My Best Friend—or My Worst Enemy?
Jeff Kominsky

All friendships have their ups and downs. Not just between girls either. Guys have complex relationships too. We just don't like to admit it.

I've known my best friend Carlos since eighth grade. He tutored me in math. He made me try out for football. He is the guy I can always count on. But no friendship free from problems.

Combine these sentences to make my writing flow better.

Last month I went to ask Kelly if she wanted to walk home with me. Kellys my girlfriend. I entered the hallway where her locker is and what did I see? She and Carlos were laughing together.

Carlos and I have been rivals at times. Take the school play last year. I wanted the lead role. I asked Carlos if he was going to try out. He didn't seem interested. Then later he decides he wants a part after all. Some friend.

Work on flow in this part, too.

Carlos knew we'd been having problems. It was weird to see him talking to Kelly. He said that maybe we weren't meant to be and if so, that was okay because most people don't stay with their high-school sweetheart forever and I would find the right girl eventually. I thought back to that conversation. Carlos obviously wanted us to break up so he could start seeing Kelly.

I started walking home in a very bad mood. Carlos and Kelly pulled up beside me near my house. He asked

Add more details and quotations to explain what happened.

When you revise, you will need to elaborate with details, improve the flow of your ideas, and work on your words and sentences. See the tips on pages 58–69.

Make Your Changes, continued

If you did your draft on the computer, you can just go into your document and start revising. If you wrote your draft by hand or work with a printout, you'll probably want to mark your changes on paper before you start keyboarding or rewriting. Use these revising marks:

Revising Mark	What It Means	Example
∧	Insert something.	like Carlos and me Even best friends ∧ sometimes compete.
⌇	Move to here.	We've been friends for over three years. (We met in algebra class.)
⌃	Replace with this.	girlfriend I saw him talking to my ~~sweetheart~~ Kelly.
ℓ	Take out.	Friendships between guys can be very ~~complicated and~~ complex.
∿	Transpose or reverse order.	I felt like I couldn't trust Kelly, Carlos, or anyone else in the world.

" With only a few revisions . . ."

My Best Friend—or My Worst Enemy?

Jeff Kominsky

All friendships have their ups and downs. ^and I'm^ Not just
^talking about friendships^ between girls either. Guys have complex relationships
too. ^even if^ We ~~just~~ don't like to admit it.

I've known my best friend Carlos since eighth grade.
He tutored me in math. He made me try out for football.
He is the guy I can always count on. But no friendship
free from problems.

Last month I went to ask Kelly if she wanted to walk
home with me. Kellys my girlfriend. I entered the
hallway where her locker is and what did I see? She
and Carlos were laughing together.

Carlos and I have ^competed with each other sometimes, such as the time^ ~~been rivals at times. Take the~~
~~school play last year.~~ ^in the school play^ I wanted the lead role. I asked
Carlos if he was going to try out. ^and at first^ He didn't seem
interested. Then later he decides he wants a part after
all. Some friend.

Carlos knew we'd been having problems. It was weird
to see him talking to Kelly. He said that maybe we
weren't meant to be and if so, that was okay because
most people don't stay with their high-school sweetheart
forever and I would find the right girl eventually. I
thought back to that conversation. Carlos obviously
wanted us to break up so he could start seeing Kelly.

I started walking home in a very bad mood. Carlos's
^car screeched to a stop^ ~~and Kelly pulled up~~ beside me near my house. He asked ^"Need a ride?"^

Combine these sentences to make my writing flow better.

Work on flow in this part, too.

Add more details and quotations to explain what happened.

Improve Your Writing: Elaboration

Rereading your paper and getting feedback from others helps you know what problems to fix. If your readers aren't clear on what you are saying, try elaborating. When you elaborate, you add details to support an idea—you add flesh and muscle to bare bones! Try these techniques.

Add Sensory Details

Tell what you saw, heard, felt, smelled, or tasted. Sensory details bring your writing to life.

Just OK

> I entered the hallway where her locker is and what did I see? She and Carlos were laughing together.

Better with Details

> I entered the hallway where her locker is and what did I see? She and Carlos were ~~laughing~~ *standing close* together. *Her cheeks were flushed, and I could hear her giggling at something he'd said.*

Add Dialogue or Quotations

Adding dialogue in fiction or quotations in nonfiction helps the reader feel as if he or she is present at the scene.

Just OK

> I entered the hallway where her locker is and what did I see? She and Carlos were laughing together.

Better with Dialogue

> I entered the hallway where her locker is and what did I see? She and Carlos were laughing together. *I heard him ask, "Are you sure it's the right thing?" "You bet," she said, "I've been planning this for a long time."*

Add Examples, Facts, and Statistics

These details help you prove your point and make your writing more powerful.

Just OK

> I entered the hallway where her locker is and what did I see? She and Carlos were laughing together.

Better with a Fact

> I entered the hallway where her locker is and what did I see? She and Carlos were laughing together. ⋀ *That kind of worried me, since two of my three previous girlfriends had a secret crush on Carlos.*

Show How You Know

It's not enough to just give an example or add a detail. Part of elaborating is to **show how** you know what you're saying. You might back up your ideas with

- memories and feelings
- personal experience
- information from people you know
- what you've learned in school or from books
- information from the media or the Internet.

Better with Added Support

> I entered the hallway where her locker is and what did I see? She and Carlos were laughing together. ⋀ *Alarms started going off in my head. Suddenly, I thought of this story we'd just read in English class in which the hero's girlfriend falls in love with another guy. I remember all the parties I'd been to with Carlos where he had girls crowded around him, hanging on his every word.*

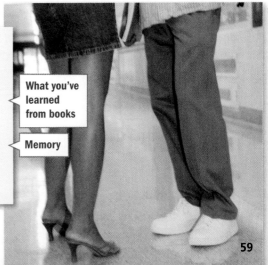

What you've learned from books

Memory

Improve Your Writing: Idea Flow

When your ideas flow, your readers stay interested and move easily from one idea to the next. Try these techniques when you need to improve the flow of your ideas.

Put Your Sentences in the Best Order

The main idea sentence in a paragraph usually sets up how the ideas in the rest of the paragraph should progress.

> Carlos and I have had a bit of a friendly rivalry going ever since we met in eighth-grade algebra class. That year, we studied together a lot, but he always got better grades. He got the lead role in the school play during our sophomore year—a role that I had wanted for myself. As freshmen, we competed for the few spots available on the football team.

This **main idea** suggests a sequential order.

The writer moved this sentence to put the ideas in order.

> Girls are attracted to Carlos for many reasons. First off, he's good-looking—six feet tall with thick black hair and muscles from working out. He's also confident and easy to be around. Sometimes hanging out with him makes me wish I knew how to charm people the way he does. And on top of all that, he's got a great sense of humor and always has a funny story to tell.

This **main idea** promises a list of examples.

The writer moved this sentence to the end to put all the examples together.

Take Out Details and Unnecessary Words

To make your main ideas come across more clearly, you may need to cut out details that don't fit.

> Carlos can be a very thoughtful person.
> In eighth grade, he spent a lot of afternoons tutoring me so I could bring my grades up in algebra class. When my car broke down a few months ago, he helped me make the repairs so I wouldn't have to take it to a mechanic. ~~Sometimes he makes plans with me and~~ ~~doesn't show up because he forgot to write it~~ ~~down on his calendar.~~

This **main idea** is about how thoughtful Carlos can be.

This detail does not fit. The writer deleted it.

Sometimes your points are watered down because your writing is too wordy. You may need to take out words to sharpen your ideas.

> Carlos is a ~~nice,~~ well-meaning person, but sometimes he can be rather thoughtless ~~and~~ ~~careless.~~ In fact, he often doesn't show up on time when we have plans to go to the movies or a concert ~~or other plans to go out and have~~ ~~a good time.~~ He's so scattered ~~and forgetful,~~ as a matter of fact, that sometimes he forgets to show up altogether.

The writer can cut words and still get the same ideas across.

Improve Your Writing: Idea Flow, continued

Use Transitions

When you use transition words, you help your reader know how the ideas in your paragraph are related so he or she can move smoothly from one idea to the next.

Transitions Between Sentences

I knew Kelly was the girl for me. *Even so,* We had been having some problems lately *because* She thought we were getting too serious. I was worried *since* she might be losing interest. I talked to Carlos about it, He was the one person I knew I could confide in no matter what.

You can also hook your paragraphs together with effective transitions.

Transitions Between Paragraphs

It was strange to see Carlos talking with Kelly since he knew we were going through a rough time. When I had talked to him about it, he'd said that maybe Kelly and I weren't meant to be together. "Even if you break up, it's not the end of the world," he'd said. Now, as I remembered that conversation, all sorts of thoughts started running through my mind.

Here are just some of those thoughts: Why were my girlfriend and my best friend hanging out together? Though I was close to both of them, I never thought they were especially close to each other.

Furthermore, Why did they leave school together? Where were they going, and why wasn't I invited to come along with them? The more I thought about it, the more worried I felt.

One way to connect paragraphs is to repeat a **key word** or phrase.

The writer starts the paragraph with a **transition word** to connect ideas.

You use different transition words depending on the direction you want to lead your reader. For example, the transitions you use to signal a comparison are not the same ones you use to signal causes and effects. The chart below shows which transitions work best for different purposes.

If you want to . . .	Use these transition words . . .	
Add new ideas	also in addition	furthermore moreover
Introduce examples	for example for instance	such as specifically
Compare	similarly likewise	in the same way also
Contrast	however but still although	in contrast despite in spite of on the other hand
Show causes and effects	because due to since	therefore as a result consequently
Show sequence	first second third	next last finally
Show time	before after in the past soon now immediately	later in the future meanwhile then until
Show place	here there next to nearby farther	above below on the other side in front of behind
Summarize ideas	all in all in summary	in conclusion in short

Improve Your Writing: Word Choice

Add energy to your writing and help your readers picture the action by using vivid and exact words. Try these techniques:

Replace Vague Words

Vague

Carlos and I both play sports. I hurt myself in last week's game.

Specific

Carlos and I both play football and basketball. I hurt my Achilles tendon in last week's game.

Use Colorful Verbs

Dull

As I walked home, I wondered whom I could trust. Carlos's car stopped beside me.

Colorful

As I trudged home, I wondered whom I could trust. Carlos's car screeched to a stop beside me.

Add Sensory Words

Limited Details

I slid into Carlos's car. I brushed against a shiny black bag from Super Tunes. When I picked up the bag, I could feel a box inside.

Sensory Details

Music blared as I slid into Carlos's car. I brushed against a shiny black bag from Super Tunes and heard a crinkling sound. When I picked up the bag, I could feel the edges of a small, flat box inside.

Avoid the Passive Voice

Passive Voice

The Super Tunes bag was quickly snatched out of my hands.

Active Voice

Kelly quickly snatched the Super Tunes bag out of my hands.

Use a Thesaurus

A **thesaurus** is sort of like a dictionary, but instead of giving the meaning of words, a thesaurus gives lists of words with similar meanings.

When you need to find a better word, use a thesaurus:

1. Look up the word you want to replace.

2. Use the sample sentence to choose the correct meaning.

3. Then read the synonyms (words with the same meaning) to find a better word.

Entry word

Sample sentence shows how word is used.

wakeful adjective **1** *he had been wakeful all night* AWAKE, restless, restive, tossing and turning. ANTONYM asleep.
2 *I was suddenly wakeful* ALERT, watchful, vigilant, on the lookout, on one's guard, attentive, heedful, wary. ANTONYM inattentive.

walk verb **1** *they walked along the road* STROLL, saunter, amble, trudge, plod, dawdle, hike, tramp, tromp, slog, stomp, trek, march, stride, sashay, glide, troop, patrol, wander, ramble, tread, prowl, promenade, roam, traipse; stretch one's legs; *informal* mosey, hoof it; *formal* perambulate.
2 *he walked her home* ACCOMPANY, escort, guide, show, see, usher, take, chaperone, steer, shepherd.
▸ noun **1** *their country walks* STROLL, saunter, amble, promenade; ramble, hike, tramp, march; turn; *dated* constitutional.
2 *the map shows several nature walks.* See TRAIL noun sense 5.
3 *he shoveled the front walk* PATH, pathway, walkway, sidewalk.
4 *her elegant walk* GAIT, step, stride, tread.
PHRASES: **walk all over** *informal* **1** *be firm or he'll walk all over you* TAKE ADVANTAGE OF, impose on, exploit, use, abuse, misuse, manipulate, take liberties with; *informal* take for a ride, run rings around. **2** *we walked all over the home team.* See TROUNCE. **walk off/away with 1** *informal she walked off with my wallet.* See STEAL verb sense 1. **2** *he walked off with four awards* WIN EASILY, win hands

These words are **synonyms** for the entry word as it is used in the sample sentence.

Antonyms are often included. These words mean the opposite of the entry word.

Improve Your Writing: Effective Sentences

Good writing has a rhythm to it. The sentences are varied and move along at a good pace. Try these techniques to improve your sentences.

Combine Sentences

If your writing sounds choppy, find some sentences to combine. There are many ways to put two sentences together. See some possibilities on pages 186–191.

Short, Choppy Sentences

> I've known my best friend Carlos since eighth grade. He tutored me in math. He made me try out for football. He is the guy I can always count on. But no friendship is free from problems.

One Way to Combine the Sentences

> I've known my best friend Carlos since eighth grade, *when* He tutored me in math *and* ~~He~~ made me try out for football. *Although he is someone* ~~He is the guy~~ I can always count on, ~~But~~ no friendship is free from problems.

This writer combined sentences 1–3 and sentences 4 and 5.

Another Way to Combine the Sentences

> I've known my best friend Carlos since eighth grade. He tutored me in math. He made me try out for football, *and has always been the guy I could count on.* ~~He is the guy I can always count~~ ~~on.~~ But no friendship is free from problems.

This writer combined sentences 3–4.

Vary Your Sentences

If all of your sentences sound alike, your writing will be bland and boring. Mix up short and long sentences and use different kinds of sentences.

Boring Sentences

> Rivalry is sometimes involved in friendship. Carlos and I compete sometimes. I wanted the lead role in the play last year. Carlos wasn't planning to try out at all at first. Then he changed his mind at the last minute. He tried out for a small part. The drama teacher was impressed with him. She gave him the lead role.

All the sentences are statements, and all are about the same length.

Varied Sentences

Short | Long

> Lots of friendships involve rivalry. Carlos and I have competed with each other sometimes, such as the time I wanted the lead role in the school play. At first Carlos wasn't planning to try out at all, but he changed his mind at the last minute and tried out for a small part. The drama teacher was impressed—very impressed, actually. Guess which role she asked Carlos to play? The lead.

Statement

Question

The writer uses this **fragment**, or incomplete sentence, for effect.

Start your sentences in different ways, too.

Too Similar	**Varied**
Everything comes easily to Carlos. He gets good grades without having to work for them. He's a natural-born athlete. He seems to make friends wherever he goes.	Everything comes easily to Carlos. He gets good grades without having to work for them. Strength and coordination make him a natural-born athlete. And wherever he goes, he makes friends quickly.

Improve Your Writing: Effective Sentences, continued

Break Up Overly Long Sentences

The reader shouldn't get lost between the beginning and the end of a sentence.

Overly Long Sentence, Fixed

> Carlos said that maybe Kelly and I weren't meant to be, ~~and if so, that was okay because~~ most people don't stay with their high-school sweetheart forever and I would find the right girl eventually.

Streamline Your Sentences

Save your reader's time and attention. Don't use three or four words when just one will do.

Wordy Sentence, Streamlined

> Carlos had told me that ~~in this~~ *today* ~~day and age,~~ lots of high-school couples don't stay together ~~due to~~ *because many* ~~the fact that a large number of~~ teenagers leave their hometown after graduation.

Instead of . . .	Use . . .
a large number of	many
at the present time	now
due to the fact that	because
in this day and age	today

Similarly, don't use three or four rambling sentences when just one well-crafted sentence will do.

Rambling Sentences, Streamlined

> I thought back to that conversation with Carlos. As I remembered that conversation, I realized that he was trying to get me to break up with Kelly. He ~~wanted us to break up~~ so he could start seeing her.

A sentence, like a donkey or a pickup truck, can only carry so much. Avoid "sentence overload."

Overloaded Sentence

As I walked home from school that dreary afternoon, I was feeling like my best friend—not just any friend, but Carlos, the guy I thought I could trust like a brother—had become my worst enemy, someone I couldn't trust at all anymore.

Streamlined Sentence

As I walked home from school that dreary afternoon, I was feeling like my best friend had become my worst enemy.

Keep your Sentences Parallel

When you compare two items or list items in pairs or in a series, use grammatical forms that are the same, or parallel.

Not Parallel

Kelly realized that it made more sense to split the cost of the present with Carlos than trying to pay for it herself.

Parallel

Kelly realized that it made more sense to split the cost of the present with Carlos than to try to pay for it herself.

Not Parallel

Not only were they not sneaking around, they just wanted to plan a cool surprise for me.

Parallel

Not only were they not sneaking around, they were planning a cool surprise for me.

Not Parallel

Carlos is my best friend, a person I look up to, and I can always count on him.

Parallel

Carlos is my best friend, a person I look up to, and the guy I can always count on.

Get It Right

When you said goodbye to Rover, he shed all over your nice black turtleneck—not good. Your date probably won't care too much, but you want to take the time to fix this. Editing and proofreading is like that: you take the time to make the little things right because you don't want them to detract from the overall impression.

Make Your Paper Ready for Your Readers

You've worked hard writing and revising your draft. Now is the time to edit it carefully to make sure your writing is the best it can be.

- Look for errors (in grammar, spelling, and punctuation) as you read your writing carefully to yourself. Or, listen carefully as you read it aloud to others during an editing conference.

- If something looks or sounds wrong, but you're not sure, check it out. Get help from a style guide, a dictionary, or your teacher.

- Fix any errors on your draft and then make a clean copy of your writing.

Gary Soto points out why he follows standard writing conventions:

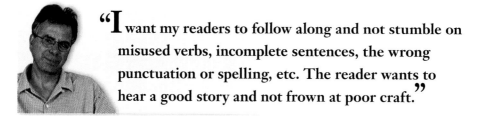

"I want my readers to follow along and not stumble on misused verbs, incomplete sentences, the wrong punctuation or spelling, etc. The reader wants to hear a good story and not frown at poor craft.**"**

FOCUS POINT Look at the edited essay on page 71. What types of changes is the writer marking at this stage?

A Friend I Can Trust

Jeff Kominsky

All friendships have their ups and downs. Im not just talking about freindships between girls either. Guys have complex relationships too, even if we don't like to admit it. competition can cause trouble, even between best friends.

I've known my best friend Carlos since eighth grade. He tutored me in Math and convinced me too try out for football. He is the guy I can always count on. But no friendship is free from problems.

Lots of friendships involve rivalry. Carlos and me have competed with each other sometimes, such as the time I wanted the lead role in the school play. At first Carlos wasn't planning to try out at all, but he changed his mind at the last minute and tried out for a small part. The drama teacher was impressed—very impressed, actually. Guess which role she asked Carlos to play? The lead. I was irritated, to say the least.

Editing and Proofreading Marks

Mark and What It Means		Mark and What It Means	
∧	Insert something.	╱	Make lowercase.
∧	Add a comma.	ℓ	Delete, take out something.
∧	Add a semicolon.	¶	Make new paragraph.
⊙	Add a period.	◯	Spell out.
⊙	Add a colon.	=	Insert hyphen.
∨ ∨	Add quotation marks.	◡	Change order of letters or words.
∨	Add an apostrophe.	#	Insert space.
≡	Capitalize.	◡	Close up, no space here.

Tools: The Dictionary

Editing and proofreading are like everything else—they're a lot easier to do if you have the right tools. The dictionary is a basic tool. It can help you check the spelling of a word, of course. But it can also tell you how to use words correctly—and much more!

Guide words: first and last entries on the page

Pronunciation

Part of speech

Origin or etymology

Special usage notes

farrier • fastball

far·ri·er \'far-ē-ər\ n : a blacksmith who shoes horses [Medieval French *ferrour*, derived from Latin *ferrum* iron]

¹**far·row** \'far-ō\ vb : to give birth to pigs [Middle English *farwen*, derived from Old English *fearh* "young pig"]

²**farrow** n : a litter of pigs

far·see·ing \'fär-'sē-ing\ adj : FARSIGHTED 1

Far·si \'fär-sē\ n : PERSIAN 2b

far·sight·ed \-'sīt-ad\ adj **1 a** : seeing or able to see to a great distance **b** : able to judge how something will work out in the future **2** : affected with hyperopia — **far·sight·ed·ly** adv — **far·sight·ed·ness** n

¹**far·ther** \'fär-thər\ adv **1** : at or to a greater distance or more advanced point **2** : more completely [Middle English *ferther*, alteration of *further*]

usage *Farther* and *further* have been used more or less interchangeably throughout most of their history, but currently they are showing signs of going in different directions. As adverbs, they continue to be used interchangeably whenever distance in space or time is involved, or when the distance is metaphorical. But when there is no notion of distance, *further* is used ⟨our techniques can be *further* refined⟩. *Further* is also used as a sentence modifier ⟨*further*, the new students were highly motivated⟩, but *farther* is not. A difference is also appearing in their adjective use. *Farther* is taking over the meaning of distance ⟨the *farther* shore⟩ and *further* the meaning of addition ⟨needs no *further* improvement⟩.

²**farther** adj **1** : more distant : REMOTER **2** : ³FURTHER 2, ADDITIONAL

far·ther·most \-ˌmōst\ adj : most distant : FARTHEST

¹**far·thest** \'fär-thəst\ adj : most distant in space or time

²**farthest** adv **1** : to or at the greatest distance in space or time : REMOTEST **2** : to the most advanced point **3** : by the greatest degree or extent : MOST

far·thing \'fär-thing\ n : a former British monetary unit equal to ¼ of a penny; *also* : a coin representing this unit [Old English *feorthung*]

far·thin·gale \'fär-thən-ˌgāl, -thing-\ n : a support (as of hoops) worn especially in the 16th century to swell out a skirt [Middle French *verdugale*, from Spanish *verdugado*, from *verdugo*

Origin or etymology

Word History The English words *fascism* and *fascist* are borrowings from Italian *fascismo* and *fascista*, derivatives of *fascio* (plural *fasci*), "bundle, fasces, group." *Fascista* was first used in 1914 to refer to members of a *fascio*, or political group. In 1919 *fascista* was applied to the black-shirted members of Benito Mussolini's organization, the *Fasci di combattimento* ("combat groups"), who seized power in Italy in 1922. Playing on the word *fascista*, Mussolini's party adopted the fasces, a bundle of rods with an ax among them, as a symbol of the Italian people united and obedient to the single authority of the state. The English word *fascist* was first used for members of Mussolini's *fascisti*, but it has since been generalized to those of similar beliefs.

Fa·sci·sta \fä-'shē-stä\ n, pl **-sti** \-stē\ : a member of the Italian Fascist movement [Italian]

¹**fash·ion** \'fash-ən\ n **1** : the make or form of something **2** : MANNER, WAY ⟨behaving in a strange *fashion*⟩ **3 a** : a prevailing custom, usage, or style **b** : the prevailing style (as in dress) during a particular time or among a particular group ⟨*fashions* in women's hats⟩ [Medieval French *façun, fauschoun,* "shape, manner," from Latin *factio* "act of making, faction"] — **after a fashion** : in a rough or approximate way ⟨did the job *after a fashion*⟩

synonyms FASHION, STYLE, MODE, VOGUE mean the usage accepted by those who want to be up-to-date. FASHION may apply to any way of dressing, behaving, writing, or performing that is favored at any one time or place ⟨the current *fashion*⟩. STYLE often implies the fashion approved by the wealthy or socially prominent ⟨a superstar used to traveling in *style*⟩. MODE suggests the fashion among those anxious to appear elegant and sophisticated ⟨muscled bodies are the *mode* at this resort⟩. VOGUE applies to a temporary widespread style ⟨long skirts are back in *vogue*⟩.

²**fashion** vt **fash·ioned; fash·ion·ing** \'fash-ning, -ə-ning\ : to give shape or form to : MOLD, CONSTRUCT — **fash·ion·er** \'fash-nər, -ə-nər\ n

fash·ion·able \'fash-nə-bəl, -ə-nə-\ adj **1** : following the fashion or established style : STYLISH ⟨*fashionable* clothes⟩ **2** : of or relating to the world of fashion : popular among those who

Synonyms and shades of meaning

Different forms of the word

Style note

fas·cism \'fash-ˌiz-əm\ n, *often cap* : a political philosophy, movement, or regime that promotes nation and often race above individual worth and that supports a centralized autocratic government headed by a dictator, severe economic and social regimentation, and forcible suppression of opposition [Italian *fascismo*, from *fascio* "bundle, fasces, group," from Latin *fascis* "bundle" and *fasces* "fasces"] — **fas·cist** \'fash-əst\ n or adj, *often cap* — **fas·cis·tic** \fa-'shis-tik\ adj, *often cap*

curving downward slope to the rear; *also* : an automobile with such a roof

fast·ball n : a baseball pitch thrown at full speed

\ə\ abut	\au̇\ out	\i\ tip	\ȯ\ saw	\u̇\ foot
\ər\ **further**	\ch\ **chin**	\ī\ l**i**fe	\ȯi\ **coin**	\y\ yet
\a\ mat	\e\ pet	\j\ **j**ob	\th\ thin	\yü\ few
\ā\ take	\ē\ easy	\ng\ sing	\th\ this	\yu̇\ cure
\ä\ cot, cart	\g\ go	\ō\ bone	\ü\ food	\zh\ vision

Pronunciation key: helps you say the word

Tools: Spell-Check

Word-processing programs usually have a spell-checking function. This function checks your words against the words it is programmed to recognize. Then it points out misspelled words and suggests alternatives.

When the spell-check program suggests several alternatives, choose the one that best fits your meaning.

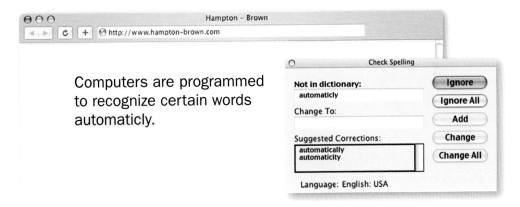

The spell-check program isn't foolproof. It can't understand the meaning of your words, so it can't tell when you've spelled a word correctly but used it incorrectly.

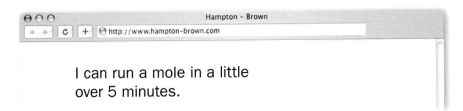

Using spell-check programs is no substitute for proofreading your paper carefully.

Tools: Personal Checklists

The English language can be tricky! It might seem like there are a million possible mistakes you have to look out for. Actually, most people repeat the same few mistakes over and over.

Reread your old papers to see which errors are marked most often, or talk with your teacher to identify your trouble spots. What kinds of errors does Michelle repeat in these papers?

Michelle MacDonald

1/4/06

English 12

The book that has had the greatest *e*affect on me is *Jane Eyre*, by Charlotte Brontë. Ever since I first read it when I was 15, it's been my favorite book. It tells the story of Jane, an orphan whose parents die*d* when she was just a baby. She live*s* with her wealthy aunt and cousins they *don't* like her. In fact they pick on her all the time they always assume she's up to no good. Her cousin John is the one, who treats her the worst.

Michelle MacDonald

3/31/06

English 12

I've always been fascinated by video games ever since I was a kid I *'ve* played them every chance I have. Last Saturday my uncle took me to the museum to see the Virtual World exhibit. I played the ultimate race car game there. It's so cool I put on special headgear and suddenly it was like I was inside a race car driving on a virtual track. The game*s* special *e*affects were awesome. The people who designed this game really knew what they *were* was doing. I decide*d* that when I finish school I want to be a video game designer.

Once you've reviewed your past work, you can create a personalized checklist of mistakes to watch out for—the types of errors you make the most. Keep changing your list to take off what you've mastered and add new things to look for.

Michelle MacDonald's Editing Checklist (3/31/06)

☑ Commas I always forget:
- Commas after introductory phrases like "Last week"

☑ Words I mix up:
- "its" and "it's"
  "It's" is a contraction for "it is." Don't forget the apostrophe!
- "affect" and "effect"
  Don't use the verb "affect" in place of the noun "effect."

☑ Mistakes I make with verbs:
- Changing verb tenses in the middle of a paragraph
- Using verbs that don't agree with the subject ("he don't," "she live")

☑ Sentence problems to look out for:
- Run-ons
  To fix: Divide into two sentences or use a conjunction.
- Comma splices
  Don't use a comma to join two sentences! Fix this mistake the same way I fix run-on sentences.

☑ Comma mistakes I make:
- Stray commas
  DO use a comma if the phrase ISN'T essential to the meaning of the sentence. DON'T use a comma if the phrase IS essential to the meaning. This is confusing! : -(

Correct Your Mistakes

When you edit and proofread, you're looking at details like grammar, spelling, and punctuation. Sometimes it can be hard to focus on these details. Some of these techniques will help you discover mistakes:

How to Discover Mistakes

- Before you edit, make a checklist of mistakes to look for. Your teacher can help you create a personalized checklist, based on your past work.

- Read your writing aloud with expression, as if you were giving a speech. (If you're doing this in class, make it a very soft, quiet speech.)

- Read your writing one line at a time. Cover up everything except the line that you're reading.

- To look for spelling errors, read your writing backward, one word at a time starting at the end. It won't make any sense, but you will catch misspellings!

- Read your writing several times, looking for a different type of error each time.

- Use a highlighter or colored pen to mark mistakes or sentences you're not sure about. Consult a dictionary, a style guide, or your teacher to see if you need to make a correction.

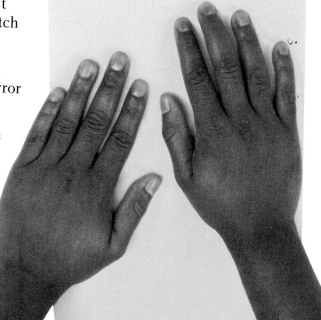

Getting there in time was essential, but I hesitated for a moment. Outside, the wind blew feircely. It

Proofreading Marks in Action

Here are the most common proofreading marks and how they are used to mark a piece of writing for corrections.

How I Learned to Prooofread

I used to think that editing my essay just meant running the computer's spell-check program and accepting whatever changes it suggested. Now I know better. A computer will not catch mistakes like correctly spelled words that are used incorrectly. In english class my teacher taught us how to use proofreader's marks to correct mistakes like words that need to be capitalized or made Lowercase. You can use a caret to insert any words that you forgot to put in.

My english teacher said Different kinds of carets are used to insert quotation marks apostrophes commas and semicolons however, dont use a caret to insert a colon. Here's how to insert a period or colon use a circle with one or two dots inside.

Also, if you accidentally type a word twice, use the delete mark to remove the extra extra word. You can use a similar mark to replace cross out words or phrases.

Finally, know what marks to use to insert a space, close up a space, and fix letters or words that are in the order wrong. Practice your proofreading skills, and soon your writing will be letter-perfect.

Get It Out There

What's It Like?

You've taken a great action shot with your new camera and you're pretty proud of the way it turned out. You pick a nice frame and mount it carefully so that you can show it to the world in the best possible light. That's how it is when you publish a piece of writing: you "dress it up" to make sure it looks its best when it faces the public.

How Do Writers Share Their Writing?

Once you're done with your writing, what's next?

- Collect your writing in a personal portfolio.

- Don't stop thinking about what you've written. Reflecting on your writing will help you improve it over time.

- Decide how you'll publish your writing and who your audience will be. Will you send your writing to a close family member or present it as a speech to the general public?

Writers have different reasons for wanting to publish their work. Gary Soto shares some of his:

"**W**hen I first started writing in the early 1970s, I was on fire to publish poems that declared that my childhood warranted description. I wanted to put life into the alleys, the playgrounds, and the streets of my childhood."

FOCUS POINT Read the poem on page 79. Does Soto's poem make you share his childhood experience?

Little League Try Out

Treading across the baseball field
beaded clods of dirt exploded,
crumbling and leveling to dust
beneath my smooth
rubber soled sneakers.
    I moved
for the kids collected
in circles sporting their mitts
and abilities, all believing
they'd make Little League.
I came prepared: equipped
with a cap, two balls of gum,
double knee jeans,
and a glove
snaked with oily lines.
Authentic necessities
I thought would make all the difference.
I remember the people
hunched in the bleachers,
stabbing their melting
snowcones with straws.
Occasionally one would point
to someone on the field
and thinking their interests
were directed toward me
I'd snap at impossible fly balls,
or zigzag furiously
to different positions
of the diamond,
attempting to appear busy
and worth their attention.
I hustled when coach
bleated instructions: filing obediently
behind the other kids,
retreiving lost balls,
loyally defending shortstop,
and even hitting
a few that year.
    Coach even
gave me a wink, pat on the butt,
the whole routine,
saying I performed well
and should expect a phone call.
After tryout I ran home
crazed with energy
through streets waving
with heat, my sneakers
slapping the soft asphalt
to await the call.

            GARY SOTO

One of Gary Soto's earliest poems—"Little League
Try Out"—as published in his college newspaper

Publish Your Writing

Suppose you've just written a great essay. You have revised it so many times that you can practically recite it from memory. You feel proud of your accomplishment and want to share your work with someone. Who will be your first audience?

Keeping It Personal

You "publish" your writing when you share it with others—with just a few people or with a large audience. If you'd prefer not to present your writing to the whole world just yet, here are some more-personal ways to share it:

- Write a letter to a friend or family member asking him or her to read your writing. Enclose a copy of your final draft.

- You can also send your writing attached to an e-mail.

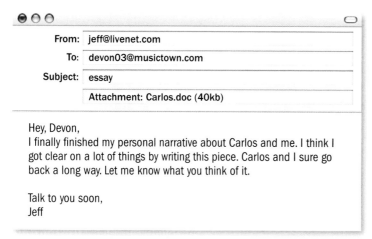

From: jeff@livenet.com
To: devon03@musictown.com
Subject: essay
Attachment: Carlos.doc (40kb)

Hey, Devon,
I finally finished my personal narrative about Carlos and me. I think I got clear on a lot of things by writing this piece. Carlos and I sure go back a long way. Let me know what you think of it.

Talk to you soon,
Jeff

- Another cool way to share your writing is to present it as a gift. Suppose you've written a poem about someone you admire. You could give this person a framed copy of your poem, typed or neatly handwritten on attractive paper.

Entering the Public Eye

Sharing your work with the public feels good! Also, feedback from others helps you improve as a writer. Are you ready to share your writing with a larger audience? If so, here are a few ways you can make it public:

- Sponsor or attend an open-mike night at your school or at a local hangout. That way, you and other writers can read your work aloud for the crowd.

- Submit a poem, short story, or essay to your school newspaper or literary magazine.

- Is there an issue that you feel very strongly about? Write a letter to the editor of your local newspaper.

- Look for writing contests in your favorite magazines or online.

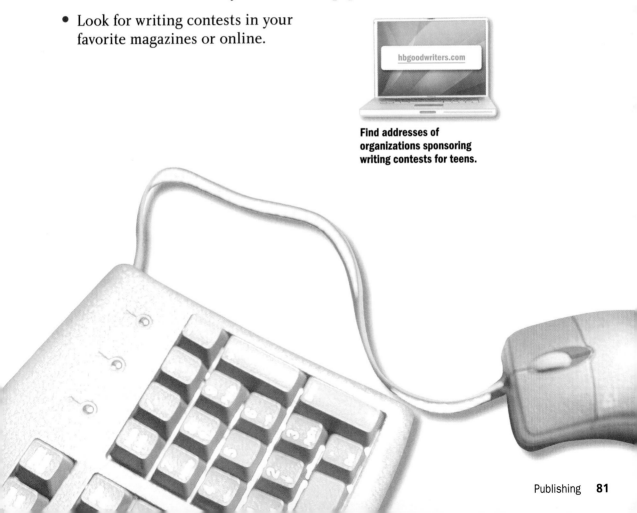

hbgoodwriters.com

Find addresses of organizations sponsoring writing contests for teens.

Publish Your Writing, continued

Enhancing Your Work with Graphics

Whether you're writing out your paper by hand or working on a computer, you have many possibilities to enhance your work with graphics.

- Add charts and tables to a science or social studies report.

- Download photos of paintings and sculptures from the Internet and insert them into an art essay.

- Scan a drawing or photo for a personal narrative.

Ready for Publishing

> The writer added a photograph to give the work a personal touch.

A Friend I Can Trust

Jeff Kominsky

All friendships have their ups and downs. I'm not just talking about friendships between girls either. Guys have complex relationships too, even if we don't like to admit it. Competition can cause trouble, even between best friends.

Carlos and me in 2004

I've known my best friend Carlos since eighth grade. He tutored me in math and convinced me to try out for football. He is the guy I can always count on, but no friendship is free from problems.

Lots of friendships involve rivalry. Carlos and I have competed with each other sometimes, such as the time I wanted the lead role in the school play. At first Carlos wasn't planning to try out at all, but he changed his mind at the last minute and tried out for a small part. The drama teacher was impressed — very impressed, actually. Guess which role she asked Carlos to play? The lead. I was irritated

Reflect on Your Writing

Finishing a piece of writing doesn't mean you stop thinking about it. One way you can improve your work over time is to reflect on what you've written. Ask yourself questions to pinpoint your writing strengths as well as the ways in which you want to improve.

Questions for Self-Reflection

1. What surprised me about my writing?

2. What unexpected questions or comments did I get from readers?

3. What makes me really proud about this piece?

4. In what ways have I become a better writer? What have I gotten really good at?

5. What was the hardest part of writing this piece?

6. What are some areas of concern? How could I improve my work?

7. What part of the writing did I learn the most from?

8. What did I discover about myself as I wrote?

9. What topics would I like to write about some more?

10. What other writing forms could I try?

Building Your Portfolio

If you like a piece of writing you've worked on, you can put it in your portfolio. A portfolio can help you organize the work you're most proud of. You may also include old drafts so that you— or others—can see how your work has changed over time. A portfolio can be a simple file folder, a loose-leaf binder, or even a briefcase.

How public should your portfolio be? It can be just as public or as private as you like. However, many writers use portfolios to showcase their talent. For this reason, you might want to keep highly personal writing, such as journal entries, in a separate notebook.

What Makes Good Writing Good?

featuring **Julius Lester**

"**G**ood writing is language that sings,
language that becomes part of the music
of a book."

The Traits of Good Writing

Julius Lester is a professional writer who has published dozens of novels, nonfiction books, articles, and stories for children, teens, and adults. Lester has also received several major writing awards during his long career. On pages 87–89, he explains what he's learned about what makes good writing good.

Inspire Your Readers:
Communicate with Good Writing

Good writing does not begin when you sit down to write something. It begins with reading—reading a lot and reading widely. I read many publications, including *People* magazine, *US Weekly*, the *New Yorker*, the *New York Times*, and my local newspaper. I read books about whatever interests me—gardening,
5   philosophy, religion, literature, and biographies. By reading, I learn how other people express their ideas.

You may not realize it, but you already know what makes writing good because, no matter what you read, you want it to be clear, organized, developed, and appropriate for the subject matter. You also expect that whatever you are
10   reading will have a distinctive voice.

Let's look at these traits more specifically.

Focus and Unity

To write clearly and be sure you are understood, focus on your subject.
Let's say you're writing an article about your school's football team. You can't write everything about the team. You have to decide what is most important.
15   Maybe it was the win in the playoffs. The focus of your writing becomes a description of that game—what players performed especially well, what the key plays were, how the crowd reacted. Anything that does not pertain directly to the game should be omitted because it will detract from your article's unity.

Don't expect to achieve focus and unity with your first draft. Everyone needs
20   to rewrite. Rewriting sharpens your focus and gives your essay a tighter unity. Sometimes I've rewritten a page more than 25 times. Be ruthless and cut out any word, sentence, or paragraph that isn't necessary. By focusing your writing, you stand a better chance of being understood. This is something all of us want.

Communicate with Good Writing, continued

Organization

The most difficult part of writing is organizing your ideas. You can have many
25 good ideas, but if you don't know how to organize them in a way that's easy for
the reader to follow and understand, your good ideas will be of no use to you or
anyone. Your goal is to communicate clearly. To do this, organize your thoughts
into sentences that move logically, one into the other.

Organizing your ideas is not easy. It is not easy even for me, and I've written
30 more than 40 books. But working at organizing your thoughts is worth the effort
because doing so will make you an effective communicator.

Development of Ideas

Let's say you want to write for your school newspaper about a concert you went
to. But what if all you can think to write is: "I went to the Funk Brothers concert
last night, and it was great"? Think about it as if you are the reader, not the
35 writer. As a reader, you want the concert review to give you details, such as "How
were the Funk Brothers dressed? What songs did they play? Did they sound as
good in person as they do on their CDs? Were people in the audience singing
along?" As a reader, you want to know the writer's opinion of the concert, but
you want the writer to support his opinion with knowledge of the subject.

40 Using details makes your writing more vivid. Using information that supports
your ideas makes what you write more convincing. Others may not agree with
everything you write. What's important is that you've given them enough details
and information to understand your point of view.

Voice

Just as we use different voices depending on whom we are talking to, we
45   use different voices in our writing. The voice we use in a letter to a friend is
different from the voice we would use in a business letter or a research paper.
Experiment with different voices, and write in the voice that is appropriate.

Notice that articles in different newspapers and magazines do not sound the
same. This difference in voices gives the publications distinct identities, so that
50   articles in *Rolling Stone*, for example, do not sound like those in *Atlantic Monthly*.

Whether we are talking or writing, the voice we use touches others. Our tone
of voice can hurt someone or create a smile. Whether the words are from our
mouths or on the page, we are communicating something about who we are.

Written Conventions

There are important differences between the spoken and written word. When
55   we talk to others, they see our facial expressions and hear our different tones
of voice. Sometimes these non-verbal cues communicate just as much as, or
more than, words. But when I write, you cannot see my face or hear my voice.
To communicate effectively, I follow accepted conventions.

This means using good grammar and correct punctuation, which are the written
60   substitutes for voice inflections and gestures. Which is the better sentence:
"He, looking sad, left," or "Looking sad, he left"? The first sentence divides the
subject, "He," from the action shown by the verb, "left." The second sentence is
better because it conveys information in two distinct, logical parts.

Learning to write well involves following the written conventions. Doing so will
65   help you to write effectively and communicate your ideas to anyone.

hbgoodwriters.com

**Find links to more
writing by Julius Lester.**

Find Your Focus

When writing isn't focused and unified, the ideas spurt out in all different directions. But when writing is focused and unifed, the ideas flow in one direction like one steady stream.

Focus Your Writing

Writing is focused and unified when you have a main point and stick to it. To keep your writing focused and unified:

- Establish a central idea, or thesis, that is clear and specific.

- Plan how each paragraph will develop the central idea. Be sure that the details in each paragraph are important and support the central idea.

- End with a conclusion about your central idea.

> "**D**on't expect to achieve focus and unity with your first draft. Everyone needs to rewrite."

FOCUS POINT Study the rubric on page 91. What is the difference between a paper with a score of 4 and one with a score of 2?

Focus and Unity

	How clearly does the writing present a central idea, opinion, or thesis?	How well does everything go together?
4 **Wow!**	The writing expresses a clear central idea or opinion about the topic.	**Everything** in the writing goes together. • The main idea of each paragraph goes with the central idea of the paper. • The main idea and details within each paragraph are related. • The conclusion is about the central idea.
3 **Ahh.**	The writing expresses a **generally** clear central idea or opinion about the topic.	**Most** parts of the writing go together. • The main idea of most paragraphs goes with the central idea of the paper. • In most paragraphs, the main idea and details are related. • Most of the conclusion is about the central idea.
2 **Hmm.**	The writing includes a topic, but the central idea or opinion is not clear.	**Some** parts of the writing go together. • The main idea of some paragraphs goes with the central idea of the paper. • In some paragraphs, the main idea and details are related. • Some of the conclusion is about the central idea.
1 **Huh?**	The writing includes many topics and does not express one central idea or opinion.	The parts of the writing do not go together. • Few paragraphs have a main idea, or the main idea does not go with the central idea of the paper. • Few paragraphs contain a main idea and related details. • None of the conclusion is about the central idea.

In Literary Works

In this passage, Julius Lester wants to set a central idea, or key point. He does not state the central idea directly. Instead, he focuses on a single incident and uses strong details to lead his readers to the central idea.

A Mother's Lesson

by Julius Lester

The writer focuses on just one **topic**.

Every summer until I was fourteen my mother took me to visit her mother, who lived outside Pine Bluff, Arkansas. I was perhaps six the day Mother and I were in a store downtown. It was hot in the store because if air-conditioning had been invented by the late 1940s, it hadn't made its way to the Arkansas delta. In a corner of the store I saw two water fountains. One was tall and above it was a sign that read WHITE. Next to it at what was the perfect height for a child was another fountain. Above it, the sign read COLORED. WHITE water didn't sound very appealing, but I imagined COLORED water would be as beautiful as Joseph's coat. I went over to the COLORED water fountain, but just as I got there my mother's hand gently grabbed my shoulder.

This event reveals the writer's central idea—the indignity of segregation.

Segregated drinking fountains in the American South, from the time that Lester is writing about

A girl leaves a cafe with separate doors for "white" and "colored." ▶

"Colored" waiting room in a bus terminal in Atlanta, Georgia, during the era of segregation

"You can't drink out of there," she said.

I didn't ask why because something in her voice conveyed that this "colored" was not a rainbow-sparkling spray. No. This COLORED was like the sign on the bus we had to take to and from town because Grandma lived too far away from town for us to walk. This COLORED was like the COLORED signs at the bus and train stations indicating what doors COLORED PEOPLE could use and at which windows they could buy tickets. That was not colored water. It was COLORED water and I think my mother would have watched me die of thirst before she let me drink from a COLORED fountain.

The **details** further develop and support the central idea.

In Newspaper Articles

Reporters use a central idea to unify their articles. This newspaper article is about what it was like to travel in the segregated South in 1961. How did the reporter stay focused and unified?

How Jim Crow Travels in South

LAWS AND CUSTOMS SLOW PROGRESS ON BUSES, TRAINS, AND AIRPLANES

by CLAUDE SITTON
special to *The New York Times*

The writer states the central idea.

MONTGOMERY, Alabama—The Negro faces a jungle of law and custom in Southern transportation despite Federal attempts to end segregation. Practices vary so widely throughout the region that uncertainty often leads him to surrender to tradition even where racial barriers are non-existent.

Each paragraph has a main idea that's connected to the central idea.

Aroused by the "freedom rides" and their sometimes violent aftermath, Attorney General Robert F. Kennedy acted this week to deal with an important facet of the problem. He asked the Interstate Commerce Commission to adopt stringent regulations against segregation in interstate bus terminals.

Details in the paragraph go with its main idea.

The progress, the lack of progress and the confusion is apparent to any Negro who travels from Atlanta to Montgomery, for example. He could catch a desegregated trolley to a desegregated Greyhound terminal in the Georgia capital and board a desegregated bus. But when the bus made a rest stop at La Grange, Ga., he would find separate waiting rooms marked "White" and "Colored."

At Montgomery

Upon arriving in Montgomery, he again would be faced with two waiting rooms, one occupied solely by Negroes and the other by whites. But he would see no signs restricting them to either race. And no one could tell him with certainty what would happen if he entered the "White" waiting room and ordered coffee.

If the hypothetical traveler decided to ride a plane, he would be struck by the even greater contrast. He would be free to sit where

In buses as well as waiting rooms, there were separate seating arrangements.

he chose, eat where he chose and drink where he chose in Atlanta's new air terminal. He might even share a seat with a white passenger enroute. But the barrier of segregation would slam down between them once they stepped off the plane.

Even Water Fountains

Illuminated signs designate the "Negro" and "White" waiting rooms and rest rooms at Montgomery's Danelly Field, which was built in 1958 with Federal

Segregated water cooler in Oklahoma City, 1939

assistance. Even the water fountains standing side by side in the ticket counter lobby are marked "White Only" and "Colored Only." The steps beside them are placed at opposite ends of the fountains as if to prevent children of the two races from brushing against each other.

In interstate travel, such practices are generally confined to terminals. Few attempts are made to enforce segregation on buses and trains themselves. Planes have never been affected.

Restrictions are still found on many bus lines and a few railroads operating within the borders of a given state. However, they are being eased as the result of voluntary action, economic pressure and Federal court orders.

In the matter of custom, many Negroes continue to sit in the rear of buses. Cases of their sharing seats with whites are rare. Leaders in the desegregation struggle have complained frequently over this failure to exercise newly-won rights.

Section heads often separate groups of paragraphs that relate to the central idea.

In Writing for Tests

When you write for tests, you also need a central idea for your paper and details to support it. Look at these papers. They have been scored using the Writing Rubric for Focus and Unity on page 91. Study each paper to see why it got the score it did.

Overall Score: 4

The writer introduces the **topic** and **central idea**.

The **main idea** of each paragraph goes with the central idea.

Water

Abraham Moreno

If I could be anything in the world, it would be water. I love water, but not necessarily to drink. What I love is water's way of being.

Water can do anything it wishes. It's a shape-shifter that changes forms with ease. If someone wants it to fit inside a cup, a vase, or a bucket, it can. However, water is not always easily molded. It can also be dense as a rock when solid. If it wants, it can form a thick glacier that's impossible to melt or penetrate. And when it doesn't want to be a changeable fluid or a hard, icy mass, it becomes an insubstantial cloud. As a vapor, it floats above the world and drifts away without being seen or touched.

Each detail relates to the main idea of the paragraph.

No one can hurt or damage water. Sure, it can get dirty and polluted. But water can change that too, by rushing along so fast that it leaves all impurities behind.

I wish I could be like water. Then I could choose whether to be strong and unyielding or flowing and adaptable. And when I wanted to, I could become an invisible escape artist.

The conclusion is also about the **central idea**.

Water

I love water, but not necessarily to drink. There are several reasons why I think water is cool.

Water can do anything it wishes. It's a shape-shifter that changes forms with ease. If someone wants it to fit inside a cup, a vase, or a bucket, it can. However, water is not always easily molded. It can also be dense as a rock when solid. If it wants, it can form a thick glacier that's impossible to melt or penetrate. And when it doesn't want to be a changeable fluid or a hard, icy mass, it becomes an insubstantial cloud. As a vapor, it floats above the world and drifts away without being seen or touched.

No one can hurt or damage water. Sure, it can get dirty and polluted. Pollution is a big problem that affects water as well as air. It's important to try to reduce the amount of pollution in our water.

I wish I could be like water. Then I could choose whether to be strong and unyielding or flowing and adaptable. And when I wanted to, I could become an invisible escape artist.

The **topic** is clear, but the **central idea** is not specific.

The **main idea** of each paragraph goes with the central idea.

These **details** do not go with the main idea of the paragraph.

The conclusion is about the **central idea.**

RAISING *THE SCORE*

The writer should make the central idea more specific and take out the details about air and water pollution, which don't belong in the paragraph. Do these details belong in the paper at all?

In Writing for Tests, continued

Overall Score: 2

Water

The writing has a **topic**, but no central idea.

Did you know that the oceans cover almost three-quarters of the Earth's surface? That's just one of many cool facts about water.

These details do not go with the **main idea** of the paragraph.

What's more, water can do anything it wishes. It's a shape-shifter that can change its form. If someone wants it to fit inside a cup, it can. But water can also be like a rock when solid. And, it can be a little cloud. There are many different kinds of clouds. Fog is actually a type of cloud, too.

Speaking of clouds, did you know that lightning could strike during the wintertime as well as during the summer? Most people associate lightning strikes with summer storms, but they can happen during snowstorms, too.

This paragraph is not about water, so it does not go with the topic.

During the big snowstorm last winter, I was amazed when I heard thunder and saw flashes of lightning. I didn't think that was possible.

The conclusion is not about the topic.

RAISING THE SCORE

The writer needs to include a central idea about the topic—water. What could the writer say? Then the writer needs to revise the third paragraph and the conclusion to go with the central idea.

Water

Did you know that the water in the oceans covers almost three-quarters of the Earth's surface? That's just one of many cool neat facts about water.

Water is a shape-shifter. I think it's so cool that water can fit inside a cup or a bucket. But water can be like a rock, too. It can become a little cloud. For me, one of the best parts of a plane ride is looking outside the window and seeing that you're actually inside a cloud.

Experts say that people need to exercise every day. You should drink even more water when it's hot out or when you are exercising. Most people do not drink enough water.

Human beings can live for days on little or even no food. But no human being can live for very long without water or other drinks.

The writing has too many **topics** and no central idea.

These paragraphs do not relate to the same topic.

This paragraph has a **main idea**, but the last detail is not related.

The conclusion does not wrap up the ideas in the paper.

RAISING *THE SCORE*

The writer should focus on one topic, instead of writing about water, plane rides, and exercise. If the writer's topic is water as a shape-shifter, which sentences can be kept?

Central Ideas Stated in Nonfiction

Whether you write fiction or nonfiction, you need a central idea about your topic. This central, or controlling, idea helps you decide which main ideas and details to include. It keeps your writing focused.

The Thesis Statement

For many forms of nonfiction writing, the central idea shows up in a **thesis statement**. A thesis statement tells your purpose for writing or gives your opinion about a topic. To create a thesis statement, narrow down your central idea so it works for what you are writing.

Here's what one writer did for a three-paragraph essay:

Central Idea:

> I want to write about the amount of water people should drink.

Sample Thesis Statements:

> Drinking water is beneficial for the human body. ⟵ Too broad
>
> Water is a good way to hydrate your skin. ⟵ Too narrow
>
> Research shows that a popular belief about how much water we should drink is a myth, not a fact. ⟵ Just right

H$_2$O: Beyond the Hype

Samara Wilson

We've all heard the same advice from nutritionists, health magazines, and even doctors: "Drink a minimum of eight 8-ounce glasses of water per day." More and more people are following this advice and carrying water bottles with them wherever they go. But do we really need to be drinking water, water, everywhere? Research shows that this popular belief about how much water we should drink is a myth, not a fact.

Recent scientific studies suggest that an average adult doesn't really need to drink 64 ounces of water per day after all. Most American adults drink plenty of juice, soda, coffee, and tea—and yes, caffeinated beverages do count toward your daily fluid intake after all.

The **thesis statement** gives your purpose for writing.

Each **main idea** supports the thesis.

Details support the main idea.

Central Ideas Unstated in Nonfiction

For some nonfiction forms like personal essays or letters, you may not state a thesis directly. However, you still need a central idea.

November 8, 2007

Dear Samara,

Thanks for the copy of your essay about the H_2O hype. I was really surprised by your research on how much water we should drink. My gym teacher always says people need tons of water to stay healthy. It sounds as if everyone should reconsider the amount of water people really need to drink.

Could you send me some of the sources you used for your essay? I'm doing a science project on "Medical Myths," and I'd like to use this as an example.

Speaking of medical myths, did you know that taking large amounts of Vitamin C does not stop you from getting a cold? As a matter of fact, too much of it can be harmful.

I really look forward to receiving the sources you used for your essay.

Sincerely,

Leticia Galliano

Leticia Galliano

Although the letter doesn't state a central idea, it's clearly all about the truth behind false popular beliefs.

Think about the writer's message in this essay. What is the central idea?

Someone To Talk To

After my dad left, Mom wanted to get me a Big Brother to hang out with. She said I needed someone to talk to. I didn't think I needed anyone, though. I wasn't a charity case. But I finally let her take me to a meeting, where I met Jamal.

I was pretty rude to Jamal at first, but I think he understood where I was coming from and let me have my space. After meeting a few more times, he asked if I wanted to go fishing on Lake Sandy outside the city. I wasn't very enthusiastic about it, but decided to go anyway.

So that Saturday, we headed out to the lake. Floating there in this little boat was so peaceful and quiet until I started talking, and talking, about everything. Jamal understood a lot. He had lost his father, too. It may sound corny, but sometimes I guess you need to let your feelings out. And if you're lucky, you'll find someone like Jamal who understands.

Central Ideas in Fiction and Poetry

Fiction and poetry also have central ideas. When you write a story, for example, you focus on those details that develop your central ideas about your characters, setting, and plot.

Fiction

A Summer at the Pool

Each summer, ever since he was little, Monté looked forward to the day the neighborhood pool would open. Now he was more impatient than ever. At 17, Monté wasn't a kid anymore. He was a certified lifeguard. Now that he'd completed his training, he would be working at the pool three days a week.

Being a lifeguard was a big responsibility, but Monté was used to protecting little kids. After all, he had three younger brothers, and ever since his mother went back to work full time, he had helped raise them.

The **details** create a unified portrait of the character, Monté.

They focus on the central idea that he's a caring, responsible teen.

For poetry, you might focus on a single theme or even a single image. A haiku, for example, is a Japanese form of poetry that focuses on one image using just three lines.

Poetry

The Pond

The sound of splashing—
A frog disturbs the stillness
Of a tranquil pond.

In this poem, the poet focuses on a single event. Each stanza adds more details to paint a colorful picture of the same event.

Going for Water

by Robert Frost

The well was dry beside the door,
And so we went with pail and can
Across the fields behind the house
To seek the brook if still it ran;

Not loth to have excuse to go,
Because the autumn eve was fair
(Though chill), because the fields were ours,
And by the brook our woods were there.

We ran as if to meet the moon
That slowly dawned behind the trees,
The barren boughs without the leaves,
Without the birds, without the breeze.

But once within the wood, we paused
Like gnomes that hid us from the moon,
Ready to run to hiding new
With laughter when she found us soon.

Each laid on other a staying hand
To listen ere we dared to look,
And in the hush we joined to make
We heard, we knew we heard the brook.

A note as from a single place,
A slender tinkling fall that made
Now drops that floated on the pool
Like pearls, and now a silver blade.

Focus Your Paragraphs

After making sure all your ideas are about the same central idea, check your paragraphs. To keep them focused and unified:

1 Use a topic sentence to state the main idea.
Although the topic sentence can be in the beginning, middle, or end of a paragraph, it is usually at the beginning or the end. Depending upon where you place your topic sentence, you may need to change the details you use or how you organize them.

- If you want your readers to know right away what your paragraph is about, place the topic sentence at the very beginning. Then add the related details.

- If you want to emphasize your point a little more, give all the details first, and then place the topic sentence at the end.

2 Be sure each detail, fact, or example relates to the main idea.
Ask yourself: Does each detail say something more about the main idea? Are all the details important?

How are these paragraphs the same? How are they different? First look at the topic sentences, and then see how the details flow.

Bottled water is a beverage company's dream product. I bet it's cheaper to make than soft drinks, since companies don't need to add sugar, flavoring, coloring, or carbonation. They just bottle water that comes from a spring. Bottled water is easy to market, too. Customers know that it's healthier than soft drinks. They also think it's purer than tap water and has a better taste.

As I opened a bottle of water after my workout today, I started thinking about how clever companies are to market and sell water that we can get for free from a tap or fountain. After all, does bottled water really taste that much better? Will drinking bottled water increase my strength or stamina? Not really, but I buy it anyway. Bottled water is a beverage company's dream product.

Focus Your Paper

Control It from Start to Finish

An essay has more detail and information than a short poem or paragraph. In a traditional five-paragraph essay for school, you can maintain your focus by following these steps:

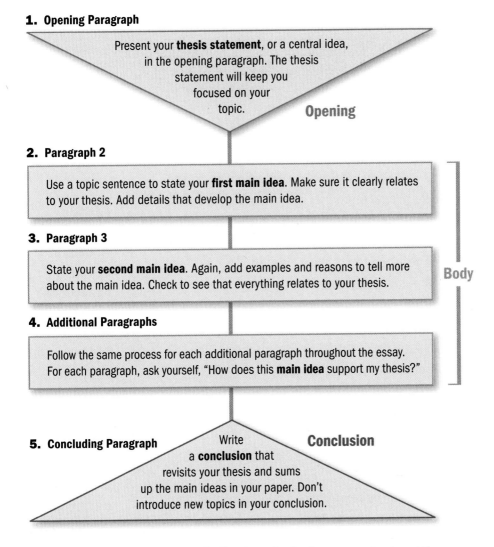

1. Opening Paragraph

Present your **thesis statement**, or a central idea, in the opening paragraph. The thesis statement will keep you focused on your topic.

Opening

2. Paragraph 2

Use a topic sentence to state your **first main idea**. Make sure it clearly relates to your thesis. Add details that develop the main idea.

3. Paragraph 3

State your **second main idea**. Again, add examples and reasons to tell more about the main idea. Check to see that everything relates to your thesis.

4. Additional Paragraphs

Follow the same process for each additional paragraph throughout the essay. For each paragraph, ask yourself, "How does this **main idea** support my thesis?"

Body

5. Concluding Paragraph

Write a **conclusion** that revisits your thesis and sums up the main ideas in your paper. Don't introduce new topics in your conclusion.

Conclusion

Remember to have a central idea in mind when you start writing. As you develop your writing, it's OK to revise it if you need to.

Focus Your Paper, continued

Test Your Focus

You can give your paper to a friend to read. If your writing is focused and unified, your friend should be able to summarize the main points in a sentence or two. Or, you can test yourself:

1 **Add a title.** The title should cue what your paper is all about.

2 **Add section headings.** Read just your title and headings aloud. If they go together, your paper is probably focused. If they don't, make the headings go together, and then fix your writing to go with each heading.

WATER MATTERS

Water is tasteless, odorless, and essential to life. We drink it, prepare food in it, and bathe in it. We may also get sick from it when it is contaminated. Water matters. Every human being on Earth should have access to clean water.

Drinking Water in the U.S.

The United States has strict water quality regulations. The Safe Water Drinking Act protects Americans against natural and man-made contaminants in the water supply.

Diseases

In many developing countries, people suffer from intestinal parasites because they don't have access to safe drinking water. Contaminated water causes disease.

Clean water is important for good health. The U.S. government needs to budget more money to help developing countries maintain a safe water supply.

" I'll change 'Diseases' to 'Water in Developing Countries' and rewrite the paragraph so it relates more to my thesis.**"**

Focus While You Edit

When you edit your work, what you take out is just as important as what you choose to include. To make your writing more focused and unified, take out:

- extraneous, or extra, details that are not about your topic.

> It's easy to conserve water. For example, you can save dozens of gallons of water if you don't wash clothes until you have a full load. ~~You should avoid wasting electricity, too.~~ When brushing your teeth, turn off the faucet until you need to rinse. These small changes can save hundreds of gallons of water per year.

- details that are not consistent with the central idea.

> Cherrapunji, a village in northeastern India, is sometimes called "the wettest place on earth." ~~Mt. Waialeale in Hawaii is also very wet, averaging about 450 inches of rain per year.~~ Over the past seventy years, Cherrapunji has averaged 450 inches per year. This village holds the record for the most rain in a year—over 900 inches!

- unnecessary repetitions of the same idea.

> Sarah Myers was soft-spoken and shy, so people were surprised at how strongly she expressed her opinions ~~and the way she felt~~ about the environment. As a sophomore, for example, she convinced more than 1500 people to sign ~~their names on~~ a petition to prevent local factories from dumping chemicals into the Clearwater River.

Structure Your Writing

Window Looking to Panarea, 2000, Leon Morrocco. Oil on canvas, The Bridgeman Art Library, New York

What's It Like ?

How does this painting make you feel? The artist carefully arranged the images so you could appreciate having a relaxing, delicious lunch as you gaze out over the water. Writers work in much the same way, arranging their ideas purposely so their writing flows and readers can appreciate the masterpiece!

Organize Your Writing

"**I**n organized writing, the sentences and paragraphs flow logically one into the other. For example, the main character is walking along a street. You expect to get some sense of what she sees, whom she might pass by, what she is thinking, and where she is going."

To help your readers know what to expect:

● Use a topic sentence and related details to organize your paragraphs for the best effect.

● Arrange the paragraphs in your essays and stories in the best possible order to get your ideas across.

● Use transitions to connect ideas and create a smooth flow from one idea to the next.

FOCUS POINT Study the rubric on page 111. What is the difference between a paper with a score of 4 and one with a score of 2?

Organization

	Does the writing have a clear structure, and is it appropriate for the writer's purpose?	How smoothly do the ideas flow together?
4 **Wow!**	The writing has a clear structure that is appropriate for the writer's purpose.	The ideas progress in a smooth and orderly way. • The **ideas** flow well from **paragraph** to **paragraph**. • The ideas in each paragraph flow well from one **sentence** to the next. • Meaningful and effective **transitions** connect ideas.
3 **Ahh.**	The writing has a structure that is generally clear and appropriate for the writer's purpose.	<u>Most</u> of the ideas progress in a smooth and orderly way. • Most of the **ideas** flow well from **paragraph** to **paragraph**. • Most of the ideas in each paragraph flow well from one **sentence** to the next. • Meaningful and effective **transitions** connect most of the ideas.
2 **Hmm.**	The structure of the writing is not clear or not appropriate for the writer's purpose.	<u>Some</u> of the ideas progress in a smooth and orderly way. • Some of the **ideas** flow well from **paragraph** to **paragraph**. • Some of the ideas in each paragraph flow well from one **sentence** to the next. • Meaningful and effective **transitions** connect some of the ideas.
1 **Huh?**	The writing does not have a structure.	<u>Few or none</u> of the ideas progress in a smooth and orderly way. The ideas in the paragraphs and sentences do not flow well together and are not connected with transitions.

In Literary Works

Writers choose different ways to organize their ideas. The organization they use depends on the kind of writing they want to do. How does Julius Lester organize the ideas in his memoir?

On Art and Writing

by Julius Lester

Lester presents events in chronological order—from high school to college.

I began studying art in high school, primarily because my homeroom teacher, Nathan Holiday, who was also the art teacher, would not accept that anyone could not draw or paint. Although I was not very talented, he helped me develop what little ability I had. I minored in art at Fisk, primarily so I could study with Aaron Douglas, who had been the leading artist of the Harlem Renaissance of the 1920s. That spring semester of my junior year I had a small exhibit of paintings and drawings. Although I have drawn and painted intermittently in the years since, my need to be creative visually found expression in photography, a passion since childhood that involves me more deeply now than ever.

Detail of *Aaron Douglas*, 1953, Betsy Graves Reyneau. Oil on canvas, Smithsonian Institution, Washington, DC

Aaron Douglas was Lester's art professor.

Julius Lester
in Atlanta,
Georgia, 1966 ▶

Studying art taught me how to rewrite. When drawing with charcoal, a black tone is not created all at once. You begin with light grays, and by applying more and more layers of gray a black tone is eventually achieved in gradations of tone. The same is true in watercolor painting where colors are layered until there is a flow from the lightest saturations of color to the most vibrant. So, when I rewrite I visualize myself back in the art studio at Fisk, hunched over a drawing board delicately shading a charcoal drawing.

The study and appreciation of art has also helped me learn to see. My wife and I go to museums and galleries as often as we can to educate our eyes and souls to what is possible when you allow your spirit to swim deep into the realm of the imagination.

Here Lester switches to logical order, starting with this **main idea**.

His ideas flow well from one sentence to the next.

Photograph courtesy of Julius Lester.

Some of Lester's photographs document life in the rural South during the 1960s.

In Literary Works, continued

MEMOIR

During my college years, I considered making a career of music or art, but neither came as easily to me as writing. I had an instinct for words, which are so real to me that I feel like I hold them in my hands and assess their weight and shape before deciding which ones to put on the page. Other times, words are like colored grains of sand, and I am not so much writing as creating a mosaic or sand painting.

I also have a patience with words that I lacked with music and art. My piano playing could be sloppy because I didn't want to devote the necessary time to reworking a phrase until I had found the best fingering. When I drew, I knew what I was supposed to do to create a rich charcoal black, but I could be impatient making layer after layer of gray. After I began photographing seriously, I loved spending eight to ten hours in the darkroom making prints, but I did not have the patience of a W. Eugene Smith, who took eight hours to make *one* print (but now I am learning). However, I will rewrite a sentence, paragraph, page, twenty-five, thirty, and more times.

Transitions move the sentences and paragraphs along in a smooth flow.

In Reports

Reports give information on a topic. The writer usually presents the information in a logical order. Transitions connect the ideas.

American Sign Language

Bringing Hearing and Deaf People Together

Ayana Dickson

One unusual talent I could use in the workplace is my knowledge of American Sign Language, or ASL. Most people are surprised that I understand ASL even though I can hear. I learned sign language when I was very young so I could communicate with my older brother, Mark, who is deaf. I hope to work with deaf students when I'm older. During my visit to the South Carolina School for the Deaf and Blind (SCSDB), I learned about an exciting program that brings hearing and deaf people together.

Our family visited SCSDB last month because Mark wants to enter their digital arts program after he graduates from high school. The school assigned a recent graduate, Carrie Pennington, to give us a tour of the campus.

The writer states the topic.

Then the writer explains how she knows about the program.

In Reports, continued

Afterward, I interviewed Carrie, who's deaf, about her own experience at SCSDB.

"I loved my time here," she said. "I went to a regular public school when I was a kid, so this was the first time I'd ever been around so many people, both hearing and deaf, who knew ASL." Carrie went on to explain, "Before I signed up for the digital arts program, I didn't know what I wanted to do. I liked photography, but I had no idea what kinds of jobs were out there." At SCSDB, Carrie took courses in photography, page layout and design, and computer technology. "Now I want to work in publishing," she said, "and use computers to design graphics for magazine pages."

Both the deaf and the hearing communities have recognized the program's students for their talent. Carrie recently won an award for some design work she did for a local magazine. She also introduced us to a friend of hers who's used his photography and design skills to create posters for businesses in Spartanburg. And in 2004, a group of digital arts students was honored by the South Carolina Senate for creating a color poster showing scenes of South Carolina life.

I asked Carrie about what skills students learn in the digital arts program. "We learn about everything!" she said. "How to plan the layout of a magazine, how to put a Web page together, even how to create animations for video. It's great because employers are really interested in hiring people with those skills. Some of my friends have managed to land a job before they even graduate. Our lab is really state-of-the-art, too. Since the technology is constantly changing, we need to keep up with all the latest advances."

The digital arts program at SCSDB is truly successful in connecting deaf and hearing people. After touring the school and interviewing Carrie Pennington, I'm now more interested than ever in putting my ASL skills to use as a teacher.

A teacher signs a lesson.

This paragraph adds information about the skills students learn.

The writer repeats key words to connect ideas within the paragraph.

In Writing for Tests

Good organization is also important when you need to write an essay for a test. These papers have been scored using the Writing Rubric for Organization on page 111. Study each paper to see why it got the score it did.

Overall Score: 4

Filling Up the Pages

Abdalla Harhara

The writer's purpose is to explain a **change**.

When I was a kid, I was never very good at keeping a journal. But when I moved to the United States with my family, my journal became my lifeline.

This paragraph describes one discovery that led to the change.

First, I discovered that writing in my journal each day helps me deal with changes in my life. Moving was hard, but my journal always comforts me. Some entries are bright and sunny, while others are gloomy. Sometimes I write slowly and carefully. Other times, I just let my thoughts and feelings pour out. Whatever my mood, writing in a journal helps me understand myself.

Transitions connect ideas.

The next paragraph describes another discovery.

Secondly, I realized that journal writing helps me write better. I used to have trouble getting started on school papers. I would stare at the blank canvas of my paper for hours. Now I just grab a pen and fill up the whiteness with ink. The more I write, the more I have to say.

Sentences move along in an orderly way.

In the past, I never thought of myself as a writer, but keeping a journal has taught me about the power of language. Now I use my journal to paint a picture of myself in both good and bad times.

The last paragraph sums up the change and its impact on the writer's life.

Filling Up the Pages

The writer's purpose is to explain a **change**.

When I was a kid, I was never very good at keeping a journal. But when I moved to the United States with my family, my journal became my lifeline.

This paragraph describes one discovery that led to the change.

First, I discovered that writing in my journal each day helps me deal with changes in my life. Moving was hard, but my journal always comforts me. Some entries are bright and sunny, while others are gloomy. Sometimes I write slowly and carefully. Other times, I just let my thoughts and feelings pour out. Whatever my mood, writing in a journal helps me understand myself.

This **transition** connects the first two paragraphs.

This is about another discovery, but it's not clear right away.

Journal writing helps me write better. I used to have trouble getting started on school papers. I would stare at the blank paper for hours. The more I write, the more I have to say. Now I just grab a pen and fill up the whiteness with ink.

Most of the sentences flow smoothly, but the fourth one is out of order.

In the past, I never thought of myself as a writer, but keeping a journal has taught me about the power of language. Now I use my journal to paint a picture of myself in both good and bad times.

The last paragraph sums up the change and its impact on the writer's life.

RAISING *THE SCORE*

The writer needs to link the paragraphs with effective transitions. How could he make a smoother transition between the second and third paragraphs?

In Writing for Tests, continued

Filling Up the Pages

The writer's purpose is to explain a **change.**

I was never good at keeping a journal when I was a kid. Then I moved to the United States with my family. My journal has become my lifeline.

The point of this paragraph is not clear, and there is no link to the first paragraph.

Moving to a new country was really hard. Writing in my journal helps me understand myself no matter what mood I'm in. My journal entries can be bright and sunny or sad sometimes. I might write slowly and carefully or just let my thoughts and feelings pour out.

The structure of the writing continues to be unclear.

The more I write, the more I have to say. Writing in my journal helps me write better. Before, I used to have trouble getting started on papers for school. Now I can grab a pen and start filling up pages. I would stare at my paper for hours.

The sentences in this paragraph do not flow in a good order.

I never used to like reading or writing. I started keeping a journal and learned about the power of language.

RAISING THE SCORE

The writer needs to arrange the sentences in each paragraph so they flow. How can the writer improve the organization within his paragraphs?

Filling Up the Pages

The writer's purpose is to explain a **change**.

I didn't write every day when I was a kid. I moved to the United States with my family. My journal became my lifeline.

These paragraphs are out of order.

The more I write, the more I have to say. Writing in my journal helps me write better. I can grab a pen and fill up a page with writing. I would stare at my paper for hours. I used to have trouble getting started on papers for school.

The sentences do not flow in an orderly way.

Paragraph 3 should be first to continue the idea about moving to the U.S.

Moving to a new country was really hard. Writing in my journal helps me deal with my new life. My journal entries can be bright and sunny or sad. My journal is always there to help me. I might write slowly and carefully or just let my thoughts and feelings out.

I never used to like reading or writing. I started keeping a journal and learned how writing can help.

Transitions are missing. The ideas within and between paragraphs are not connected.

RAISING *THE SCORE*

The writer needs to reorganize the paragraphs and the sentences within each paragraph. How should the writer rearrange the paragraphs? How can he improve the progression of ideas?

How to Organize Your Paragraphs

When you write an essay, it's easier for your reader to understand your ideas if every paragraph is carefully organized. See the Writer's File in Chapter 1 on pages 30–37 for some text structures you might use to organize your paragraphs.

Connect the Main Idea and Details

Have you ever read a paragraph and wondered, "What point is this writer trying to make?" You can help your readers figure out your point right away if you use these techniques:

1 **Decide on a main idea for each paragraph and state it in a topic sentence.**

Most of the time, your topic sentence will be at the beginning or the end of the paragraph. But, depending upon your purpose, it might show up in the middle.

2 **Add details that tell more about the main idea.**

Use an order that makes sense for your purpose. Choose details that logically follow from your main idea if it's at the beginning. Or, you can lead up to your main idea if it's at the end.

❝ Let me show you my dream car. It'll have . . . ❞

Paragraphs can be organized in many different ways, but they all need a main idea and related details.

Topic Sentence at the Beginning

This is how I learned to do a "blind" charcoal drawing of a figure. First, I perch on the edge of a low stool with one knee on the floor. I hold my charcoal stick at arm's length. As I draw, I keep my eyes on the model the whole time, and outline the model's figure without looking down at the paper. I concentrate very carefully on the model, and my final drawing ends up looking very much like the subject—even though I haven't looked at my paper at all!

After presenting the main idea in a topic sentence, the writer uses a logical order to add the details.

Topic Sentence at the End

I perched on the edge of a low stool with one knee on the floor, holding my charcoal stick at arm's length. "Don't look at your sketchbook!" said my art teacher, Mrs. Bain. "Keep your eyes on the model while your hands do the drawing." I nervously outlined the figure without looking down at my paper. At the end of class, I was surprised to find that my drawing looked very much like the model. That's how I learned to do "blind" charcoal drawings.

The writer describes an experience first to lead up to the main idea. The topic sentence comes last.

Topic Sentence in the Middle

I perched on the edge of a low stool with one knee on the floor, holding my charcoal stick at arm's length. "Don't look at your sketchbook!" said my art teacher, Mrs. Bain. "Keep your eyes on the model while your hands do the drawing." I nervously outlined the figure without looking down at my paper. Could I really learn how to do "blind" charcoal drawings? At the end of class, I was surprised to find that my drawing looked very much like the model.

The writer creates a different effect by placing the topic sentence in the middle.

Logical Order in Paragraphs

When you choose an appropriate way to order your details, creating a well-organized paragraph is a snap. A paragraph organized by logical order may contain a main idea and details in any of the following arrangements:

- from general statements to specific details

- from specific details to more general statements

- from least important ideas to most important ideas

- from most important ideas to least important ideas.

Number 22, 1949, Jackson Pollock. Mixed media on paper, private collection

The Colors of a Festival

General ▷ From a distance, it was like an abstract Jackson Pollock painting. It looked like the artist had splattered colors all over the canvas, just as Pollock had done. When I got closer, though, the splotches of color began to look like a **More specific** ▷ scene. At first I thought it was a garden, but then realized it was a festival. I saw people with a parade of floats winding **Most specific** ▷ between them. Each float was covered in flowers, and the spectators were dressed in colorful costumes.

Jackson Pollock created abstract images by dripping or pouring paint on canvas.

Chronological Order in Paragraphs

Use chronological order to organize a series of events or the steps in a process.

Traditional methods of developing photographs involve a darkroom and chemicals.

How to Develop a Photo

I love the process of developing photos in the darkroom. First, I make a contact print by placing the negatives on a sheet of photo paper and exposing them to light for a specific amount of time. Then I put the photo paper in the developing solution. When the print is "done," I slide it into the fixer—a chemical that binds the images to the paper. Finally, I study the contact print and choose the image I want to work with.

> First step

> Step 2

> Step 3

> Last step

A contact print shows all the photos taken so you can choose a favorite. ▶

Cause and Effect in Paragraphs

Cause-and-effect writing explains why something happened. Depending on your topic, you can choose among several different ways to organize your writing:

- Discuss the effects that resulted from one cause.

- Discuss how several causes led to an effect.

- Present a causal chain, in which each effect becomes the cause of another effect.

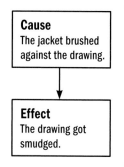

Cause
The jacket brushed against the drawing.

↓

Effect
The drawing got smudged.

A Careless Mistake

After I drew the daisies in pastels, I left my drawing on the kitchen table. The next day, when I came home from school, I unthinkingly tossed my jacket over a chair. It brushed against my drawing and smudged it. That made me feel pretty irritated with myself. As a result, I resolved not to be so careless in the future.

What other causes and effects can you find?

Spatial Order in Paragraphs

Use spatial order to describe something so your reader can picture what it's like—from inside to outside, left to right, or bottom to top.

Man Loaded with Lilies, 1950, Diego Rivera. Water color on rice paper, The Bridgeman Art Gallery, NY

Photo © Christie's Images, Private Collection

Man Carrying Calla Lilies

A man seems to be walking across a tile floor carrying a straw basket high near his waist. His strong hands grip the top rim of the basket, holding it steady. Blossoming yellow calla lilies stretch up and out of the basket to form a giant canopy that completely hides his head.

In what order does the writer describe the painting?

Location words clarify where things are.

Comparison and Contrast in Paragraphs

When you want to compare or contrast two things, you can tell how they are alike or different on each point. Or, you can present all of the information about one thing before telling all about the other.

Art and Writing Communicate!

The writer compares art and writing on each point.

Comparison words signal that the two things are alike.

It's easy to see why people who are attracted to art are also attracted to writing. Both art and writing are strong ways of communicating. Visual artists express themselves in a variety of ways—drawing, painting, sculpture. Similarly, writers choose among many different genres, such as poetry, fiction, or journalism. Both forms of communication take patience, practice, and talent. Moreover, both need an audience.

Art and Writing Communicate!

The writer presents the points about art first and then tells how writing is the same.

Comparison words signal that the two things are alike.

It's easy to see why people who are attracted to art are also attracted to writing. Art is a strong way of communicating. Visual artists express themselves in a variety of ways—drawing, painting, sculpture. They need patience, practice, and talent, and an audience to appreciate their work. Writing is a strong way to communicate, too. Like artists, writers express themselves in a variety of ways: poetry, fiction, or journalism. They also need patience, practice, and talent, and an audience to appreciate their work.

Problem and Solution in Paragraphs

Use this structure to tell about possible solutions to a given problem.

The writer states a **problem** and then explores a **solution** in detail.

Your Perfect Profession

If you think you want to be a communicator, but you don't yet know what kind, be sure to take a variety of classes. A class on current events or journalism might help you realize an interest in news reporting. Learning about contemporary literature might lead you toward writing novels or short stories. Taking classes on media communications might inspire you to work in television or radio. Consider your interests and abilities, and combine them with what you learn. You just might come up with the perfect profession for you.

Reporters gather around cricket player Rahul Dravid prior to a 2003 World Cup match between India and Pakistan.

Opinions and Support in Paragraphs

Use this structure when you want to convince readers to agree
with your point of view.

Sailor Kissing Nurse, 1945, Alfred Eisenstaedt. Photograph.

A sailor kisses a nurse
on the streets of
New York City at the
end of World War II. ▶

Reuters © Time, Inc.

Photography IS Art

The writer states
a **position** and
then presents
**supporting
arguments**.

Some people think that photography is a craft,
but artists use creativity and technical skill to
affect people's emotions. By that definition, I think
photographers are artists. They make creative
decisions when they frame a subject, decide how
to use light and shadow for effect, and choose the
type of print to make—black-and-white or color,
smooth or grainy. Photography also requires
technical skill, whether the artist is working in
a darkroom or manipulating a digital image on
a computer. Finally, a good photograph provokes
an emotional response. Think about Alfred
Eisenstaedt's photo of a sailor kissing a nurse in
the street when World War II ended. It took a true
artist to preserve that moment forever.

What other
arguments
support
the writer's
position?

Getting Your Paragraph to Flow

Choosing a suitable structure is the first step in building a good paragraph. The next step is getting your ideas to flow. A little doodling before you start writing may help. For example:

- Sketch out a quick graphic organizer with the specific points you intend to cover.

- Note some transition words that can connect your sentences when you write. (See the Writer's File on pages 136–139 for transitions that work for different purposes.)

	however	unlike	in contrast
	Watercolor Painting	**Oil Painting**	
in addition	easy for beginners	takes a long time to learn	such as
for example	materials are cheap	materials are expensive	
	done on paper	done on canvas	
	almost any brush is okay	worth getting a good brush	

As you write, follow your plan and use transitions to achieve a coherent paragraph with ideas that flow.

Effective Paragraph with a Good Flow

Like most kids, I started my "artistic career" with watercolors. (After crayons, of course!) Painting with watercolors is easy for beginners. In addition, materials are relatively cheap. For example, watercolor is done on paper, almost any old brush will do a decent job, and you use plain water to mix colors and for cleanup. When I "graduated" to oil painting, I was in for a surprise or two. Unlike watercolors, oil painting is done on canvas, and the paints and solvents are expensive (such as that shocking $35 brush!). My early watercolors were fun and satisfying. My early oils, however, were a sticky mess. Ultimately, climbing the learning curve of oil painting was worth it for me, but it isn't for the faint of heart or the faint of pocket!

Organizing Longer Works

Longer works like essays and stories need a clear organization, too. Here are some ways to keep your writing well organized no matter how many paragraphs you have!

Check the Order of Your Paragraphs

How well do your paragraphs go together? Here are some ways you can check the organization.

- Highlight the topic sentence of each paragraph as in the essay on page 133. Then reread your essay. The topic sentences should read like a summary of your essay. Ask yourself: Does the order make sense?

- Write your main ideas on sticky notes so you can easily rearrange them to plan or improve the order of the paragraphs in your paper.

1 Aaron Douglas: artist who used African design/ subject matter

2 Became a popular painter and magazine illustrator

3 Painted murals at NYC Library

4 Taught art at Fisk University

Aaron Douglas taught at Fisk University from 1940 to 1969.

A Pioneering Artist

Painter Aaron Douglas emerged in the 1920s as one of the exciting new artists of the Harlem Renaissance. After earning a degree in fine arts and teaching in Kansas City schools, Douglas began illustrating books and magazines. The African designs and subject matter in his artwork caught the attention of leading artists and writers of the day.

Douglas's work became very well known during his lifetime. It was published in popular magazines such as *Vanity Fair*. His paintings, which also adorned book jackets, became so famous that he was called a "pioneering Africanist." His style featured flat, hard-edged patterns that included African-influenced motifs of jazz music and dance.

During the 1930s, Douglas painted a series of murals at a New York City library. The murals showed figures fleeing slavery and domination. They also showed a musician who symbolized the creativity of the Harlem Renaissance of the 1920s.

Douglas joined the faculty of Fisk University in Nashville, Tennessee, in the late 1930s. He taught art there until his retirement nearly three decades later. His murals adorn the walls of some of the university's buildings. Douglas's tenure at Fisk was the culmination of a successful career as the "Dean of African American painters."

Aspects of Negro Life: An Idyll of the Deep South, 1934, Aaron Douglas. Oil on canvas, The New York Public Library, NY

An Idyll of the Deep South is one work in the series of murals Douglas created for the New York Public Library.

Organizing Longer Works, continued

Transitions help your readers follow your train of thought. They are like signposts that point out what direction you're heading in.

Make Frequent Use of Transitions

You can use transitions for many purposes such as:

- showing contradictions

> In much of the South in the early 1920s, it was a time of racial persecution and segregation for African Americans. But In Harlem, in New York City, it was a time of great literary excitement and creativity.

- pointing out cause-and-effect relationships

> Many came to Harlem to share their culture, racial pride, and talent with the world. As a result, There was an explosion of artistic works.

- introducing examples

> There were many novelists and poets who started their careers during this period. For example, Langston Hughes published his first collection of verse, The Weary Blues, in 1926.

- emphasizing a point

> Other talented people like the painter and muralist Aaron Douglas also became very successful during the Harlem Renaissance. In fact, You'll probably recognize some of these musicians' names: Louis Armstrong, Duke Ellington, Bessie Smith.

Look at the difference transitions make in the essay on page 135.

The Harlem Renaissance

During the early twentieth century, African American art and culture flourished in New York City within the mostly black neighborhood of Harlem. Overnight, it seemed, there was an explosion of new talent and artistic works in literature, drama, music, and the visual arts.

Today, these artistic works still resonate. For example, the writings of Langston Hughes, Zora Neale Hurston, and James Weldon Johnson are now considered classics. People everywhere enjoy listening to jazz musicians such as Duke Ellington and Louis Armstrong, and blues singers such as Bessie Smith. When you experience these works of art, you can connect to this exciting period in African American history.

These **time words** help the writer transition from the past to today.

A **repeated phrase** connects ideas in different paragraphs.

These **transitions** let you know to expect a list or an example.

The Harlem Renaissance

During the early twentieth century, African American art and culture flourished in New York City within the mostly black neighborhood of Harlem. Overnight, it seemed, there was an explosion of new talent and artistic works in literature, drama, music, and the visual arts.

The writings of Langston Hughes, Zora Neale Hurston, and James Weldon Johnson are considered classics. People everywhere enjoy listening to jazz musicians Duke Ellington and Louis Armstrong, and blues singer Bessie Smith. You can connect to this exciting period in African American history.

Without transitions, the writing seems dull and choppy.

Without a transition to the new paragraph, the writer's shift in time is not clear.

For more about using transitions, see the Writer's File on pages 136–139.

Louis Armstrong

Transition Words and Phrases

Techniques for Connecting Ideas

Think about how the ideas in a paragraph are related. Then use transitions to show the connection. The transition you use depends on what you want to accomplish.

Add Related Ideas
When you add related ideas or details, you can use these words and phrases:

in addition   **furthermore**   **moreover**

> Joelle signed up for a modern dance class at school, **in addition** to her weekly ballet lessons. **Furthermore**, she plans to major in dance when she goes to college.

Introduce Examples or Lists
These transitions will introduce examples or lists that support your ideas:

for example   **to illustrate**   **including**
for instance   **such as**   **in one case**

> Many instruments played around the world resemble the guitar. **For instance,** a long-necked, stringed instrument called a sitar is common in India.

Show Events or Ideas in Sequence
Some words can show the order of events or the steps in a process:

before   **second**   **after**   **last**
first   **third**   **next**   **finally**

> Learning how to play the piano is complicated. **First** you spend hours just practicing scales and other exercises. **Next** you have to start learning how to read music. **After** a few weeks of lessons, you'll **finally** be ready to learn your first song.

Show Time
Use words like these to show when events occur:

before	**now**	**soon**
earlier	**today**	**after**
back then	**meanwhile**	**later**
in the past	**immediately**	**in the future**

> **In the past, before** there were digital cameras, photographers would spend hours in a darkroom to perfect their work. The process is much easier **today**. Both amateur and professional photographers use computers to edit digital images.

Show Place

Here are some words to use when you want to show where things are located in relation to each other:

here	above	nearby
there	across from	farther
next to	below	in front of
behind	on the other side	inside

One of M.C. Escher's best-known works is his 1935 lithograph, "Hand with Reflecting Sphere." **Inside** the sphere is the reflection of the man who holds the sphere in his hand. His distorted bookshelves are visible **above** him. **Farther back** is a window.

Hand with Reflecting Sphere, 1935, MC Escher. The MC Escher Company, Holland

Compare

When you want to show how two or more things are alike, use these words to connect ideas:

similarly	like
in the same way	also
likewise	both

Georgia O'Keeffe and her husband, Alfred Stieglitz, were among the most important artists of the twentieth century. O'Keeffe's bold, original paintings attracted attention throughout her lifetime. **Like** O'Keeffe, Stieglitz was **also** a pioneer. His work showed people that photography could be an art form.

Contrast

You can use these words to show how two or more things are different:

in contrast	however	unlike
on the other hand	but	different

Unlike earlier painters, who used themes from history and mythology, the Impressionists focused on everyday subject matter. Classical painters often used dark, somber hues. **In contrast**, Impressionists preferred light, intense colors.

Transitions, *continued*

Show Causes and Effects or Logical Connections

These words show how one event leads to another and how events or ideas are logically connected:

because	therefore	as a result
due to	the effect was	it follows that
since	consequently	thus

Because Langston Hughes is one of the best-known poets of the Harlem Renaissance, his work is included in many anthologies. **Thus,** many people are familiar with his poems "The Weary Blues" and "Dreams."

Like other artists, writers may have to struggle for years before their talent is recognized. **It follows that** many writers have trouble finding a publisher for their first book.

Emphasize an Important Idea

Do you want to make sure your reader understands an important point? Use one of these transitions for emphasis:

more importantly	in fact
most importantly	in particular
as a matter of fact	above all

Beginning writers need to be very persistent and not give up. **In particular,** they should try sending their work to multiple publishers. Even if one publisher rejects it, someone else might accept it.

Wrap Up Your Ideas

These transitions will help you wrap up your ideas at the end of an essay:

in conclusion	in summary	all in all
in short	to sum up	

Czech-born writer Franz Kafka had a day job at an insurance agency. The American poet William Carlos Williams was also a medical doctor, and George Orwell, the English novelist and essayist, briefly supported himself as a dishwasher. **In short**, many writers have had second jobs or even second careers.

Restate an Idea

Use these transitions when you want to restate an idea in slightly different words:

that is	to put it simply
in other words	to put it another way

> Whether you write short stories, poetry, or nonfiction, it takes a lot of time and effort to develop your craft. **In other words**, practice makes perfect.

Present Different Possibilities

These transitions come in handy when you want to present two possible outcomes or choices:

either ... or	alternatively	otherwise
instead	rather than	

> He was a talented artist, but he chose to pursue a writing career **instead** of studying art. **Otherwise**, he might have become a famous painter.

Show How One Outcome Depends on Another

Use these words to show how one outcome depends on another:

if ... then	unless	assuming that

> Carmen applied for a scholarship for art school. **Assuming that** she receives it, she won't need to work full-time while going to school.

Introduce an Unexpected Idea

To introduce an unexpected idea, or an idea that contradicts something you said earlier, try these transitions:

however	actually	even though
yet	but	despite
although	even so	on the contrary

> Vincent van Gogh was an unknown artist during his lifetime, **yet** his work became famous in the decades after his death.

Self-Portrait, 1889, Vincent van Gogh. Oil on canvas, Musée d'Orsay, Paris

Expand on Your Ideas

When you spread a tasty tomato sauce on a pizza and add a lot of toppings, you have a dish that everyone wants to eat. Applause for the chef! You can get applause for your writing, too, if you develop your ideas as deeply as a deep dish pizza and pile it high with details.

How Do You Develop Ideas in Depth?

"**Y**ou expect that the author is going to tell you who the character in a story is and what happens. But to be truly involved in the story, the author needs to tell you everything about the character— the way the character speaks, acts, feels, and thinks—that way you won't want to put it down!"

To be sure your readers stay engaged with your writing:

- Use different ways to capture your readers' attention right from the start.

- Elaborate on your ideas by adding details, dialogue, examples, or graphics.

- Revisit the most important ideas in your conclusion. Leave your reader with something to remember.

FOCUS POINT Study the rubric on page 141. What is the difference between a well-developed paper and an undeveloped one?

Development of Ideas

	How thoughtful and interesting is the writing?	How well are the ideas explained and supported?
4 **Wow!**	The writing engages the reader with worthwhile ideas and an interesting presentation.	The ideas are fully explained and supported. • The ideas are well developed with important details and examples. • The writing feels complete, and the reader is satisfied.
3 **Ahh.**	<u>Most</u> of the writing engages the reader with worthwhile ideas and an interesting presentation.	<u>Most</u> of the ideas are explained and supported. • Most of the ideas are developed with important details and examples. • The writing feels mostly complete, but the reader is left with some questions.
2 **Hmm.**	<u>Some</u> of the writing engages the reader with worthwhile ideas and an interesting presentation.	<u>Some</u> of the ideas are explained and supported. • Only some of the ideas are developed. Details and examples are limited. • The writing leaves the reader with many questions.
1 **Huh?**	The writing does <u>not</u> engage the reader.	The ideas are <u>not</u> explained or supported. The ideas lack details and examples, and the writing feels incomplete.

In Literary Works

Writers use plenty of details to develop the setting, plot, and characters in stories. How does Julius Lester develop the plot in this folktale?

Often, the title cues the idea the writer will develop.

WHY MEN HAVE TO WORK

from Black Folktales
by Julius Lester

The sky used to be very close to the ground. In fact, it wasn't any higher than a man's arm when he raised it above his head. Whenever anybody got hungry, all he had to do was reach up and break off a piece of the sky and eat it. That way, no one ever had to work.

Well, it was a fine arrangement for a while, but sometimes people would break off more than they could eat, and what they couldn't eat they just threw on the ground. After all, the sky was so big there would always be enough for everybody to eat. What did it matter if they broke off more than they actually wanted?

Maybe it didn't matter to them, but it mattered to the sky. In fact, it made the sky angry to see itself lying on the ground, half-eaten, like garbage. So one day the sky spoke out and said, "Now, look-a-here! Can't have this! Uh-uh. Can't have you people just breaking off a piece of me every time your stomach growls and then taking a little bite and throwing the rest away. Now if y'all don't cut it out, I'm going to move so far away no one will ever touch me again. You understand?"

The writer gives plenty of details to introduce the problem and explain events.

The writer uses dialogue to tell even more about the plot in an interesting way.

Well, people got the message. In fact, they were pretty scared, and for a while they made sure that no one ever broke off more of the sky than he could eat. But slowly they began to forget. One day, a man came by and broke off a chunk big enough to feed forty people for a month. He took a few little bites, licked around the edges, threw the rest over his shoulder, and walked on down the road just as happy and dumb as anything you've ever seen. Well, the sky didn't say a word, but with a great roar, the sky lifted itself up as high as it could, and that was pretty high.

When the people realized what was happening, they began crying and pleading with the sky to come back. They promised that they would never do it again, but the sky acted like it didn't hear a word.

The next day, the people didn't have a thing to eat, and they had to go to work to feed themselves, and that's why man is working to this very day.

These details are so rich that the reader has no question about what's happening.

The conclusion sums up what finally happens so readers don't have to wonder.

In Nonfiction Books

In nonfiction books and articles, writers use examples, facts, and statistics to develop ideas. How did the writer of this book elaborate on his ideas?

from

What Color Is Your Parachute?

A Practical Manual for Job-Hunters & Job-Changers
by Richard N. Bolles

EATING UP THE MILES AND MINUTES

The writer grabs your attention with an engaging example.

Back in 1985, the late John Crystal used to describe the ridiculousness of our traditional job-hunting "system." A job hunter would be walking down a street, despairing of ever finding the work he wanted; and brushing past him would be an employer who was hunting for exactly that man or woman with exactly those traits and experience.

The writer introduces the main idea he'll develop in depth.

But now it is the year 2004, or later, and we have fixed all that. We have invented the worldwide Internet—first for military purposes, then for educational and research purposes, and now for every purpose under the sun, including job-hunting.

No one agrees on the *number* of Internet sites currently devoted to job-hunting—some experts say 1,000; some say 5,000; some, 10,000; some, 40,000; and some, 100,000 or more. But all agree on the *purpose* of Internet sites devoted to job-hunting. And that is, to make it easier for job-hunter and employer to find each other. It is, indeed, far easier than it was back in 1985. Also faster. It is now *possible* for you and an employer to find each other in one day—sometimes, even, in one hour.

THE GROWING IMPORTANCE OF THE INTERNET IN THE TRADITIONAL JOB-HUNT

Internet access is available to more and more job-hunters, month by month. Currently, in the U.S. at least, more adults have access to the Internet than don't. Of regular users, some can access it from their home; the remainder, from work. But, except in remote and undeveloped regions, many more *could* access it if they wanted to.

The writer develops another important idea with facts.

Internet Access

If you don't have access at home or at work, you can usually find it by going to one of the following:

- One of the increasingly popular commercial Internet cafes. Though known by a different name in virtually every city, village, and hamlet around the world, there are currently more than 4,000 of them, in over 149 countries (475 in the U.S. alone).

- Your local public library; local, state or government employment center; or local large bookstore.

- Internet kiosks in airports, bookstores, stationery stores, coffee shops, and local print shops.

Just look around you. You might find a place with access that you'd never think of, like a rest area along a freeway!

The writer further elaborates with examples of places to go to access the Internet and with statistics.

In Writing for Tests

Good essays have well-developed ideas, too. Study these papers. They have been scored using the Writing Rubric for Development of Ideas on page 141. Why did each paper get the score it did?

Overall Score: 4

Thanks, Mom!

Andy Grossman

The question gets readers interested in a worthwhile **central idea**.

   Don't you just want to scream when you hear, "You can do that yourself. It'll help you learn how to be independent"? That's what Mom said whenever I wanted something. For example, if I asked her how to spell a word, she made me look it up in the dictionary. I always had to finish my chores before I could go out. And when I wanted more money for CDs, Mom didn't say, "Okay, I'll raise your allowance!" Instead, she said I should get a job. Little did I know that my restaurant job would help me appreciate all she had taught me.

The writer uses plenty of examples to explain how he became so independent.

The writer presents a related idea to add depth to the writing.

   When I first started waiting tables, I realized how much Mom had taught me about acting responsibly and relying on myself. Thanks to her, I could handle busy shifts and cranky customers without the manager's help. I didn't need anyone telling me what to do—I just did it. My boss even said, "Andy, you're one of my best employees. You know how to work independently!"

Interesting **details** *and* **dialogue** *show exactly what the writer means.*

   I still lose my patience with my mom sometimes, but now I know she is just looking out for me. I know she is proud of the person she's raised me to be—a person who knows how to take care of himself.

The conclusion wraps up the important ideas, so the writing feels complete.

Thanks, Mom!

Don't you just want to scream when you hear, "You can do that yourself. It'll help you learn how to be independent"? That's what Mom said whenever I wanted something. For example, if I asked her how to spell a word, she made me look it up in the dictionary. I always had to finish my chores at home before I was allowed to go out. And Mom didn't just agree to raise my allowance when I asked. Instead, she decided it was time for me to get an after-school job.

When I first started waiting tables, I realized how much Mom had taught me about acting responsibly and relying on myself. I didn't need to have anyone telling me what to do—I just did it. My boss even said I was one of the best employees.

I still lose my patience with my mom sometimes, but now I know she is just looking out for me. I know she is proud of the person she's raised me to be.

RAISING *THE SCORE*

The writer should add details and dialogue to expand on what his boss said and show how his mother's actions affected his job performance. What could he add?

In Writing for Tests, continued

Overall Score: 2

Thanks, Mom!

The paper seems to be on a worthwhile **central idea**, but the opening isn't too interesting.

My mom used to say, "You can do that yourself. It'll help you be independent." That was always what she said whenever I wanted something. I have lived with my mother all my life, and when you have lived with a person that long you know when she's frustrating. Not to mention the fact that all my friends agree with me that my mom nags me way too much. When I asked for a raise in my allowance, she said no. Instead, she made me get an after-school job.

The writer used only one example to explain how he became so independent.

The writer presents a related idea, but the **details** are vague and uninteresting.

I guess my job waiting tables showed me how to be responsible. Mom probably had a lot to do with that. At work I didn't leave a lot of extra work for other people. I didn't need to be told what to do—I just did it. My boss even said I was a good worker.

I still get frustrated with my mom sometimes, but not as often. I know she's proud of me.

The conclusion leaves the reader with questions about the point of the essay.

RAISING THE SCORE

The writer needs to elaborate on each important idea with specific examples and interesting details. What additional ideas should the writer add to the conclusion?

Thanks, Mom!

Mom was always talking about how I should do things. I have lived with her all my life, and when you have lived with a person that long you know when she's frustrating. However, I've learned some things from her.

She helped me when I started my first job. While I was waiting tables, I found out that Mom had taught me a lot about doing things on my own. The boss said he liked the way I did whatever I had to without being told. That's why I say I learned a lot from my mom about responsibility.

I still get frustrated with my mom sometimes, but not as often. I know that the only reason she nags me is that she cares a lot about me.

Development of Ideas   **149**

Engage the Reader from the Start

When it comes to reading, people have millions of choices. How does a writer reel readers in? The best writers do it with the first few sentences. In fact, a strong opening is called a "hook" because it catches readers' attention and leaves them wanting to read more.

Baiting the Hook

When you write, think about how you can use the first paragraph to capture your readers' interest and make them want to read on. Keep in mind that some types of beginnings are better "bait" than others.

Look at this opening paragraph about the work of Dr. Samuel Lee Kountz, Jr.

> Samuel Lee Kountz, Jr., was born in 1930 in Lexa, Arkansas. He attended Arkansas Mechanical and Normal College and became a doctor.

Does the writing make you want to read more? Probably not. To get your interest, the writer needs to find a way to make the first paragraph more interesting and exciting.

Better Beginnings Use Better Bait

So, what types of beginnings will help hook your readers?
Try these techniques to catch their attention:

- Start with a thought-provoking question or statistic.

Question

How did a young man who failed his college entrance exam go on to develop an important new kidney transplant technique?

Statistic

Before Samuel Lee Kountz, Jr., invented a new kidney transplant technique, fewer than 5% of kidney transplant patients survived for more than two years.

- Start with an interesting quotation that relates to the topic.

Quotation

"I had been living with dialysis for three years or so, and the new kidney felt like a reprieve, a new gift of life," said transplant patient Peter Wright. The work of Samuel Lee Kountz, Jr., helped make this transplant and all modern kidney transplants possible.

- Start with an unusual metaphor or analogy.

Analogy

The human body is like a machine. If one part breaks, the whole thing can stop running. Doctors like Samuel Lee Kountz, Jr., have found ways to keep people's bodies running smoothly once a part breaks down.

- Start by referring to an experience familiar to your readers.

Personal Connection

Failing an important test or losing a big game can make a person want to give up. Fortunately, Samuel Lee Kountz, Jr., didn't give up when he failed his college entrance exam. Instead, he asked for a second chance.

Develop Ideas in Nonfiction

Once you capture your readers' attention with a good beginning, keep them interested by elaborating on your ideas. In nonfiction, for example, don't just state the main points— tell more about them.

Elaborate in Your Paragraphs

You can elaborate on ideas by adding specific explanations, details, and examples. Some examples may come from your knowledge and experience. Others may come from research.

Suppose you want to develop the following idea:

> Part-time jobs can help high school students gain important real-world skills, but working more than part time may hurt students' academic performance.

To develop that idea, add specific examples, facts, and explanations:

Part-Time Jobs

Thinking of getting a part-time job? That's great. Jobs teach teens responsibility and give them an inside view of the working world. For example, Dave Thomas, who started working part-time jobs at age 12, said his early experiences taught him important lessons. He became a multimillionaire owner of a national chain of fast-food restaurants.

Although having a job helps prepare teens for adulthood, working too many hours can leave them with no time for studying. For example, one study found that students who worked 21 hours or more per week had lower standardized-test scores in science. Education as well as work experience is crucial for later career success. If you take on a part-time job, be careful not to let it interfere with your schoolwork.

Explanation

Example

Fact

Elaborate With Visuals

You can further develop your ideas by adding visuals like photographs and graphics. Graphics get readers' attention and help make complicated ideas clear. Here are some techniques you might try:

- Use a bar graph or a pie chart to present data.

Weekly Hours Worked by Students

None
27%

Over 30 hours
7%

Less than 6 hours
6%

26-30 hours
9%

6-10 hours
9%

21-25 hours
13%

11-15 hours
10%

16-20 hours
18%

Pie Chart

- Present related information in a table.

How Hours Worked Affects Scores on Science Test
(500 Total Points Possible on Test)

Hours Worked per Week	Average Student Scores
None	149 points
Less than 6 hours	156 points
6-10 hours	151 points
11-15 hours	152 points
16-20 hours	149 points
21-25 hours	144 points

Table Source: National Assessment of Educational Progress (2000)

- Remember: a picture can be worth a thousand words. How does this visual communicate the same idea as the essay on page 152?

 **+**  **= SUCCESS**

Develop Ideas in Fiction

Nonfiction writers elaborate with facts, statistics, and examples. Fiction writers, however, expand on their ideas using dialogue and sensory details to develop a theme, show what a character or setting is like, or reveal important plot events.

Fiction writers don't just tell you their ideas—they show you. What helps you picture the scene in this story?

THE DILEMMA

"Hey, what do you think you're doing?" Ricardo blurted out. "That's all the money we have to buy the decorations and food for the Valentine's Day dance." The last bell had rung, and the hallway was eerily quiet. Max and Ricardo were the last students minding the booth that sold tickets for the dance.

Max looked at Ricardo and sneered, "What are you going to do about it? Would a computer nerd like you have the nerve to turn in the football captain? Besides, I lost my job and I need some cash for my date tonight." He grunted and pulled on his expensive leather coat.

Ricardo felt his heart pounding and adrenaline pumping. He knew that Max had been fired from the video store because he was always late—that's why he was the one who always had to cover Max's shift. As Max's footsteps echoed down the hall, Ricardo tried to decide what to do. He was so furious that it was hard for him to think straight.

How to Show and Not Tell

1 Use Dialogue

You can use dialogue to develop a character's personality or to reveal plot events. Which piece of writing below is better developed and more interesting?

Without Dialogue

> Lisa was a grouchy, unfriendly woman. She was easily irritated by everyone around her. If a waitress forgot the sugar for her coffee, Lisa would be very rude and make a scene.

With Dialogue

> "You nitwit!" Lisa snapped at the hapless waitress. "I asked for black coffee with two sugars. If you can't remember a simple order like that, maybe you should find another line of work!"

2 Use Sensory Details

Sensory details will help readers imagine how something looks, sounds, feels, smells, or tastes.

Just OK

> His first day on the job, Julio arrived early. When he knocked on the door, nobody answered, so he just went in. The room was gross! A cat was there, but no people. He checked the address that he had written down the day before. He thought he was in the wrong place.

Much Better

> His first day on the job, Julio arrived early. He knocked but no one answered. The big oak door creaked in protest as he forced it open. The dusty, cluttered room reeked of old, burnt coffee. Rustling came from behind a file cabinet, and a small black creature leaped out. Julio was relieved it was only a cat. "Where's everyone?" he muttered. "Did I get the address right?"

Build a Strong Conclusion

You've worked hard to capture your readers' interest with a good beginning, and you have developed your essay by elaborating. Now put on the final touches by adding a strong conclusion!

Ways to Create a Strong Conclusion

A good conclusion scores major points with readers. It makes all your hard work worthwhile by ensuring they'll remember what you've said.

Suppose the thesis, or central idea, of your paper is:

> People are happier and more successful when they choose a career that fits their interests and skills.

Here are some ways you could write a satisfying conclusion:

- Relate ideas in the conclusion to your thesis.

    Tie to Your Thesis

    > To ensure that you find a job you love, first explore your interests and evaluate your skills. Then consider which jobs make sense for you.

- Summarize the major points you made.

    Sum Up

    > The most important thing to remember about career planning is that every person is an individual. One person's perfect job is another person's nightmare. That's why it's so important to find a job that fits your talents and interests. You're much more likely to be successful in a job you enjoy and are good at.

A satisfying job is one you enjoy and are good at. These animal health workers are treating an injured sea turtle. ▶

- Answer a question you posed at the start or pose a new one based on what you've said.

Answer a Question

> Is there really a good way to make sure your job is a joy rather than a grind? Research suggests that exploring your interests and skills helps to ensure that you'll find a job you enjoy.

Pose a New Question

> Now that you know what it takes to find a satisfying career, what line of work would you like to explore?

- End with a memorable quote from a famous person or someone you admire.

Use a Quote from a Famous Person

> As President Theodore Roosevelt said, "Far and away the best prize that life has to offer is the chance to work hard at work worth doing."

Use a Quote from Someone You Admire

> As my grandfather always says, "Work is easy when you love what you do." So, choose work you love and work you are good at.

- Conclude with a dramatic or personal example.

Use a Personal Example

> My own experience has taught me how important it is to find work that suits your interests and abilities. For many years, I worked as a lifeguard because that's what my friends did. But the truth is, I didn't like it much. I always got sunburned. I also felt anxious about being responsible for little kids' safety. I like caring for animals, though, so last summer I worked in a veterinarian's office. Now I know I'd like to be a veterinarian when I'm older.

Make Your Writing Sound Like You

Develop Your Own Voice and Style

> "**If** you were writing a report to your boss, would it be appropriate to begin by writing, 'Yo, boss man. I checked into them sales figures you wanted to see, and look-a-here.'? Obviously, such a voice is inappropriate in a business environment."

When you write, use a voice that's appropriate for the situation, but that still sounds like you. Show your readers who *you* are as a writer. Develop your own voice and style using these strategies:

- Use precise nouns and action verbs, effective modifiers, and figurative language. Write with colorful language to make your work lively and exciting.

- Vary your sentences to keep your readers engaged.

- Change voice to suit your form, audience, topic, and purpose.

FOCUS POINT Study the rubric on page 159. What's one surefire way to improve a paper's score for voice and style?

Voice and Style

	Does the writing sound real, and is it unique to the writer?	How interesting are the words and sentences? How appropriate are they to the purpose and audience?
4 Wow!	The writing fully engages the reader with its individual voice and style. The tone is consistent throughout.	The words and sentences are interesting and appropriate to the purpose and audience. • The words are powerful and engaging. • The sentences are varied and flow together effectively.
3 Ahh.	<u>Most</u> of the writing engages the reader with a voice and style that are unique. The tone is mostly consistent.	<u>Most</u> of the words and sentences are interesting and appropriate to the purpose and audience. • Most words are powerful and engaging. • Most sentences are varied and flow together.
2 Hmm.	<u>Some</u> of the writing engages the reader, but the voice and style are not unique.	<u>Some</u> of the words and sentences are interesting and appropriate to the purpose and audience. • Some words are powerful and engaging. • Some sentences are varied, but the flow could be smoother.
1 Huh?	The writing does <u>not</u> engage the reader.	<u>Few or none</u> of the words and sentences are appropriate to the purpose and audience. • The words are often vague and dull. • The sentences lack variety and do not flow together.

In Literary Works

Julius Lester likes to retell familiar stories, such as the one about a rabbit who races a tortoise. Though the plot is familiar, notice how the language reflects Lester's unique voice and style.

BRER RABBIT FINALLY GETS BEATEN

from Uncle Remus: The Complete Tales

by Julius Lester

They got Brer Buzzard to be the race judge and hold the bet money. It was to be a five-mile race, with posts set a mile apart. Brer Turtle claimed he could race faster going through the woods. Everybody told him he was out of his mind. How could he expect to beat Brer Rabbit, who would be running on the road! Brer Turtle said, "Watch me."

Brer Rabbit went into training. He bought a red jogging suit, a green sweatband, and some yellow Adidas sneakers, and he jogged ten miles every day. Then he'd come home and do a whole mess of push-ups, sit-ups, and skip rope to his records. Some folks wondered if he was training for a race or for "Soul Train."

Brer Turtle didn't do a thing. You see, it's a strange thing about the turtle family. There were six of 'em, including Brer Turtle, and they all looked alike. The only way to tell them apart was to put 'em under a magnifying glass, and even then you could make a mistake.

On the day of the race, folks was there from all over. Even the TV networks were there, so the folks on the Moon could see it. Miz Meadows and the girls brought lunch baskets and

The informal language fits Lester's purpose to entertain.

Lester's retelling shows his unique voice and style.

lots of Dr. Pepper to drink. Brer Rabbit showed up in his shades, wearing a gold jogging suit with a tan stripe, and when he took that off, he had on emerald-green racing shorts. Everybody ooohed and aaahed and rushed to get his autograph.

Meanwhile, Brer Turtle and his family had been up with the sun. He had put his wife in the woods at the starting line, and he stationed each of his children near the other posts. Brer Turtle hid himself in the woods at the finish line.

Race time came and Brer Rabbit hollered, "You ready, Brer Turtle?"

Miz Turtle was off a little ways in the woods and, disguising her voice, hollered, "Let's go!"

Precise **verbs** and colorful language make the writing lively and interesting.

In Literary Works, continued

FOLKTALE

Brer Turkey Buzzard fired the gun and the race was on. Brer Rabbit took off like a 747 jet. Miz Turtle went home.

Brer Rabbit came to the one-mile post. "Where you at, Brer Turtle?"

Brer Turtle's young'un crawled on the road and said, "Right with you, Brer Rabbit."

Brer Rabbit started running a little faster. He came to the two-mile post. "Where you at, Brer Turtle?"

"Right with you," came the answer.

Brer Rabbit ran a little faster. He passed the three-mile post, the four-mile post, and every time he hollered for Brer Turtle, the answer came back, "Right with you!"

The finish line was in sight now, a quarter mile away. Brer Rabbit could see Brer Buzzard with the checkered flag, but he didn't see Brer Turtle come out of the woods and hide behind the post marking the finish line.

"Give me the money, Brer Buzzard! Give me the money!" Brer Rabbit started hollering, and Miz Meadows and the girls started cheering like they'd lost their senses.

Brer Rabbit was a hundred yards from the finish line when Brer Turtle came from behind the post and crossed the line. "Soon as I catch my breath, I be pleased to take that fifty dollars, Brer Buzzard."

Brer Buzzard handed over the money, and Brer Turtle went home.

The writer uses a **simile** to help readers picture Brer Rabbit in motion.

The varied sentence lengths and structures keep the story from getting dull.

In Magazine Articles

People who write for magazines choose language that will appeal to their readers. Different magazines have a different voice and style depending on their purpose, audience, and topic. The article below appeared in a magazine for young people.

TALES AND LORE

from *Footsteps* magazine, May/June 2006

Native Americans tell stories that link humans with animals.

by Kimberly N. Ruffin

Once upon a time, long before the days of television, DVDs, computers, and MP3s, people used a broad range of creative tools to teach and entertain. These methods included "folklore," which means the teachings (lore) of a group of people (folk). For folklore to survive, it must be told and retold in ways that not only capture the attention of those who listen but also inspire them to spread the tales.

To inform young people about folklore, the writer uses a clear, straightforward style.

In Magazine Articles, continued

The writer uses precise nouns and clear language to engage the reader.

Peoples throughout the world have their own folklore, with stories about everything from animals and historical and mythical people to imaginary figures. Riddles, proverbs, myths, stories, legends, and jokes all contribute to a culture's folklore. Because folklore is older than writing itself, it is considered *oral tradition*, that is, customs that are shared through words and sounds. Through *oral traditions*, which continue even today, people reflect on the world and learn about community values, hopes, and history.

Oral traditions from many different geographic and cultural areas came into contact with each other in early America. People of African, European, and Native American backgrounds heard stories that were new to them. Native Americans told creation stories that often linked humans with animals such as the coyote and the eagle.

Folklore is often shared through music.

Leprechaun

European tales made connections between humans and a hidden world of imaginary beings, such as leprechauns and fairies. African folklore gave meaning to human life with its animal tales, particularly those involving the leopard and the tortoise.

Key to the African legacy is the role of the griot. Griots and griottes (male and female storytellers) serve as community historians and, in African societies, keep the past and present connected. It is their responsibility to memorize and recount creatively—through words, song, and music—their people's history. Because of their extensive knowledge, griots and griottes enjoy high social status and often give advice to everyone, from royalty to everyday people. With reverence for community storytellers, especially for those who found creative ways to enliven their stories, African Americans continued many African folklore customs.

Griots are community storytellers.

All the sentences are statements, but the writer varies the beginnings and lengths for interest.

In Writing for Tests

Even when you write for tests, use your own voice and show your personal style. These papers have been scored using the Writing Rubric for Voice and Style on page 159. Study each paper to see why it got the score it did.

Overall Score: 4

Say What You Mean
Tony Mevoli

The writer uses specific, precise words.

Saying what you mean is harder than it sounds. For instance, how much teenage heartache has "So-and-so likes you" caused? The problem is that the word "like" can refer to friendship, affection, or attraction. If someone misinterprets it, watch out! Feelings will be wounded and egos will be shattered.

The varied sentence length and structure makes the writing interesting.

Friends can read you wrong, and so can adults. Sometimes I've gotten into trouble not because of what I said, but because of my tone. Once, for example, my math teacher scolded me for my "inappropriate" T-shirt. I said, "Okay, okay, I won't ever wear it to school again." Unfortunately, my teacher thought I showed some serious attitude. I didn't mean to be sarcastic; I was just grumpy and stressed out that day. Luckily, she let me explain myself, and then she understood.

Does that mean I obsess over each word I say? No. I won't spend every waking moment worrying about what I say. I'm just more careful now that I know what sounds right to me might strike someone else the wrong way—just like my "inappropriate" T-shirt.

The informal language illustrates the writer's voice and style.

The language fits the writer's purpose to share a personal experience.

Say What You Mean

Saying what you mean is harder than it sounds. For instance, how much teenage heartache has "So-and-so likes you" caused? The problem is that the word "like" can refer to friendship, affection, or attraction. If someone misinterprets it, watch out! Egos will be shattered.

The writer uses some **specific verbs**.

Friends can read you wrong, and so can adults. Sometimes I've gotten into trouble not because of what I said, but because of my tone. Once, for example, my math teacher scolded me for my "inappropriate" T-shirt. I said, "Okay, okay, I won't ever wear it to school again." Unfortunately, my teacher thought I showed some serious attitude. I didn't mean to be sarcastic. I just felt grumpy and stressed out that day. I got lucky, though. I explained myself. She understood.

This part of the essay is dull because each sentence begins the same way.

Does that mean I obsess over each word I say? No. I won't spend every waking moment worrying about what I say. I'm just more careful now that I know what sounds right to me might strike someone else the wrong way—just like my "inappropriate" T-shirt.

The **informal language** fits the writer's purpose and has a unique voice and style.

RAISING *THE SCORE*

If all the sentences sound alike, it's hard to keep a reader's interest. The writer needs to rewrite some of the sentences in the second paragraph. How could the writer vary the sentence structure?

In Writing for Tests, continued

Overall Score: 2

Say What You Mean

The writer uses too many **vague words**.

Saying what you mean is harder than it sounds. For instance, how many teenagers have felt bad when they hear "So-and-so likes you"? The problem is that the word "like" can mean anything. If someone doesn't understand what you mean, feelings can be hurt.

Friends aren't the only people who might sometimes read you wrong. Adults can also read you the wrong way. Sometimes I've gotten into trouble because someone read me the wrong way. Once a teacher told me she didn't like my T-shirt. I said, "Okay, okay, I won't ever wear it to school again." She said she didn't like my attitude. I didn't mean to sound that way. I was just unhappy that day. I was able to explain things. She didn't get mad then.

The language is too formal. It doesn't go with the personal nature of the topic.

Teenagers should not worry about every word they use. It is important, however, for them to pay attention to how they say things.

The writer repeats the **same idiom** too many times. That's boring.

The writer begins all the sentences the same way. That's boring, too.

RAISING *THE SCORE*

The writer needs to use language more precisely and to avoid repetition. What nouns, verbs, and idioms would add color to the essay?

Say What You Mean

Saying what you mean is hard. For instance, how many teenagers have had a problem with the words, "So-and-so likes you"? The meaning of the word "like" isn't easy for people to know. It can mean liking someone a little or a lot. It's easy for your meaning to be read the wrong way and then the person will be hurt.

Friends aren't the only people who can read you wrong. Adults might also read you the wrong way. I've had problems because my words were read the wrong way by someone else. For instance, I was told by a teacher that my T-shirt was wrong. My answer was, "Okay, okay, I won't ever wear it to school again." Her belief was that I had a bad attitude. I wasn't doing it on purpose. I was just unhappy that day. I was able to explain. She didn't get mad.

I'm not going to worry about everything I say. I know people might not understand everything I say. But I'm not going to spend time worrying about it. I'm learning to be more careful about what I say. I'm also learning to be careful about how I say things. Sometimes, something might seem right to me but seem wrong to someone else.

Choosing the Right Voice

Writers often adapt their voice to go with their form, audience, topic, and purpose.

Adapt Your Voice for Your Form and Topic

Your form can determine what voice you'll use. For poems, for example, you'll often use colorful imagery to show strong emotion. For a report, you'll present facts in an unemotional way. How is the voice of the announcement different from that of the letter?

Join us for
Tales of Muskrats and Alligators
Saturday, August 5 8 p.m.
Franklin High Auditorium

An announcement has to present information in just a few words, so it is brief and straightforward.

May 31, 2007

Sally Masters
Bayou High School
Fifth Avenue
Baton Rouge, LA 70895

Dear Ms. Masters:

Franklin High is hosting a storytelling session in our school's auditorium on August 5 at 8 p.m. This event will be unique because the storyteller is my uncle, Philip Johnson! He has some fascinating Louisiana lore to share. Please join us.

Sincerely,
Patrick M. Johnson
Franklin High Class President

The letter allows the writer to give more details and make a personal connection.

You can adapt your voice for the topic, too. A serious topic, like "the Louisiana fishing industry," would have a different voice from a humorous one like "eating my first crayfish."

Adapt Your Voice for Different Audiences

When you're writing to a friend, it's okay to use informal language. For other audiences, such as a teacher, use a more formal voice. Which of these uses an informal voice?

Hey Jessie,
   Uncle Phil is here this week. He's so cool! He tells these wild stories. Like this one time, he said, "Did I ever tell you about the time I wrestled sixteen fierce Mama 'gators?" I thought he was pulling my leg.

One reason Uncle Phil is my favorite relative is that he tells the most amazing stories. He'll prop his feet up on the table and say something like "Did I ever tell you about the time I wrestled sixteen fierce Mama 'gators?" I know then that it is time to settle back and listen.

Adapt Your Voice for Your Purpose

When you write to inform, you use different language than when you write to persuade. How does the writer change the language to fit the purpose?

Purpose: To Inform

My uncle, Philip Johnson, was born in 1961 in a small Louisiana town. Despite many other accomplishments, he's best known around town as a storyteller. He will present Louisiana lore next Saturday.

Purpose: To Persuade

Everyone in Louisiana needs to connect with our heritage. Next Saturday, you'll have your chance when Phil Johnson shares some fascinating Louisiana lore. Be there on time — 8 p.m. sharp!

Choosing Effective Words

Each sentence you write will have at least one verb and one noun. When you enrich your sentences with effective verbs and nouns and use other vivid words, your readers will know exactly what you mean and will stay interested in your ideas.

Precise Nouns

Precise nouns help your reader understand exactly who or what you're talking about. Choose nouns that pack a lot of information into one word.

Look at these examples. Which sentence in each group gives you the best picture of the writer's ideas?

Vague	More precise	Most precise
The girl saw a movie.	Valerie watched a biopic.	Valerie, a straight-A student, watched *The Last King of Scotland.*
I finished the work.	I finished my homework.	I finished my critique of the new movie.
Terrell surprised the girls with flowers after the show.	Terrell surprised Shannon and Tess with flowers after the movie.	Terrell surprised Shannon with a bouquet of roses and Tess with a handful of daisies after the movie.

Vague nouns don't tell the whole story!

Precise and Vivid Verbs

No matter what you're writing, verbs help your reader to picture the action. Verbs, like nouns, can also pack a lot of information into one word. That's why using precise and vivid verbs will make your writing exciting and lively.

Which sentence in each group below gives you the best picture?

Vague	More precise	Most precise
Scott went down the street to the theater.	Scott raced down the street to the theater.	Scott sprinted down the street to the theater.
He liked everything about the movie.	He enjoyed everything about the movie.	He relished everything about the movie.

To really make a scene come alive, use precise nouns and verbs together:

Vague

One day we went to the city. The weather was warm, and there were a lot of people in the park. Uncle Frank went by all the people and got us tickets for the movie.

Precise

Last Friday, we traveled to New York City. May breezes warmed the midday air, and people crowded into the park. Uncle Frank weaved his way through the crowd and bought tickets for the new movie *Frozen in the Night*.

For more ways to make your language precise, see Chapter 3, pages 240–247.

Choosing Effective Words, continued

Use Lively Modifiers

An adjective modifies, or tells more about, a noun. An adverb modifies a verb, an adjective, or another adverb. Add adjectives and adverbs to a boring sentence to make it more lively, but don't overload the sentence.

Boring—No Modifers	Lively	Overloaded
The boy watched the movie.	The delighted boy eagerly watched the movie.	The grateful, delighted boy very eagerly watched the amazing movie.

You can replace overused adjectives with alternatives like these:

Overused Adjective	Effective Alternatives
small	tiny, petite, diminutive, slight
big	enormous, cumbersome, massive, immense
dark	shady, murky, dim, gloomy
bright	sunny, sunlit, radiant, brilliant
fast	rapid, swift, hasty
slow	sluggish, unhurried, deliberate, leisurely

Use a thesaurus to find synonyms for overused adjectives.

Thesaurus Entry

good adjective **1** *a good product* FINE, superior, quality; excellent, superb, outstanding, magnificent, exceptional, marvelous, wonderful, first-rate, first-class, sterling; satis-factory, acceptable, not bad, all right; *informal* great, OK, A1, jake, hunky-dory, ace, terrific, fantastic, fabulous, fab, top-notch, blue-chip, blue-ribbon, bang-up, killer, class, awesome, wicked; smashing, brilliant. ANTONYM bad.

2 *a good person* VIRTUOUS, righteous, upright, upstand-ing, moral, ethical, high-minded, principled; exemplary,

from *Oxford American Writer's Thesaurus.* Christine A. Lundberg. By permission of Oxford University Press, Inc.

Adding Color to Your Language

Writers use figurative language—similes, metaphors, and idioms—to say things in vivid and imaginative ways.

Figurative Language: Similes

A **simile** compares two unlike things using the words *like* or *as*. Which paragraph gives a more vivid impression of the stepsisters?

Without Similes

> When the wicked stepsisters learned that the prince was looking for Cinderella, their faces crumpled. They were very angry.

With Similes

> When the wicked stepsisters learned that the prince was looking for Cinderella, their faces crumpled like wadded-up pieces of paper. They were as angry as wasps whose hives were being destroyed.

When you edit, you can turn an adjective into a comparative adjective and add on a simile to paint a better picture.

> Meaner than a pack of rabid dogs,
> ⌃The ~~mean~~ stepsisters could not imagine why the prince wanted to see Cinderella instead of them.

When you use similes, try to come up with original comparisons.

Overused	Fresh
feels as cold as ice	feels as cold as the Arctic wind
roars like a lion	roars like a supersonic jet breaking the sound barrier
sparkles like a diamond	sparkles like the moon's reflection on the deep blue ocean

Adding Color to Your Language, continued

Figurative Language: Metaphors

Like a simile, a **metaphor** compares two unlike things, but it does not use the words *like* or *as* to make the comparison. Instead, it says that one thing *is* the other thing. How does the paragraph with the metaphor help you see how Cinderella's stepsisters acted?

Without a Metaphor

The stepsisters were very angry when they heard the news about Cinderella and the Prince. As they walked through the cottage, nasty words came out of their mouths every time they spoke.

With a Metaphor

The stepsisters were fire-breathing dragons when they heard the news about Cinderella and the prince. Lumbering heavily through the cottage, they spewed flames from their mouths every time they spoke.

The writer builds an extended metaphor, comparing the stepsisters to dragons.

Figurative Language: Idioms

Idioms are another kind of figurative language. In an idiom, the words mean something different from what they say.

Idiom	What You Really Mean
He was really steamed.	He was very angry.
You're off the hook.	You're out of trouble.
Juan laughed his head off.	Juan laughed very hard.

Idioms can enliven your writing, but use them sparingly. Since idioms are familiar expressions, your writing will sound clichéd or too casual if you use too many. Here's how one writer made his paragraph livelier by using idioms:

> In order to finish our English assignment, my study partner and I ~~stayed up late~~ *burned the midnight oil* last night. We were ~~looking at Internet sites about~~ *surfing the Net for* folktales. I said that the morals in fables were always stated at the end, but I had to ~~admit I was wrong~~ *eat my words* because that's not always the case. Sometimes to understand the moral of a fable, you have to ~~look for the hidden meaning.~~ *read between the lines.*

Check out the Writer's File on pages 178 and 179 for more idioms you might want to use in your writing.

Common Idioms

Idioms from A to Z

Idioms add color to your writing. When you write, you may want to keep this list of idioms handy to help you spice up your writing.

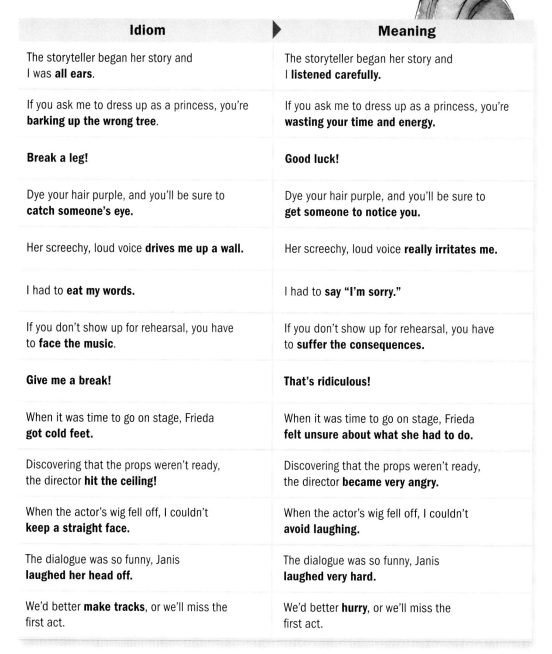

Idiom ▶	Meaning
The storyteller began her story and I was **all ears**.	The storyteller began her story and I **listened carefully.**
If you ask me to dress up as a princess, you're **barking up the wrong tree**.	If you ask me to dress up as a princess, you're **wasting your time and energy.**
Break a leg!	**Good luck!**
Dye your hair purple, and you'll be sure to **catch someone's eye.**	Dye your hair purple, and you'll be sure to **get someone to notice you.**
Her screechy, loud voice **drives me up a wall.**	Her screechy, loud voice **really irritates me.**
I had to **eat my words.**	I had to **say "I'm sorry."**
If you don't show up for rehearsal, you have to **face the music**.	If you don't show up for rehearsal, you have to **suffer the consequences.**
Give me a break!	**That's ridiculous!**
When it was time to go on stage, Frieda **got cold feet.**	When it was time to go on stage, Frieda **felt unsure about what she had to do.**
Discovering that the props weren't ready, the director **hit the ceiling!**	Discovering that the props weren't ready, the director **became very angry.**
When the actor's wig fell off, I couldn't **keep a straight face.**	When the actor's wig fell off, I couldn't **avoid laughing.**
The dialogue was so funny, Janis **laughed her head off.**	The dialogue was so funny, Janis **laughed very hard.**
We'd better **make tracks**, or we'll miss the first act.	We'd better **hurry**, or we'll miss the first act.

Idiom	Meaning
Matt confessed to ripping the costume, so you're **off the hook.**	Matt confessed to ripping the costume, so you're **not in trouble**.
Michele forgets her lines **once in a blue moon**.	Michele forgets her lines **very infrequently**.
Before making the costumes, she wanted to **pick someone's brain** about the design.	Before making the costumes, she wanted to **get advice from someone** about the design.
Each actor **put his best foot forward**.	Each actor **did his best**.
I knew I'd seen the play before, but I had to **rack my brain** to remember where and when.	I knew I'd seen the play before, but I had to **think very hard** to remember where and when.
Often, actors and directors don't **see eye to eye**.	Often, actors and directors don't **agree with each other**.
After Ross explained the joke to me three times, I began to **see the light**.	After Ross explained the joke to me three times, I began to **understand**.
Katie was really **steamed** when Fran was chosen to play Juliet.	Katie was really **angry** when Fran was chosen to play Juliet.
No matter what you do, you should always try your best to **toe the line**.	No matter what you do, you should always try your best to **follow the rules**.
Without the scenery for our play, we're **up the creek without a paddle**.	Without the scenery for our play, we're **in trouble and unable to do anything about it**.
After his active scene, Ray went backstage to **veg out**.	After his active scene, Ray went backstage to **relax**.
The **walls have ears** so you should be very careful about what you say.	**People might be listening secretly** so you should be very careful about what you say.
You can say that again.	**I totally agree with you.**
Zip your lips!	**Be quiet!**

Staying Mostly Active

As a writer, you want your sentences to be interesting and exciting for your readers. One way you can keep your writing lively is by using the active voice and avoiding (for the most part) the passive voice.

What's the Difference Between Active and Passive Voice?

In the **active voice**, the subject of the sentence performs the action expressed by the verb:

> **Active Voice**
>
> The handsome prince rode a white stallion. The three stepsisters greeted the prince. Dismounting from his horse, the prince pulled a shimmering glass slipper from his saddlebag.

In the **passive voice**, the subject doesn't perform the action. Whoever performs the action is buried in a <u>phrase</u> after the verb:

> **Passive Voice**
>
> A white stallion was ridden <u>by the handsome prince</u>. The prince was greeted <u>by the three stepsisters</u>. A shimmering glass slipper was pulled <u>by the prince</u> from his saddlebag.

The passive voice often slows down the pace of the writing and makes it hard to picture the action.

Does that mean you should never use the passive voice? No. Like scientists, technicians, and journalists, you may want to use the passive voice when:

- the material studied is more important than the person or people doing the studying.

> A culture's customs are shared by its people through words, songs, and music.

- you want to sound objective and impersonal.

> Historically, storytellers were respected by the community for sharing their culture's history.

How to Change from Passive to Active Voice

Check for the passive voice in your sentences. Look for any two-part verbs that begin with *is, are, was,* or *were* followed by a phrase beginning with *by.*

Change sentences to the active voice by making the subjects perform the action. That way your sentences will be interesting and lively.

> The prince asked the stepsisters,
> ~~The stepsisters were asked by the prince~~, "Does the lovely creature who owns this slipper live here?"
> Each sister gave the same answer.
> ~~The same answer was given by each sister.~~ "That's my slipper. Let me try it on." So, one by one, each sister's
> the prince pushed and squeezed
> right foot ~~was pushed and squeezed~~ into the slipper ~~by the prince.~~ But it was just too small.

Avoiding Repetition

Why is Repetition a Problem?

When writing repeats the same words too many times, readers might have to stop often to ask themselves, "Didn't I just read that?" or, "Didn't that already happen?" Keep your readers from getting confused—avoid repetitious language.

How to Fix Repetitive Sentences

As you check your writing for repetitious language, try these strategies to keep your writing clear and interesting:

- Take out words or phrases that say the same thing.

- Replace repeated nouns with pronouns.

- Use synonyms for words you need to repeat to keep the meaning clear.

The pronoun *its* replaces an overused word.

A synonym replaces the repeated word *slipper*.

The prince was relieved that the slipper didn't fit any of the ugly stepsisters. ~~Even though he was relieved the sisters couldn't wear the slipper~~, ^But^ he was disappointed that he hadn't found ~~the slipper's~~ ^its^ true owner. ~~He wondered if he'd ever find her.~~ "Where could she be?" he ^wondered^ ~~thought~~ as he put the ^tiny shoe^ ~~slipper~~ back into the saddlebag.

One word conveys the idea.

One sentence, not two, presents the idea.

Varying Your Sentences

Are all your sentences statements? Do they all begin the same way? Are they all about the same length? Vary your sentences to avoid boring your reader.

Use Different Sentence Types

Turn some of your statements into questions, exclamations, or commands.

All Statements

The prince got back on his horse and picked up the reins. He turned to gallop away, but something caught his eye. It was Cinderella in rags coming out to scrub the porch. The prince wondered if he should ask her to try on the slipper.

Varied Sentence Types

The prince got back on his horse and picked up the reins. He turned to gallop away, but something caught his eye. It was Cinderella! She was dressed in rags coming out to scrub the porch. "Should I ask her to try on the slipper?" he wondered.

> Statement

> Exclamation

> Question

Begin Your Sentences in Different Ways

Don't always start with the subject!

Same Beginnings

The prince reined in the stallion and headed back to the house. He pulled up to the steps and dismounted. He said, "Excuse me, miss, but I think I have something that belongs to you." The prince pulled out the slipper once again from his saddlebag.

Varied Beginnings

Suddenly, the prince reined in the stallion and headed back to the house. After pulling up to the steps and dismounting, he said, "Excuse me, miss, but I think I have something that belongs to you." Once again, the prince pulled out the slipper from his saddlebag.

Varying Your Sentences, continued

Use a Mix of Sentence Lengths

Your writing will be more lively and sophisticated if you make some sentences short and some long. On this page and the next, compare the monotonous passage with the professional model. What makes the professional models better?

Monotonous Passage

Timoteo reached her. He dismounted. He asked, "I have been searching for a girl called Domitila. Do you know where I can find her?"

Timoteo looked down. He still held the carved strip of leather. He saw the girl. She was wearing sandals with a matching design. She looked up at him. A gentle breeze blew. It lifted her hair from her beautiful face. They looked into each other's eyes. It was the first time they had seen each other. It felt the way it does when the sun comes up. Timoteo found Domitila!

Professional Model

from

DOMITILA:

A Cinderella Tale from the Mexican Tradition

adapted by Jewel Reinhart Coburn
illustrated by Connie McLennan

When Timoteo reached her, he dismounted and asked, "I have been searching for a girl called Domitila. Do you know where I can find her?"

Still holding the carved strip of leather, Timoteo looked down and saw the girl wearing sandals with a matching design. As she looked up at him, a gentle breeze lifted her hair from her beautiful face. For the first time, they looked into each other's eyes. Just as the sun bursts above the Sierra peaks to start a new day, Timoteo's search had come to an end. "You are Domitila!" he exclaimed.

The moon hid behind a cloud. It was the blackest part of night. It was then that Yeh-Shen dared to show her face at the pavilion. She tiptoed timidly across the wide floor. The girl in rags sank down to her knees. She examined the tiny shoe.

First, she made sure that the shoe was the missing mate to her own gold slipper. Then she dared to pick it up. At last she could return both little shoes to the fish bones. Surely then her beloved spirit would speak to her again.

from

Yeh-Shen:
A Cinderella Story from China

retold by Ai-Ling Louie
illustrated by Ed Young

It wasn't until the blackest part of night, while the moon hid behind a cloud, that Yeh-Shen dared to show her face at the pavilion, and even then she tiptoed timidly across the wide floor. Sinking down to her knees, the girl in rags examined the tiny shoe.

Only when she was sure that this was the missing mate to her own gold slipper did she dare pick it up. At last she could return both little shoes to the fish bones. Surely then her beloved spirit would speak to her again.

The sentences by the professional writers are much more interesting and lively. A big part of the reason is that the pros know how to craft sentences of different lengths and complexity. They mix up short and long sentences to create a nice rhythm and flow for their stories. You can, too!

Combining Sentences

Sentence variety doesn't always happen on a first draft. But you can make it happen during the revising step if you know how to combine sentences effectively. Pages 186–191 present various techniques for combining sentences.

1. Join Neighboring Sentences

Look to see how the ideas in two sentences are related. If the ideas are equally important, join the complete sentences with a word that cues the relationship: *and*, *but*, or *or*.

I had to rewrite a fairy tale for English class ,and I chose "Cinderella." My version resembled the tale told by the Grimm brothers in some ways ,but It was different in others. In it, Cinderella lived with her evil stepmother and two cruel stepsisters. Cinderella worked very hard to please the family ,but They still treated her badly.

As I wrote, I thought about Cinderella's alternatives. She could run away from home ,or She might stay and take control of her life. Would she defy her family openly , or Would she secretly plot against them?

Use *and* to join related ideas.

Use *but* to contrast two ideas.

Use *or* to present different possibilities.

Throughout history, artists have illustrated the Cinderella story. This 1911 illustration appeared in a famous book of fairy tales.

Cinderella Appears at the Ball, 1911, Charles Robinson. Illustration, The Big Book of Fairy Tales.

2. Join Related Ideas

Often the ideas in your sentences are closely related, but one idea is more important than the other. To show the relationship, turn one sentence into a clause that gives additional information about the more important idea. Use a connecting word to join the sentences.

- Use these words to show a time connection:

when	**until**	**after**	**once**
whenever	**before**	**while**	**as soon as**

> *When*
> ⌄The Grimm brothers told the story in the 1800s⌄Cinderella
> *until*
> was spineless. She never stood up for herself⌄ Her fairy
> godmother came along.

- Use these words to connect causes and effects:

because	**since**	**as**	**so**	**so that**

> *Since*
> ⌄I didn't want my heroine to be a wimp⌄I thought how
> *so*
> Cinderella could take charge. She did all of the chores⌄She
> had the power to make the household fall apart.

- Use these words to show other relationships:

if	**even if**	**although**	**as if**
wherever	**unless**	**even though**	**whereas**

> *unless*
> Cinderella's stepsisters couldn't do anything⌄Cinderella
> *Although*
> helped them. She was miserable and overworked⌄She knew
> *If*
> she could make her stepsisters miserable, too. ~~Suppose~~ she
> stopped doing the laundry⌄They'd have nothing to wear to
> the ball.

Use *although* or *even though* to contrast ideas.

Use *if* to show how one thing depends on another.

Combining Sentences, continued

3. Move Details from One Sentence Into Another

Whenever one sentence adds just a little more information about something, try moving that detail into the main sentence. That way you can keep your sentences concise and effective.

- You can move words or phrases from one sentence into the other.

> **Choppy**
>
> The stepsisters kept hassling Cinderella. They were demanding. "Bring me my tea!" shouted one stepsister. Cinderella brought the tea. She used salt instead of sugar.

> **With Sentences Combined**
>
> The demanding stepsisters kept hassling Cinderella. "Bring me my tea!" shouted one stepsister. Cinderella brought the tea with salt instead of sugar.

- You can use appositives to rename a person, place, or thing.

> **Choppy**
>
> Breakfast was the stepsisters' favorite meal. It was ruined. Now the family was confused. Cinderella was their servant. But she had dared to defy them.

> **With Sentences Combined**
>
> Breakfast, the stepsisters' favorite meal, was ruined. Now the family was confused. Cinderella, their servant, had dared to defy them.

4. Use *Who, Whose, Which,* and *That*

Look for a sentence that adds more detail about a noun or pronoun in another sentence. Turn the sentence into a clause that begins with *who, whose, which,* or *that* and move it into the other sentence.

Choppy

Cinderella's stepsisters wanted to be the loveliest girls at the ball. They were very vain. They had spent all their time choosing clothes and hairstyles. They wanted to wear the outfits to the ball. They finally found just the right dresses. The dresses were very expensive.

Cinderella did the laundry that day. She added too much detergent to the clothes. The clothes quickly disintegrated. The stepsisters' dresses were ruined. They burst into tears.

With Sentences Combined

Cinderella's stepsisters, who were very vain, wanted to be the loveliest girls at the ball. They had spent all their time choosing clothes and hairstyles that they wanted to wear to the ball. They finally found just the right dresses, which were very expensive!

Cinderella did the laundry that day. She added too much detergent to the clothes, which quickly disintegrated. The stepsisters, whose dresses were ruined, burst into tears.

Use **who** or **whose** for people.

Use **that** for people, places, or things.

Use **which** for places or things.

Combining Sentences, continued

5. Condense Ideas and Details

As you combine sentences, you might discover that you can use fewer words to say the same thing. Try some of these techniques to make your writing crisp and concise.

- Cut unnecessary words so your details get right to the point.

Wordy

Cinderella gathered the mop and pail. The pail was filled with water and some soap. Today was the day Cinderella had to scrub the dirty floors. The stepsisters wanted all the floors in the house to be sparkling clean.

Concise

Cinderella gathered the mop and pail of soapy water. Today Cinderella had to scrub the dirty floors because the stepsisters wanted them to sparkle.

- Use fewer words to say the same thing. Try summarizing the ideas in the details. Or, replace two or more words with just one precise word that conveys the same meaning.

Wordy

Cinderella started to scrub the floors in the house. It was the biggest house in town and the largest in the land. But she wasn't thinking about what she had to do. She knew she'd clean off all the dirt and dust on the floors. Cinderella had one thing on her mind. What other tricks could she play on her stepsisters?

Concise

Cinderella started to scrub the floors in the colossal house. But she wasn't thinking about cleaning the filthy floors. Cinderella had one thing on her mind. What other tricks could she play on her stepsisters?

- Use a verb's *–ing* or *–ed* form as a modifier. Just place the verb near the word it describes.

Wordy

Cinderella put her plan for revenge into action. Cinderella hid frogs under the stepsister's quilts. When the stepsisters flopped onto their beds, the frogs leaped out. The frogs terrified the stepsisters. They screamed.

Concise

Putting her plan for revenge into action, Cinderella hid frogs under the stepsister's quilts. When the sisters flopped onto their beds, the frogs leaped out. Her terrified stepsisters screamed.

- Also try using a verb's *–ing* form as a noun.

Wordy

From that day on, Cinderella didn't do any housework. She didn't cook. She didn't clean. Those chores were no longer her responsibilities.

Concise

From that day on, Cinderella didn't do any housework. Cooking and cleaning were no longer her responsibilities.

- Or, try using *to* plus a verb as a noun or a modifier.

Wordy

Cinderella would leave the house for good. That was her plan. At last, she was free. She could do as she pleased.

Concise

To leave the house forever was Cinderella's plan. At last, she was free to do as she pleased.

Play by the Rules

Learning how to play an instrument takes practice. You'll probably make several mistakes until you can play the right notes together to create a pleasing rhythm. As you write, you'll probably make mistakes in grammar and punctuation, too. But once you learn the basic rules, you'll know just how to make your writing flow along smoothly.

Follow Written Conventions

"**W**riting a sentence with good grammar and correct punctuation is no different from making a car; the car won't run if the gas tank is put where the oil should go. Every part of a car or a sentence has to be in the right place to move along smoothly."

Get to know the conventions of writing and do what good writers do:

- Edit and proofread your work carefully. Be aware of spelling and grammar "trouble spots" that writers often have.

- Use tools like dictionaries, writing handbooks, and spell-check programs.

- Ask someone else to look over your work.

FOCUS POINT Study the rubric on page 193. What is the difference between a paper that gets a score of 4 and one that gets a score of 2?

Written Conventions

	Are the sentences written correctly?	Does the writing show correct punctuation, capitalization, and spelling?
4 Wow!	The sentences are complete and correct. Fragments may be used on purpose to achieve an effect.	The writing is free of major errors in punctuation, capitalization, and spelling.
3 Ahh.	<u>Most</u> of the sentences are complete and correct.	The writing has <u>some</u> errors in punctuation, capitalization, and spelling.
2 Hmm.	<u>Few</u> of the sentences are complete and correct, but the reader can understand the meaning.	The writing has <u>many</u> errors in punctuation, capitalization, and spelling.
1 Huh?	The sentences are <u>not</u> complete and correct. The writing is difficult to read and understand.	The errors in punctuation, capitalization, and spelling make the writing difficult to read and understand.

In Literary Works

Fiction writers develop their own style, but nevertheless they still have to play by the rules and follow written conventions.

from

Pharaoh's Daughter

NOVEL

A Novel of Ancient Egypt

by Julius Lester

As I watched Almah leap and spin and somersault across the porch, something odd happened. I stopped seeing her as my sister, and she became someone who merely *looked* like my sister. I was enthralled by her beauty, her joy, her lack of self-consciousness, and no longer cared who she was. I cared only that she never stopped leaping and spinning to the beat of the drums, the *shesheset*, and the music of the flutes and horns.

My eyes widened and my heart beat faster as the rhythms pounded at me like the heartbeat of the sun. I felt like I, too, wanted to dance, could dance—and more, should. The crowd below started clapping their hands in rhythm to the drums. I closed my eyes, and my body began swaying from side to side. Nothing existed anymore except the melodies and rhythms filling the air, and I thought I could feel the passion throbbing in the hearts of everyone in the crowd.

The writer uses **italics** for emphasis and to indicate that a word is from a foreign language.

A **dash** signals an abrupt change of thought or interruption.

The writer uses a **comma and** *and* to form compound sentences.

In Magazine Articles

Writers for newspapers, magazines, and other publications also follow written conventions. Editors review the writers' work for errors.

Mirkovich's paintings aim to capture musicians' emotions. ▶

MAGAZINE ARTICLE

For the Love of Dance and Music
Painters Strive to Capture the Emotions and Energy of Musicians and Dancers

from Art Business News, April 2006
by Audrey S. Chapman

It happened in 1968. But Belgrade-born painter Nenad Mirkovich remembers it to this day. He remembers the people and the pigeons. He remembers the beggars on the street.

But most of all he remembers the violin player who, in the midst of it all, was simply lost—lost in the moment and the music as the maze of people and pigeons surrounded him.

"It was like a little miracle," Mirkovich says.

That miracle struck such a chord in Mirkovich that he not only painted this violinist once, he's painted him again and again, looking to re-create the magic he witnessed on that long ago, but not forgotten, day. This desire comes from the same place as that of people who want to surround themselves with music and dance in their art. Just as looking at that violinist inspired 56-year-old Mirkovich to paint, looking at paintings of musicians and dancers stirs something in people, which may be why artists such as the French Impressionist Edgar Degas, whose 19th-century paintings of ballerinas are among the most well-known depictions of dance in art, have always found an audience for their work, says Mirkovich.

When it comes to music depicted in art, Los Angeles painter Clifford Bailey says, "It can make you cry. It can make you think. It can make you laugh. It can make you remember a moment in time."

"It reminds them of moments of joy in life, moments of celebrating," adds Israeli-born artist David Schluss.

"It's seductive. It's haunting. It affects people," says Sausalito, CA, painter Mark Keller.

The writer capitalizes **proper names**.

The writer uses **quotation marks** to show a speaker's exact words.

In Writing for Tests

Following the conventions of good writing is important for tests, too. Study these papers that have been scored with the Written Conventions Rubric on page 193. Why did each paper get the score it did?

Overall Score: 4

Peace

Kelly Sánchez

The writer uses complete sentences: each has a subject and a predicate.

Have you ever stopped to think about what makes you happy and gives you peace? Some people might say that a nice warm day on the beach with family is the most relaxing thing ever. The only thing I have to say about that is, "Ha!"

When I was young, we took family trips to the shore. We had to get up at 5:00 in the morning, which made everyone cranky. Nobody slept the night before; we had to stay up fixing food for the trip. Then, during the car ride, I fought with my cousins. When we got there, the heat irritated us, and we fought even more. All of this was supposed to be relaxing; it wasn't.

The writer consistently uses commas and semicolons correctly.

The writing does not have spelling errors.

The place I found peace and relaxation was at home when we watched movies on Sunday nights. We talked and played jokes on each other. One night, when we were watching an older movie that had a lot of dancing, my little sister got up and started dancing, too. Then, my cousins stood up and joined her! It was very entertaining. My best family memories come from these evenings of movie-watching. True heaven. Everyone felt completely peaceful, and nobody fought or argued.

The writer uses a sentence fragment on purpose for effect.

Peace

The writer uses complete sentences throughout the essay.

Have you ever stopped to think about what makes you happy and gives you peace? Some people might say that a nice warm day on the beach with family is the most relaxing thing ever. The only thing I have to say about that is, "Ha."

When I was young, we took family trips to the shore. We had to get up at 5:00 in the morning, which made everyone cranky. Nobody slept the night before, we had to stay up fixing food for the trip. Then, during the car ride, I fought with my cousins. When we got there, the heat irritated us, and we fought even more. All of this was supposed to be relaxing, it wasn't.

The writer makes some punctuation errors. Here a **comma** is used where a semicolon should be.

The writer consistently uses **past-tense verbs** to describe past events.

All the words are spelled correctly, but the writer misuses the word *two*.

The place I found peace and relaxation was at home when we watched movies on Sunday nights. We talked and played jokes on each other. One night, when we were watching an older movie that had a lot of dancing, my little sister got up and started dancing, two. Then, my cousins stood up and joined her! It was very entertaining. My best family memories come from these evenings of movie watching. It was true heaven. Everyone felt peaceful and nobody fought or argued.

RAISING THE SCORE

The writer needs to replace the commas that separate two sentences with semicolons. What can the writer do to fix the error in word usage?

In Writing for Tests, continued

Overall Score: 2

The writing has incomplete sentences— missing a subject or a verb.

Peace

Have you ever stopped to think about what makes you happy? A nice warm day on the beach with family. The most relaxing thing ever, right? Maybe for some people. The only thing I have to say about that is, "Ha."

We took family trips to the shore. We had to get up at 5:00 in the morning that made everyone upset. Nobody slept the night before. We had to stay up fixing food for the trip. On the car ride I always fought with my cousins. When we got there the heat bothered us and we fought even more. All of this was supposed to be relaxing it wasn't.

I liked it better at home when we watched movies on Sunday nights. We talked and played jokes on each other. One night we were watching an older movie that had a lot of dancing. My little sister got up and danced, too. Then my cousins stood up and joined her! It was great. Most of my family memories are about watching those movies. It was wonderful because everyone was happy.

The writing has some **run-on sentences.**

Several commas are missing after **introductory clauses and phrases.**

RAISING THE SCORE

The writer needs to revise many of the sentences to make the ideas clear for the reader. How can the writer fix the sentence fragments? The run-ons?

Peace

Had you ever stopped to think about what makes you happy A nice warm day on the beach with famly. The best thing ever right. Maybe for some people. The only thing I have to say about that is Ha.

We took family trips to the shore we had to get up at 5:00 in the morning, that made everyone upset. Nobody slept the night before we had to stay up preparing food for the trip. During the car ride I always fought with my Cousins. When we got their the heat bothered us so we fought more. All of this was suppose to be relaxing it wasnt.

I was happier at home watching movies. We talked and play jokes on each other. One night when we was watching an older movie that had alot of dancing my little sister gets up and started to dance, too. Then my cousins stood up and joined her, it was very funny. Most of my family memories are from watching movies. they where happy times because everyone was happy.

▲

RAISING *THE SCORE*

With all the sentence fragments, run-ons, and punctuation and spelling errors, it's difficult to understand what the writer means. How could the writer revise the sentences to make the meaning clear?

Use Modifiers Carefully

Modifiers are descriptive words and phrases that tell more about nouns and verbs. Some modifiers are verb forms, called *participles,* that end in *-ed* or *-ing.*

Participles often start a phrase that can add great color, flavor, and voice to your writing. But if you use them carelessly, they can also add confusion and unintended humor. To be sure your readers don't get confused:

- Place each participle phrase close to the word it describes.

Confusing	Is the guitar leaping?

Jim began to play his guitar leaping onto the stage.

Clear

Leaping onto the stage, Jim began to play his guitar.

- Add or change words so that the participle phrase clearly describes what you want it to.

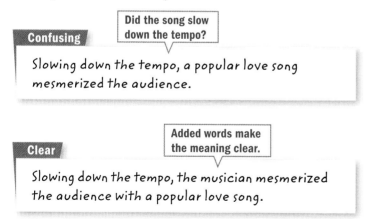

Confusing	Did the song slow down the tempo?

Slowing down the tempo, a popular love song mesmerized the audience.

Clear	Added words make the meaning clear.

Slowing down the tempo, the musician mesmerized the audience with a popular love song.

Use the Right Word

Some words in English are frequently confused because they look or sound similar. Look at this sentence. What does the writer mean?

> Everyone on the committee agreed that farther discussion about where to hold the homecoming dance was necessary.

The meaning of the sentence isn't clear because the writer confused the word *farther* with *further*. *Farther* has to do with distance, but *further* refers to something additional. The writer meant to say that the committee needs to talk more, or *further* discuss, where to have the dance. What words are confused in the examples below?

Confused

Are gifts required?

Your presents is requested at the dinner and dance.

Correct

Your presence is requested at the dinner and dance.

Confused

Who eats sand?

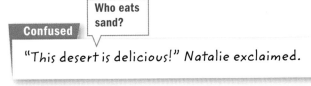

"This desert is delicious!" Natalie exclaimed.

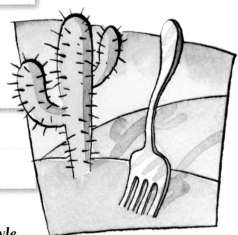

Correct

"This dessert is delicious!" Natalie exclaimed.

You can find a guide to using words correctly in the ***Handy Handbook of Grammar and Style***, pages 532–537.

Use Punctuation Correctly

When you speak, your listeners know what you mean by the words you say and how you say them. When you write, your readers can't hear you, so you need punctuation to make your meaning clear.

Confusing

> The people that I find most inspiring are my parents, Mikhail Baryshnikov and Martha Graham.

> Are these famous dancers really the writer's parents?

Clear

> The people that I find most inspiring are my parents, Mikhail Baryshnikov, and Martha Graham.

> Adding commas for the series makes your meaning clear.

Take a look at Jill's letter below. It doesn't sound like she's very fond of Jack, does it? See if you can play around with the punctuation (and capitalization) to make Jill have a change of heart. (Turn the book upside down to see what a difference punctuation can make.)

She Loves Him Not

from *Eats, Shoots & Leaves* by Lynne Truss. Used by permission.

> Dear Jack,
>   I want a man who knows what love is. All about you are generous, kind, thoughtful people, who are not like you. Admit to being useless and inferior. You have ruined me. For other men I yearn! For you I have no feelings whatsoever. When we're apart I can be forever happy. Will you let me be?
>
>   Yours,
>   Jill

She Loves Him!

> Dear Jack,
>   I want a man who knows what love is all about. You are generous, kind, thoughtful. People who are not like you admit to being useless and inferior. You have ruined me for other men. I yearn for you. I have no feelings whatsoever when we're apart. I can be forever happy—will you let me be yours?
>
>   Jill

You can read about the correct uses of punctuation marks on pages 527–530. You can also think of punctuation marks as "stage directions" for your reader. Imagine your reader reading your writing aloud. How can you "coach" him or her through punctuation? Here are some ideas.

Punctuation Mark	What Does It "Coach" Your Reader to Do?
, comma	Slow down or pause. Maybe the pauses show the items in a list. Maybe the comma shows how groups of words are separated from other groups of words.
. period	Stop—a much longer, more definite pause than for a comma.
! exclamation point	Show excitement, surprise, or deep emotion. Don't overuse the exclamation point!
? question mark	Raise the pitch of the voice at the end of the sentence to indicate a question, or maybe just to show confusion or puzzlement.
• • • ellipses	If this is at the end of the sentence, make the voice drift away. . . . If it's in the middle, make it drift away . . . and come back.
( ) parentheses	Lower the voice to show an interruption or an aside. Parentheses can signal a quiet secret (the same way that some people put a hand over their mouth to whisper).
— dash	A single dash signals a longer pause than a comma—but shorter than a period. In pairs, dashes signal an interruption—like parentheses—but bolder.
" " quotation marks	Most often, speak in the voice of a character or person: "Me?" she asked. "No, someone else," he answered.
: colon	Pause longer than a comma but not as much as a period. Pause about as long as a single dash. Colons can signal something coming: a list, an announcement, or something you need to look at closely.
; semicolon	Pause a little bit longer than for a comma. Semicolons are often used to join two sentences. They also sometimes work like super-commas to separate groups of phrases that may already have commas in them.

Use Complete Sentences

Like interrupted phone calls when you can only hear parts of a message, incomplete sentences can be frustrating and confusing for your readers.

Make sure that each sentence you write has a subject and a verb. A fragment is not a sentence, but you can add information to it to make it a complete sentence.

Fragments	Complete Sentences
played a woodwind instrument	Have you ever played a woodwind instrument?
	A woodwind instrument is played by blowing air through a tube or a long barrel.
Clarinet lessons since I was five years old.	I have taken clarinet lessons since I was five years old.
I like music. Because it makes you want to move.	I like music because it makes you want to move.

Look out for sentences with more than one subject and verb. Be sure the sentence is correctly punctuated.

Confusing

To start a new band, you need equipment keyboards and guitars are essential.

Clear

To start a new band, you need equipment; keyboards and guitars are essential.

How to Catch Your Mistakes

Both beginning and experienced writers use different strategies for detecting errors in their writing. Here are a few you might try:

1. Proofread Your Paper Backwards

Move from the last sentence to the first. The writing won't make much sense that way, but you won't get distracted by the content. Changing the direction will help you focus on only spelling and mechanics.

2. Slowly Read Your Work Aloud

Sometimes your brain thinks so fast that your writing hand can't keep up. When your thoughts are way ahead of what you are writing on the page, you may leave out punctuation or use it incorrectly.

Punctuation gives you signals, or cues. When you are reading aloud, punctuation tells you what to do with your voice. As you represent these marks in your oral reading, you may hear mistakes that you might not see as you look at the writing on the page.

3. Ask Others to Read Your Work

Let a friend, family member, or classmate read your writing.

- Have someone read your writing silently and note the errors.

- Make copies and have someone read your work aloud as you listen and mark the errors.

- Give copies to two people. Have them read your work and mark any mistakes. Review the copies and combine the errors onto a master copy for you to correct.

How to Catch Your Mistakes, continued

4. Take a Close Look

Here are two more tricks that might help you "see" any mistakes in your writing:

- If you're using a computer, print your paper out. Sometimes it's easier to catch mistakes on paper than on-screen.

- Place a ruler, blank sheet of paper, or index card underneath each line, moving it down line by line as you read. That way you can focus on one line at a time.

5. Recognize Common Errors

Do you have trouble with commas, pronouns, or run-on sentences? A lot of writers do. Take a look at the Writer's File on pages 208–211 to see the kinds of errors writers make most often.

When you know what your trouble spots are, you can be on the lookout for them as you check your paper. You might want to create a checklist for your most troublesome areas. Use your checklist along with a dictionary, a grammar book, or other tools to help you correct your mistakes.

Last night's Battle of the Bands at the Community Center was incredible it was a great success! For over three hours the audience was mesmerized by several local bands. Teens and parents alike especially enjoyed the rocking rhythms of the Bluesuits and they gave the drum solo by Joel Ignacio of the Grass Roots a standing ovation.

My Watch List
Check the Commas
✓ *run-ons*
✓ *in compound sentences*
✓ *after introductory words*

Use Spell-Check

Sometimes writers rely on computer spell-check programs to catch mistakes. Although these programs can help you fix spelling errors quickly, they can't do all of the proofreading for you!

Computers can be programmed to point out any words they don't recognize. However, computers may not be smart enough to know whether you've used a word correctly. Look at the errors this student's computer didn't catch:

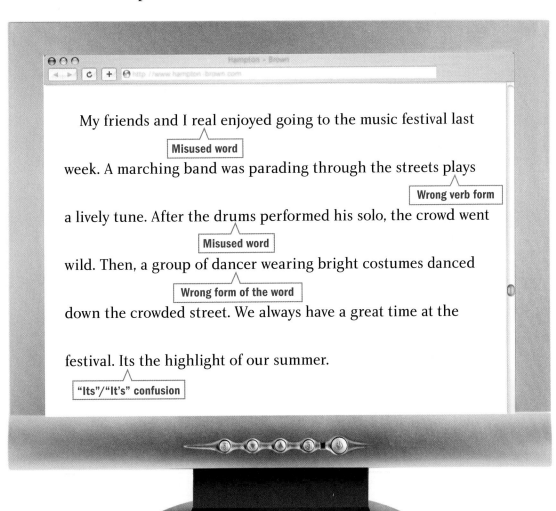

My friends and I real enjoyed going to the music festival last

Misused word

week. A marching band was parading through the streets plays

Wrong verb form

a lively tune. After the drums performed his solo, the crowd went

Misused word

wild. Then, a group of dancer wearing bright costumes danced

Wrong form of the word

down the crowded street. We always have a great time at the

festival. Its the highlight of our summer.

"Its"/"It's" confusion

20 Common Errors

Avoiding Common Errors

Here are some mistakes that writers often make. Compare the examples to see how you can fix errors in your writing.

ERROR 1 The comma after introductory words is missing.

Wrong	Right
As a matter of fact I do like to dance.	**As a matter of fact, I do like to dance.**

Why fix it? The comma sets off the introductory words from the main part of the sentence.

ERROR 2 It's not clear to whom a pronoun refers.

Wrong	Right
Max called John. John's brother answered and said he had gone to a concert.	**Max called John. John's brother answered and said John had gone to a concert.**

Why fix it? Readers will better understand your meaning if you clarify which noun a pronoun refers to.

ERROR 3 The comma in a compound sentence is missing.

Wrong	Right
We planned an outdoor festival for today but the weather was rainy.	**We planned an outdoor festival for today, but the weather was rainy.**

Why fix it? Using a comma alerts your reader to expect a related idea.

ERROR 4 The wrong word is used.

Wrong	Right
You can't feel the affect of your words.	**You can't feel the effect of your words.**

Why fix it? Your readers will better understand what you mean if you use the correct word.

ERROR 5 Commas are missing around a clause that is not necessary for the sentence's meaning.

Wrong	Right
Yolanda who is a very good ballet dancer got a part in "The Nutcracker."	**Yolanda, who is a very good ballet dancer, got a part in "The Nutcracker."**

Why fix it? Your readers won't know which information is the most important unless you set off unnecessary information with commas.

ERROR 6 The verb endings are wrong or missing.

Wrong	Right
After stop at the bookstore, she walk to the music shop.	After stopping at the bookstore, she walked to the music shop.

Why fix it? When the verb endings are correct, your readers won't get distracted and will know when events happen.

ERROR 7 The wrong preposition is used or a preposition is missing.

Wrong	Right
Instruments are sold on that store.	Instruments are sold at that store.

Why fix it? Using correct prepositions will convey the right meaning.

ERROR 8 A comma is used to separate two complete sentences.

Wrong	Right
Troy works hard in school, he won a scholarship.	Troy works hard in school; he won a scholarship.

Why fix it? Using a comma between two complete sentences creates a run-on sentence that can confuse your readers. Use a semicolon or period instead.

ERROR 9 An apostrophe is missing in a possessive noun.

Wrong	Right
Julies guitar lesson starts at 3 p.m. on Thursday.	Julie's guitar lesson starts at 3 p.m. on Thursday.

Why fix it? An apostrophe makes ownership or possession clear.

ERROR 10 Different verb tenses are used to tell about the same action.

Wrong	Right
Brian lifts up his dance partner and placed her on the stage.	Brian lifted up his dance partner and placed her on the stage.

Why fix it? Consistent verb tenses let readers know when things happen.

ERROR 11 The point of view changes and is not consistent.

Wrong	Right
He was bored, because you get that way sometimes.	He was bored, because he gets that way sometimes.

Why fix it? Writing in the same person makes it easy for your readers to know to whom you are referring.

ERROR 12 The writing has sentence fragments that don't express a complete thought.

Wrong	Right
Although the dress for the prom was expensive.	Although the dress for the prom was expensive, it was worth the money.

Why fix it? To express a complete thought, a sentence must include an independent clause with both a subject and a predicate.

ERROR 13 The verbs are in the wrong tense or form.

Wrong	Right
Mr. Gregory has spoke often about his daughter's accomplishments.	Mr. Gregory has spoken often about his daughter's accomplishments.

Why fix it? Using the correct verb tenses and forms makes it clear when the action takes place.

ERROR 14 The subject and verb in the sentence don't agree.

Wrong	Right
The band's manager pay Emily once every two weeks.	The band's manager pays Emily once every two weeks.

Why fix it? When the form of a verb doesn't agree with its subject, the reader could be confused.

ERROR 15 The commas are missing for items in a series.

Wrong	Right
Tuan can play the violin clarinet and cello.	Tuan can play the violin, clarinet, and cello.

Why fix it? Commas separate specific items and clarify the number of items in a category.

ERROR 16 A noun and the related pronoun do not agree in number.

Wrong	Right
Mary is not speaking to me. They think I behaved badly.	**Mary is not speaking to me. She thinks I behaved badly.**

Why fix it? A pronoun needs to agree with the noun it refers to. That way, your readers know which person you are talking about.

ERROR 17 Commas are used to separate an essential clause from the rest of the sentence. A clause is essential if it can't be taken out without changing the basic meaning of the sentence.

Wrong	Right
Everyone, who participated in the raffle, had a chance to win tickets to the show.	**Everyone who participated in the raffle had a chance to win tickets to the show.**

Why fix it? The sentence just doesn't sound right when essential clauses are set off by commas.

ERROR 18 Two or more sentences are joined together without punctuation to form a run-on sentence.

Wrong	Right
Anne tried out for the play she got the part of Juliet.	**Anne tried out for the play. She got the part of Juliet.**

Why fix it? Using the correct punctuation between ideas will let readers know when one idea ends and another idea begins.

ERROR 19 A modifier is misplaced.

Wrong	Right
Driving through New England, the colorful fall foliage was admired by all of us.	**Driving through New England, we all admired the colorful fall foliage.**

Why fix it? When a modifier is placed near the word it modifies, the sentence's meaning will always be clear.

ERROR 20 *Its* and *it's* are misused.

Wrong	Right
The dog jumped up and licked it's owner.	**The dog jumped up and licked its owner.**

Why fix it? Ideas won't make sense unless *its* and *it's* are used correctly. *Its* is a possessive adjective; *it's* is a contraction that stands for *it is*.

Troubleshooting Tips

featuring **Marian Haddad**

"Writing is sometimes harder than we expect. The important thing is that we don't give up on our writing. Good writing takes time, energy, focus, and desire.**"**

IN THIS CHAPTER

Growing as a Writer

Nothing and nobody is perfect. And there's always room for improvement. That goes for writers and writing as much as for anything else. It takes time, practice, and constructive criticism from others to achieve your best work.

When your writing is not all you wish it could be, it's easy to get discouraged. But a little attention devoted to finding out exactly what's wrong, and then a little work to correct it, can produce big results. This chapter will suggest solutions for some of the common writing problems described on page 217. Learning how to write well is a journey, as writer and teacher Marian Haddad describes on pages 215–216.

My Journey as a Writer

I grew up loving words. My parents were immigrants from the Middle East (my mother spoke only Arabic). And we lived by the Texas/Mexico border, immersed in a soup of English and Spanish. Even as a little girl, I was called upon to act as my
5   mother's translator. I was only six when I began to write as a form of communication, as a form of entertainment, and as a form of friendship. When no one was available to hear about my happenings that day at school, I wrote them down. I quickly became "the writer" of the family.

10   I continued in that tradition through high school, where I began to take creative writing classes. I loved creating new places out of old words or reviving old places through new words. And it seemed like I received mostly positive comments from teachers and students alike. Writing was almost effortless—I was told I had a gift; I was told I was "a natural." So when I went on to college
15   and enrolled in my first writing courses, I thought I had smooth sailing ahead. I had found my voice, and I was ready to share it with the world! Little did I know I had only just begun to grow as a writer.

I recall the first story I submitted in my freshman creative writing class. I had put so much work into it. I thought it was just what the teacher wanted, and that
20   the other students would be impressed. To my great surprise, they were not. In fact, they told me they couldn't quite get what I was trying to do in the story, and that I needed to be "clearer."

I held my disappointment and hurt pride inside and decided to listen to what my teacher and my peers had to say. I had a pretty good storyline, they said,
25   but they were *confused* about the main character. They said they wanted to *see* him better. That is when I learned that writers have to write as if they are film directors. Our words have to create mini-movies for the reader.

My Journey as a Writer, continued

"Marian, show me. Don't tell me," my teacher
said. "If Jason is in love with Sarah, I don't want
30   to hear him saying, 'Sarah, I love you.' I want to
see his actions, his expression, the tone of his voice,
even the clothes he's wearing, proclaiming that love for Sarah."

I was confused. I felt bombarded by all the suggestions. But in all
honesty, mostly I was just disheartened. Through all of my schooling,
35   I had only heard good things about my writing. Both friends and family
had always been very positive and supportive; I was not quite prepared
to hear my college classmates and my professor tell me I needed to "work
on my writing."

A wounded ego can be a pretty tall obstacle. But if you want to improve
40   as a writer, you have to get over it. After days—maybe even weeks—of feeling
slightly sorry for myself and doubting my future as a writer, I became a
little tougher and decided to see the new course (and those unimpressed
students and teacher) as learning opportunities, paths to growth. By
the end of the semester, I had truly taken in a number of good ideas for
45   making my writing stronger. With that course, and those comments, taken
to heart and accepted, began my true apprenticeship as a writer—an
apprenticeship that, I hope, still continues.

I am so grateful to that writing instructor and those fellow students
(fellow writers) for being real with me, being honest. Part of my work today
50   includes the teaching of writing. In my head, that voice still rings: "Show me.
Don't tell me. You can show me 'love' in a relationship without ever using
the word *love*." I hear myself say to my students, young and old alike, "Show
me. Don't tell me. Take me there." And they do.

Some Common Writing Problems

The problems with your writing may be unique to you—but probably not! Chances are you're coming up against some of the problems that puzzle all writers. This chapter will give you some good solutions.

WHAT YOU CAN DO . . .

► If Your Writing Wanders

Do you set out to write about one thing and then end up writing about another? Do you find it hard to stay focused on your topic?

► If You Can't Write Enough

Do you seem to run out of things to say after only a sentence or two? Do you hand in assignments that are mostly blank paper?

► If Your Writing Is Not Connected

Does your writing sound like a collection of loose sentences? Do your readers lose the thread of what you're saying?

► If Your Writing Is Too Vague

Is your writing long on generalities and short on specifics? Is it hard for your reader to see clearly what you're describing?

► If Your Writing Sounds Like a List

Does your writing sound like this: *This happened and then this other thing happened and then something else happened and then the last thing happened.*

► If Your Writing Is Too Wordy

Is your writing thin and "lite"? Do you write a whole page and then find out you haven't said very much after all?

hbgoodwriters.com

► If Your Sentences Are Boring

Do your sentences leave you (and others) cold? Do you wish you could put more zip and style into your sentences?

Find more examples of writing problems and solutions.

If Your Writing Wanders

What happens if you drive a car that has no steering wheel? It weaves all over the place and you have no control over where you go. Writing that wanders is a lot like that. It goes in many different directions, making it difficult for your readers to follow.

How Can You Fix Writing that Wanders?

"**S**ometimes when I write, my brain revs up and I think of many things at once. To help me focus on one topic at a time, I make a list of ideas about the topic first, then develop each idea as I write."

Making a list is one way to keep your writing from wandering. Here are a couple of others:

• Concentrate on just one thing you believe is true about your topic—or about life or the world in general. Keep your writing focused on that truth.

• Picture how your mind arrived at your truth. Map out your thoughts one step at a time. Then write a sentence to tell more about each thought. When you put the sentences together, they'll all tell about the same idea.

FOCUS POINT What is the main point of Frank's letter on page 219? What makes it difficult to figure out?

> Imagine that your school has to cut one of its sports programs. Write a persuasive letter to your principal about which sport should not be cut. Include support for your arguments.

March 31, 2008

Dear Principal:

I've heard that our school will have to cut one of the sports programs for next year. I am writing to urge you not to cut football. Football helps so many students. My sister plays soccer. Soccer is an even better sport, actually, though soccer players get injured often. Lots of other athletes get hurt too. I saw a TV show about gymnasts, and they live in pain. Football does take a lot of money, so maybe football should be cut after all. Our cafeteria has not improved lately, and what we eat deserves some attention too. It's horrible to go through the day hungry!

Sincerely,
Frank Takahashi
Tenth-grade student

Marian's Advice for Frank

Your letter tries to do what the prompt asks, but it wanders all over the place. What does the cafeteria have to do with sports? To stay focused, try these techniques:

- Choose one thing to write about, and get clear on your main point.

- Before you start writing, make a list of arguments or evidence that supports your main point.

- As you write, stay focused on your destination. Don't turn off onto every side road.

Solution #1: Speak Your Truth

Some things, like science or spelling, you know in your head. Other things, about people or the world, you know in your heart. That's your truth. When you write about one thing you believe in your heart, your writing will not wander.

Start With a Photograph

What do you believe is true about people or the world? You may already have an idea in your head, but sometimes looking at a photograph can help you discover your truth. What truth would you add to this list?

Truths

1. Everyone needs help to learn new things.

2. Families spend time together.

3. Not everyone can get things right without some help.

4. People change as they get older.

5. There are many ways to define a family.

Something that is true for one person is not necessarily true for others. When you look at these photographs, does a different truth come to mind?

Working together is so much better than working alone.

Communication mistakes can cause serious problems.

Sometimes you have to look from a distance to see something clearly.

Shopping is like searching for treasure; you never know what you're going to bring home.

Solution #2: Explain Your Truth

Knowing your truth is the first step in keeping your writing from wandering. But, how did you arrive at your truth? Try mapping out your thought process, and then write a sentence to tell about each thought. This will give you a writing plan that will keep you focused.

Use an Idea Organizer

To show how you arrived at your truth, map your thoughts with an **idea organizer**. This will help you plan how to present your writing. Start with your truth. Then show how you know it's true using an idea organizer. See the example below. You can find more idea organizers on pages 224–225.

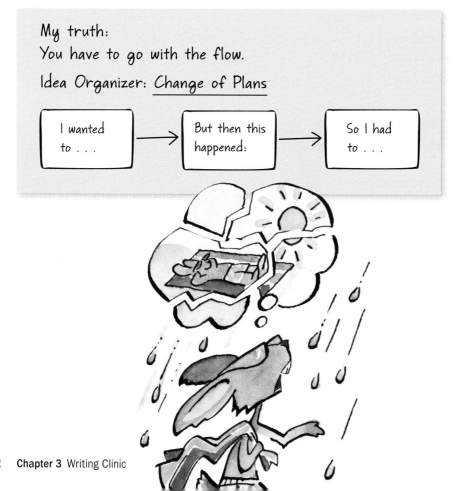

My truth:
You have to go with the flow.

Idea Organizer: Change of Plans

| I wanted to . . . | → | But then this happened: | → | So I had to . . . |

Write Kernel Sentences

A **kernel sentence** is like a summary—it tells the most important idea about each part of an experience. When you write a kernel sentence to tell more about each part of your thought process, you show what happened to lead you to your truth.

Idea Organizer

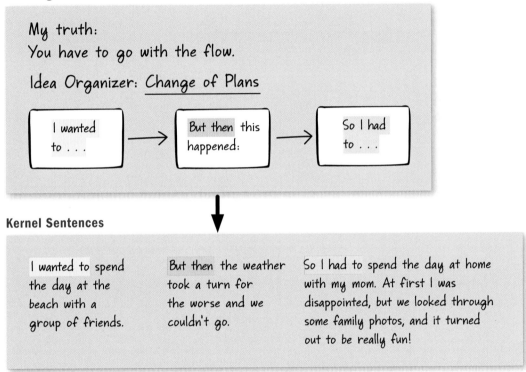

My truth:
You have to go with the flow.

Idea Organizer: Change of Plans

I wanted to . . . → But then this happened: → So I had to . . .

Kernel Sentences

I wanted to spend the day at the beach with a group of friends.

But then the weather took a turn for the worse and we couldn't go.

So I had to spend the day at home with my mom. At first I was disappointed, but we looked through some family photos, and it turned out to be really fun!

Put all your kernel sentences together and you'll end up with a **kernel essay**—a compact plan for focused, coherent writing. Read your kernel essay aloud and hear how it sounds. Pretty good, huh? A kernel essay is a great cure for a case of the wanders.

Idea Organizers

Choose an Organizer

Idea organizers can help you plan how to present your ideas. They help the reader (and the writer—you!) follow your thinking process.

The Story of My Thinking

I used to think... → Then this happened: → So now I think...

Life Lesson

A life lesson I've learned → One way I know it → Another way I know it → Another way I know it → What I'd like to remember about this lesson

Comparing Notes

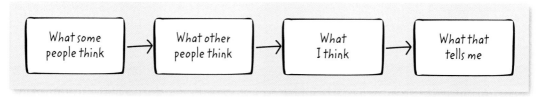

What some people think → What other people think → What I think → What that tells me

Memory Reflections

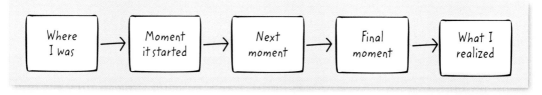

Where I was → Moment it started → Next moment → Final moment → What I realized

Wrong Assumption

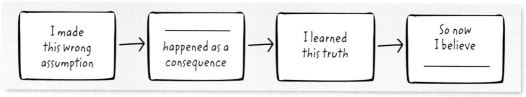

I made this wrong assumption → _____ happened as a consequence → I learned this truth → So now I believe _____

Sensory Associations

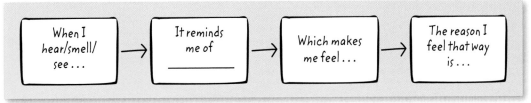

| When I hear/smell/ see... | → | It reminds me of _____ | → | Which makes me feel... | → | The reason I feel that way is... |

Something Big

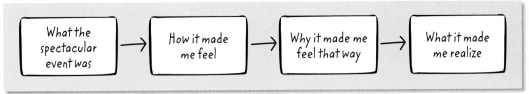

| What the spectacular event was | → | How it made me feel | → | Why it made me feel that way | → | What it made me realize |

Finding Out for Sure

| I've never been sure if... | → | But I've always suspected that... | → | Because once I experienced... | → | Which made me think that... | → | And finally I realized that... |

Making a Change

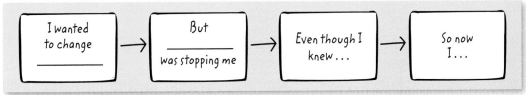

| I wanted to change _____ | → | But _____ was stopping me | → | Even though I knew... | → | So now I... |

Learning From Mistakes

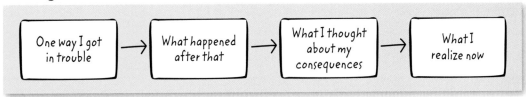

| One way I got in trouble | → | What happened after that | → | What I thought about my consequences | → | What I realize now |

If You Can't Write Enough

Do you sometimes start writing and feel like you've said everything after just three lines? It's like you've run out of gas. A car won't get anywhere without gas. And your writing won't go anywhere unless you fuel it with developed ideas and interesting details.

How Can You "Fuel Up" Your Writing?

Marian Haddad suggests that to keep your writing from running on "empty," you should:

"**A**dd details, details, and more details. That's what enlivens writing and makes it meaty, not skeletal."

You have more to write about than you may think. Here are some ways to put gas in your writing tank:

- Imagine that someone challenges what you say. Use what you know and how you know it to prove your point.

- Recreate a moment in your life. Tell where you were, what you saw, and what you thought.

FOCUS POINT Look at the article on page 227. How would you develop and expand this article?

> Your school is considering adopting mandatory school uniforms. Write a persuasive article for your school paper. State your position clearly and include facts to support your arguments. Make clear what you want students to do in response.

NO UNIFORMS!
An article by Samantha Tran

Will students at our school be required to wear uniforms next year? I hope this is not true. Many schools require uniforms for boys and girls. But uniforms are expensive, they're ugly, and they harm our creativity. We should all vote not to have uniforms.

Marian's Advice for Samantha

Your opinion about school uniforms is clear, but to persuade your readers you need to elaborate! Details, reasons, and support will strengthen your letter. For example:

- Tell exactly how much uniforms cost.

- Explain what makes them ugly to you.
- Just how do uniforms harm students' creativity? Give a full explanation.

Details, reasons, and evidence will get readers on your side!

Solution #1: Get Into an Argument

If you tell your friend something and your friend totally agrees with you, that part of the conversation is usually over. On the other hand, if your friend argues with you and challenges you to prove your ideas, there's a lot more to say! You can think of a lot more to say in your writing if you imagine how you would respond to someone who's arguing with you.

How Do You Know?

To argue with confidence, you have to know **how** you know things. Your sources of information are all around you.

Ways You Know Things

👁 **1. You go places and experience things.**	📰 **5. You read things in newspapers.**
💡 **2. You have feelings and thoughts.**	👄 **6. People tell you things.**
📺 **3. You see things on television.**	📻 **7. You hear things on the radio.**
📖 **4. You read things in books.**	🖱 **8. You learn things online.**

How Do You Prove It?

Once you get into an argument, you can reveal your sources to prove your ideas. Tell what you know and how you know it. For example:

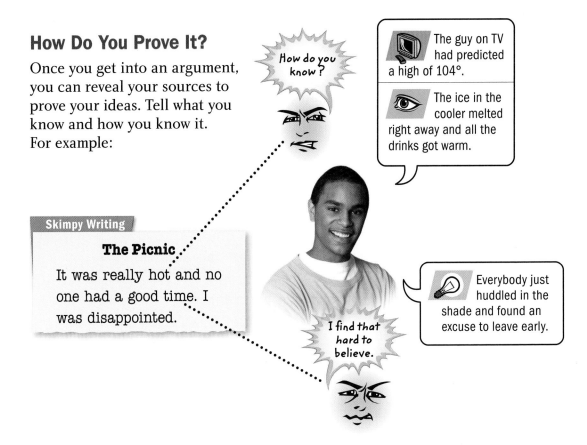

How do you know?

The guy on TV had predicted a high of 104°.

The ice in the cooler melted right away and all the drinks got warm.

Everybody just huddled in the shade and found an excuse to leave early.

I find that hard to believe.

Skimpy Writing

The Picnic

It was really hot and no one had a good time. I was disappointed.

Then use your proof to add interesting details to your writing.

Developed Writing

The Picnic That Wasn't

The guy on TV had predicted that the high would hit 104° the next day. I guess he was right, because by 10 o'clock all the ice in the coolers had turned to warm water and the cold drinks were like soup. The few people who showed up hung around listlessly in the shade for a while, and soon remembered that they had to be somewhere else. I had been looking forward to that picnic ever since February, and I was really disappointed.

Solution #2: Prove It On Your Own

There will always be places in your writing where you can add more information or details. Use the Ways You Know Things to develop your ideas fully.

Ways You Know Things

👁	1. You go places and experience things.	📰	5. You read things in newspapers.
💡	2. You have feelings and thoughts.	👄	6. People tell you things.
📺	3. You see things on television.	📻	7. You hear things on the radio.
📖	4. You read things in books.	🖱	8. You learn things online.

Figure Out Where to Add Details

Compare the two examples on page 231. If you think like an arguer, you'll find places where you can add information or details. Challenge yourself, and you'll find yourself writing proof. This will make your writing more developed and much more convincing.

I don't think so!

PROVE IT!

Too Much TV

Teenagers in the United States watch too much TV. This can cause problems with weight, vision, and sleep. Teens must limit their TV time and interact more.

Too Much TV

Teenagers in the United States watch too much TV. This can cause problems with weight, vision, and sleep.

Last spring, I visited my cousins in Arizona. All they did was watch TV and eat pizza. I pictured them as I read *Fast Food Nation*, a book on the obesity problem in the U.S. Being overweight is not just a social problem; according to www.medicalprofessionals.com, extra weight can cause diabetes, heart disease, and respiratory problems.

Too much TV can also harm our vision. My coach said that every hour we spend running track sharpens our vision, while every hour we spend lying down and watching TV weakens our eye muscles.

Finally, I saw a TV special about sleep disorders. It connected watching late-night TV with that problem.

There are many more important things teens can do with their time and energy. As a society, we should make TV something that teens do only in between sports and interacting with others.

Solution #3: Ba-Da-Bing!

When you want to supplement skimpy writing, add a Ba-Da-Bing.
A Ba-Da-Bing answers these questions about an event:

1. Where were you? What physically were you doing?

2. What, exactly, were you seeing?

3. What words went through your head as it was happening?

How Does It Work?

When you know you need to write more, think **BA** and add
where you were, think **DA** and tell what you saw, think **BING** and
write what you thought about it all. Try beefing up this sentence:

My mom and I saw some students.

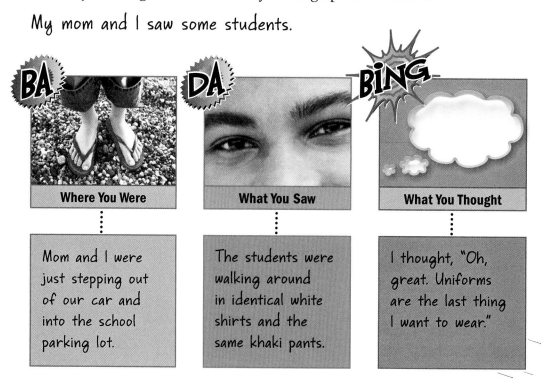

Where You Were	What You Saw	What You Thought
Mom and I were just stepping out of our car and into the school parking lot.	The students were walking around in identical white shirts and the same khaki pants.	I thought, "Oh, great. Uniforms are the last thing I want to wear."

You can use your Ba-Da-Bing to give the writing more depth.
It will help your readers see through your eyes so that they can
relive a moment that you experienced.

Fixed with Ba-Da-Bings

Compare these examples. How did the Ba-Da-Bings help?

Before

My mom and I saw some students.

After

When my mom and I stepped out of our car and into the school parking lot, I saw students walking around in identical white shirts and the same khaki pants. I thought, "Oh, great. Uniforms are the last thing I want to wear."

Before

My media award made me feel good.

After

When I walked into Warren High for my media award, I saw the biggest crowd of people I've ever seen, like at a concert. Then I thought to myself, "This is a bigger deal than I thought it would be."

You can use Ba-Da-Bings at the beginning, middle, or end of your writing. Remember Samantha's article about school uniforms from page 227? Here's an example of using a Ba-Da-Bing to turn an okay lead-in into a great one.

Just OK

Will students at our school be required to wear uniforms next year? I hope this is not true.

Much Better

When I stepped into class last week and saw my teacher writing the words "school uniforms" on the board, I thought she was speaking about other schools. Soon the other students settled in, and I watched my teacher's face as she explained the uniform policy for next year. I thought, "She's serious! School uniforms? At our school? This must be for a writing assignment, and not reality!"

If Your Writing Is Not Connected

When driving, you can get into trouble if you don't signal or if you give the wrong signal. Other drivers won't know where you're heading. Writing works the same way—without the proper signals, your readers won't be able to follow what you are trying to say.

Why Connect Your Ideas?

"**W**hen you read writing that isn't connected, it feels like a bumpy ride in a car. The car jerks down the street, instead of smoothly gliding along."

To avoid bumps and jerks, writers use words and phrases called **transitions** that move the reader smoothly from one idea to the next. The reader knows what is about to happen and follows along effortlessly. To tell your readers where you are going:

- Think about the parts of your message.

- Add transitions to signal connections or changes in your thoughts and ideas.

- Check that you've used the correct transition. Don't lead your reader in the wrong direction.

FOCUS POINT Is it easy or hard to follow the writer's thinking in the essay on page 235? What's missing?

> Members of our families or people we meet can have a profound impact on our lives. Write an essay explaining how people can make a difference in each other's lives.

How Others Affect Your Life
by Adrianne Dibartoli

Other people can affect your life. The impacts they make on you can be positive. Some impacts are negative.

Just like in the movie Napoleon Dynamite. Napoleon was friendly to a new kid in school. The new kid became his best friend because of it. It had a major impact on him.

People have made a difference in my life, especially my classmates. When I was in the sixth grade, people made fun of me and called me names. I didn't like it. This one girl named Brianna made fun of my haircut one day. After that day, her friends all laughed and pointed at my hair every time they saw me. It ruined my whole year.

These are some examples of how people can affect you. In conclusion, people can make a difference to each other in life.

Marian's Advice for Adrianne

As writers, we know what the connections are, but our readers may need help along the way.

- Try adding transitions to make your sentences flow. For example:

  Sometimes the impact people have on your life can be positive. Other times, it can be negative.

- Use transitions between paragraphs to move from one idea to the next. For example:

  . . . The new kid became his best friend because of it. It had a major impact on him.

  Likewise, people have made a difference in my life. Especially . . .

Solution #1: Take Time for Transitions

A **transition** is any word or phrase that serves to connect ideas. When you add transitions, the sentences in your writing work together as a team to get your ideas across.

Keep Your Ideas Flowing

Just like drivers, readers don't want to stop and go, stop and go; they want to get somewhere. Create a smooth path for your readers to follow by adding transitions.

Which of these is easier to follow?

Without Transitions

> Sometimes the kind things people do can surprise you. I took the train to visit my family in New Jersey. I'd never ridden on a train. I felt nervous about missing my stop. I didn't. I met Jim on board. We started talking. We became friends. He made sure I didn't miss my stop. He was kind to me. I can do the same for someone else.

The short, choppy sentences make the writing hard to follow. Ideas are not well connected.

With Transitions

> Sometimes the kind things people do can surprise you. Last week, for example, I took the train to visit my family in New Jersey. Because I'd never ridden on a train, I felt nervous about missing my stop. I didn't, though. I met Jim on board. We started talking, and soon we became friends. He made sure I didn't miss my stop. He was kind to me. Maybe I can do the same for someone else sometime.

With **transition words and phrases**, the writing flows smoothly from one idea to the next.

Choose the Right Transitions

Transition words and phrases signal how your ideas are related:

Cause	Time	Order	Emphasis
because	afterward	to begin with	in fact
since	earlier	second	more importantly
therefore	as time passed	finally	amazingly

Examples	Contrast	Comparison	Summary
for instance	though	also	all in all
to illustrate	yet	likewise	finally
in some cases	however	similarly	in summary

For a more complete list of transitions, see pages 136–139. Here are some transitions in action:

> Other people can affect your life in significant ways. In some cases, these people are family members or friends. In other cases, they may be complete strangers. Only yesterday, my life was changed by someone I met on the street. It was cold and the sidewalk was icy. Just when I started to fall, Mrs. Maggie P. Zimmerman caught me. I'm sure she saved me from a broken leg. That's why I'll still be playing basketball on Saturday!

To signal examples

To signal time

To signal cause

Repeat Key Words

Another way to connect your ideas is to repeat a word or phrase.

> Sometimes a complete stranger can affect your life. Just yesterday, a stranger kept me from breaking my leg on the street. Now Mrs. Maggie P. Zimmerman and I are great friends.

A **repeated word** links the sentences.

Solution #2: Connect Your Paragraphs

Just as transition words help you connect your sentences, they can also help you tie your paragraphs together. Effective transitions between paragraphs tell your reader what to expect next.

Transitions Get Your Reader Ready

In this essay, the writer gets his points across and makes us understand the complexity of his relationship with his brother, but he does not use transitions.

Without Transitions

My younger brother and I are friends. We do things together frequently. He even looks up to me in some ways, I think.

Our relationship is not perfect. My brother and I are not immune to a bit of sibling rivalry now and then. We even get into fights—usually only verbal! There are a few things that seem to set us off.

Whenever report cards come out, my brother's grades always outshine mine. As a result, my brother gets praise from my parents, and I get jealous. I don't like to admit it, but I hate having my little brother show me up like that.

My brother's athletic achievements also tend to eclipse mine. He made both the football and baseball teams at school, and I couldn't make either. I'm happy for him and all, but sometimes it's hard to be the star's brother.

I have a pretty complex relationship with my little brother. I love him and admire his talent, but sometimes I also envy and resent him. I wonder if it would be any easier if I were the younger one.

Now look at how a few paragraph **transitions** connect the whole essay and make it easier for the reader to follow.

My younger brother and I are friends. We do things together frequently. He even looks up to me in some ways, I think.

However, our relationship is not perfect. My brother and I are not immune to a bit of sibling rivalry now and then. We even get into fights—usually only verbal! There are a few things that seem to set us off.

> Prepares the reader for a contrast

Whenever report cards come out, **for instance**, my brother's grades always outshine mine. As a result, my brother gets praise from my parents, and I get jealous. I don't like to admit it, but I hate having my little brother show me up like that.

> Prepares the reader for an example

Similarly, my brother's athletic achievements also tend to eclipse mine. He made both the football and baseball teams at school, and I couldn't make either. I'm happy for him and all, but sometimes it's hard to be the star's brother.

> Signals a similar example

All in all, I have a pretty complex relationship with my little brother. I love him and admire his talent, but sometimes I also envy and resent him. I wonder if it would be any easier if I were the younger one.

> Prepares the reader for a summary

If Your Writing Is Too Vague

What's It Like ?

Have you ever driven with a dirty windshield? You just can't see where you're going. Vague writing is like that. You sort of see that there's something there, but you can't make it out clearly. That's when you need to turn on the wipers and get a clear view!

How Can You Fix Vague Writing?

"The poet William Carlos Williams spoke about 'the photographic eye' in writing—seeing things through a lens, having a focus on all you see, being ready to deliver the images in language as you would in a freeze-frame."

Using a "photographic eye" is one method writers use to keep their writing as clear and sharp as possible. Here are some other ways to fight vague writing:

- Replace dull, general words with sharp, precise words.

- Add sensory details and your own thoughts, to help the reader imagine being right there with you.

- Build layers into your writing, to give it depth and dimension.

FOCUS POINT Read the student essay on page 241. What makes it difficult to picture the writer's ideas?

> Write an essay about a memory triggered by a place, object, or sound.

Memories Last Forever
by Pedro Flores

A life doesn't last forever, but the memories can. And sometimes memories aren't just in your head. There are a lot of things that can trigger a memory. Some day, for example, you can develop a relationship with someone. As you spend time with that person, you'll probably give each other keepsakes like pictures, notes, or clothing. Whenever you look at those items, you'll probably think about the person and the special times you had. Other memories can be triggered by just walking down the street, going out, or hearing a certain sound. Even seeing an animal can help you remember something important in your life.

All kinds of things can make couples think about their relationships. There are many common or personal objects and places that can remind you of the things you love. These are the things that never go away.

Marian's Advice for Pedro

As a writer, I love to create scenes that my readers can picture—scenes that help them make a movie in their minds. Pedro could help create that movie by including details and being more specific. For example, he could:

- name some of the keepsakes, such as *a class ring on a gold chain*
- tell what some of the notes said, like *I will never forget you*
- describe some of the special times, like *dancing at the prom*.

Being specific and adding details will give the essay color and personality.

Solution #1: Use the Intensity Scale

To keep your writing from being vague and uninteresting, use words that say exactly what you mean. Using specific, precise words will capture—and keep—your readers' interest.

Check Your Words on an Intensity Scale

"Weighing" your words on an Intensity Scale will help you choose precise, colorful language. Here's how it works:

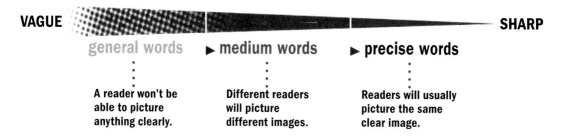

When you use words that fall toward the right end of the scale, your writing will be clear, sharp, and interesting!

Try it. Draw an Intensity Scale and place words in each section.

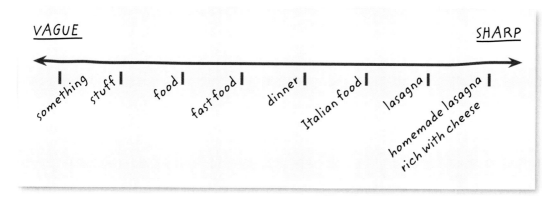

Replace General Words and Vague Details

Which of these paragraphs gives the best picture of what the writer did after school? Why?

If you use **generic nouns**, each reader will picture something different.

> After school, Shawn came to get me in his car. On the way to my house, we stopped at the store for a few things, and then we went home, ate, and watched TV. It was fun.

Vague details don't convey the feeling of "being there."

Specific nouns help each reader "see" the same thing.

> After school, Shawn cruised by the bus circle in his famous rusty red convertible and picked me up. On the way to my house, we stopped at Randy's Corner Market for our favorite snack combination: tortillas and fresh peanut butter. Then we went to my living room, turned on Comedy Club, munched down on our feast, and laughed hysterically for an hour.

Sharp, clear details help readers picture being at the scene.

Solution #2: Add Snapshots and Thoughtshots

Another way to keep your writing from being too vague is to add plenty of detail using **snapshots** and **thoughtshots**. Here's how it works:

- Read your writing to yourself. Pick just one moment and visualize it in your mind. What do you see, hear, smell, and taste? When you write down every detail from your mental photograph, you'll create a snapshot in words.

- Revisit the same moment you pictured. This time, write down everything you thought about at that moment, as it was happening. This description of your thinking is called a thoughtshot.

Imagine that you are going through a ropes course with a bunch of friends. What details would you add to the sentences to create a **snapshot**? A **thoughtshot**?

Vague Writing

Matt helped me with all the gear. Then I attached the rope. I went to the edge and looked down.

Snapshots

Where were you?

Was anyone else with you? Who?

What time of day was it?

What was happening? Did you see anything unusual? What was it?

Thoughtshots

How did you feel while you were there?

Did you want to get away or stay there?

What were you thinking about as you stood there?

See how the snapshots and thoughtshots turned into effective writing in this description.

Grabbing the Ring
by Kimberly Goss

Matt helped me with all the gear. Then I attached the rope. I went to the edge and looked down.

"I can't do it!" my mind exploded. So many things could go wrong. The harness could break, the rope could snap, the man who was supposed to catch me might forget. My heart pounded. I stood atop the pole, swaying, gazing at my friends thirty feet below. I fixed my gaze on the gold ring I had to jump and grab.

My friend Jake called up, "Are you ready?"

"No!" my mind screamed, but I kept my arms up for balance and replied, "Yes!"

"Jump on three, okay?" I felt people's stares as I nodded.

"One!" My knees started to shake. "Two!" My breathing got heavy as I felt my whole body trembling.

"Three! Jump!" I leapt into the air, my eyes still focused on the gold ring. I stretched my arm out and felt my fingers close around the cold, hard metal. Did I get it? The harness caught, and for a moment I wasn't sure what was happening. But as I lifted my right hand, I knew. I had just conquered my greatest fear and lived to tell the tale. The gold ring was my trophy.

— Thoughtshot

— Snapshot

Solution #3: Get on Target

Effective writing has many layers or dimensions. These help a reader enter the writer's world. When you read an effective piece of writing, you will be able to answer these questions:

1. What is the memory or event mostly about?

2. What details do you remember?

3. What feelings are obvious in the piece?

4. What's a life lesson that you hear dawning on the writer?

Vague writing, on the other hand, leaves those questions unanswered.

> **Vague Writing**
>
> I had waited forever to get my driver's license. One cold morning, Dad and I got into the truck. As I pulled out of the driveway, I almost hit our other car.

To avoid or correct vague writing, try completing a target diagram. Draw the diagram and fill in the rings with the answers you plan for your paper. This will help you write in layers.

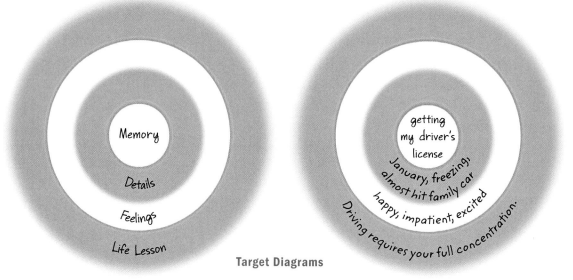

Target Diagrams

Take a look at the paper below. How did the notes in the diagram lead to effective writing? Notice how the layering makes the paper more interesting.

Off into Tomorrow
by Clayton Graham

When my alarm clock's annoying chime sounded at 7 a.m., I was already wide awake. "Hey, Bell," I said to my dog as I jumped out of bed. "Guess who's getting his driver's license today?"

I walked into the kitchen, where my dad greeted me wryly, "So, do you have any special plans for this morning?"

"Yes—that is, if someone takes me!"

"I will, but remember that driving is a privilege, not a right."

"Yes, Dad, I know, and yes, I will be a responsible driver, and yes, I will do my best to stay safe. But can we please go soon?"

After a quick breakfast, we stepped outside into the January chill. "Man, I hope we don't freeze on the way over," I said, shivering in our frost-covered van. I was so excited, knowing that I was just hours away from being a licensed driver. In fact, I was so excited that as I pulled out of the driveway, I almost hit the family station wagon. It's a good thing no one was testing me just then. I know at least one question I'll get right: Driving does require your full concentration!

When you're ready to revise, ask someone to read your paper and answer the four questions at the top of page 246. If a reader cannot answer some of the questions, you will know where to target your revision.

If Your Writing Sounds Like a List

What's It Like

In a traffic jam, all you can see is car after car after car. Jammed traffic does not move. Writing that is just a string of sentences one after the other doesn't go anywhere either. It sounds like a list and can be very boring! In a traffic jam, you're stuck, but there are things you can do to get your writing moving!

How Can You Fix Listy Writing?

"**T**o avoid having my readers fall asleep, I try my hardest not to create what I call 'grocery-list writing': *I did this. I did that. Afterward, I did that. Then, I did this!* To heal the most boring of essays, I like to use a lot of details to 'show,' not tell, more about each event."

To avoid listy writing, you can:

- Pick out one or two exciting events and tell more about them. Leave out unimportant or boring parts.

- Give more details, so your readers feel they have experienced one event before you go on to tell about the next one.

FOCUS POINT Does your writing ever sound like the essay on page 249? How can you improve the essay?

> Write a brief essay telling about a favorite place.

<u>My Favorite Place</u>
<u>by Danisha Williams</u>

As the barn door opened, Bryan began to slide into a pile of hay. Marita and I were laughing because Bryan kept on trying to stand up. Then we joined him and all slid into the pen down below. We fed the cows and headed out to the pasture. Marita showed us how to ride her horse.

After that, we went back into the house and Marita's grandmother gave us some fresh-baked cookies. We ate and decided to play some music. We heard noise outside and so we ran out there to see what it was. It was Marita's boyfriend showing off a new tractor his family had just bought. I didn't know the first thing about tractors, but it sure looked like an impressive machine.

After sunset, we all drove into town for ice cream and a movie.

Marian's Advice for Danisha

How can Danisha change this essay so it isn't listy? She can:

- Get more quickly to the horseback ride. That's the most interesting part, and I want to know a whole lot more about it.

- Add dialogue and details to round out one event before going on to the next. For example:

"Man, that's slippery," laughed Marita as she watched Bryan fall and stand, stand and fall, in the big pile of hay.

Solution #1: Add Meat to the Bones

Listy writing goes from one event to the next too quickly.

> On Friday, Mike and I spent all afternoon looking for a job. I left school, and then got into my car. Then I noticed I had no gas.
>
> So I filled up and then drove to Mike's high school and picked him up. Then we went to the mall and got some job applications.
>
> We went to a restaurant and filled out a couple of them, and then we left. I dropped off my friend and then I went home.

The writer simply lists the events, repeating the same **time words**.

Listy writing is like a skeleton—bare bones. When you add concrete details, you add meat to the bones and fix listy writing.

How to Add Concrete Details

As a writer, you have a variety of tools available for rounding out your writing: dialogue, sensory details, snapshots, and thoughtshots. Study the examples to see how these tools work to add meat to this bare-bones sentence:

> When my mother picked me up from school, there was a baby in the car with her.

1. Use Dialogue

Dialogue tells the actual words people or characters say. Adding dialogue makes your writing more like a movie or a play.

> "Hi," my mom whispered as I got into the front seat. She pointed into the back seat and I looked.
>
> "A baby?" I couldn't believe my eyes.
>
> "She's your cousin," my mom nodded.

2. Use Sensory Details

Sensory details tell what you hear, smell, see, taste, or feel. They give your reader the sense of "being there."

> I slid onto the soft velour seat and felt the quiet air conditioner blowing cool air into my hair. The door swung closed, latched, and locked. I caught a whiff of baby powder as I looked around.

3. Use Snapshots

A snapshot gives a complete description of everything in the scene, as if you were looking at a photograph.

> The afternoon sunlight streamed through the car, lighting up the dashboard. My mother looked rested and ready to go, her hands lightly resting on the steering wheel of the old car. In back, a gray plastic baby carrier was snuggled into the middle of the back seat, surrounded by boxes of books. In the middle of the baby carrier, a tiny infant slept, its head barely visible through a cloud of soft blankets.

4. Use Thoughtshots

A thoughtshot tells what the narrator or the characters are thinking. It lets the reader "get inside people's heads."

> Mom had a strange look on her face, I thought, as I got into the car. And what was that in the back seat, I wondered, looking around. A baby?! Whose? What was my mom doing with it? And what's that smell? Someone had some explaining to do, I thought.

Solution #2: Zero In on a Moment

If your writing is listy, the repetition and choppiness will make your readers lose interest. You'll do better if you concentrate on just the most important moment.

Choose the Best Moment

To find the most important moment of your writing, try "index-card narrowing." Start by telling your story on index cards. When you can see each part of the story separately, it'll help you find the most important part to focus on and expand.

1 **Summarize the Story on Index Cards**
Write a one-sentence summary of each event on each card. You'll need at least three cards, but use as many as you need. Some writers also like to draw pictures on the cards.

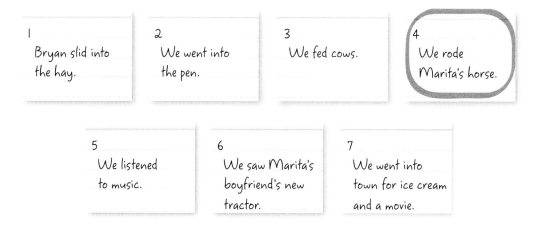

1 Bryan slid into the hay.

2 We went into the pen.

3 We fed cows.

4 We rode Marita's horse.

5 We listened to music.

6 We saw Marita's boyfriend's new tractor.

7 We went into town for ice cream and a movie.

2 **Choose the Best Card**
This will probably be your favorite part of the story. You might read aloud your cards and ask a listener to help you decide which part promises to be the most interesting.

3 **Collapse the "Before" and "After" Cards**
Combine into one sentence all the cards before your best card. Do the same for the "after" cards.

4 Zero In on the Best Card

Write a lot about the moment on your best card. Use plenty of specific details. Help your reader imagine having the same experiences you did.

Have someone read your writing. You may want to revise some parts, but chances are your writing won't be listy! Does the writing below sound listy now?

My Favorite Place

Marita, Bryan, and I were in the barn, sliding in the hay and feeding the cows. Then Marita looked out into the field.

"There's Buster," she said, pointing at the palomino grazing in the distance. Marita whistled and he galloped toward us, mane and tail flying, until he reached the fence where we stood.

"Let's ride bareback," she said as she looped a rope over Buster's neck and led him into the corral. After attaching his halter, Marita leaped onto the horse's back and nudged him with her knees until he started trotting. Off they went, riding in circles. Soon Marita pulled up, slid smoothly off his back, and asked "Who's next?"

I'd never ridden a horse before, but Bryan gave me a boost and there I was on Buster's back. Marita handed me the rope and said, "Just kick him softly with your heels till he gets going." So I did, and I felt his powerful stride beneath me as we circled the corral. We stopped, and I slid off the way I saw Marita do it. It was so easy!

The day wasn't over until we listened to music for a while and then drove into town for some ice cream and a movie. What an incredibly mellow day!

The writer combined the ideas on cards 1–3 to start the story. She got to the important idea quickly.

She then added plenty of details to explode the important idea on card 4.

The writer covered all the ideas in cards 5–7 in one short paragraph.

If Your Writing Is Too Wordy

What's It Like?

As a driver, you can drive your passengers crazy if you go on and on about the driving experience. Your passengers don't need to hear a lot of fluff—they just want to get where they're going without having their ears talked off. Writing works the same way. If you ask your readers to wade through too many words, they will stop reading.

Make Every Word Count

"Telling your readers that you are going to tell them something just wastes words. I try to remember: 'Marian, don't waste time and space telling the reader what you're going to do. Just simply begin—and then get to the point!'"

Talking about your writing—instead of about your topic—is one cause of wordiness. This is known as **throwaway writing**. Another cause of wordiness is simply writing more than you need to make your points. For effective writing, you will see in this section that using fewer words is often better.

FOCUS POINT Can you find the "throwaway writing" parts in the essay on page 255? Do you see any other words that are unnecessary?

Write a short essay explaining what character means to you.

Do You Have Character?
by Jason Gilpin

I am a person who has thought a lot about what character means. I have two ideas about what character means: the ability to tell right from wrong, and independence. These two qualities combine together to make character.

The first characteristic that I will cover is the fact that a person of strong character has the ability to tell right from wrong. This ability to tell right from wrong means that the person looks inside himself or herself, instead of at what different other people would do. It means that he or she follows an internal guide.

The second characteristic I'll explain is independence. If a person is independent, he or she will act a certain way even if nobody else does. If a person is independent, that person follows his or her conscience, no matter what anyone else does.

In conclusion, I've told you what it is that character means to me and about the two parts of character. One more time, they are the ability to tell right from wrong and independence. Thank you.

Marian's Advice for Jason

You've spent too much time and space introducing your ideas and "coaching" your reader. And you haven't always said things in the most economical way. Streamline your essay by:

- replacing the "coaching" with details or examples that show what character looks like in action

- eliminate any words that don't add substance to your argument. For example, instead of

  I am a person who has thought a lot about what character means.

  how about just

  I have thought a lot about character.

Solution #1: Take Out Throwaway Writing

Imagine if you went to a play and the author felt it necessary to inform you of all the production details in advance.

When you write, you don't need to announce the structure of your writing to your audience. Letting your writing speak for itself actually makes it *easier* to get your message across.

How to Recognize Throwaway Writing

Some throwaway writing consists of polite phrases and formulas that are fine in a social setting, but are out of place in a formal essay—things like

Hi, my name is . . .

Thank you for reading my paper.

Worse are useless phrases that announce the writer's intentions or give the reader hints about the structure or purpose of the writing. Look for sentences that begin like this:

Now I will tell you about . . .

My paper will focus on . . .

It is my belief that . . .

I have proved that . . .

How many different kinds of throwaway writing can you find in the letter to the editor below? How would it sound without it?

Dear Editor,

I'll introduce my topic with a question. Who is to blame for the price of gas? American consumers have pointed angry fingers at rich oil executives. However, I believe that oil company executives don't have that power because they are governed by supply, demand, and political risk.

First I'll discuss supply. Our nation's oil refineries are running at capacity, according to news reports. Supply cannot be increased without building more refineries. The next paragraph will talk about demand.

Demand for oil in the world is skyrocketing. American consumption alone continues to increase each month. America's not the only country that uses oil, so I'll mention another one. Other countries are now competing to buy the oil we want, too, especially China.

I have discussed supply and demand. I must also point out the troubles in the Middle East. Political instability in the Middle East and the resulting investment risk also affect gas prices. Much of our gas starts out as crude oil produced there. When world events interrupt production, it changes the way oil prices are set.

As we Americans become frustrated with rising fuel costs, we need to be part of the solution instead of blaming the most convenient target. Thank you for reading this letter.

—Artemis Briceño

It's not necessary to **announce what's to come.**

Good writing speaks for itself. Readers don't need to be told **how it's organized**.

Good manners are important, but are not necessary to include in most writing.

◄ Refineries process crude oil to make gasoline and other fuels.

Solution #2: Use Fewer Words

Even after you throw away throwaway writing, you may have more words than necessary. Read the example below. How many words can you take out without affecting the meaning?

> The question as to whether romantic love is a good thing or not is an interesting one. This is a question that many writers have tried to give an answer to in the past. The reason why is that love can make you happy, but at the same time it can also make you miserable.

The writer of the passage has something to say, but the reader has to fight a blizzard of words in order to get to the meaning.

Types of Too-Muchness

Knowing how to identify the two most common sources of too-muchness can help you get to lean and meaningful writing.

1. Saying the Same Thing Again

If a word (or phrase or sentence) adds no meaning to a piece of writing, it may be because you say the same thing elsewhere.

> Love can make you happy, but ~~at the same time~~ it can also make you miserable.

"at the same time" and "also" express the same idea

Many phrases in common use can be shortened without any loss of meaning. Here are just a few examples:

Wordy/Redundant	▶ Streamlined	Wordy/Redundant	▶ Streamlined
advance warning	warning	join together	join
appear to be	appear	lift up	lift
he is a man who	he	the reason why	the reason

2. Wandering All Around the Point

It may seem more sophisticated to use a lot of words where just one or two will do. Which of the following examples would you rather write? Which would you rather read?

Wordy

During the time that I was visiting my cousin in Maine last summer, I had occasion to meet a friend of his by the name of Tony. This meeting gave rise to a series of letters and phone calls between us before I called a halt to the long-distance romance.

Concise

While I was visiting my cousin in Maine last summer, I met a friend of his named Tony. This meeting started a series of letters and phone calls between us before I stopped the long-distance romance.

Sometimes writers wander because they are trying to fill up the page. But the most interesting way to fill up the page is to elaborate by giving additional information, not simply to use more words to give the same information.

Take Out the Deadwood

Now that you know what to look for, make it part of your revision process to look for "deadwood"—the extra words that clutter up your writing. Here's the passage from page 258 made lean and meaningful by taking out the deadwood:

Many writers have tried to answer the interesting question of whether romantic love is a good thing. Love can make you happy, but it can also make you miserable.

If your writing seems skimpy after taking out the deadwood, build it up with meaningful details and elaboration. (See pages 152–155.)

If Your Sentences Are Boring

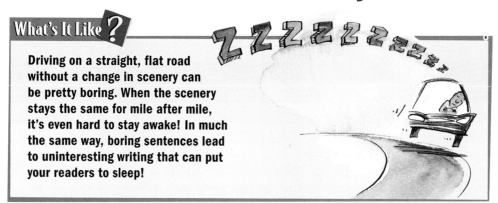

What's It Like?

Driving on a straight, flat road without a change in scenery can be pretty boring. When the scenery stays the same for mile after mile, it's even hard to stay awake! In much the same way, boring sentences lead to uninteresting writing that can put your readers to sleep!

How To Keep Your Writing Interesting

"**I** like to think of my sentences as paintbrushes. Sometimes I need a long brush stroke followed by a medium brush stroke, punctuated by a short brush stroke. I always pay attention to how variety makes the canvas of my story come alive."

Good writers experiment with their sentences to make their writing come alive. Here are a few techniques you can try with your sentences to avoid boring your readers:

- Mix up the length of your sentences until you get a good rhythm to your writing, a pace that carries your readers along.

- Play with the placement of your words and phrases.

- Enrich your sentences with powerful words and engaging language.

FOCUS POINT Would the speech on page 261 keep you interested? Explain your answer.

Your city has some extra funds. Write a speech presenting one idea for spending the money in a way that would make the city a better place to live. Back up your opinions and ideas with evidence that supports your arguments.

Speech to the City Council
by Angeline Dimaggio

Mayor Brown, council members, and citizens of Riverton:

I have heard that you have some extra funds. I have an idea for the extra money. Our city needs more skate parks. We don't have any skate parks now. Many of my friends skate. They don't have any good places to go. They take their skateboards to parking lots and concrete ditches. Owners make them leave all the time. This makes my friends feel like criminals. That is not fair. We should give them a safe place to skate. This would make us all very happy.

Marian's Advice for Angeline

If this were my speech, I'd challenge myself to:

- Add color and excitement by starting my sentences with the names of real people, places, and things instead of *we, they, that,* and *this.*

- Create full-bodied sentences such as *Because teens don't have a place to go, they end up skating in parking lots where angry owners kick them out.*

But, I'd use some short, powerful ones, too, like *We aren't criminals!*

Solution #1: Vary Your Sentences

Recognize Boring Sentences

Sentences can be boring when they are all too similar. They could be similar in length or they could all have a similar pattern, such as two parts linked together with *and* or *but*, as in the following example:

Boring Writing

> We need a skate park in this town, and we have a good idea for how to start planning for one. The Wheels Club at school met and decided to hold a fundraiser at the upcoming International Food Festival. Some of my friends have tried my dad's chili, and they think we can sell lots of it. Dad offered to cook for us, but this is something we want to do on our own. So he'll be our consultant for the recipe, and we're going to do all the cooking ourselves.

A mix of long and short sentences in an unpredictable pattern helps prevent "reader's rut." The following sentences have varied patterns, and even include some intentional sentence fragments. This variety keeps the reader from getting bored.

Interesting Writing

> We have been without a skate park in this town for far too long. We need to get one. Now! The Wheels Club at school came up with a great idea: a fundraiser at the upcoming International Food Festival! What do we sell? Easy! Some of my friends have tried my dad's chili, and they are confident we can sell lots of it. Dad generously offered to cook for us. Even though we appreciate his help, this is something we want to do on our own. He'll be our recipe consultant. All the actual cooking we'll do ourselves. Watch out!

Cooking up a piece of writing that will keep your reader's interest is a little like following a recipe. See the steps on page 263.

Recipe for Sentence Variety

1 **Prepare some longer sentences.**

Make sure you use full-flavored sentences, full of meaty content. Craft them well, until juicy and robust. When revising, you can create longer sentences by combining shorter ones or adding details. (See pages 184–187.)

2 **Mix with some shorter sentences.**

Choose only ones with good, solid construction, to add structure and chunky flavorfulness. Mix these with your longer sentences in an unpredictable pattern, so your reader is always surprised.

3 **For extra crunchiness, add a fragment or two.**

A **fragment** is an incomplete sentence, missing either a subject or a predicate. Fragments can be the result of careless writing. But careful writers often include them intentionally for effect. They can add energy and a conversational tone.

Careful with fragments! Make sure they are intentional and that you can defend their use. And don't overuse them—a few fragments can go a long way; overuse will make them lose their punch. Enough said.

Here's an example of "the recipe" put to work to fix a piece of boring, predictable writing:

Boring

> The bee landed on Natalie's hand. She started screaming. The chili spilled. Her eyes bulged and her arms flailed. Every head at the fairgrounds turned. People were staring at us.

Fixed with "The Recipe"

> The bee landed on Natalie's hand and, without warning, she screamed like a siren, her eyes bulging and her arms flailing. The plastic bowl of chili flew across the booth. Every head at the fairgrounds turned at once. People stared shamelessly. Cold, disapproving stares.

Solution #2: Spice Up Your Verbs

What's an Action Verb? .

Many verbs tell what someone or something does—*eats, munches, gulps, devours.* These action verbs can be bland, like *eats*, or give a vivid picture, like *devours*. If your sentences are boring, take a look at your action verbs. You may need to spice them up.

Bland

> Emily looked inside the bubbling pot; her chili smelled like it was almost ready.

Pepped Up with Vivid Verbs

> Emily **squinted** as she **peered** inside the bubbling pot; she **inhaled** the pungent aroma— her chili was almost ready.

Change to Spicy Verbs

The following chart shows the most overused, general verbs, as well as a few of the verbs that you can substitute to make your writing more lively and interesting. A thesaurus (see page 65) is a great resource for finding precise, specific, and vivid verbs.

Instead of . . .	How about . . .
cry	weep, whimper, whine, sob, bawl, wail
give	provide, supply, contribute, furnish, grant, confer
go (fast)	race, rush, hurry, dash, hasten, scamper, hustle
go (slow)	walk, meander, trudge, hobble, stroll, amble
go (other)	crawl, leap, jump, march, skip, hop, trundle
laugh	grin, giggle, chuckle, cackle, howl
learn	study, grasp, master, memorize, understand
like	enjoy, appreciate, relish, treasure, love, adore, admire
pull	drag, haul, draw, lug, tug, yank
talk	chat, chatter, discuss, communicate, speak, converse
write	record, compose, scrawl, scribble, inscribe

Solution #3: Pepper Your Writing with Prepositional Phrases

Another way to enrich your sentences is to add prepositional phrases that offer interesting details.

What's a Prepositional Phrase?

Prepositional phrase is a mouthful of a term for something that you use all the time. It refers to phrases that begin with words such as *above, behind, after, before, in, for, with,* and many others.

> Tells about the cousin

My cousin is the one **with the blue shirt.**
She came to visit me **from El Salvador.**

> Tells where the cousin is from

Add Them Anywhere!

Because prepositional phrases can modify both nouns and verbs, you can add them virtually anywhere in your writing, wherever a sentence seems too bare or you need to spark your writing with an interesting detail.

Plain (and Boring)

Vendors sell food. My cousin has a booth. She sells *pupusas.*

Peppered with Prepositional Phrases

Vendors **at the International Food Festival** sell food **of many types from all around the world.** My cousin has a booth **in the middle of the fairgrounds.** She sells *pupusas* **to the huge crowd at the fairgrounds.**

Solution #4: Move a Modifier

What's a Modifier?

A modifier is a word or phrase that tells more about another word. Adjectives and adverbs are common types of modifiers.

- An adjective tells more about a **noun** and usually appears before the noun it modifies:

> My buddies don't like crowded parks.

- An **adverb** can modify a **verb**, an adjective, or another adverb. When used with a verb, an adverb often appears just before or just after the verb it modifies:

> Mike **strongly** dislikes having a large audience of gawkers while he skates, though he **manages fine** with just a few people.

Adding adjectives and adverbs to your sentences can make your writing more colorful and interesting. To call special attention to them, try placing the adjectives and adverbs in unusual places.

Placing Adjectives

Plain

> Superathletic Julian placed second in a competition.

One **adjective** before one **noun**

Better

> Superathletic Julian placed a strong second in a statewide competition.

More **adjectives**, but all in the usual place, before **nouns**

Even More Interesting

> Julian, superathletic and confident, stepped onto the half-pipe.

Adjectives after the **noun**

> Superathletic and confident, Julian glided up to the half-pipe.

Adjectives at the beginning of a sentence

> Julian skated down into the half-pipe, slick and steep and treacherous.

Adjectives at the end of the sentence, after a **noun**

Placing Adverbs

Plain

> Leeanne skated on the sidewalk.

No adverbs

Better

> She skated fast but cautiously in and out of the walkways.

A pair of **contrasting adverbs** added after the **verb**

Even More Interesting

> Smoothly, steadily, she glided to the end of the street.

Adverbs at the beginning of the sentence, before the **verb**

> She glided around the trees smoothly, steadily.

Adverbs at the end of the sentence

Solution #5: Elaborate with Participles

What's a Participle?

A **participle** is a verb form that often ends with *-ed* or *-ing*. It often comes at the start of a phrase, which is called a **participial phrase**. The participle or the participial phrase acts as an adjective to describe a noun in a sentence.

Examples

1. Needing a break from the skate-park scene, the friends piled into Nadine's van and headed out to the river.   Describes what the friends are thinking

2. The water, gurgling softly over the rocks, sparkled in the sun.   Tells more about the water

3. After two hours, refreshed, Ricardo emerged from the river.   Tells how Ricardo feels

4. He sat on a rock sizzling in the early afternoon sun.   Describes the rock

Questions and Answers

You can ask yourself questions to uncover additional details to include in your sentences. Then you can answer the question using participles. Here's how it works:

1 **Ask an interesting question about a noun.**
Who knows the most about your writing topic? You do! So, when a sentence seems a little boring, try asking yourself a good question about one of the nouns. (A noun is the name of a person, place, thing, or idea.)

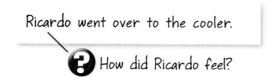

Ricardo went over to the cooler.

? How did Ricardo feel?

❷ Answer with a participle or participial phrase.

Here are a couple of examples:

With a participle

> Exhausted, Ricardo went over to the cooler.

With a participial phrase

> Beginning to get hungry, Ricardo went over to the cooler.

To avoid confusion, be sure to place a participle or its phrase right next to the noun it tells about.

Going up the steep mountainside, Mike and Lin were hot and sweaty from the sun.

Mike and Lin were hot and sweaty from the sun going up the steep mountainside.

Participles and participial phrases may be placed before or after a noun. Use commas to set them off from the rest of the sentence.

Before the Noun

> Wearing a Hawaiian shirt and jeans, ∧Mrs. Lott climbed into her
>   Relieved to find a ride home,
> pickup truck.∧Mike and Lin
>
> smiled gratefully at Mrs. Lott.

After the Noun

> , wearing a Hawaiian shirt and jeans,
> Mrs. Lott∧climbed into her
>   , relieved to find a ride home,
> pickup truck. Mike and Lin∧
>
> smiled gratefully at Mrs. Lott.

Solution #6: Elaborate with Clauses

What's a Clause?

A **clause** is a group of words with a subject and a verb. Some clauses function as adjectives; some as adverbs. Professional writers bring additional sparkle and interest to their sentences by using adjective and adverb clauses. You can, too!

How to Add an Adjective Clause

Adjective clauses begin with a word like *who, that, which,* or *where* and modify a **noun** or pronoun.

> My friend, who is an expert rock climber, will be an instructor at the Climb Gym this summer.

To enrich a skimpy sentence, you can ask yourself a good question about one of the nouns and then answer it with an adjective clause.

Skimpy Sentence

My friend will be an instructor at the Climb Gym this summer.

 Where is he from?

 What is at the gym?

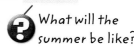 What will the summer be like?

Enriched with Adjective Clauses

, who is from Nepal,
My friend ⋀ will be an instructor at the Climb Gym this summer.

To tell about a **person**, start the clause with *that* or *who.*

, where they have the tallest indoor wall in the state,
My friend will be an instructor at the Climb Gym ⋀ this summer.

To tell about a **place**, start the clause with *that, which,* or *where.*

My friend will be an instructor at the Climb Gym this summer ⋀ *, which is going to be an awesome three months.*

To tell about a **thing**, start the clause with *that* or *which.*

How to Add an Adverb Clause

Adverb clauses begin with a word like *after, before, if,* or *because* and modify a verb, adjective, or adverb.

> Before he became an expert climber, my friend used to be scared of heights.

To enrich a skimpy sentence with an adverb clause, ask yourself questions that begin with words like *why* or *when* and then answer it with good details.

Skimpy Sentence

My friend used to be scared of heights, but he got over it.

When was he
scared
of heights? Why was he
scared
of heights?

Enriched with Adverb Clauses

Before he became an expert climber,
ᴧMy friend used to be scared of heights, but he
got over it.

Clause tells **when** the friend used to be scared.

because he fell from a tree as a child
My friend used to be scared of heights, but he
got over it. ᴧ

Clause tells **why** the friend was scared.

Solution #7: Elaborate with Absolutes

Are you ready to use absolutes to add density and sophistication to your writing? Absolutely!

How Do Absolutes Work?

Here are two complete sentences:

> His hands were clenched into two tight fists.
>
> He climbed nervously into the boxing ring.

Here the two sentences have been combined by deleting the word *were* in the first sentence:

> His hands ~~were~~ clenched into two tight fists,
>
> ~~He~~ climbed nervously into the boxing ring.

The phrase *His hands clenched into two tight fists* is an example of an **absolute**. An absolute is a phrase that is almost a complete sentence, missing only some form of the verb *to be*. Below are some more examples:

Forms of *Be*	
In the Present	In the Past
am	was
is	were
are	

> He looked straight ahead, **his muscles working visibly in his jaw.** He stood there, **hands tightly gripping the top rope,** for what seemed an interminable time.

The addition of an absolute can bring excitement and sophistication to a borderline boring sentence.

Working with Absolutes

You can combine sentences to create an absolute, or you can add an absolute anywhere you need to craft a long, full-bodied sentence. Absolutes can appear at the beginning, in the middle, or at the end of a sentence.

Boring

Stan's muscles were still sore from the fight. He shuffled toward the kitchen. He drank some juice. His mind was still fuzzy from sleep. Suddenly he realized that his life had changed irretrievably yesterday. He stepped onto the patio. His eyes were blinking. They were trying to adjust to the dazzling light.

Sentences Combined to Create Absolutes

~~Stan's~~ *His* muscles ~~were~~ still sore from the fight. ~~He~~ *Stan* shuffled toward the kitchen. He drank some juice. His mind ~~was~~ still fuzzy from sleep. Suddenly he realized that his life had changed irretrievably yesterday. He stepped onto the patio. His eyes ~~were~~ blinking. ~~They were~~ trying to adjust to the dazzling light.

Boring

Stan very briefly stood up by the ropes; then he threw in the towel.

❓ How did Stan look?

❓ What was he feeling?

Absolutes Added

Stan very briefly stood up by the ropes—**eyes swollen, legs wobbling**—then he threw in the towel, **his hopes of an easy victory now a quickly fading dream.**

The Many Writers You Are

featuring **David Yoo**

"**W**riting well is all about making adjustments depending on the situation, just like everything else in life."

Writing for Real

As a writer, you take on different roles depending on the situation. Sometimes, you just want to draw your readers into a good story. You write to make readers live your characters' feelings and adventures. Other times, you might write about an important issue that affects your community, or to persuade an employer to hire you for a summer job.

David Yoo makes his living writing stories—but at various times he takes on all of the other roles described on page 279, and more! On pages 277–278, he explains why understanding your role as a writer is so important.

Know Your Role:
Why Are You Writing? And for Whom?

People often underestimate the careful thought that's required to write well because they've been writing since they were little kids. Maybe they figure that if they've been doing it that long, they must be pretty good at it. As a result, one mistake people often make is that they write without thinking very much about whom they're writing for. They ignore the fact that your role as a writer in any given situation shapes how you write for that particular audience. Knowing your role and understanding your audience's needs can make all the difference in getting your point across effectively.

For example, you don't write a letter to your boss the same way you write a letter to your girlfriend. For one thing, it'll probably get you fired. (Either that or it will land you a date with your boss, which probably isn't a good idea.) You don't write a poem the same way you write a lab report for chemistry class, either. (Well, a truly talented poet can probably manage it, but most of us can't.)

When I wrote a best man's speech for my buddy's wedding a few years back, I knew that I obviously couldn't write it as if I were a restaurant critic. Restaurant critics have no obligation whatsoever to make their subject feel loved, to be sensitive and balance the negative with the positive. In fact, they're often encouraged, for the entertainment's value, to trash their subject—definitely *not* something you should do at a wedding. My point is, knowing your audience and your role as a writer is crucial to writing effectively.

The fact is, writing well really does require this level of careful thought. Not paying attention to your role and your audience is like getting up to bat in a baseball game and just swinging away, assuming every pitch is going to be a fastball down the middle. Or to put it another way, it's like running into a burning building without thinking about how you're going to get the flames

under control. Firefighters don't just charge into each fire the same way; they carefully analyze what kind of fire it is and how best to deal with it before taking action. Writers should treat their subjects with as much
30 consideration.

Also, there are often important consequences to what you write and how well you write it. You write a résumé hoping to get a job. You write a best man's speech hoping to communicate to your buddy how much you value him and wish him well. You write a letter to your landlord
35 complaining about a leak in the ceiling and hoping to get it fixed. You write a class assignment hoping to get a good grade. No matter what you're writing, there's usually a lot at stake, so it's all the more important to consider your audience and your role. When you develop a sense of who your audience is and what you want to accomplish, you can be that much
40 more effective.

Why is this important? It's important because good writing will lead to your getting the job, being the highlight of the wedding, having your leaky ceiling fixed, getting a good grade
45 in class. Not to sound melodramatic, but learning to understand your role as a writer can
50 change your life ... forever. Okay, I'm being slightly melodramatic.

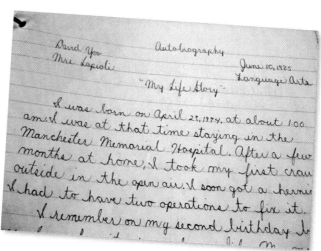

The beginning of David Yoo's autobiography, written when he was 11 years old.

Writing Roles and Forms

You can take many roles when you write, and you can write in many forms. Take a closer look at how you can write . . .

► **As a Family Member**

Share memories with the people closest to you.
Featured form: Reflective Essay

► **As a Consumer**

Request information, or ask to have a problem solved.
Featured form: Letter of Problem Solving

► **As a Storyteller**

Grab your readers with a good story—funny or serious.
Featured form: Short, Short Story

► **As a Citizen**

Bring changes to your community, city, or country.
Featured form: Persuasive Essay

► **As a Critic**

Evaluate something, and share your opinions.
Featured form: Literary Critique

► **As an Employee**

Find a job or do the job you have well. Featured form: Résumé

► **As a Reporter**

Tell the world about a topic or an event.
Featured form: News Article

► **As a Poet**

Share your personal feelings in poems or songs.
Featured form: Poem

Examples of many other forms you can write appear in the "All You Can Write" section, beginning on page 346.

hbgoodwriters.com

Link to sites with writing that exemplifies these roles.

Write as a Family Member

What's It Like

How is every home like a skyscraper? It's got lots and lots of stories—family stories! Families are an endless source of writing topics, and relatives give writers every reason to write. That's why when you write as a family member, you can write anything, from an e-mail to an essay.

Close to Home

Do you remember the first time you made a birthday card for your mom or wrote a note home when you were away? Chances are, some of your first experiences with writing involved your family. When you write as a family member, you may write about or to someone in your family or people closest to you. You might write to:

- stay in touch through short notes, e-mails, letters, and cards

- honor a relative or close friend by writing a speech for a wedding or a poem for a parent's birthday

- share family memories through reflective essays, diary entries, or memoirs

- describe your day-to-day life in a blog that family and friends can read online.

FOCUS POINT Read David Yoo's account of his experience delivering a best-man speech on page 281. What similiar celebrations with family or friends does it remind you of? Have you ever spoken, sung, or recited something at a gathering of family or friends?

David Yoo on . . .

Writing as a Family Member

After going to a dozen or so weddings I realized that there's a formula to the "best man's speech." He rambles about the groom's "wild ways" back in college, then switches gears to explain how the bride (whom he's just met for the first time that weekend) changed the groom's life, and finishes up with a sappy cliché that—despite its sappiness—brings tears to the bride's eyes and makes the groom nod in earnest approval.

I didn't want to give that typically corny speech when I was best man at my buddy Joe's wedding; I wanted to be original. But as I struggled to write it over several weeks, I realized that all best-man speeches inevitably end up sounding pretty similar because there are mandatory "pre-reqs" to this type of speech. You can't really stray too far from them because your audience is made up of the friends and family of the couple and, fact is, you're not writing this for yourself, you're writing it for them!

Still, I tried my hardest to write something that didn't sound formulaic, because I still thought those speeches usually sounded terrible! Whether or not I succeeded in transcending the genre is debatable, but I at least tried to be authentic while working within the conventions.

Reflective Essay

One kind of family writing is a **reflective essay.** In a reflective essay, the writer captures the most important parts of a memory and shares new thoughts, or reflections, about the experience.

What memory does Carlos capture in his essay? What does he think today about the experience?

◀ Frio River
in South Texas

REFLECTIVE ESSAY

A Moment for Life

Carlos Santiago

Opening
Introduces the **topic**. Tells what Carlos remembers.

Last summer, when my family decided to leave the city and go on a camping trip, I wasn't all that excited at first. I'd never been out in the wilderness before. But I'll always remember what a fantastic trip it turned out to be.

Body
Gives specific details about the trip.

We chose a campsite by the Frio River, near the town of Uvalde. We pitched our tents in a really quiet, isolated spot with no electricity. Setting up the tents took forever because there were so many pieces! We kept getting the poles, ropes, and canvas all tangled up. It was just crazy!

Camping by
the water ▶

Body
Also includes
sensory details
about what
Carlos saw,
heard, and felt.

Once the tents were up, my cousins and I jumped into the crystal-clear water. The day was hot, but the water felt like ice! In fact, the river's name, "Frio," means "cold" in Spanish. It took us a few minutes to get used to the chill, but then we spent hours splashing around and floating down the rapids. It was great just to hang out and relax.

Later on, we walked through the woods and then came back to camp for dinner. My aunts and uncles had three or four grills going all at once. The cooking smells made me so hungry, it was hard not to grab the burgers right off the hot grill! Finally we ate.

That night it got really dark because there was no light from any houses nearby. We all sat around the campfire looking up at the stars. That was really cool because we never get to see stars in the city. Everyone felt so content.

Voice
Uses
slang
and shares
personal
feelings
with the
audience.

Conclusion
Presents
Carlos's
thoughts as
he reflects on
the experience.
Explains why
the memory is
important.

After three days, we had to pack everything up and drive home, but I'll remember that trip forever. I had so much fun and, even better, I got to reconnect with my family. Being around the people you care for can be incredible, even if you're in the middle of nowhere. All of the Santiagos agree: we need to come back next summer.

How to Write a Reflective Essay

1 **Choose a Memory**

Think about moments in your life that you don't want to forget. If you need some reminders, try looking in your writer's notebook, journal, or collection of souvenirs. Family photos will definitely give you some ideas, too. Choose one moment or one memory for your topic.

▲ Roasting marshmallows over the campfire

2 **Trap the Unforgettable Ideas**

Write down everything from your memory you'd like to include, just as you remember it. Make sure to include clear descriptions so your memory is preserved, even if you forget some of it.

Here are two ways you can trap ideas:

I saw . . .	• stars I never see in the city • the Frio River rapids • lots of trees
I heard . . .	• water rushing over the rocks • frogs and crickets at night
I smelled . . .	• food cooking on the grill • crisp, clear air
I tasted . . .	• grilled hamburgers • corn on the cob
I touched or felt . . .	• icy cold water • fresh, warm breezes

Five-Senses Diagram

City Life	Camping Trip
I hear noise from traffic, sirens, and music.	I hear sounds of water, crackling fire, and animals.
I'm always busy and on the move.	I feel calm and relaxed.
There are many people around.	There are few other people around.
I see billboards and neon signs.	I see trees and stars.

Comparison Chart

3 Plan How Your Ideas Will Flow

Write down words or phrases that describe the most unforgettable parts of the memory. These will be the parts of the event that came back into your memory first.

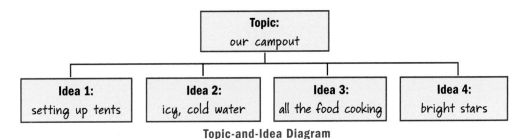

Topic-and-Idea Diagram

4 Start with a Good Beginning Sentence

Write an opening sentence that makes your reader want to find out more. Hook the reader with an interesting detail.

Boring

> My cousin Dolores asked
> the family if we would all
> like to go on a camping
> trip together.

Better

> "Familia." Even through e-mail,
> we could hear my cousin
> Dolores's signature Spanglish.
> "¿Qué tal if we go camping?"

5 Keep Going—Tell the Story in Your Own Voice

Use your plan to write the essay. Try different techniques to find the style that feels right to you.

Technique	Example
Write as if nobody is going to read it but you.	Because of Dad's attitude about crowds, we set up camp in the middle of nowhere.
Write as if you're telling the story to a new friend of the family.	My father doesn't care for crowds, and so we chose an isolated spot.
Write as if you are talking to a close family member who wasn't there.	You know how Dad is about crowds, right? So we got a campsite with as much space as Uncle Frank's backyard.

How to Write a Reflective Essay, continued

6 **Use Effective Transition Words**

Transition words serve to show relationships between ideas and help guide your reader.

Confusing

The water of the Frio River felt like ice. We got used to it, and we swam all afternoon.

Clear

At first the water of the Frio River felt like ice, but after we got used to it, we swam all afternoon.

7 **End with a Good Conclusion that Includes Your Reflection**

Finish your essay on a strong note. Don't just restate what you've said—leave the reader with something to remember. Explain what you value now about the memory. If you're not sure, try answering these questions:

- What makes this memory important to you?

- What is one life lesson you learned because of that memory?

- What is one thing you know now that you didn't know then?

Just Okay

In conclusion, I had a great time going camping with my family. It was a lot more fun than I had expected it to be. I enjoyed every part of the trip, from the moment we started setting up our tents to the day we packed up our things and went home. I would love to do it again next summer.

Much Better

I'll remember that trip forever. I had so much fun and, even better, I got to reconnect with my family. Being around the people you care for can be incredible, even if you're in the middle of nowhere. All of the Santiagos agree: we need to come back next summer.

More Ways to Write As a Family Member

A reflective essay isn't the only kind of family writing you can do. See the models in "All You Can Write" for other forms you might choose from.

Write to Stay in Touch

Blog (page 354)

Tell your family about the events of each day.

Friendly Letter (page 370)

Share what's going on in your life.

Write to Share a Family Memory or Honor a Relative

Memoir (pages 380–381)

Write about an unforgettable experience with your family.

Poems and Songs (pages 390–395)

Write a poem or song to honor a family member on a special occasion.

Write as a Consumer

What's It Like ?

Have you ever been surprised by something you purchased? Maybe it was better than you expected, or something was terribly wrong with it. As a consumer, you can write to a company to show how you feel about its products or services, good or bad. Most companies welcome feedback from their customers, so don't be shy about speaking your mind.

A Satisfied Customer

Teenage consumers purchase everything from CDs to soft drinks to shoes ... the list is endless. In a few years, you'll be spending money on big-ticket items like your first car, your own apartment, or your education. As a consumer, you might need to write to a company to:

- ask for information about an item you plan to buy

- solve a problem you have with a person, product, or service

- request a missing or replacement part

- thank someone for giving you great service.

By writing as a consumer, you can influence how a company does business—and ensure that you're a satisfied customer.

FOCUS POINT Have you ever experienced problems of the type described by David Yoo on page 289? What did you do about them? What experiences have you had writing as a consumer?

David Yoo on . . .

Writing as a Consumer

Part of the reality of renting an apartment is having to on occasion write letters of complaint. The roof starts leaking during a thunderstorm, the toilet backs up, paint chips regularly fall from the ceiling and shatter on your head as you're watching TV after dinner on a weeknight . . . .

These are all problems that need to be dealt with, and I've learned from experience that the key to a successful letter of complaint is to not only point out the problem but suggest a specific solution as well. And you should always date each letter, because the landlord never responds to the first couple of letters—in fact, you have to be of the mindset that the point of writing the landlord a letter at first is to merely start a paper trail that will eventually guilt the landlord into fixing what needs to be fixed. That's all a letter of complaint is, really. A hard copy of guilt.

Letter of Problem Solving

A good way to tell a company or business about a problem with a product or service is to write a letter. In a letter of problem solving, the writer describes the problem and suggests how the company can fix it.

What problem did Katie have? How does she expect the company to solve the problem?

LETTER OF PROBLEM SOLVING

816 Monterey Drive
Atlanta, GA 30326
(404) 555-6587
July 24, 2007

Inside Address
Addresses a **specific person**, if possible.

Mr. Daniel Whaley
Customer Service Representative
Summer Shoes, Inc.
300 Stafford Road
Mitchell, NC 28777

Dear Mr. Whaley:

Introduction
Gives **information** about the date and location of the purchase.

On July 10, 2007, I purchased a pair of cute Summer Shoes flip-flops from Suzie's Sandals in Kenton, FL, where I was vacationing with my family. I planned to wear them to a water park the next day.

On July 11, I wore the flip-flops. But after walking around the water park for just two hours, one of the straps on my right flip-flop broke. As a result, the flip-flop would not stay on my foot. The rest of the day I had to walk around with only one shoe. I was very uncomfortable and upset that my brand-new purchase was already useless.

I am enclosing the flip-flops and a copy of my receipt. Please send me a new pair of blue flip-flops in a women's size 7 as soon as possible.

Thank you for your time and attention. Please feel free to call me at (404) 555-6587 if you have any questions. I look forward to receiving my new pair of Summer Shoes flip-flops.

Sincerely,

Katie Chiang

Katie Chiang

Problem
Describes the problem and explains how Katie was inconvenienced by it.

Solution
Describes how the company can solve the problem.

Closing
Uses a **polite tone**.

How to Write a Letter of Problem Solving

1 Plan What You'll Say About the Problem

Organize your facts. Focus on information that will help someone understand and solve your problem. Use a list of questions and answers to help you remember all the details.

Question	Answer
What did I buy?	blue flip-flops, Summer Shoes brand
When did I buy them?	July 10, 2007
Where did I buy them?	Suzie's Sandals, Kenton, Florida
What was the problem?	strap broke after a couple of hours
Why was it a problem?	The flip-flop kept falling off of my foot! I had to walk around with only one shoe.

Then get the name of a specific person to contact. Call the company's service department, or use the Internet to find out who handles customer complaints.

2 Decide on the Solution You Want

What can the company do to solve the problem? What will it take to make you feel okay? You have to be clear on what you want before you ask.

www.summershoes.com

SUMMER SHOES

CUSTOMER SERVICE DEPARTMENT
300 Stafford Road
Mitchell, NC 29078
(363) 555-SHOE

Refunds and Exchanges Contact:
Daniel Whaley
Customer Service Representative
Extension 4117

❸ Make Your Letter Look Professional

Format your letter as a business letter, preferably on a computer. Be sure to include your address, the date, and the company's address. Don't indent the body paragraphs.

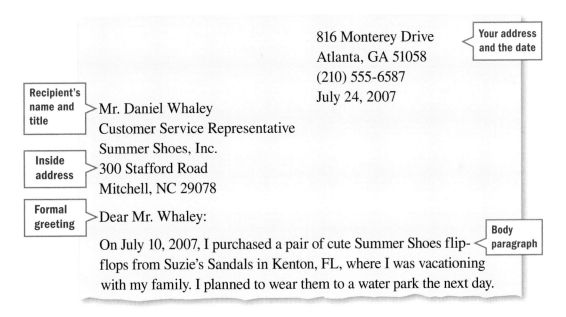

816 Monterey Drive
Atlanta, GA 51058
(210) 555-6587
July 24, 2007

Your address and the date

Recipient's name and title

Mr. Daniel Whaley
Customer Service Representative
Summer Shoes, Inc.

Inside address

300 Stafford Road
Mitchell, NC 29078

Formal greeting

Dear Mr. Whaley:

Body paragraph

On July 10, 2007, I purchased a pair of cute Summer Shoes flip-flops from Suzie's Sandals in Kenton, FL, where I was vacationing with my family. I planned to wear them to a water park the next day.

❹ Describe the Purchase and the Problem

Use your list of questions to give all the important details. Be specific about the problem and how it affected you.

Vague

A few weeks ago, I was on vacation with my family in Florida. While I was there, I bought a pair of your company's shoes. Then I wore them to a water park the next day. Unfortunately, they started falling apart right away. I tried to fix them but I couldn't. My whole day was ruined.

Specific

On July 10, 2007, I bought a cute pair of Summer Shoes flip-flops from Suzie's Sandals in Kenton, FL. On July 11, I wore them to a water park. After just two hours, the strap on my right flip-flop broke. As a result, it would not stay on my foot. The rest of the day I had to walk around with only one shoe.

How to Write a Letter of Problem Solving, continued

❺ Propose Your Solution

Explain how you want the company to solve the problem. Do you want the company to replace the product, or to give you a refund? Be clear about exactly what the company can do to satisfy you, the customer.

Unclear	Clear
Please send me a new pair of shoes.	Please send me a new pair of blue flip-flops in a women's size 7.

Unclear	Clear
Please refund what I spent on my shoes.	Please send me a refund in the amount of $10.61 to cover the cost of the flip-flops and the cost of shipping them back to you.

❻ End Your Letter Politely

Even if you're really upset, stay cool and calm while you write. Avoid harsh words. Instead, use a polite but firm tone. Be sure to thank the person you're writing to for taking the time to read about and address your problem.

Effective Endings	Ineffective Endings
• Thank you for your time. I look forward to receiving my new pair of flip-flops.	• Your products are the worst ones I've ever used. I'll never buy from your company again!
• Thank you in advance for your cooperation.	• If you care at all about your company's image, you'd better respond to me.
• Thank you for your help. I am eagerly awaiting your reply.	• Thanks a lot for making a terrible product.

More Ways to Write as a Consumer

Consumers write for many different reasons, not just to solve problems. See other kinds of letters you might write for different purposes in "All You Can Write."

Write for Information

Letter of Inquiry or Request (page 371)

Ask questions about something you plan to spend money on. Ask for something to be sent to you.

Write to Show Appreciation

Letter of Praise (page 372)

Thank someone for a good product or service.

Write as a Storyteller

What's It Like ?

Before they ever walk onto a stage, comedians decide how to craft a funny story so it will get the most laughs from the audience. Of course, writers tell other kinds of stories, too. They might write about real people or invented characters, ordinary places or imaginary worlds, their own lives or other people's lives. When you write to tell a story—real or made-up—you can make your audience laugh, cry, or just appreciate what you have to say.

In Touch with Your Audience

To tell a good story—or to tell a story well—you appeal to readers' emotions. You make them laugh, make them cry, or keep them on the edge of their seat with suspense. Here are some effective ways to interest readers in your stories:

- Make a person, object, or place come alive in a word portrait or character sketch.

- Amuse readers with a parody of a famous book, movie, or TV show; or create an imaginary world with a short story or play.

- Draw readers into the past or the future by writing historical fiction or science fiction.

- Tell readers the story of your life by writing your autobiography.

FOCUS POINT The process of writing to tell a story can be daunting. Read David Yoo's account of his bout with "writer's block," on page 297. Sound familiar? Share with a partner what you do to get "unblocked" when writing or telling a story.

Writing as a Storyteller

I was stuck trying to write a short story for my fiction workshop in college. It was frustrating because I had an idea that I was excited about, and in fact I knew every little scene and even knew how the story ended, but I just couldn't write a lick. Anytime I sat at the computer to bang out a rough draft, I'd end up just sitting there feeling totally lost.

The weekend before my story was due I ran into my creative-writing professor. He asked me how my story was coming, and I admitted my situation. His advice? He told me to go back to my room and write the story as an instruction manual. It was abstract advice, and he refused to elaborate, but I did as he said. I sat down at my computer and tried to write my story—about a guy trying to ask a girl out—as an instructional piece about how to ask a girl out.

An hour later, having quickly dropped the idea of writing an instruction manual, I'd written five pages at a feverish pace and realized the point of his advice. The point of the exercise was simply to get me to start writing something down, because figuring out a story often is easier once you're in the trenches and have pages to work with. Sometimes the best way to figure out how to crack a story is to just start writing it.

Short, Short Story

A short, short story is REALLY short—just a page or two, sometimes even less. But you can pack a lot of story into this compact form. You'll need to set the scene quickly and center the plot on a single main event.

What event does Rochelle capture in her story? What emotional response does she want from her readers?

SHORT, SHORT STORY

The Mailman's Adventure

Rochelle Riley

Beginning introduces the **setting** and **characters.**

Back when I was eight, the neighborhood girls and I liked to spy on people. Most people in our neighborhood were boring, but we always had fun spying on the mailman. He was a mean little man who scuttled around like a crab, always looking over his shoulder. If he caught us spying, he'd jump and scold us. It was scary but funny to get yelled at by someone other than our parents.

On one sunny summer day, he had a package for the neighborhood busybody, Miss Watts. She was a prissy lady who always wore a pinched expression, as if she'd just bitten into a lemon. We hid behind the bushes bordering her immaculate yard and watched to see what would happen.

WATTS

Middle
Introduces the
main plot event.
Moves quickly
to the **turning
point**.

The mailman knocked on the door. When she opened it, he announced, "A package for Miss Watts!"

Miss Watts tore open the package right away. Her sour expression turned into a delighted smile as she pulled out a beautiful handmade quilt, a nice gift from somebody. "Oh, my! Thank you!" she exclaimed excitedly. Before we knew it, prissy old Miss Watts leaned forward and kissed the mailman on the lips.

Immediately afterward, her eyes got big and her face flushed with embarrassment. She turned and rushed back into her house, slamming the door. Meanwhile, the mailman stood motionless on the front porch, staring at the closed door. We held our breaths as we crouched behind the bushes, waiting to see what would happen next.

He began to back up slowly until we were sure he'd fall off the porch. Then he turned and strolled down the steps with a dreamy look on his face.

"My first kiss!" he whispered as he skipped toward his truck. "Hooray!" From that day forward, he was the sweetest mailman around. After all, he was in love.

End
Tells how a
problem is
resolved or how
a **character
changes**.

How to Write a Short, Short Story

1 Consider Your Audience

Is your story for adults, other teens, or young children? Think about your readers and decide how to tell it in a way that would interest them.

2 Plan Your Plot

Usually a short, short story focuses on a brief series of events with one clear turning point. Use a flow chart to plan the events that will lead up to the turning point and to show what happens next.

Beginning

A group of little kids likes to spy on their neighbors (mean mailman, prissy lady)

↓

Before the Turning Point

1. The kids hide in the prissy lady's yard.
2. They see the mailman deliver a package.
3. It's a quilt from the prissy lady's sister.

↓

Turning Point

The lady is so excited that she kisses the mailman on the lips without thinking.

↓

After the Turning Point

1. The lady runs back into her house.
2. The mailman acts dazed.

↓

End (Resolution)

The mailman walks away and whispers, "My first kiss."

Flow Chart

❸ Choose the Point of View

Decide in whose "voice" you will tell the story. If the narrator is part of the action, use *first-person*. If the narrator is <u>not</u> a character in the story, use *third-person*.

First Person

> We held our breath as we crouched behind the bushes, waiting to see what would happen next. The mailman began to back up slowly until we were sure he'd fall off the porch.

Third Person

> The children held their breath as they crouched behind the bushes, waiting to see what would happen next. The mailman began to back up slowly until they were sure he'd fall off the porch.

❹ Start by Briefly Describing the Setting

In a short, short story, the plot is the main focus. There's no room for long, detailed descriptions of the setting. Use just a few words to tell quickly where and when things happen.

Too Long

> It was a gorgeous summer day in our neighborhood. The weather was sunny but not too hot. As I walked down the quiet, tree-lined streets I thought, "This is a perfect day to spy on the mailman."

Just Right

> It was a warm, sunny day in our neighborhood—perfect weather for spying on the mailman.

❺ Use Key Details to Develop the Characters

You can paint a character quickly with just a few brushstrokes. Add dialogue to help develop the characters, too.

Detail	What It Reveals
neighborhood busybody	The character interferes in other people's business.
always wore a pinched expression, as if she'd just bitten into a lemon	The character has no sense of humor and doesn't know how to relax.

How to Write a Short, Short Story, continued

6 Keep Going—And Maintain the Tone

Use your flow chart to finish the story. In a short, short story, you should strive for one overall emotional effect. Do you want to go for laughs? Do you want to tug at the heartstrings? Choose one and maintain that tone throughout.

For Laughs

Why did I start spying on my neighbors when I was eight? For the same reason that inspires anyone to get into the exciting world of neighborhood espionage: sheer boredom. Through an exhausting and highly demanding process we called "waiting in the bushes," my friends and I would give new meaning to the term "neighborhood watch."

Wistful and Evocative

When I was eight, I remember I went through a stage of "spying" on the neighbors. What excitement for me to watch them going about their very ordinary lives! I was especially fond of trailing our old mailman, expecting him to turn around and "discover" me at any moment.

7 Make the Ending Short and Sweet

Don't linger too much over your ending. To leave your reader satisfied, give answers to questions like:

- What happened to the characters after the turning point?

- Did the characters learn anything from what happened?

Weak Ending

After that day, my friends and I still walked around sometimes to spy on the mailman the way we did before. But it just didn't feel the same. He never bothered to yell at us anymore. He was in love with Miss Watts, and he barely even noticed us.

Strong Ending

"My first kiss!" he whispered as he skipped toward his truck. "Hooray!" From that day forward, he was the sweetest mailman around. After all, he was in love.

More Ways to Write as a Storyteller

A short, short story isn't the only kind of "story" you can tell. See the following models in "All You Can Write" for some other possibilities.

Tell the Real Story

Biography (page 353)

Tell the story of a person (famous or not) that you admire or find fascinating.

Autobiography (page 352)

Tell readers the story of your own life.

Magazine Feature Article(page 378)

Write about an important event, or about traveling to an interesting place.

Use Your Imagination

Historical Fiction Story (pages 406–407)

Invent a story based on real places and events from history.

Parody (page 385)

Write a humorous imitation of a well-known work.

Play (pages 386–389)

Write a story that's meant to be acted onstage.

Write as a Citizen

When you were a child, your family was your whole world. Then that world expanded to include school. Now that you are in your teens, you are ready to take on a role as citizen of your community, your state, your country and the whole world.

Share Your Views

Do you have opinions about the issues that affect you? Of course you do! When you write as a citizen, you write about those issues. Often you try to persuade other people to agree with your views. You may even try to get them to take a specific action. You'll probably write in a variety of forms, such as:

- a persuasive speech at a public meeting
- a letter to the editor of your local newspaper
- a newspaper editorial about an issue that affects readers
- a persuasive essay about how to solve a problem

Writing as a citizen gives you the chance to make your voice heard and change your community for the better.

FOCUS POINT Read David Yoo's account of his high school political campaign, on page 305. Have you ever won an argument or convinced someone to do something by taking an unusual approach? Talk about it with a partner.

David Yoo on . . .
Writing as a Citizen

My junior year of high school I decided to run for class secretary. I was running against two very popular girls, so at first I thought I didn't stand any chance of winning. But since I rarely won anything in high school, I decided to just go for it. And I thought I saw an opening, a way to win.

The opening was this: those two girls were about equally popular, and they were even part of the same group of popular girls. I thought that if I angled my speech a certain way I could win simply by being "something else."

So for my persuasive speech I wrote about how similar the two girls were (trying not to sound accusatory). I described how they were both on the field hockey team, they were both in the same clubs, etc., and by the end of my speech I'd made it clear that the two were basically interchangeable. As a result, I won the election in a landslide. The lesson? A persuasive speech can be really persuasive.

Persuasive Essay

Writing as a citizen often involves writing to persuade. In a persuasive essay, you try to convince others to agree with your position on an important issue—and to take action.

What position does Mike take in his essay? What arguments does he use to try to convince his readers?

PERSUASIVE ESSAY

End the Curfew Now

Mike Bozarth

Opening
Provides background on the issue. States the writer's **position.**

The city officials in San Antonio believe that imposing a curfew on teenagers makes our city a better place. I disagree. Lifting the curfew would help local businesses by encouraging people to visit downtown stores at night. Furthermore, it would help make our city safer and reduce crime. It would also reward the city's hard-working students by allowing them to hang out with their friends at more comfortable times of day. Ending the curfew would improve life in San Antonio.

Body
Gives **reasons** for the writer's position and provides supporting evidence.

Ending the curfew would benefit our city's economy. Right now, our town is nearly empty at night because there aren't any teenagers around. But if the curfew were lifted, more people would spend time shopping downtown at night. That would help local businesses to grow and encourage stores to stay open longer. Longer store hours, in turn, would lead to better wages and more jobs available for retail workers.

Furthermore, although many people think the curfew reduces crime, it actually doesn't. In fact, since the curfew began last year, vandalism and theft have been on the rise. Officer Cheryl Williams of the San Antonio Police Department says that most of these crimes occur in quiet areas when no one's around. So, if more people were outside during

A view of San Antonio, Texas, at sunset ▶

the evenings, our town would be safer. People would think twice about committing a crime, since more potential witnesses, including teenagers, would be around to report it.

Finally, dropping the curfew would benefit the city's students. Right now, by the time they finish their homework and want to see their friends, it's too late to do anything. Some people say, "Why can't teenagers hang out downtown after school?" The problem with that suggestion is that it's really hot here in Texas. In the daytime, when it's 100 degrees outside and super sunny, people just want to stay in. At night, it's cooler, and the sun isn't hurting your skin. Students should be allowed to enjoy a nighttime social life.

Persuasive essays often include a response to an anticipated objection.

The curfew law penalizes good kids and does nothing to benefit local businesses or to make our city safer. People should write to the mayor and urge her to lift the curfew on teens. It's the right thing to do.

Conclusion Includes a **summary** of the writer's ideas and a **call to action.**

Writers use many different techniques to try to convince readers to agree with their point of view. See pages 308–309 for some ideas.

How to Use Persuasive Appeals

Persuasive writing can appeal either to logic or to emotion.

Appeals to Logic

Include the following in your essay, and you will appeal to your readers' sense of logic.

Solid Reasons

Back up your point of view with at least two or three solid reasons. Present them in order—from strongest to weakest (as shown below) or from weakest to strongest.

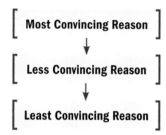

[**Most Convincing Reason**]
↓
[**Less Convincing Reason**]
↓
[**Least Convincing Reason**]

Facts and Statistics

Sometimes specific facts and statistics can be more convincing than words alone.

With Facts and Statistics

Somerville dropped its curfew two weeks ago, but no one has since been arrested for disorderly conduct. Bordentown lifted its teen curfew last year and has actually seen a 10% decrease in crime since then.

Examples

To make your reasons convincing, include supporting examples.

Unconvincing—No Examples

Local store owners depend on business from teenagers.

Convincing—With Example

Store owners depend on business from teenagers. Carol Matthews, owner of Carol's Cool Threads on George Street, says business is down since the curfew.

Backup from an Expert

Including an expert's opinion is a great way to support your point of view. You might do research to find out the experts' opinions or talk to people in your community.

With Backup from Experts

The Bureau of Crime Statistics found that curfews have little effect on violent crime rates. Police Chief Tom Garcia himself says he doesn't think the curfew has had much of an effect on local crime rates.

Appeals to Emotion

Emotional appeals can help get your readers to take action. Include the following and you can harness emotions to convince your readers.

Persuasive Language

Use language that shows you believe strongly in your position. Don't overdo it, though. Using harsh words and exclamation points is like shouting on paper. Try to sound reasonable but committed.

Boring—No Emotion

The new curfew isn't good for teenagers. Lots of local teens don't like it.

Effective Appeal to Emotions

The new curfew is unfair to teens. Sure, it might keep some troublemakers off the streets. But it also affects teenagers who aren't causing any problems.

Overly Emotional

The new curfew is a terrible idea! Why can't these stupid city officials mind their own business instead of punishing kids who haven't done anything wrong?

Personal Examples

You can appeal to readers' emotions by talking about the people who are affected by an issue. These examples don't take the place of facts and statistics, but they help get readers to care more about what you're saying.

With Use of Personal Examples

- Record store owner Carl Pulaski says he's worried about his falling sales figures. "I have to admit, it looks like this curfew is hurting my business," he said.

- High school junior Joelle Sullivan says the curfew doesn't make her feel safer. "I work at the ice cream shop until 8:00," she says, "and I don't like walking home by myself through empty streets."

- Amy Ling, a teacher at Jefferson High, says she thinks the curfew is unfair to students. "My kids work hard," she commented, "especially with SATs coming up. They should be allowed to hang out and goof off a little at night."

How to Write a Persuasive Essay

1 **Choose an Issue and a Position**

Some issues may directly affect you or your friends. Others may be global issues, such as pollution or climate change. Choose an issue you care about and know something about. Then decide what your position is—and what you want people to do about it.

> Mike is against the city's curfew for teens. He wants people to write to the mayor asking her to end the curfew. ▶

2 **Gather Evidence—Facts and Details**

Choose the best evidence to support your arguments. You might include evidence based on personal experience, facts and statistics, or what experts have to say. Use a chart to help you organize the evidence. (The chart will also help you see whether you have enough.)

Argument	Evidence
The curfew is hurting businesses.	Stores are closing earlier. Many now close before 8 P.M.
Curfews don't reduce crime.	According to Officer Williams of the San Antonio Police Department, vandalism and theft have increased by about 10% over the past year. Several neighboring towns with no teen curfew actually have lower crime rates than San Antonio.

❸ Organize Your Main Supporting Points

Plan how you will support your position. What reasons will you give to convince readers to agree with you? In a persuasive essay, reasons are often presented in order of importance. Use a graphic organizer to show the order.

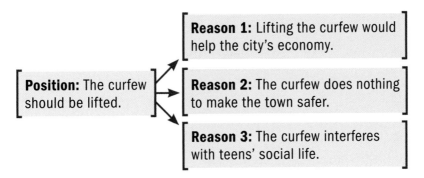

Position: The curfew should be lifted.

Reason 1: Lifting the curfew would help the city's economy.

Reason 2: The curfew does nothing to make the town safer.

Reason 3: The curfew interferes with teens' social life.

❹ Write an Introduction With a Thesis Statement

In your introduction, give your readers some background information about the issue. Then present your position in a **thesis statement**. Keep your thesis statement short and simple. Remember, you can explain more in the body of your essay.

Too Complicated

Because the curfew hurts our city's economy, doesn't reduce crime, and interferes with teens' ability to socialize, I think it causes more problems than it solves and should be ended immediately.

Short and Simple

In many ways, ending the curfew would improve life in San Antonio.

How to Write a Persuasive Essay, continued

⑤ Keep Going—Build Your Case

Use your list of reasons and evidence to write your essay.
Include appeals to logic as well as to emotions.

Build Your Case	Examples
Support your reasons with facts.	Three stores on Houston Street have gone out of business since the curfew began.
Develop your reasons with details.	Movie theaters and record stores rely on teenage customers to make a profit.
Use persuasive language.	Shouldn't our town do something to help struggling local businesses?
Get readers on your side.	My friends and I have never been in trouble with the law, but the curfew still applies to us. Is it fair to treat all teenagers like potential criminals?

⑥ Anticipate and Address Objections to Your Arguments

Answer readers' possible objections to your point of view.
Use a calm, reasonable tone to explain your position.

⑦ End with a Strong Conclusion and a Call to Action

In your final paragraph, summarize your position and major
supporting points. Present a call to action by telling your
audience what you want them to do. Be clear and specific.

> The curfew law penalizes good kids and does nothing to
> benefit local businesses or to make our city safer. People should
> write to the mayor and urge her to lift the curfew on teens. It's
> the right thing to do.

More Ways to Write as a Citizen

A persuasive essay isn't the only kind of writing you can do as a citizen. See the following models in "All You Can Write" for some other possibilities.

Share Your Point of View

> ### Advertisement (page 349)
> Write to convince people to buy a product or service.

> ### Newspaper Editorial (page 382)
> Write a newspaper editorial about an issue that readers care about.

Speak Your Mind

> ### Speech (pages 400–401)
> Write a speech about an issue that matters to you and your audience.

Write as a Critic

What's It Like?

At the Olympics, judges evaluate an athlete's performance based on what's expected in the sport and on what's been accomplished in the past. When you write as a critic, you also evaluate someone's performance—but you have to come up with a lot more than just a number!

A Reasoned Opinion

When you critique a poem in English class or contribute a movie review to your school paper, you're writing as a critic. Basically, you're telling others your judgment or opinion about someone else's creative work.

But a simple "I like it" or "I don't like it" doesn't really cut it. Good critical writing offers reasoned, supported opinions. You'll have to:

- give enough information about the piece you are critiquing—a summary of the plot or storyline, for example—to familiarize the reader with it

- offer reasons to explain and justify your opinions

- cite details from the work you are critiquing that support your reasoning and your overall judgment.

FOCUS POINT Read David Yoo's account of one of his first experiences in writing as a critic, on page 315. Have you had a similar experience? How do you balance writing as a critic with writing as a friend?

David Yoo on . . .
Writing as a Critic

When I was a senior in high school one of my best friends asked me to preview a short film he'd made. "Don't tell me your opinion right now," he suggested. "Let all the symbols sink in overnight, then write me a real review!"

I thought the film was terrible, and wrote him a scathing review, channeling my inner Ebert, pointing out everything about it that was awful, which was, well, everything. From writing my first-ever movie review I realized an important lesson, not about writing movie reviews, but about writing a review of something a *friend* has created: No matter how bad it is, you need to have at least as many sentences praising the work as you do slamming it, because people are usually really sensitive to negative comments. They're apt to feel that you're not just critiquing their work—you're critiquing *them*.

My aspiring filmmaker buddy and I are no longer friends, after I slammed his film. But, to quote from my original review of his film back in high school, "It really did stink!"

THE CRITIC'S CORNER

| Home | Search | Post a Review | Contact Us | Links |

What Teens Are Saying About

- ▶ Movies
- ▶ Television
- ▶ Books & Magazines
- ▶ Music
- ▶ Games & Technology
- ▶ The Web
- ▶ Fashion

Literary Critique

In a literary critique, the writer evaluates a work of literature, such as a poem, story, or essay, supporting his or her opinion with evidence and details from the text.

What is Carrie Chun's opinion of Amy Tan's autobiographical piece "Fish Cheeks"? How does Carrie support her opinion?

LITERARY CRITIQUE

Proud to be Different

Carrie Chun

Introduction
Introduces the **literary work** and briefly states Carrie's **opinion.**

    Although mothers sometimes embarrass their teenage children, they are often the wisest people in their children's lives. In her autobiographical essay "Fish Cheeks," Amy Tan describes a painful social experience from her adolescence and tells about what she learned from her mother's response. I highly recommend this powerful essay.

Body
Supports Carrie's **opinion** with details and quotations from the essay.

    Although she is a well-known adult author, Tan is able to remember what it was like to be a fourteen-year-old Chinese-American girl. She vividly describes the embarrassment she feels when her parents invite a white minister and his handsome son, Robert, to share in a holiday dinner of traditional Chinese food. When her mother serves the guests a whole fish, Robert, whom Amy has a crush on, makes a face. Tan writes:

> Then my father poked his chopsticks just below the fish eye and plucked out the soft meat. "Amy, your favorite," he said, offering me the tender fish cheek. I wanted to disappear.

These details help the reader understand how mortified the teenaged Amy Tan felt.

Tan perfectly portrays how hard it is to be caught between two cultures—Chinese and American. She tells how, at the end of the meal, her father "leaned back and belched loudly" to show his appreciation of the food. Although this detail adds some humor to the story, Tan admits that she didn't see the humor at the time. In fact, she says, she was "stunned into silence."

Tan ends the essay by describing what she learned from her experience. She tells how, after the guests leave, her mother gives her a miniskirt and tries to comfort her. "You want be same like American girls on the outside," her mother says. "But inside, you must always be Chinese. You must be proud you different." Tan says that as an adult, she realizes the wisdom of her mother's words. She also realizes that her mother had lovingly prepared all of Amy's favorite foods for the dinner.

Amy Tan's authentic and sensitive essay shows how hard it is to be a teenager and feel like you don't fit in with the people around you. It also gets across her mother's important message: being different is something to be proud of. For some, this message may be stated too obviously, verging on preachiness. For me, the essay had a powerful effect because I am half Chinese, and I have experienced some of the things Tan experienced. After reading "Fish Cheeks," I see the importance of being true to myself.

Conclusion
Sums up Carrie's balanced evaluation. Ends with a personal reaction.

How to Write a Literary Critique

1 **Choose a Literary Work That's Important to You**

Choose a work of literature that you know well and have strong opinions about. (If you're writing on a work that's been assigned in class, get to know it and form an opinion about it!)

2 **Read It (or Reread It) and Jot Down Your Opinions**

What is your overall opinion of the work?
Are some parts better than others? What's good about this work? What's not so good? Would you recommend this book to a friend? Why or why not?

Literature
Amy Tan's "Fish Cheeks"

Opinions and reactions
I can totally understand how Amy feels, especially since she has a crush on Robert. Parents don't always realize when they're embarrassing their kids.

What's good about it?
Authentic dialogue
Sensitive description of feelings
Nails feeling of being in two cultures at once

What could be better?
The lesson or "moral" of the story can seem too pat—almost preachy.

Would I recommend this to other people? Why or why not?
Yes, because many teenagers could relate to the events and feelings Amy Tan describes.

3 **Gather Support for Your Opinions**

Look at the text carefully. Note specific passages that support your first impressions.

> **Opinion**
> Amy Tan shows what it's like to be embarrassed by your family.
>
> **Supporting Examples**
> • young Amy's feelings when her family cooks traditional Chinese foods that seem strange to their American guests
> • her description of how she feels when her father belches

4 **Start Writing: Introduction**

In your introduction, name the title and author of the work. Hook your readers with a detail that makes them want to learn more. Briefly state your overall opinion of the work.

Strong Beginning

> In her autobiographical essay "Fish Cheeks," Amy Tan describes a painful social experience from her adolescence and tells about what she learned from her mother's response. I highly recommend this powerful essay.

5 **Keep Going—Pile on the Evidence**

Support your opinions with specific details and direct quotations from the text.

Weak—No Text Support

> Amy Tan's mother is wiser than her teenage daughter. She knows it's important to be true to your heritage. Amy shouldn't have felt ashamed of her family's traditions.

Strong—With Text Support

> Amy Tan's mother knows it's important to be true to your heritage. She wisely tells her daughter, "Inside, you must always be Chinese. You must be proud you different."

How to Write a Literary Critique, continued

⑥ Present a Balanced View

A good work is seldom perfect. And there are usually some bright points even in a disappointing piece. Try to present a balanced, objective view. Avoid both raving and snarling.

⑦ Restate Your Opinion in the Conclusion

Your parting words should remind the reader of your overall opinion. You can also add a personal reflection that answers one of these questions:

- What's one thought from this piece that's likely to stay with you? Why?

- How does this work relate to your own experience?

- What life lesson could other people learn by reading this work?

Strong Conclusion

> For me, the essay had a powerful effect because I am half Chinese, and I have experienced some of the things Tan experienced. After reading "Fish Cheeks," I see the importance of being true to myself.

More Ways to Write as a Critic

A literary critique isn't the only kind of critical writing you can do. See the following models in "All You Can Write" for some other possibilities.

Write to Share Your Opinion

Comparison-Contrast Essay (pages 360–361)

Compare two different creative works.

Literary Response (pages 376–377)

Write about your personal response to a work of literature.

Review (page 399)

Share your opinion with the public. Write about a recent book, movie, CD, concert, or art exhibit.

Write as an Employee

Joining a business is a lot like joining a sports team. First you send in your résumé and application, to let them know you're interested in trying out for the team. Once you're in, a lot of the job revolves around teamwork and good communication.

Getting the Job Done

Before you can get the job done, you need to get the job! So a big part of writing as an employee is writing as a potential employee. This role requires you to:

- present your skills and experience in a résumé that will appeal to employers

- use the job application to point out how your skills fit with the company's needs, and to specify your pay and schedule requirements

Once you're hired, you'll need to write as an employee to:

- communicate clearly with your boss, customers, or coworkers through e-mails and memos

- explain business procedures accurately and in detail, so that others can follow them

FOCUS POINT Read David Yoo's advice about résumés, on page 323. Does it ring true to you? What is your own experience with résumés and job applications?

David Yoo on . . .
Writing as an Employee

I rarely ask for help, and therefore I usually fail the first time I try something. When I try again, I have learned a lot from failing that first time, but still I fail again. Each time I fail, I gain a new insight into how to do what I'm not yet quite able to do. At some point—after I've failed enough times to learn all there is to learn about what I'm trying to do—I finally succeed!

This is what's known as learning through experience. Case in point: my résumé. The biggest lesson I've learned through my numerous résumé failures is that you need to highlight whatever it is the employer's looking for. You can't assume your résumé is golden, no matter how stunning your list of achievements. Valedictorians still get refused jobs, and it's often because they're overly confident that their résumé will "speak for itself." You have to make your résumé or job application speak for you and make you stand out from the pile of papers your potential employer has to go through.

That said, you also don't want to inflate your résumé too much. In particular, never claim expertise at computer programs that you barely know. It could make for a really embarrassing situation.

Résumé

A résumé is like a self-portrait that presents your education, work experience, and accomplishments. Its purpose is to persuade an employer that you're the right person for a job.

How well does Jada present herself in her résumé?

Contact Information
Tells how to get in touch with Jada.

Objective
Explains the job Jada wants.

Profile
Summarizes Jada's qualifications.

Experience
Uses **active verbs** to describe her experience.

Jada Wilkes
13316 Crescent Avenue, Chicago, Illinois 60601
(773) 555-6789
jada_w@orion.com

OBJECTIVE

A summer job with *Odessa Tours of Chicago*

PROFILE

An articulate, quick learner with four years experience in public speaking

EXPERIENCE AND RELATED ACTIVITIES

School Newspaper (2002–2006)
- Met deadlines consistently
- Designed pages for monthly 8-page newspaper
- Communicated with writers, editors, and teachers to design effective layouts

Debate Team (2002–2003)
- Member of the Forensic Society of America (2002–2003)
- Lincoln-Douglas debate team leader, Tournament of Champions (2005, 2006)

HONORS   **Academic**
- Awarded four-year scholarship to Northern Illinois University, De Kalb
- Awarded Midwest Regional High School Award for Academic Excellence (2005–2006)

Debate
- Won 1st Place in the Novice Lincoln-Douglas debate at Churchill HS 2005 tournament
- Won two 1st Place speaker awards in local tournaments (2003–2004)
- Given Degree of Distinction (2003)

SPECIAL SKILLS
- Familiar with word-processing and desktop publishing software
- Working knowledge of Spanish

EDUCATION
- Anticipated May 2006 graduation from Midwest Regional High School, Chicago, Illinois
- Ranked 61 out of 675 students
- Attending Northern Illinois University in the fall of 2006

REFERENCES   Available upon request

Honors
Describes accomplishments and awards with the most recent ones listed first.

Education
Describes Jada's educational background.

How to Write a Résumé

1 **Think About What the Employer is Looking For**

Some jobs don't require a résumé. If the job you want does, then it's important to tailor your résumé to what the employer is looking for. Jada was responding to this ad in the paper.

Help Wanted

Summer Interns needed for *Odessa Tours*. 20 hrs/wk. Duties include guiding indiviuals or groups of tourists on cruises through places of interest in the Chicago area. Excellent opportunity for those who enjoy communicating with others, and for recent grads interested in pursuing a career in tourism. Send résumé and writing samples to K. Becker.

2 **Take Inventory—Think About What You Have to Offer**

Take a personal inventory. List the skills and accomplishments that would make you a great employee. Don't misrepresent yourself, but be sure not to sell yourself short, either.

Personal Inventory: Jada Wilkes

Education
1. Graduate HS this year
2. Rank in class: 61 of 675
3. Accepted at Northern Illinois University

Work Experience
1. Design experience on school paper
2. R-X drugstore (quit after a week)
3. Volunteered at Center St. Community Center

School Activities
1. School newspaper
2. Debate team
3. Spanish club

Hobbies
1. Being outdoors
2. Guitar
3. Public speaking

Accomplishments/Honors
1. Debate trophies
2. 4-year scholarship to NIU
3. Academic Excellence award

Other
1. Pretty good in Spanish
2. Familiar with word-processing and desktop publishing software
3. Enjoy meeting new people

Personal Inventory

❸ Present Information Briefly and Clearly

Use your personal inventory to write your résumé. Be sure to include all the information the employer needs, in a way that's clear and easy to read. It's a good idea to start with these points:

- **contact information** that includes your name, address, phone number, and e-mail address

- an **objective** that describes your job goals

- a **profile** that summarizes your qualifications

Unclear and Incomplete

> **Jada Wilkes**
> Chicago, Illinois
> jada_w@orion.com
>
> **OBJECTIVE**
> A summer job
>
> **PROFILE**
> A good student and a quick learner

Clear and Complete

> **Jada Wilkes**
> 13316 Crescent Avenue
> Chicago, Illinois 60601
> (773) 555-6789
> jada_w@orion.com
>
> **OBJECTIVE**
> A summer job at *Odessa Tours of Chicago*
>
> **PROFILE**
> An articulate, quick learner with four years of experience in public speaking and journalism

❹ Keep Going—Organize Your Information

Organize your résumé into sections with headings. Emphasize the skills and accomplishments related to the job you want. You might:

- List your work experience first if it relates closely to the job you're seeking.

- List your educational background first if it is strong and you don't have much work experience.

Within each section, list information in reverse chronological order—that means you list the most recent items first.

How to Write a Résumé, continued

5 Be Specific and Use Strong Verbs

Use precise language to describe your past jobs and special honors. Use strong, active verbs to tell about your job duties, so the employer gets a clear sense of what makes you unique.

Vague

- On the debate team
- Won trophies

Specific

- Lincoln-Douglas debate team leader
- Placed nationally in Tournament of Champions

6 Make Your Résumé Look Serious and Professional

Use a computer to give your résumé a professional look. Don't be cute—use black type in a standard font. Ask a relative, teacher, or friend to look over the final draft for typos or misspellings.

7 Send Your Résumé or Post It Online

Before you send or post your résumé, find out the answers to these questions:

- To whom should you send your résumé? Make sure you have the correct name and address.

- Do you need to include a cover letter?

- Should you send your résumé by mail, attach it to an e-mail message, or upload it to a Web site?

- Have you included all the documents the employer has asked for, such as letters of recommendation?

MONDAY, JUNE 12

✓ Finish cover letter and ask Dad to proofread it
✓ Call Odessa Tours about where to send résumé
✓ Copy my History of Chicago essay to send with résumé

TUESDAY, JUNE 13

More Ways to Write as an Employee

A résumé isn't the only kind of writing you might do when you write as an employee. See the following models in "All You Can Write" for other forms.

Write to Find or Apply for a Job

Job Application (page 369)
Complete a job application with personal and work-related information online.

E-mail (page 357)
Write to introduce yourself to an employer and find out more about a job you might want.

Write on the Job

Memo (page 379)
Share information with your coworkers or supervisor.

Procedure (pages 396–397)
Tell someone how to complete a specific task or job.

Write as a Reporter

What's It Like ?

When people travel, they often send postcards to show and tell the folks back home what they've seen and learned. When you write as a reporter you do something very similar. You "take a trip", and report back to the folks "back home" about what you've learned and discovered.

Tell It Like It Is

When you write as a reporter, you research and share information about a topic. The topic could be anything of interest to your community. To get information, you might interview your new school principal, analyze the letters of a famous writer to better understand his or her life, or read other writers' reports of what is currently known about animal cloning, for example.

No matter what topic you decide on, the process will always consist of three basic steps:

1. **Gather** information through observation or by reading.

2. **Digest** the information, to weave it into a coherent presentation.

3. **Present** the information, in an interesting way while remaining true to the facts.

FOCUS POINT Read David Yoo's story of his early experience writing a report, on page 331. Which of the steps above did the young Yoo have trouble with? Which step do you have the most trouble with? Which is easiest?

David Yoo on . . .
Writing as a Reporter

The first time I had to write a research report for history class in ninth grade, I was surprised to find that inserting lots of quotes into the paper actually made writing the paper all the more *difficult*. I found that I was merely linking quotes together. When I tried to offer up my own thoughts, I had trouble finding a way to say things that wasn't just rephrasing what the quotes already said! What could I possibly add that was original?

Finally, it dawned on me—the reason I couldn't figure out what to say was that I hadn't allowed myself to form my own opinion. I had focused so much on doing the research and finding quotes to support my initial idea that I had stopped thinking on my own. So I waited for the *point* of the paper to come back to me. I let the research I'd done settle in my head. Eventually I realized what I wanted to say, and I produced a solid paper. (I still got a C+, though, because I turned it in two weeks late!)

News Article

Writing for a newspaper is one way to write as a reporter. When you write a news article, you spend time gathering and verifying information before you create the article. Anna Torres published this article in her high school newspaper.

Headline
Sums up the main idea.

Energy Drinks Spark Controversy at Brockwood High

by Anna Torres

Lead Paragraph
Answers the questions *who, what, where, when,* and *why.*

Inverted Pyramid Style
Each subsequent paragraph gives additional information from most to least important.

The Brockwood Township Parent-Teacher Association met in the Brockwood High School Conference Room last night to discuss a proposal to ban caffeinated "energy drinks" from school vending machines.

Concerned parents asked the school board to ban certain beverages, including Hi-Octane and Supernova, from campus vending machines. PTA President Carol Manzarek argued, "Some of these drinks contain twice as much caffeine as a cup of coffee. Students are getting hooked on a caffeine-and-sugar buzz. Our school should provide healthier choices."

Brockwood High Principal Dr. Patricia Johnson countered that contracts with national beverage vendors provide much-needed revenue for the school's theater and music departments. "Without the extra funds," says Johnson, "the budget for our arts programs would have to be cut dramatically. If that happens, students would lose out on valuable opportunities."

Marcus Richie, a theater arts teacher at Brockwood, added, "Parents don't realize that most extracurricular programs operate on a shoestring budget. We depend on that extra outside revenue." Other teachers, however, echoed Ms. Manzarek's concerns about the caffeine and sugar content of the beverages available.

The PTA will reconvene on January 19 to vote on the proposal.

Dr. Johnson leads the PTA meeting in the Conference Room last night.

Students discuss a controversial topic at school. ▶

Tone
The reporter's job is to present facts, so the tone of the article is objective.

Good reporters trap the exact words of the people they interview so they can include quotes from people affected by the event.

Brockwood junior Toshio Nakama sees nothing wrong with selling energy drinks at school, including his own preferred brand, Bolt Juice. He commented, "It is the students' responsibility to limit their consumption. Our arts programs should not lose funding due to a few students' bad choices."

Other students who attended last night's meeting say it made them reconsider whether energy drinks are potentially harmful. "I won't stop drinking Hi-Octane entirely, but I'm going to try to cut back," said senior Mina Shahlapour.

Thanks to their popularity among teens, energy drinks are now a 3.4 billion-dollar industry. Worldwide, dozens of new beverages marketed as energy drinks have been introduced over the past few years. A study by Schmittner Research found that 31% of teens surveyed consume energy drinks at least twice a week. Some teens drink them daily before and after school.

Like soft drinks, energy drinks are high in sugar and caffeine. However, energy drinks typically contain two to four times the caffeine found in soft drinks. The extra caffeine can cause nausea, heart palpitations, and insomnia. Even without these side effects, frequent caffeine consumption can be habit-forming.

Most energy drinks also contain vitamins, some of which trigger harmful side effects when consumed in excess. Some teens have experienced an increased heart rate or numbness of the extremities after consuming energy drinks. On rare occasions, these symptoms may require a trip to the emergency room.

While nutrition facts–such as calories and sugar content–are listed on most energy drinks, the caffeine content is sometimes missing from these labels. Even though students can determine the amount of calories and sugar they are consuming, they may be missing important information to help them control their caffeine intake.

How to Write a News Article

1 Choose a Newsworthy Topic and Get the Facts

A reporter gathers and reports the facts. The best kind of fact gathering happens when you're at the scene and can see, hear, and experience the events yourself. Essential to a news article are the 5 Ws: *Who, What, Where, When,* and *Why.*

PTA Meeting—the 5 W's	
WHAT happened?	meeting to discuss proposal to ban energy drinks from school vending machines
WHO was involved?	Brockwood High School Parent-Teacher Association plus a few students
WHEN did it happen?	last night
WHERE did it happen?	Brockwood High Conference Room
WHY did it happen?	Parents, students, teachers, and administrators disagree about whether energy drinks should be sold in our school.

2 Gather Background Information

Reporters don't just give their readers the bare facts. They also put those facts in context. To get that context, you may have to do some additional research. For example, you might interview an expert, verify facts on the Web, or look at what other school districts have done about high-energy drinks.

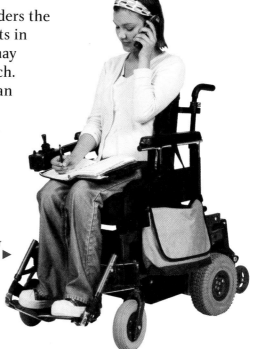

Anna Torres conducts a phone interview to verify facts for her news article. ▶

③ Organize Information

Plan to state the most important information in the headline and lead paragraph. Your readers should be able to get the gist of the story by reading just the headline and first paragraph. You can use the rest of the article to provide additional background. Here's how Anna Torres organized her news article.

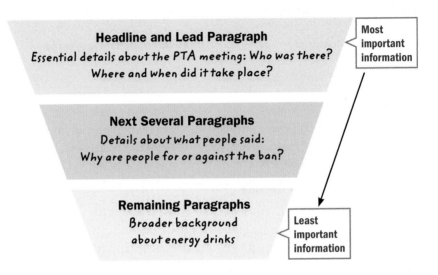

Headline and Lead Paragraph
Essential details about the PTA meeting: Who was there? Where and when did it take place?

> Most important information

Next Several Paragraphs
Details about what people said: Why are people for or against the ban?

Remaining Paragraphs
Broader background about energy drinks

> Least important information

④ Start Writing: Headline and Lead Paragraph

Craft a headline that gets the reader's attention and sums up what happened. Then write a lead that provides the essential facts about the event.

Vague Headline and Lead

Should Teens Have a Choice?

In a recent heated debate, parents and school administrators argued over whether energy drinks should continue to be available at our high school.

Precise Headline and Lead

Energy Drinks Spark Controversy at Brockwood High

The Brockwood Township Parent-Teacher Association met in the Brockwood High School Conference Room last night to discuss a proposal to ban caffeinated "energy drinks" from school vending machines.

How to Write a News Article, continued

5 **Keep Going—Focus on the Facts**

In your article, present specific details that show why the story matters. You might include background information from your research or quotes from people involved in the events. Maintain an objective tone throughout. Focus on the facts, and let readers form their own opinions.

Weak: Subjective, Opinionated

> Although both energy drinks and soft drinks are pumped full of sugar and caffeine, some energy drinks contain more caffeine than anyone should consume in one sitting.

Strong: Objective, Fact-based

> Like soft drinks, energy drinks are high in sugar and caffeine. However, energy drinks typically contain two to four times the caffeine found in soft drinks.

6 **Wrap Up with Additional Details**

The closing paragraphs of your article should present information that's relevant to the story, but not essential. (Your editor may cut it, or your reader may not finish reading the article!)

Closing Paragraph

> While nutrition facts–such as calories and sugar content–are listed on most energy drinks, the caffeine content is sometimes missing from these labels. Even though students can determine the amount of calories and sugar they are consuming, they are missing important information to help them control their caffeine intake.

More Ways to Write as a Reporter

There are many ways you can write as a reporter. Look in "All You Can Write" for examples of the following forms.

Write to Inform

Analysis of an Issue (pages 350–351)

Explore a fascinating or controversial issue.

Biography (page 353)

Tell the story of someone else's life.

Cause-and-Effect Essay (pages 358–359)

Explain why something happened.

Interview (page 368)

Learn by asking questions of someone else and then write up the questions and answers.

Observation Report (page 384)

Report on an experiment you conducted.

Write as a Poet

What's It Like ?

Glasses don't just help people see well or protect their eyes from the sun. Like clothing, glasses can also be used as a means of self expression, as an element of style. Language can work that way, too. When you use language intentionally to go beyond just clear communication to embody feelings and emotions, you're using language as a poet.

Language That Lets You Know It's There

Scientists and mathematicians like to make language disappear. They are happiest when they can get down to a formula:

$$E = mc^2 \qquad C = 2\pi r$$

For poets, on the other hand, language is the whole point of the exercise. Poets bring language front and center, to trigger memories, evoke emotions, and express the whole messy complexity that comes with being human. As a poet, you might:

- work to condense a lot of complex meaning into a few simple-seeming words

- use figurative language—words that don't mean exactly what they say—for emotional effect

- choose words for their sound value—to create a powerful rhythm or a memorable rhyme

- set words to music

FOCUS POINT Read David Yoo's thoughts on *feeling* poetry versus understanding it, on page 339. Do you agree with his thinking? What is your favorite kind of poetry? Do you think you need to understand what a poem is saying in order to appreciate it?

David Yoo on . . .
Writing as a Poet

I usually can't explain what it is about a poem that I like. All I know is that it somehow moves me. Some turn of phrase or rhythm in a line can literally give me shivers. Poems remain a mystery to me to this day.

In the one poetry class I took in college, I'd turn in poems every week. One week I tried to write a poem that rhymed. Another week I tried to mimic Bukowski. They'd always get panned by my classmates. Finally, one night, I just rearranged my roommate's poetry magnets on the refrigerator door until they looked interesting to me, and wrote down the resulting "poem." My classmates loved it, said I was finally getting it.

You'd think the point I'm trying to make with this anecdote is to disprove poetry, to suggest that there's no rhyme or reason to what makes it work or not. Rather, this anecdote illustrates the one thing I do understand about writing and reading poetry, and it's the one thing I suppose you really need to know. It's not about understanding it.
It's about *feeling* it.

what can you say
about a summer day
with a sweet wind
you will soar away

blue friend dream

Poem in Free Verse

When you write free verse, you make up the rules. You don't have to use any special rhyme scheme or rhythm. For a poem written in free verse, you can:

- explore a single image or emotion
- break up the lines to look a certain way on the page
- use repetition for rhythm or effect
- bend or break the rules of grammar and punctuation.

Which of these techniques does Alison use in the free-verse poem below?

Title and Opening
Introduces the **topic**: Adam's music.

For Adam
by Alison Wing

Your music
Speaks your mind
Your soul
Your spirit

When you play, you take the rhythm of
   your heart
And translate it into melody—

Body
Explores the topic without using traditional stanzas, rhyme, or a regular rhythm.

I listen and lose myself
In the language of your world
(Foreign but familiar)

It makes me think,
Expands the horizons of my mind
And of my heart

No one tells you how to play
    your song
You express yourself
With improv rhythm
And swaying chords resounding

No lies as you harmonize
Energize
Words rising to new truths
With every note

When you play, your melodies
Start beating in my heart
A rhythm shared

Your music
Speaks your mind
Your soul
Your spirit

How to Write a Poem in Free Verse

1 **Choose a Topic and Narrow It Down**

Choose a topic you feel deeply about, such as someone or something you admire, feel angry toward, or want to protect. Narrow it down to make it specific. On pages 340–341, Alison didn't write about all of Adam's talents—just the quality of his songs.

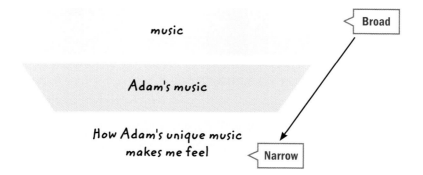

music   **Broad**

Adam's music

How Adam's unique music makes me feel   **Narrow**

2 **Jot Down Ideas and Impressions**

Without stopping, write everything you can think of that describes your topic. What details stand out in your mind? What emotions do they stir? Don't worry about complete sentences—just get your thoughts down on the page.

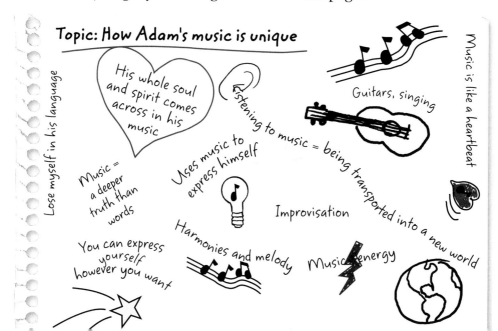

Topic: How Adam's music is unique

His whole soul and spirit comes across in his music

Lose myself in his language

Guitars, singing

Music is like a heartbeat

Music = a deeper truth than words

Uses music to express himself

Listening to music = being transported into a new world

Improvisation

You can express yourself however you want

Harmonies and melody

Music energy

3 Play with Words as You Draft

Then start putting words together, paying attention to how they sound. Try a lot of versions until you land on ones you like.

Your soul, your mind, your spirit

Your mind, your soul, your spirit

Your music speaks your mind
It shows your soul
It lifts your spirit

Your music speaks your mind
Your soul, your spirit

Play with line breaks. They often cue the rhythm of the poem.

Your music
Speaks your mind
Your soul
Your spirit

In free verse, the lines of your poem do not all rhyme, but you can use rhyme within the lines for an appealing sound.

No lies as you ~~sing~~ harmonize

With energy in every word

343

How to Write a Poem in Free Verse, continued

4 **Read Your Draft Aloud Before Revising It**

Poetry is meant to be read aloud. So put a listener on it and think about these questions as you get feedback from other people:

- Does my poem get and keep listeners' attention?

- Does it have a good rhythm and appealing sounds?

- Does my main idea come across?

- Do I need to add details or use more vivid words to liven up my poem?

- Does the poem produce the emotional effect I want?

In this revision, Alison improves the rhythm, the sounds, and the word choice.

Draft

No lies as you harmonize
Energize,
Words rising to new truths
With every note.

Revised

No Lies as you harmonize
With energy in every word
With every note
You speak a new truth.

5 **Enjoy the Process**

The painter Paul Gardner famously said:

> "A painting is never finished—it just
> stops in interesting places."

The same is true of a free-verse poem. Only you can tell when the poem expresses just what you want it to express, so keep tweaking the language and the structure until you're satisfied that the emotion is just right.

More Ways to Write as a Poet

Free verse isn't the only kind of poetry you can write. See the following models in "All You Can Write" for other forms to try.

Write to Express Yourself

Song Lyrics (pages 394–395)

Write a song to honor a friend or family member.

Rhymed Verse (page 390)

Use rhyme to make your poem memorable.

Blank Verse (page 391)

Follow the rhythm that Shakespeare used.

Haiku (page 393)

Focus on a single moment or image.

All You Can Write

Writing Forms A–Z

Advertisements

Analysis of
an Issue

Autobiography

Biography

Blog

Character Sketch

Description

E-mail

Essays

Interview

Job Application

Letters

Literary Critique

Literary Response

Magazine

Memo

Memoir

Newspaper

Observation Report

Parody

Play

Poetry

Procedure

Résumé

Review

Speech

Stories

Summary

Web site

Advertisements

Print Ad

Advertisements are a powerful form of persuasion. They can be used to "sell" almost anything—food, clothes, vacation spots, even political candidates. Print ads appeal to readers by combining text with eye-catching visual images.

"Whistle" was a soft drink popular in the 1920s. ▼

Attracts readers' attention with images

Uses descriptive words to appeal to consumers

The Best on the Beach!

At the end of a perfect swim—"Whistle". It's great! And refreshing! And dee-licious! Something to be glad about? You said it! It's bottled sunshine.

Just drift to some nearby place where you can pucker up your lips and

WHISTLE

TV Ad Script

Advertisements on television get viewers' attention and present a brief, persuasive message, often with catchy phrases and vivid images. Some ads try to sell a product. Others, like the public-service announcement below, try to persuade viewers to take action on a community concern.

Crushed aluminum cans ready for recycling ▶

"Recycling" PSA

Scene: A living room with doorway to the kitchen visible in background. JAMAL is taking a nap on the couch in the living room.

KEVIN begins wrestling a heavy garbage bag from the trash can in the kitchen. JAMAL wakes up.

JAMAL *(annoyed)*: Why does taking out the trash have to make so much noise?

KEVIN: It's all these soda cans.

JAMAL: What are those doing in the garbage?

KEVIN: Making noise, I guess.

KEVIN puts the heavy bag down. It drops loudly.

JAMAL: No, I mean, why are they in the trash when they aren't garbage? Those cans could be melted down and reused. Recycling metal cans saves energy and resources.

Cut to a recycling bin full of cans.

VOICE-OVER: If it clinks, it's not garbage. Recycle.

Cut to CCFEA logo and URL.

VOICE-OVER: For more information about recycling in your neighborhood, visit www.ccfea.org. Paid for by Concerned Citizens for Environmental Activism.

Stage directions tell what happens on-screen.

Dialogue defines what the actors will say.

A clear persuasive message often uses brief, memorable language.

Analysis of an Issue

An issue analysis may appear in a book, a news article, or an essay. In an issue analysis, you examine a topic about which there is some disagreement. You may take a position, but you should give information about both sides of the issue.

As Obesity Rates Rise, Schools Reconsider Vending-Machine Contracts

by Camille Ricketts

Nov. 2—WASHINGTON—

Juvenile obesity may begin at home, but thousands of U.S. schools have signed contracts that feed the growing problem.

Over half of all high schools and junior high schools nationwide have struck deals with soft-drink companies or vendors, giving them exclusive marketing rights to their students, according to the Institute of Medicine, a health policy adviser to Congress. In exchange, the schools often get five- or six-figure payments that cover benefits their budgets don't, such as SAT test fees for low-income students, new scoreboards, uniforms and even proms.

The problem is that the marketing deals often promote consumption of foods that are a nutritionist's night-mare. Pennsylvania school food-service directors, for example, reported in June that their cafeterias' best sellers were, in rank order: pizza, hamburgers and sandwiches; cookies, crackers, cakes and pastries; french fries; potato chips and cheese puffs; and sodas and sugary sports drinks.

The cafeteria at George Washington Middle School, in Silver Spring, Md., has been trying to serve healthier entrees.

Since, according to the institute's study, 40 percent of kids' daily food intake occurs while they're at school, schools are implicated in a worrisome trend: Childhood obesity has doubled among teens and tripled for kids ages 6 to 11 since the 1970s. That's according to the Institute of Medicine's study, "Preventing Childhood Obesity," which was released Sept. 30.

That's no surprise to Diana Frey, a junior at Montgomery-Blair High School in Silver Spring, Md. "A lot of kids don't even have time for breakfast, then they eat a crappy lunch here," she said. "That's a good eight hours without eating anything healthy at all."

School meals served as part of the National Lunch and Breakfast programs aren't the problem. Schools must provide specified amounts of vitamins and nutrients to be reimbursed by the Department of Agriculture under these programs.

Rather, it's food sold in vending machines and lunchtime a la carte lines that often has no nutritional standard and is intended to be popular—and profitable.

At Montgomery-Blair, a school that's trying—largely in vain— to shift student tastes toward healthful fare, nutritional value isn't what sells food, according to students.

"It's really just what's available and what tastes good," said Elena Pinsky, a junior. "We get inundated with information about healthy eating, the food pyramid and whatever, but in the end you can choose whether or not to listen and most people don't."

Senior Nick Falgout agreed. "Kids just don't see how what they eat now will affect them in the immediate short term, so they don't really pay attention," he said. A case in point, Falgout noted, was his own lunch of a sugary popcorn snack.

Includes **data** to support opinions

Often quotes people affected by the issue

Autobiography

An autobiography is the story of someone's own life. When you write an autobiography, you tell about the experiences that made you who you are today.

At age 7, Firoozeh Dumas moved to the U.S. from Iran. ▶

20   FUNNY IN FARSI | Firoozeh Dumas

Often includes background about family history and childhood experiences.

Moving to America was both exciting and frightening, but we found great comfort in knowing that my father spoke English. Having spent years regaling us with stories about his graduate years in America, he had left us with the distinct impression that America was his second home. My mother and I planned to stick close to him, letting him guide us through the exotic American landscape that he knew so well. We counted on him not only to translate the language but also to translate the culture, to be a link to this most foreign of lands.

Uses first-person pronouns.

Once we reached America, we wondered whether perhaps my father had confused his life in America with someone else's. Judging from the bewildered looks of store cashiers, gas station attendants, and waiters, my father spoke a version of English not yet shared with the rest of America. His attempts to find a "vater closet" in a department store would usually lead us to the drinking fountain or the home furnishings section. Asking my father to ask the waitress the definition of

Tells about specific memorable events.

"sloppy Joe" or "Tater Tots" was no problem. His translations, however, were highly suspect. Waitresses would spend several minutes responding to my father's questions, and these responses, in turn, would be translated as "She doesn't know." Thanks to my father's translations, we stayed away from hot dogs, catfish, and hush puppies, and no amount of caviar in the sea would have convinced us to try mud pie.

Character Sketch

A character sketch may appear in fiction or nonfiction writing. It's like a quick word portrait of another person. A character sketch may portray a real person or a fictional character.

THIS BOY'S LIFE | Tobias Wolff 15

Dwight was a short man with curly brown hair and sad, restless brown eyes. He smelled of gasoline. His legs were small for his thick-chested body, but what they lacked in length they made up for in spring; he had an abrupt, surprising way of springing to his feet. He dressed like no one I'd ever met before—two-tone shoes, hand-painted tie, monogrammed blazer with a monogrammed handkerchief in the breast pocket. Dwight kept coming back, which made him chief among the suitors. My mother said he was a good dancer—he could really make those shoes of his get up and go. Also he was very nice, very considerate.

I didn't worry about him. He was too short. He was a mechanic. His clothes were wrong. I didn't know why they were wrong, but they were. We hadn't come all the way out here to end up with him. He didn't even live in Seattle; he lived in a place called Chinook, a tiny village three hours north of Seattle, up in the Cascade Mountains. Besides, he'd already been married. He had three kids of his own living with him, all teenagers. I knew my mother would never let herself get tangled up in a mess like that.

Includes **descriptive details** about appearance, actions, and personality.

The writer tells his opinion of the character.

Description

A description uses specific details to help readers picture whatever is being described. Use words that appeal to the reader's senses.

42   THE WATSONS GO TO BIRMINGHAM—1963 | C. P. Curtis

Includes vivid sensory details.

It was one of those super-duper cold Saturdays. One of those days that when you breathed out your breath kind of hung frozen in the air like a hunk of smoke and you could walk along and look exactly like a train blowing out big, fat, white puffs of smoke.

It was so cold that if you were stupid enough to go outside your eyes would automatically blink a thousand times all by themselves, probably so the juice inside of them wouldn't freeze up. It was so cold that if you spit, the slob would be an ice cube before it hit the ground. It was about a zillion degrees below zero.

Word pictures create a memorable image of this very cold day.

It was even cold inside our house. We put sweaters and hats and scarves and three pairs of socks on and still were cold. The thermostat was turned all the way up and the furnace was banging and sounding like it was about to blow up but it still felt like Jack Frost had moved in with us.

E-mail

People write e-mail messages for many different reasons—to chat with friends and family, communicate with coworkers, sometimes even to apply for a job. Therefore, they can be as informal as a note left on the fridge or as formal as a business letter—make sure you get the tone right!

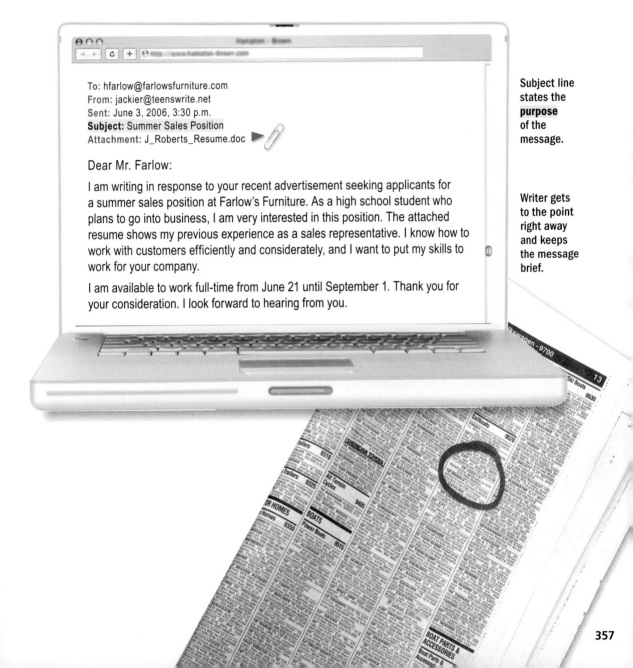

To: hfarlow@farlowsfurniture.com
From: jackier@teenswrite.net
Sent: June 3, 2006, 3:30 p.m.
Subject: Summer Sales Position
Attachment: J_Roberts_Resume.doc

Dear Mr. Farlow:

I am writing in response to your recent advertisement seeking applicants for a summer sales position at Farlow's Furniture. As a high school student who plans to go into business, I am very interested in this position. The attached resume shows my previous experience as a sales representative. I know how to work with customers efficiently and considerately, and I want to put my skills to work for your company.

I am available to work full-time from June 21 until September 1. Thank you for your consideration. I look forward to hearing from you.

Subject line states the **purpose** of the message.

Writer gets to the point right away and keeps the message brief.

Essays

Cause-and-Effect

A cause-and-effect essay tells why something happened. When you write a cause-and-effect essay, you may focus mainly on causes or mainly on effects, or you may discuss both.

The introduction in column 1 introduces the **topic**.

The first section of the body explains the causes of the "freshman 15."

BEATING THE FRESHMAN 15

Everyone's heard warnings about the "freshman 15," but is it true that many college students pack on 15 pounds during their first year at school? Recent studies find that some first-year students are indeed likely to gain weight. Researchers at Cornell University found that students gained an average of 4 pounds during the first 12 weeks of their freshman year—a rate of gain that is 11 times higher than the typical weight gain for 17- and 18-year-olds.

Not everyone's destined to gain the full frosh 15, though: A multi-year study by researchers at Tufts University found that, on average, men gain 6 pounds and women gain 4.5 during their first year of college.

WHAT'S BEHIND FIRST-YEAR WEIGHT GAIN?

College offers many temptations. You're on your own and free to eat what you want, when you want it. You can pile on the portions in the dining hall, eat meals of french fries and ice cream, and indulge in sugary and salty snacks to fuel late-night study sessions. In addition, you may not get as much exercise as you did in high school.

College is also a time of change, and the stress of acclimating to school can trigger overeating.

College students often eat on the run.

SHOULD I WORRY ABOUT THE WEIGHT?

Some weight gain is normal as an adolescent body grows and metabolism shifts, but pronounced or rapid weight gain may become a problem.

Weight gain that pushes you above your body's normal range carries health risks. People who are overweight are more likely to have high blood pressure, high cholesterol, breathlessness, and joint problems. People who are overweight when they're younger have a greater likelihood of being overweight as adults. Poor diet and exercise habits in college can start you on a path that could later lead to heart disease, Type 2 diabetes, or obesity, and may increase your risk for developing certain cancers.

Unhealthy food choices also won't give you the balance of nutrients you need to keep up with the demands of college. You may notice that your energy lags and your concentration and memory suffer. The Tufts study found that most students earn failing marks when it comes to good nutrition: Almost 70% of students get fewer than the recommended five servings of fruits and vegetables each day.

If you do gain weight, don't freak out. Take a look at your eating and exercise habits and make adjustments. Cutting out one can of soda or a midnight snack and being more active will help you get back on track.

The second section describes the effects of diet and weight gain.

The conclusion leaves the reader with something to think about.

Essays, continued

Comparison-Contrast

A comparison-contrast essay describes how two things are alike and different. You may choose to describe one item completely before you move on to the next. Or, you might organize your essay according to the specific points you're comparing.

FOOD AND FUN

MANGIA!

Italian Cuisine on Both Sides of Town
by Rick Bevilacqua

With the senior and junior proms coming up soon, it's time to think about where to take your date for dinner. I decided to check out the two most popular Italian restaurants in town: **Paolo's** on Main Street and **Café Salato** on Poplar Avenue. The verdict: Paolo's is an affordable choice for traditionalists. Café Salato is modern and flashy, but the prices will quickly empty your wallet.

ATMOSPHERE
Recently renovated, Café Salato has an elegant, modern décor. Dim lighting and soft music create a romantic atmosphere that's perfect for a big date. A word to the guys: If you're planning to dine here, dress to impress. Jackets and ties are required.

In contrast to Café Salato, Paolo's décor is more traditional, with checkered tablecloths and rustic Old World oil paintings on the walls. The somewhat noisy kitchen and tables placed close together contribute to the lively, casual atmosphere.

FOOD
Paolo's serves traditional Italian fare. My appetizer of fried eggplant with homemade basil marinara was delicious. The breading was spicy and the eggplant fresh. Unfortunately, my entrée didn't quite live up to its promise. I ordered Spaghetti alla Bolognese (in other words,

Paolo's on Main Street

Cheese raviolis at Cafe Salato

spaghetti with meat sauce) and the sauce was definitely on the salty side. Dessert, however, was excellent. My date and I had coffee gelato, which is similar to ice cream but a little bit sweeter.

While the food at Paolo's was hit-or-miss, the food at Café Salato was consistently very good. I ordered minestrone, a Caesar salad, and baked ravioli, and every bite was perfectly seasoned and delicious. Dessert, a chocolate cake with raspberry sauce, was out of this world.

SERVICE AND PRICE

I suppose Café Salato must have overspent on their renovations, because their prices were through the roof. If you are looking at Café Salato for prom, don't blow all of your money on the tux or dress—you will need extra cash for dinner! However, with the large price tag comes excellent service. Our waitress was friendly and attentive. She went out of her way to make us comfortable.

Paolo's is a bit easier on the wallet. While Café Salato is the kind of place I could afford to visit only on a very special occasion, Paolo's prices are far more reasonable. However, the service needs improvement. Our waiter was nice, but disorganized. He brought out the wrong appetizer at first, and he took forever to bring us our check.

WHERE SHOULD YOU GO ON PROM NIGHT?

If you want to impress your date and get a taste of the modern, Café Salato is for you. Just make sure you save up for it, because eating at Café Salato is a splurge. If you prefer to save money and enjoy decent, traditional Italian food, head to Paolo's.

These **transition words** show a contrast.

The conclusion sums up the major differences to help the reader make a decision.

Essays, continued

Opinion

An opinion essay tells what you think about something and why. You need to state your point of view clearly and precisely, and back up your opinions with examples and facts.

The title summarizes the writer's opinion.

The first sentence grabs the readers' attention.

The rest of the introduction presents the problem concisely.

Opinion is supported with specific examples.

Prom Costs Too High

By Cesar C., teenink.com

It's that time of the year: prom. As students flock to stores to prepare for what is supposedly the "most important" dance of their high school years, what ensues is pandemonium. Students, male and female, think nothing of spending hundreds of dollars on whatever luxury they feel is necessary to enjoy their prom night. Every year this night gets more expensive; some spend so much that it is laughable. Isn't there a limit to how much money people will waste on this "special night"? It seems that its true meaning has been forgotten.

As prom approaches, half the school's population goes wild. For the typical female, the prom dress is the most important item to spend money on, with an average cost of $200. For some teens, this may not seem like a big price tag, but consider what else the money could be used for.

The expenses don't stop there—the perfect dress must have perfect accessories, among them long gloves and tiny purses that will hold nothing. These costly items will rarely (if ever) be worn again.

Prom night also costs a lot for many male students. While guys don't need to stress out about the perfect dress, they worry about other expenses, including taking their date for a nice dinner. Most plan on showing up in a luxury car, which isn't cheap. Since there is rarely an alternative, the expensive limo is the favorite.

Prom night used to mean something. It was one of the highlights of high school, since it involved friends dancing and genuinely having fun. Today, prom is neither of these. It has become a competition, where everyone compares dresses and cars with others. Most teenagers don't even stay for the whole evening, leaving early in search of parties. So why spend so much money on preparing for the prom?

As the pandemonium of prom befalls us once again, most teens plan to spend tons of hard-earned cash. Can't we try to focus on having a good time instead of spending money to impress each other? The high cost of prom night has truly taken the enjoyment out of an otherwise fun dance.

Concludes by restating opinion.

Essays, continued

Persuasive

A persuasive essay aims to change the way people think and to inspire them to take action. When you write to persuade, be specific about what you believe and why. Back up your opinions with examples and facts.

Building a Better Future

Natasha Bellari

The introduction gets readers' attention and presents **a position statement**.

No one likes being stuck in a crowded space. Just think of how stressed-out people get when they're sitting in a traffic jam. Unfortunately, trying to learn in an overcrowded classroom can feel a little like sitting in a traffic jam for seven hours a day. At Fairville's Kennedy High School, overcrowding reduces the quality of the education students receive. Some administrators have proposed solving the problem by implementing a "split-session," or staggered, schedule, while others try to minimize the educational effects of overcrowding. The best solution to the problem, however, is the one proposed in County Referendum 29: build an additional high school within the next three years.

The argument includes examples and **facts**.

A quick walk through Kennedy High, with its 2500 students, shows that one high school is not enough to serve Fairville's needs. Class sizes have increased dramatically over the past few years, and the student population is increasing each year. It's not uncommon for classes to have 35 or more students, and due to the lack of space, many classes are now held in makeshift trailers outside of the school building.

Each paragraph in the body gives an argument that supports the position.

This environment negatively affects student learning. Individual students easily get lost in the shuffle when class sizes average 30 or more. The lack of one-on-one attention is especially frustrating for students who are struggling in a subject or have special needs. Classroom discipline also suffers when teachers must manage huge classes. Finally, holding classes in trailers at the edge of the school property makes it all too easy for students to cut class. No wonder some overcrowded county high schools face dropout rates as high as 30%.

How can Kennedy High School's overcrowding problem be solved? Surprisingly, some high-level administrators don't recognize it as a problem at all. Assistant Principal Joanne Arbus comments, "Creative teachers know how to work successfully with large classes." Teachers disagree. "There's no substitute for individualized attention," notes math teacher Mark Gonzalez, "and that's just not possible in a classroom of 35 students."

Other administrators and school-board members have proposed implementing split sessions, with half of the students attending classes from 7 a.m. to 12 p.m. and the remainder attending classes from 12:30 to 5:30. On the surface, this might seem like a viable solution. However, this schedule creates further problems. Research has shown that teenagers are most alert and productive after 9 a.m., and it's all too likely that most students will doze through any early-morning classes. (Two county high schools that experimented with split sessions last year reported a decline in students' grades.) Split sessions are also a problem for students attending afternoon classes, since the 5:30 p.m. dismissal time interferes with after-school activities, such as jobs and sports.

Clearly, the best solution to this problem is to build a new high school to accommodate the increased student population. Although this would result in a slight increase in property taxes, the benefit to our students cannot be ignored. Two high schools could easily accommodate up to 4,000 students. Class size would be reduced significantly, which would allow students to receive the individual attention they all deserve. I urge members of the Fairville community to support our students and teachers by voting in favor of County Referendum 29 on November 4.

The first two paragraphs on this page address objections to the position and explain why they are not valid.

The essay ends with a **call to action**.

Essays, continued

Reflective

A reflective essay presents the writer's thoughts and feelings about a particular subject. Often it focuses on a powerful personal experience. In a reflective essay, you may use a less formal structure and tone than you would for other types of essays.

36 ～ *Fish Cheeks*

The writer sets the scene and gives background.

I fell in love with the minister's son the winter I turned fourteen. He was not Chinese, but as white as Mary in the manger. For Christmas I prayed for this blond-haired boy, Robert, and a slim new American nose.

The writer shares her feelings.

When I found out my parents had invited the minister's family over for Christmas Eve dinner, I cried. What would Robert think of our shabby Chinese Christmas? What would he think of our noisy Chinese relatives who lacked proper American manners? What terrible disappointment would he feel upon seeing not a roasted turkey and sweet potatoes but Chinese food?

Vivid sensory details help you picture the event.

On Christmas Eve, I saw that my mother had outdone herself in creating a strange menu. She was pulling black veins out of the backs of fleshy prawns. The kitchen was littered with appalling mounds of raw food: A slimy rock cod with bulging fish eyes that pleaded not to be thrown into a pan of hot oil. Tofu, which looked like stacked wedges of rubbery white sponges. A bowl soaking dried fungus back to life. A plate of squid, crisscrossed with knife markings so they resembled bicycle tires.

And then they arrived—the minister's family and all my relatives in a clamor of doorbells and rumpled Christmas packages. Robert grunted hello, and I pretended he was not worthy of existence.

Dinner threw me deeper into despair. My relatives licked the ends of their chopsticks and reached across the table, dipping into the dozen or so plates of food. Robert and his family waited patiently for platters to be passed to them. My relatives murmured with pleasure when my mother brought out the whole steamed fish. Robert grimaced. Then my father poked his chopsticks just below the fish eye and plucked out the soft meat. "Amy, your favorite," he said, offering me the tender fish cheek. I wanted to disappear.

At the end of the meal my father leaned back and belched loudly, thanking my mother for her fine cooking. "It's a polite Chinese custom, to show you are satisfied," he explained to our astonished guests. Robert was looking down at his plate with a reddened face. The minister managed to muster a quiet burp. I was stunned into silence for the rest of the night.

After all the guests had gone, my mother said to me, "You want be same like American girls on the outside." She handed me an early gift. It was a miniskirt in beige tweed. "But inside, you must always be Chinese. You must be proud you different. You only shame is be ashame."

And even though I didn't agree with her then, I knew that she understood how much I had suffered during the evening's dinner. It wasn't until many years later—long after I had gotten over my crush on Robert—that I was able to appreciate fully her lesson and the true purpose behind our particular menu. For Christmas Eve that year, she had chosen all my favorite foods.

First-person pronouns contribute to the authenticity.

Dialogue makes the experience seem more immediate.

The conclusion tells what the writer learned.

Interview

An interview presents a conversation in question-and-answer format. When you write an interview, prepare your questions beforehand and record carefully the answers of the person you are interviewing.

Molding Troubled Kids into Future Chefs

An Interview with Neil Kleinberg
by Kathy Blake

Neil Kleinberg is the culinary-arts training manager at a tiny, 12-seat, takeout cafe operated by Covenant House, a shelter for runaway teen-agers in New York City. Kleinberg says his job at Ezekiel's Cafe involves being father, mother, brother, counselor, teacher, and adviser, as well as a tough boss to the 17- to 21-year-old trainees who work with him.

Starts with background information about the person interviewed.

How do you work as executive chef and culinary-arts trainer?

A place this small doesn't need an executive chef. My real job is teaching. Ezekiel's Cafe exists to give kids who live at Covenant House hands-on training in food service so they can get good jobs. Of course, when you say Covenant House, you know that these are kids with troubled pasts who need a lot of training in life skills, not just job skills. We screen the kids to try to get the ones who really have the desire to work in the industry, because to work this hard takes a lot of commitment.

When did you know you wanted to cook?

I always wanted to be a chef, and this was before it was trendy. When I was a kid growing up in Brooklyn, I'd go to Lundy's, which was the largest restaurant in the world at one time, and I'd think, "I want to be the chef here someday." That's why I tell the kids to be careful what they wish for! I got my wish, and it was really hard work. We did 1,500 dinners on Saturday nights. I essentially gave up my life for two years.

Was that immediately before you went to Ezekiel's?

Yes. I'd worked really hard my whole career; and when I left Lundy's, I needed some soul-searching time. So I took about a month and a half off and traveled to Australia, Thailand and Europe. When I got back, I wanted to teach but I still wanted to cook. I knew I'd always been good at directing people.

Lists the interviewer's questions and the interviewee's responses.

Job Application

Many companies ask job candidates to fill out applications before they can be considered for a position. When you fill out a job application, make sure that the information is clear, accurate, and easy to read.

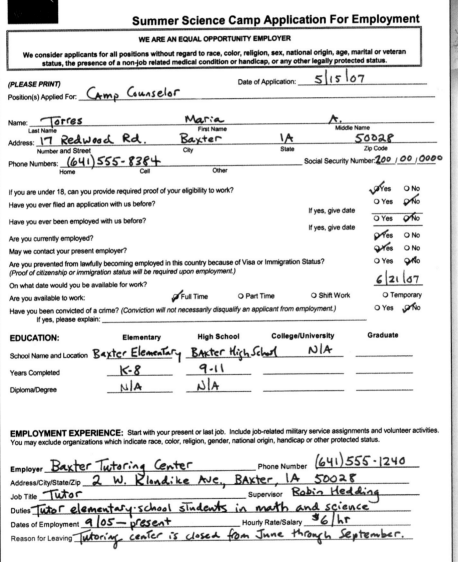

Summary Science Camp Application For Employment

WE ARE AN EQUAL OPPORTUNITY EMPLOYER

We consider applicants for all positions without regard to race, color, religion, sex, national origin, age, marital or veteran status, the presence of a non-job related medical condition or handicap, or any other legally protected status.

(PLEASE PRINT)

Position(s) Applied For: Camp Counselor

Date of Application: 5/15/07

Name: Torres (Last Name) Maria (First Name) A. (Middle Name)

Address: 17 Redwood Rd. (Number and Street) Baxter (City) IA (State) 50028 (Zip Code)

Phone Numbers: (641)555-8384 (Home) (Cell) (Other) Social Security Number: 200/00/0000

If you are under 18, can you provide required proof of your eligibility to work? ☑Yes ○No

Have you ever filed an application with us before? ○Yes ☑No If yes, give date

Have you ever been employed with us before? ○Yes ☑No If yes, give date

Are you currently employed? ☑Yes ○No

May we contact your present employer? ☑Yes ○No

Are you prevented from lawfully becoming employed in this country because of Visa or Immigration Status? ○Yes ☑No
(Proof of citizenship or immigration status will be required upon employment.)

On what date would you be available for work? 6/21/07

Are you available to work: ☑Full Time ○Part Time ○Shift Work ○Temporary

Have you been convicted of a crime? *(Conviction will not necessarily disqualify an applicant from employment.)* ○Yes ☑No
If yes, please explain: _____

EDUCATION:

	Elementary	High School	College/University	Graduate
School Name and Location	Baxter Elementary	Baxter High School	N/A	
Years Completed	K-8	9-11		
Diploma/Degree	N/A	N/A		

EMPLOYMENT EXPERIENCE: Start with your present or last job. Include job-related military service assignments and volunteer activities. You may exclude organizations which indicate race, color, religion, gender, national origin, handicap or other protected status.

Employer Baxter Tutoring Center Phone Number (641)555-1240

Address/City/State/Zip 2 W. Klondike Ave., Baxter, IA 50028

Job Title Tutor Supervisor Robin Hedding

Duties Tutor elementary-school students in math and science

Dates of Employment 9/05 — present Hourly Rate/Salary $6/hr

Reason for Leaving Tutoring center is closed from June through September.

Provides personal information.

Writes "N/A" in any section that does not apply.

Tells about past work experience.

Letters

Friendly

In a friendly letter, you write to someone you know, using an informal tone. A friendly letter often tells about recent events in the writer's life.

August 31, 2007

Dear Amber,

How are you? My family and I just got back from our vacation late last night. We had such a great time out west. It was like nothing I had ever seen before.

We traveled all over Colorado and Arizona. First we went to a National Park near the Rocky Mountains in Colorado. We hiked all day until I thought my legs were going to fall off. I was really surprised by how many deer we saw along the trails. The mountains themselves were incredibly beautiful. Some of them are over 12,000 feet high!

Believe it or not, Arizona was even more amazing. We went to see the Grand Canyon. I'd seen pictures of it before, but looking at pictures is nothing like seeing it in person. The pictures don't show all the different colors in the rocks and soil, and they definitely don't show how huge the canyon really is. It's truly an awesome sight.

Write to me and tell me about your summer. Hopefully we can get together sometime before school starts.

Your "best pal,"
Kelsey

Include the date. It is not necessary to include your address.

Tell your news in an informal tone.

Use an affectionate closing.

Inquiry/Request

When you write a letter of inquiry or request, you ask for specific favors, materials, or information. Use business-letter format when making an inquiry or request.

423 Wadsworth St., Apt. B
San Diego, CA 92020
April 20, 2007

Includes your address as well as the date.

Dr. Maria Todd
Dept. of Graphic Design
Rising Crest College,
32 Bayview Ave.
San Diego, CA 92020

Dear Dr. Todd:

    I am writing to request information about the graphic-design program at Rising Crest College. I read about the program on the college's website and would like to know more about it.

States the reason for writing.

    I'd appreciate your sending me more information about the program and an application for admission. I would also appreciate any available information about scholarships and financial aid programs.

Requests specific information or materials.

    Thank you for your time. I look forward to hearing from you.

Sincerely,

Jerome Martin

Jerome Martin

Closes formally with full signature.

EXPRESS

Letters, continued

Praise

A letter of praise expresses appreciation for the actions of a person. When you write to offer praise, be specific about why you are pleased.

37 Scotson Road
Parkville, OR 97086
October 6, 2007

Mr. Fred Simms
Parkville Youth Athletic League
1100 Carey Lane
Parkville, OR 97086

Dear Coach Simms:

Thank you so much for your patience, caring, and hard work this summer. Your efforts have made my teammates and me into better players and made this year's baseball season one to remember.

When the season started, most of us didn't know each other and we didn't work together very well. In only a few weeks, you brought us together and taught us how to play as a team. Under your coaching, my skills greatly improved. Even when I made a bad play in the field, you didn't get upset. Instead, you taught me how I could learn from my mistakes and do better next time.

Thanks again for making this baseball season so memorable. I can't wait to play on your team again next year!

Sincerely,
Tony Lopez
Tony Lopez

Tells why the person mattered to the writer.

Provides specific details.

Problem-Solving

Consumers write problem-solving letters to inform a company or organization about a problem. State your complaint and explain how the problem can be solved.

714 Almond Road
Fresno, CA 93707
August 1, 2007

Mr. Gary Zimmer, Chairman
Green Grass Teen Craft Fair Committee
43 Howard Avenue
Fresno, CA 93707

Dear Mr. Zimmer:

On June 23, 2006, I paid to reserve a table to sell my handmade jewelry at the upcoming Green Grass Teen Craft Fair. However, I recently read on your website that the date of the fair has been moved forward a week. Unfortunately, I will be out of town during the festival's new date, and I will not be able to attend.

I am enclosing a copy of my approved reservation application and my receipt. I would like you to send me a refund for the price of my reservation.

Thank you for your time and attention. Please feel free to call me at 555-6784 with any questions.

Sincerely,

Beth Vaden

Beth Vaden

Politely states the complaint.

Tells how the writer wants the problem resolved.

Often includes contact information.

EXPRESS

Literary Critique

A literary critique evaluates a work of literature. Give your opinion and support it with details and quotations from the text. You may discuss the literary merit of the work, how it is connected to historical events, or how it is impacted by the author's life.

THE BEAN TREES

by Barbara Kingsolver

Reviewed by Alexa U.

Opens with lively details about the plot and main characters.

It's the 1980s. A young woman travels from Kentucky to Arizona in an old VW that requires the driver to take a running start to make it budge. Halfway through her trip, she finds herself the "mother" of an infant who is thrust into her arms at a bar. She changes her name and sends a postcard to tell her mother. In Arizona, she works at a burger joint and encounters illegal immigrants and a blind woman.

Marietta, who decides to be known as Taylor, does all this and more in The Bean Trees, Kingsolver's compelling tale of self-discovery and independence.

Her life begins anew, as she wanted, since she now must mother the abused, mute infant she affectionately names Turtle. She also befriends the owner of a tire shop and bonds with another single mother.

Taylor must take on the roles of mother and friend. After years of feeling isolated, she suddenly has a sense of belonging. She must adjust, which is quite a challenge since she

admits she never thought the world could be as unjust as it is. She believes that "if the truth was a snake, it would have bitten [her] a long time ago."

Kingsolver brings her characters to life with vivid descriptions and alarming imagery. Taylor, who narrates the story, tells her tale in a lively Kentucky dialect, which adds incredible depth and realism to the novel. She and her friend Lou Ann, who is also from a small Kentucky town, share stories about their families and form a "family" of their own. Later, when Taylor meets Estevan and Esperanza, illegal immigrants from Guatemala, she can relate to their sense of displacement.

Kingsolver's portrayal of these characters opened my eyes to situations I never understood before, including Central American immigration and the differences between various regions of the United States.

I highly recommend Kingsolver's novel, and am happy to have had the pleasure of reading it. Taylor's characterization conveys hope, understanding and love. The book is an extraordinary tale of common occurrences brought to life by a gifted author.

Quotes from the text to support a point.

Closes with the writer's overall evaluation of the book.

Literary Response

A response to literature is similar to a literary critique, but it focuses more on the writer's personal, individual reactions to the work. You still need to support your response with concrete details from the text.

States opinion and summarizes the book.

When I Was Puerto Rican
by Esmeralda Santiago

Reviewed by Jennifer K.

This is a delightfully woven story of immense passion and unconquerable spirit. In this extraordinary autobiography, Santiago, an immigrant to New York from rural Puerto Rico, tells the story of her trials and triumphs, defeats and heartaches, in vivid detail.

Santiago grew up in what her *mami* calls "savage" conditions, dutifully obeying her parents as they constantly moved. Her greatest relocation occurred when a "metal bird" flew her, her mother, and two of her siblings to the rough city of New York. . . .

Using words as her medium, Santiago paints a beautiful picture of her life. I smelled the spices and herbs emanating from the special Puerto Rican dishes her *mami* prepared. Mesmerized, I watched as her *abuela* delicately stitched her needlework. . . . Santiago writes with such clarity and fierceness that it is impossible for any person not to see, feel, and understand what she went through in her remarkable journey.

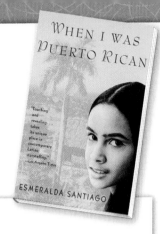

Santiago's unique style is easy to follow. When I read the book, I was immediately hooked and could not stop until I read the last word. The stories are interesting and full of insight. Santiago addresses fears and trials of all people. I especially related to her conflicts with her cultural identity. Anyone who has lived in between two cultures can relate to her story. Santiago wrote, "When I returned to Puerto Rico after living in New York for seven years, I was told I was no longer Puerto Rican. . . . In writing the book I wanted to get back to that feeling of Puertoricanness I had before I came here. Its title reflects who I was then, and asks, who am I today?"

Santiago's book provides a sense of hope. The narrator is transformed from a confused and frightened child into a spirited woman full of courage and hope. Her success in life—acceptance into New York City's High School of Performing Arts and graduating from Harvard with highest honors—proves she is capable of achieving her dreams.

Santiago's strong will and courage are evident throughout her story. *When I Was Puerto Rican* describes the remarkable journey that her life has been.

Describes the writer's emotional response to the book.

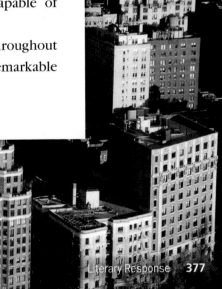

Magazine

Feature Article

A magazine feature informs the reader about a topic in a dramatic or entertaining way. It often begins with an anecdote that relates to the topic.

> # Laugh Your Way to Good Health
>
> *How laughter affects every part of your body*
>
> ## Positive Convulsions
>
> **K**evin Lee Smith bounds to the front of the room, grabs a microphone and utters a few words. Then something comes over him: A cascade of chemical messengers in his brain throws Smith into convulsions.
>
> For several seconds, he loses voluntary control over most of his body. His legs, arms, back and chest tense. His facial muscles squeeze upward. His stomach muscles and diaphragm spasm. His heart races. His blood pressure spikes. Someone call 911; give the man a sedative!
>
> But Smith's audience is also experiencing the same phenomena: They are, of course, laughing.
>
> ## Value of a Giggle
>
> Laughter is so common a human experience, we forget how bizarre it is. When aliens first see us laugh, they'll think we're having some sort of fit (and they probably won't get the punch line either). Smith causes the hilarity by talking about his growing forehead: "My hairline is making a beeline for my behind." Those chemicals cascade, bodies convulse, laughter erupts.
>
>
>
> Smith informs the audience that he's a male nurse: "Some people think it's unusual for a man to be a nurse. But there are male nurses throughout the country. Every once in a while the seven of us get together to talk about things." He teaches a course on humor and medicine at the University of Minnesota.

Dramatic opening grabs readers' attention.

Headings break up the text into small chunks.

Memo

A memo presents important information to other members of a company or organization. When you write a memo, write clearly and concisely, and use a professional tone.

Camp Kiwago

To: All Counselors at Camp Pakuna
From: Erin Margolis, Head Counselor
Date: June 27, 2006
Subject: Opening Day on July 3

Summer season at Camp Pakuna is rapidly approaching! Please review the opening-day instructions below.

Registration
All counselors must arrive by 12:30 p.m. on July 3. Campers will arrive between 1:00 p.m. and 3:00 p.m. Campers should register before removing their luggage from the trucks. Please guide campers to the registration station in front of the office. Bunk assignments will be announced during registration.

Unloading and Unpacking
Following registration, help your campers unload their belongings from the camp trucks. Lead the campers to their bunkhouses and help them settle in.

Orientation
After campers are settled in, direct them to the camp meetinghouse to await orientation at 4:00 p.m.

I hope that this will be the beginning of a fantastic summer!

Memos always start with this basic information.

Headings organize the text for easy understanding.

Information is brief and clear.

Usually, memos are not signed.

Memoir

The word *memoir* comes from the same root as *memory*. A memoir is a first-person narrative about the writer's memories and experiences. Memoirs often fill an entire book and tell about many events in the writer's life.

50   *Father*

<table>
<tr>
<td valign="top" width="30%">

Offers a reflection on a childhood experience.

</td>
<td valign="top">

My father was showing me how to water. Earlier in the day he and a friend had leveled the backyard with a roller, then with a two-by-four they dragged on a rope to fill in the low areas, after which they watered the ground and combed it slowly with a steel rake. They were preparing the ground for a new lawn. They worked shirtless in the high summer heat, and talked only so often, stopping now and then to point and say things I did not understand—how fruit trees would do better near the alley and how the vegetable garden would do well on the east side of the house.

</td>
</tr>
<tr>
<td valign="top">

Includes sensory details.

</td>
<td valign="top">

"Put your thumb like this," he said. Standing over me, he took the hose and placed his thumb over the opening so that the water streamed out hissing and showed silver in that dusk. I tried it and the water hissed and went silver as I pointed the hose to a square patch of dirt that I soaked but was careful not to puddle.

</td>
</tr>
<tr>
<td valign="top">

Explodes a moment of everyday life.

</td>
<td valign="top">

Father returned to sit down with an iced tea. His knees were water-stained and his chest was flecked with mud. Mom sat next to him, garden gloves resting on her lap. She was wearing checkered shorts and her hair was tied up

</td>
</tr>
</table>

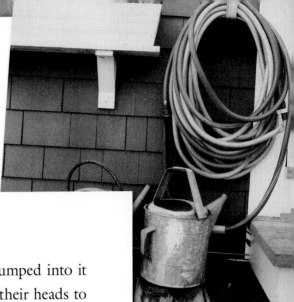

in a bandanna. He patted his lap, and she jumped into it girlishly, arms around his neck. They raised their heads to watch me—or look through me, as if something were on the other side of me—and talked about our new house, the neighbors, trees they would plant, the playground down the block. They were tired from the day's work but were happy. When Father pinched her legs, as if to imply that they were fat, she punched him gently and played with his hair.

The water streamed, nickel-colored, as I slowly worked from one end to the next. When I raised my face to Father's to ask if I could stop, he pointed to an area that I had missed. Although it was summer I was cold from the water and my thumb hurt from pressing the hose, triggerlike, to reach the far places. But I wanted to please him, to work as hard as he had, so I watered the patch until he told me to stop. I turned off the water, coiled the hose as best I could, and sat with them as they talked about the house and stared at where I had been standing.

Uses first-person pronouns like *my* and *I*.

Newspaper

Editorial

An editorial expresses the writer's opinion about an issue of local, national, or international importance.

deseretnews.com

Safeguarding Tanning Teens

So they tanned his hide when he died, Clyde, and that's it hanging on the shed.
—From "Tie Me Kangaroo Down"

Puts the issue in context and gives the writer's opinion.

For those who relish irony, one current example involves teenagers who often ruin their health and skin by going to tanning salons in order to look "sun-tanned and healthy." Like smoking, getting tanned has gone from being personal choice to a national health concern. And, like smoking, tanning is still legal and available.

The key is to make sure those with enough mental firepower are making the decision. Overdoing things can lead to tragedy. Beauty may be only skin deep, but bad tanning goes all the way to the bone.

That's why we applaud the Davis County Board of Health and a new rule that insists a parent in Davis County not only give consent but must drive a child under age 18 to the salon for a tanning session. The new rule not only forces teens to think twice about their decision,

Develops the thinking behind the opinion.

but it forces parents to take an active role in the routines of their kids. Many parents will not bother. Among those who do, who knows? That lift to the salon may generate some conversation which, in turn, may lead to understanding. Davis County plans to study the effects of the regulation over the next 18 months and work with other county health departments and the Utah Department of Health

to come up with other regulations.

Tanning salon operators even signed off on the new approach. One claimed that some day the redeeming qualities of getting tanned will come out—such as keeping teens from lying out in the sun and getting burned to a crisp.

Until that day, however, shielding young children from ultraviolet rays and other ill effects makes perfect sense.

Will young people simply scoot to another county to "bootleg" a tan? Probably. But at least they're on the run. And the approach Davis County has taken might serve as a model for other communities. It's a plan that allows for freedom of choice but factors in the wisdom of a guardian as a filter for any rambunctious thinking.

It shows bureaucratic creativity at its best.

That may sound like more irony, but it seems to be the way Davis County has been going about its business.

Tanner's eyes are protected by anti-UV goggles.

EVACUATION ROUTE

News Article

A news article tells about a recent event. It covers the "5 Ws": who, what, where, when, and why. A news article uses an "inverted pyramid" structure: it states the main points in the beginning, and then provides less important details in later paragraphs.

Tropical Storm Florence Forms in Atlantic

Weather system intensifies but poses no immediate threat to land

States the main point.

MIAMI, FL—Tropical Storm Florence formed today in the open Atlantic, becoming the sixth named storm of the 2006 hurricane season.

Tells what happened and when.

Florence had top sustained winds near 40 mph, 1 mph over the 39 mph threshold for a tropical storm, and it was expected to slowly intensify over the next few days, according to the National Hurricane Center.

Tells where and who might be affected.

Its tropical storm force winds extended 115 miles from its center, but posed no immediate threat to land.

At 11 a.m., the storm was centered 935 miles east of the Lesser Antilles and was moving west at about 12 mph, forecasters said.

Florence follows Tropical Storm Ernesto, which was briefly the season's first hurricane before hitting Florida and North Caro-

lina last week as a tropical storm.

At least nine deaths have been attributed to Ernesto, and the aftereffects were still being felt early today. About 75,000 people remained without power in New York's Westchester County.

Last year's Atlantic storm season set a record with 28 named storms and 15 hurricanes, including Katrina, which devastated the Louisiana and Mississippi coasts.

Often connects the story to a broader subject.

Radar image of hurricane approaching west coast of Florida.

May include photos and captions.

Observation Report

An observation report describes the procedure and the results of an experiment. The writing in an observation report is clear and concise. It uses an objective, impersonal tone.

Light and Moisture Preferences of Pillbugs

Research Question: What light and moisture conditions will pillbugs seek in a laboratory setting?

Tell what you want to know.

Hypothesis: Pillbugs will seek out low light and high moisture.

Tell what you think will happen.

Procedure: Four tube environments were created within a plastic container, with various combinations of light and moisture as outlined in the **Results** section. Low light was created by wrapping the tube in black paper. High moisture was created by placing a damp paper towel inside the tube. Twenty active pillbugs were obtained and placed in the container.

Describe how you set up the experiment.

Results: After 15 minutes, the tubes were removed and the pillbugs were counted. Observations are summarized in Table 1 below.

Report what you observed.

Tube	Light	Moisture	Number of pillbugs after 15 minutes
1	high	low	0
2	high	high	2
3	low	low	1
4	low	high	17

Conclusion: Pillbugs clearly seemed to prefer a low light, high moisture environment. It is possible that they sought out the tubes with the paper towels not because they were moist, but because they offered a soft material that the pillbugs could hide under.

Tell what your results mean.

Parody

A parody imitates a famous work or a particular style of writing. The purpose is either to make fun of it, or to just have fun! When you write a parody, think of the specific characteristics you plan to imitate.

Ricardo and Julie

An Updated Balcony Scene

Setting: Outside Julie Capilli's family's downtown apartment

RICARDO:

[*aside*] It's easy to say love is nothing, until you're *in* love.

[JULIE *appears above at a window, cell phone in hand.*]

Whoa! Check out those neon lights in the sky!
It's a million-megawatt arena,
and my girl Julie is the rock star.
Julie, walk onto the stage like you own it,
and just ignore the other girls,
who aren't even fit to be your backup singers.
They're just jealous of you anyway.
Ditch them. You can do better.
Oh look, there she is!
It's my sweetheart, oh, it's my love!
She's holding her cell phone,
yet she does not speak—
Could she be sending a text message?
If I could just make eye contact with her. . . .
Oh, what's the use? She's way out of my league,
For her eyes flash like the brightest of strobe lights,
and her cheeks have such a perfect pink glow
that I swear she's hired her own personal make-up artist.
See! how she dabs more gloss upon her lips:
Oh! if I could be that tube of gloss
So I might touch those lips.

Closely follows the work on which it's based. Which play is the writer parodying?

Uses a mock-serious tone.

Play

Plays are meant to be performed onstage. They are organized into **acts**, each of which may include several **scenes**. The script for a play tells what actors will say and do during the performance.

Like/Love

by Kristen Dabrowski

At the beginning of a script, there is usually a list of characters.

Characters

MITCHELL, a young man in his late teens

VICTORIA, Mitchell's girlfriend

A note at the start of each scene tells where it takes place.

Scene 5

Mitchell's bedroom on a Sunday afternoon. Victoria has made herself at home and is reading in Mitchell's chair.

MITCHELL *(impatient)*: You're in my study chair again.

VICTORIA: Yeah. I was thinking about that.

MITCHELL: You were thinking about my chair?

VICTORIA: I was thinking about you.

MITCHELL: Me?

VICTORIA: Yep.

MITCHELL: Why?

VICTORIA: I think you'd look good with a
haircut and a style makeover.

MITCHELL *(sarcastically)*: Thanks. That's very
flattering. Now, my chair? Get off of it.

VICTORIA: No.

MITCHELL: What?

VICTORIA: I don't think so.

MITCHELL: You're killing me. I have a math test, and,
as I've explained in the past, I must study in
my study chair!

VICTORIA *(pretending to yawn as if she is bored)*:
Yes, yes, yes. You get A's on your tests when
you sit in The Chair. You know, you'd be cute
if you weren't so high-strung.

A script identifies
each **speaker**
and shows the
speaker's exact
words, or dialogue.

Stage directions
tell what the actors
do onstage.

Play, continued

Stage directions can also tell how characters deliver their lines.

MITCHELL (*raising his voice*): I'm not high-strung!

VICTORIA: Oh, no. I can see that now.

MITCHELL: What can I do to make you move?

VICTORIA: Cut your hair.

MITCHELL: Sure. Fine. But I can't do that now because I have to study. . . .You're not moving!

VICTORIA: There's more. Also, shop with me.

MITCHELL: Oh, this is too much.

VICTORIA: I'm telling you, with a little tweaking I could change your whole life.

MITCHELL: How very generous. Maybe it never occurred to you that I like how I am.

VICTORIA: I like how you are, too, mostly. I just want to get you a haircut and a new pair of jeans or something.

MITCHELL: Very generous. Fine.

VICTORIA: And maybe a tux.

MITCHELL: What?? You've lost it. Stop messing with me and get out of my chair!

VICTORIA: Prom.

MITCHELL: What?

VICTORIA: Prom.

MITCHELL: What? Can you speak in full sentences?

VICTORIA (*speaking with exaggerated slowness*):
Take. Me. To. The. Prom.

MITCHELL: Me.

VICTORIA: You.

MITCHELL: But only if I get a haircut.

VICTORIA: Right.

MITCHELL: Then I'll get my chair.

VICTORIA: Who cares about your chair?
(*VICTORIA stands up and kisses him suddenly.*)

VICTORIA: There. There's your stupid chair. If you
want to talk haircut and prom, I'll be in *that*
chair, over *there*. OK?

MITCHELL (*taken aback*): O—OK.

(*VICTORIA exits. MITCHELL sits in the chair and
opens a book. Beat. He slams the book shut.*)

MITCHELL: Women! Now I'll get a B on the test for
sure!

The scene builds
to a dramatic
turning point.

Poetry

Rhymed Verse

Rhymed verse follows a set rhyme scheme and often uses a regular rhythm as well.

Stopping By Woods on a Snowy Evening

by Robert Frost

Whose woods these are I think I know.	*a*
His house is in the village, though;	*a*
He will not see me stopping here	*b*
To watch his woods fill up with snow.	*a*
My little horse must think it queer	*b*
To stop without a farmhouse near	*b*
Between the woods and frozen lake	*c*
The darkest evening of the year.	*b*
He gives his harness bells a shake	*c*
To ask if there is some mistake.	*c*
The only other sound's the sweep	*d*
Of easy wind and downy flake.	*c*
The woods are lovely, dark, and deep,	*d*
But I have promises to keep,	*d*
And miles to go before I sleep,	*d*
And miles to go before I sleep.	*d*

This poem has an interesting rhyme pattern, shown by the letters.

Blank Verse

Blank verse does not rhyme, but it has a definite rhythm. A line of blank verse has ten syllables, with every other syllable stressed. The "music" of a line of blank verse sounds something like this:

daDUM daDUM daDUM daDUM daDUM

This rhythm is called *iambic pentameter.* Here's an example of a line written in iambic pentameter:

And why should I believe the things you say?

A poem in blank verse—such as the one below— follows the general pattern of iambic pentameter, but has many small variations for the sake of interest and emphasis.

Elevator Music

by Henry Taylor

A tune with no more substance than the air,
performed on underwater instruments,
is proper to this short lift from the earth.
It hovers as we draw into ourselves
and turn our reverent eyes toward the lights
that count us to our various destinies.
We're all in this together, the song says,
and later we'll descend. The melody
is like a name we don't recall just now
that still keeps on insisting it is there.

Poetry, continued

Free Verse

Free verse has no fixed rhythm and uses irregular rhyme or no rhyme at all. However, free verse often includes other poetic devices, such as repetition, imagery, or figurative language.

MOTHER

by Maya Angelou

During the years when you knew nothing
And I knew everything, I loved you still.
Condescendingly of course,
From my high perch
Of teenage wisdom.
I grew older and
Was stunned to find
How much knowledge you had gleaned
And so quickly.

Haiku

A haiku is a brief poem that focuses on a single image or emotion. The haiku form originated in Japan and often describes images found in nature. The form traditionally uses three lines with five, seven, and five syllables, respectively.

by the noonflower
a rice-pounder cools himself:
a sight so moving

—*Bashō*

the cathedral bell
is shaking a few snowflakes
from the morning air

—*Nicholas Virgilio*

heat before the storm:
a fly disturbs the quiet
of the empty store

—*Nicholas Virgilio*

A bitter morning:
sparrows sitting together
without any necks.

—*James Hackett*

Poetry, continued

Song Lyrics

Song lyrics are a form of poetry set to music. Usually, the lines rhyme. People write songs for many reasons—to express their feelings, to entertain people, or to honor a loved one.

84 ～ *Jenny*

Simple rhyme and rhythm.

Jenny is upside down in a giant cocoon
Floating around this town like a crazy balloon
All the neighbors stand on the grass
Pointing up as she passes all of them by

Jenny is overhead like a blimp on the go
Cruising around this town like a strange embryo
There's a blip up there in the sky
Radar can't seem to identify

She's soaring up above the evergreens
She's on her way, on her way now
Wonder woman pushing seventeen
She's on her way, on her way
Now the clouds all part in the sky
Town is waving goodbye
Everything she wants will happen soon

Paparazzi rubbing their eyes
Waiting for her to fly back down

MATT BROWN 〜 85

She's soaring up above the evergreens
She's on her way, on her way now
Wonder woman pushing seventeen
She's on her way, on her way
Now the clouds all part in the sky
Town is waving goodbye
Everything she wants will happen soon

Jenny is upside down in a giant cocoon
Waiting to touch new ground on an alien moon
Wake up now, look around
You're infinity bound, oh yeah

She's soaring up above the evergreens
She's on her way, on her way now
Wonder woman pushing seventeen
She's on her way, on her way
Now the clouds all part in the sky
Town is waving goodbye
Everything she wants will happen soon

Contains a *refrain* that is repeated.

Procedure

A procedure is a list of steps that must be followed to complete a task. When you write a procedure, clearly describe, in order, what needs to be done.

Headings help organize the instructions.

Gives clear, specific, step-by-step instructions.

PROCEDURE FOR HOUSE SITTER

When Entering

Open door and close it quickly. Rufus will try to escape if the door is left open!

In the Morning

1. Give Rufus fresh water and dry kibble.
2. Play with Rufus and let him outside for $\frac{1}{2}$ hour.
3. Water plants on kitchen windowsill.
4. Feed fish with flakes next to tank.
5. Bring in the morning's newspaper and leave on kitchen table.

In the Afternoon

1. Bring in the day's mail and leave on kitchen table.
2. Feed Rufus $\frac{1}{2}$ can of dog food.
3. Play with Rufus and walk him for at least 20 minutes.
4. Check the tomato plants and place any ripe tomatoes on the kitchen table.

When Leaving

1. Close windows.
2. Turn off lights and fans.
3. Don't forget to lock the door and deadbolt.

Emergency Phone Numbers

Mr. & Mrs. Rhoades (cell): (212) 555-7834

Dr. Sternberg (vet): (212) 555-4700
Annandale Police Dept.: (212) 555-2299

Résumé

People write résumés to persuade an employer to hire them. A résumé presents details about your education, work history, and achievements. It also makes a strong first impression! Make sure it's organized, carefully edited, and professional-looking.

Provides contact information.

CHRIS KRAMER

90555 ROCKY MOUNTAIN WAY
FT. COLLINS, COLORADO 80526
Cell phone: (970) 555-1234
E-mail: chrisk@me.com

CAREER GOAL:

To gain relevant work experience using my education, prior experience, and strong technical skills toward my goal of becoming a commercial airframe mechanic.

Describes educational background.

EDUCATION:

Rocky Mountain High School, Ft. Collins, CO, Class of 2006

Completed Technical Program, focusing on Industrial Design and Automotive Diagnostics and Repair. **Courses included:** Industrial Physics, Welding, Machining, Drafting, Automotive Drives Train/ Heating/AC, and Diagnostics and Electrical.

Lists most-recent jobs first.

EMPLOYMENT:

Auto Technician

Highline Motors, Ft. Collins, CO – Summer 2007. Repair and maintain high-end import cars.

Installer

Vanworks, Ft. Collins, CO – Summer 2006. Installed leather interiors, running boards, custom electronics, and aftermarket accessories for custom conversion van company.

Craftsman

Wood Shop, Ft. Collins, CO – Summer 2005. Crafted custom dashboards from quality hardwoods and veneers.

Autotech Trainee

Wilf's European Motors, Mead, CO – Summer 2004.

Review

In a review, the writer states and supports his or her opinion of a book, movie, music CD, or other creative work. Reviews that appear in newspapers and magazines are usually written by professional critics. You might write a review for your school newspaper or literary magazine, or for a Web site that solicits reviews from the general public.

AT THE MOVIES

The Devil Wears Prada

Reviewed by Brittany Howe

Opening
Engages the reader and states the reviewer's opinion.

Think your job at the burger joint is a pain in the neck? Go see The Devil Wears Prada, and you'll never complain about your job again. This frivolous-but-fun flick stars Anne Hathaway as Andy Sachs, a naïve college grad who wants to become a journalist, but takes a job at Runway, a glitzy fashion magazine, to pay the bills. Meryl Streep is unforgettable as Miranda Priestly, the magazine's ruthless editor. Based on the bestselling novel of the same name, The Devil Wears Prada provides an entertaining look at the ultimate nightmare workplace.

Body
Summarizes the plot and gives important details.

From the moment Andy walks into Runway's offices, sporting a lumpy sweater and uncombed hair, it's obvious that she doesn't fit in. The other staffers sneer at her. In Miranda's eyes, however, they're all equally inept. Miranda expects employees to be on-call 24 hours a day. She makes ridiculous demands like "Find me that piece of paper I had in my hand yesterday morning" and dismisses excuses by declaring, "The details of your incompetence do not interest me."

Closing
Restates the reviewer's opinion.

Andy hates the job, but she's determined to stick it out for a year, knowing it could be a stepping stone to something much better. As she's gradually lured into Runway's superficial world, you find yourself wondering just how far she'll go in pursuit of her dream. The ending is somewhat predictable, but thanks to the actors' strong performances and snappy one-liners, this movie is consistently fun and entertaining.

Speech

Speeches can entertain, inform, or persuade—and some speeches do all three. Speechwriters often use highly charged language and repeated phrases to appeal to listeners' emotions. When you write a speech, think about its purpose. What impact do you want to have on your audience?

from **Senate candidate Barack Obama's remarks at the Democratic National Convention, July 27, 2004**

…I stand here today, grateful for the diversity of my heritage, aware that my parents' dreams live on in my precious daughters. I stand here knowing that my story is part of the larger American story, that I owe a debt to all of those who came before me, and that, in no other country on earth, is my story even possible. Tonight, we gather to affirm the greatness of our nation, not because of the height of our skyscrapers, or the power of our military, or the size of our economy. Our pride is based on a very simple premise, summed up in a declaration made over two hundred years ago, "We hold these truths to be self-evident, that all men are created equal. That they are endowed by their Creator with certain inalienable rights. That among these are life, liberty, and the pursuit of happiness."

Uses repetition for effect.

That is the true genius of America, a faith in the simple dreams of its people, the insistence on small miracles. That we can tuck in our children at night and know they are fed and clothed and safe from harm. That we can say what we think, write what we think, without hearing a sudden knock on the door. That we can have an idea and start our own business without paying a bribe or hiring somebody's son. That we can participate in the political process without fear of retribution, and that our votes will be counted— or at least, most of the time.

Barack Obama became a U.S. Senator for Illinois in 2005. ▶

This year, in this election, we are called to reaffirm our values and commitments, to hold them against a hard reality and see how we are measuring up, to the legacy of our forebears, and the promise of future generations. And fellow Americans—Democrats, Republicans, Independents—I say to you tonight: we have more work to do. . . . More to do for the father I met who was losing his job and choking back tears, wondering how he would pay $4,500 a month for the drugs his son needs without the health benefits he counted on. More to do for the young woman in East St. Louis, and thousands more like her, who has the grades, has the drive, has the will, but doesn't have the money to go to college.

Don't get me wrong. The people I meet in small towns and big cities, in diners and office parks, they don't expect government to solve all their problems. They know they have to work hard to get ahead and they want to. . . . Go into any inner city neighborhood, and folks will tell you that government alone can't teach kids to learn. They know that parents have to parent, that children can't achieve unless we raise their expectations and turn off the television sets and eradicate the slander that says a black youth with a book is acting white. No, people don't expect government to solve all their problems. But they sense, deep in their bones, that with just a change in priorities, we can make sure that every child in America has a decent shot at life….

Uses examples that appeal to the audience's emotions.

Stories

Short Story

Short stories entertain readers and appeal to their emotions. When you write a short story, you create characters and put them in a setting—the time and place of the story. The plot unfolds as you tell about a conflict and the events that lead to its resolution.

THE CENSORS

Luisa Valenzuela

The writer introduces the main character.

Poor Juan! One day they caught him with his guard down before he could even realize that what he had taken as a stroke of luck was really one of fate's dirty tricks. These things happen the minute you're careless and you let down your guard, as one often does. Juancito let happiness—a feeling you can't trust—get the better of him when he received from a confidential source Mariana's new address in Paris and knew she hadn't forgotten him. Without thinking twice, he sat down at his table and wrote her a letter. The letter that keeps his mind off his job during the day and won't let him sleep at night (what had he scrawled, what had he put on that sheet of paper he sent to Mariana?).

The character has an internal conflict that motivates his actions.

Juan knows there won't be a problem with the letter's contents, that it's irreproachable, harmless. But what about the rest? He knows that they examine, sniff, feel, and read between the lines of each and every letter, and check its tiniest comma and most accidental stain. He knows that all letters pass from hand to hand and go through all sorts of tests in the huge censorship offices and that, in the end, very few continue on their way. Usually it takes months, even years, if there aren't any snags. All this time the freedom, maybe even the lives, of both sender and receiver are in jeopardy. And that's why Juan's so down in the dumps: thinking that

something might happen to Mariana because of his letter. Of all people, Mariana, who must finally feel safe there where she always dreamed she'd live. But he knows that the Censor's Secret Command operates all over the world. . . . There's nothing to stop them from going as far as that hidden Paris neighborhood, kidnapping Mariana, and returning to their cozy homes, certain of having fulfilled their noble mission.

Well, you've got to beat them to the punch, do what everyone tries to do: sabotage the machinery, throw sand in its gears, get to the bottom of the problem so as to stop it.

This was Juan's sound plan when he, like many others, applied for a censor's job—not because he had a calling or needed a job: no, he applied simply to intercept his own letter, a consoling but unoriginal idea. He was hired immediately, for each day more and more censors are needed and no one would bother to check on his references.

Ulterior motives couldn't be overlooked by the Censorship Division, but they needn't be too strict with those who applied. They knew how hard it would be for those poor guys to find the letter they wanted, and even if they did, what's a letter or two when the new censor would snap up so many others? That's how Juan managed to join the Post Office's Censorship Division, with a certain goal in mind.

Juan's actions move the plot ahead.

Creates suspense about the story's outcome.

38   THE CENSORS | Luisa Valenzuela

The building had a festive air on the outside which contrasted with its inner staidness. Little by little, Juan was absorbed by his job and he felt at peace since he was doing everything he could to get his letter for Mariana. He didn't even worry when, in his first month, he was sent to *Section K* where envelopes are very carefully screened for explosives.

It's true that on the third day, a fellow worker had his right hand blown off by a letter, but the division chief claimed it was sheer negligence on the victim's part. Juan and the other employees were allowed to go back to their work, albeit feeling less secure. After work, one of them tried to organize a strike to demand higher wages for unhealthy work, but Juan didn't join in; after thinking it over, he reported him to his superiors and thus got promoted.

You don't form a habit by doing something once, he told himself as he left his boss's office. And when he was transferred to *Section J*, where letters are carefully checked for poison dust, he felt he had climbed a rung in the ladder.

By working hard, he quickly reached *Section E* where the work was more interesting, for he could now read and analyze the letters' contents. Here he could even hope to get hold of his letter which, judging by the time that had elapsed, had gone through the other sections and was probably floating around in this one.

Soon his work became so absorbing that his noble mission blurred in his mind. Day after day he crossed out whole paragraphs in red ink, pitilessly chucking many letters into the censored basket. These were horrible days when he was shocked by the subtle and conniving ways employed by people to pass on subversive messages; his instincts were so sharp that he found behind a simple "the weather's unsettled" or "prices continue to soar" the wavering hand of someone secretly scheming to overthrow the Government.

His zeal brought him swift promotion. We don't know if this made him happy. Very few letters reached him in *Section B*—only a handful passed the other hurdles—so he read them over and over again, passed them under a magnifying glass, searched for microprint with an electronic microscope, and tuned his sense of smell so that he was beat by the time he made it home. He'd barely manage to warm up his soup, eat some fruit, and fall into bed, satisfied with having done his duty. Only his darling mother worried, but she couldn't get him back on the right road. She'd say, though it wasn't always true: Lola called, she's at the bar with girls, they miss you, they're waiting for you. Or else, she'd leave a bottle of red wine on the table. But Juan wouldn't overdo it: any distraction could make him lose his edge and the perfect censor had to be alert, keen, attentive, and sharp to nab cheats. He had a truly patriotic task, both self-denying and uplifting.

His basket for censored letters became the best fed as well as the most cunning basket in the whole *Censorship Division*. He was about to congratulate himself for having finally discovered his true mission, when his letter to Mariana reached his hands. Naturally, he censored it without regret. And just as naturally, he couldn't stop them from executing him the following morning, another victim of his devotion to his work.

Creates suspense about the story's outcome.

The turning point comes when he sees the letter he wrote. Then the story ends suddenly and ironically.

Historical Fiction

Historical fiction presents a story set in the past, with specific details that bring the setting to life for modern readers. To write historical fiction, you need to research the time period and make sure the details you present are accurate.

102   *Resistance*

This story takes place during the early 1940s, when the Germans occupied Paris, France.

▲ A Nazi soldier from World War II

Characters use words typical of the time period.

Philippe sticks out a booted foot, and Michel sprawls on the ground. The beret topples into a puddle, and the broom skips across the cobblestones. Philippe's pals, gathered like vultures, squawk with delight.

Can they really be so stupid? Or just cruel, like Colonel Bloch? They know perfectly well Michel can't hear them. Michel is stone-deaf. It happened four years ago when he was ill with scarlet fever. I stayed at the café with Great-aunt Pauline so I wouldn't catch it too. . . .

The day I went home again, Michel was in the parlor bundled in a blanket by the fire. Out in the kitchen the enamel washbowl slipped from Maman's wet hands into the stone sink with an almighty clang. Michel didn't flinch. Didn't even blink. Just kept on reading. I yelled. Clapped my hands. But Michel heard nothing.

Papa immediately set to work creating a silent language we could all use. Each evening for months and months, we sat around the table forming and reforming our awkward fingers into letters and words. . . .

"Buffoons!" I yell, a tidal wave of anger in my gut. "Pick on someone your own size!" I retrieve the broom and shake it at them. "Go home!"

The soldiers smirk. How dare Philippe embarrass Michel in front of the Germans. He does it all the time. Never misses an opportunity. How I despise him.

Nazi forces march by the Eiffel Tower and the Arc de Triomphe in Paris, 1942.

JANET GRABER ∼ 103

Flushed with success, the boys continue to taunt Michel as they saunter past the shuttered shops bordering the square. The shopkeepers rarely have much to sell beyond the rations allotted us by the government. Except M. Fournier, the butcher, of course. Philippe's father groveled and scraped when the Germans marched into town. He secured a lucrative contract to supply the local troops with meat, and in so doing, secured the contempt of almost everyone in town. . . .

"I'm sorry, Michel," I sign. "They're just ignorant louts."

Michel shrugs. "Do you have a message? Am I needed tonight?"

I don't want to tell him. I never do. He's three years younger than me. Only twelve years old. Far too young to be risking his life on such dangerous missions for the Resistance.

"Well?" he signs.

"There's a delivery. Yes."

"What time?"

"One o'clock."

He nods.

"Will you have far to go" I ask.

"I can't tell you . . . You know that."

I do. My country, my village, and even my family are filled with secrets now. I hate the scheming. We must not divulge more than necessary, even to one another.

Details accurately reflect daily life during WWII.

Summary

A summary condenses into just a few sentences the main ideas and most important details of a longer text. You might write a summary when you do research or when you study for an exam. Page 409 shows notes from the following textbook article and a summary of the notes.

Senate Leadership

The official leader of the upper house is the president of the Senate, a position held by the Vice President of the United States. This role includes such routine powers as calling on members to speak and putting questions to a vote. In practice, however, the Vice President has little real influence in the Senate. As an elected member of the *executive*, rather than legislative, branch, the Vice President cannot debate issues on the Senate floor or vote, unless there is a tie.

Because the Vice President is rarely available to preside over the Senate, a **president pro tempore** is elected to perform those duties. Chosen by the whole Senate after being endorsed by the majority party caucus, the president "pro tem" usually the majority party member who has served the longest.

Other leadership positions are organized around political parties, too. The **majority leader** heads the party in power and holds the most powerful office in the Senate. The leader plans the Senate's daily agenda and has considerable influence over the party's committee assignments. Working closely with individual senators, key committee leaders, and various congressional groups, the majority leader also organizes other party members to support legislation favored by their party.

On the Senate floor, it is the majority leader's duty to see that business flows smoothly. The most powerful part of the job is scheduling which bills will be debated and *when* they will be debated. The success or failure of a bill often hinges on where it falls on the schedule.

The other leader elected by the political parties is the **minority leader,** who heads the opposition party. Although not as powerful as the majority leader, he or she has similar duties. The minority leader is always present on the floor during consideration of bills and has a strong voice in committee assignments for minority party members. His or her primary duty, however, is to lead fellow party members in their struggle to change or defeat the policies and programs of the majority party. It is the minority leader who persuades influential minority party members and committee leaders to follow the party's position. In addition, if the minority leader belongs to the same political party as the President, he or she usually acts as the President's spokesperson on the floor.

The two floor leaders are aided by party whips, or assistant leaders, who are chosen by party caucuses. Whips keep track of their party's support on various issues and try to "whip up" more backing by persuading members to vote for or against a particular piece of legislation. They provide information on bills for members, advise floor leaders on how much support their party has for certain bills, and ensure that their members are in full attendance during important floor votes.

president pro tempore member of the Senate who temporarily presides over the Senate when the Vice President is absent

majority leader member of a legislative house elected by members to lead the majority party

minority leader member of a legislative house elected by members to lead the minority party

Section Review

1. How are senators chosen today?

2. Why is the Senate known as a continuous body?

3. What qualifications must a person meet to be a senator?

4. **Challenge:** In your opinion, should the Vice President have less power or more power in the Senate? Why?

U.S. Senate Leadership

<u>Vice President</u>   The Senate's official leader, but cannot debate issues on the floor unless there is a tied vote. Usually is not present to preside over the Senate.

<u>President Pro Tempore</u>   Senator elected to preside over the Senate. Usually the member of the majority party who has served the longest in the Senate.

<u>Majority Leader</u>   Most important and powerful role. Plans the Senate's day-to-day activities, assigns committee memberships, schedules debate of bills, and works to pass laws favored by the majority party.

<u>Minority Leader</u>   Similar to majority leader, but not as powerful. Heads the minority party. Assigns committee membership for senators of minority party.

<u>Whips</u>   There is one whip for each party. Each whip assists his or her party leader. Whips make sure senators from their party support or oppose certain bills.

Summary
The business of the U.S. Senate is carried forward by leaders from both parties, each of whom has special duties and responsibilities.

Headings make organization visible.

Uses note-taking style to condense information.

Sums up the details in a statement that is easy to grasp and remember.

Web Site

A Web site can be personal or professional and can be about any subject. Web sites often include images, sound files, video, and links to related pages or sites.

As a Web-site "writer" you have to think "in time."
What happens when you click a link?
How do you get back "home" after listening to a song?

Writing Modes

Writing can be classified into one of five modes: narrative, expository, descriptive, expressive, and persuasive. A mode defines the broad purpose of a piece of writing.

It gets a little complicated, because a single mode may take several different forms—for example, a story and a narrative poem might both be in the narrative mode. Also, a single form of writing may encompass several modes—a novel usually contains some narrative parts and some descriptive parts.

Find out more about the five writing modes in the pages that follow.

All You Can Write

Writing Modes

Narrative

Expository

Descriptive

Expressive

Persuasive

Narrative Mode: Tell a Story

The purpose of **narrative writing** is to tell your readers a real or made-up story. Fiction and nonfiction narratives usually present events in chronological order, with a clear beginning, middle, and end. Narratives may be written to explain actual events or for an artistic purpose.

Some common narrative forms include short stories, novels, biographies, memoirs, and autobiographies.

Short Story

David Yoo's story "Turning Japanese" is narrative fiction. It's about a Korean American whose boss assumes he is Japanese and expects him to teach her the language.

42   TURNING JAPANESE | David Yoo

"I'm going to need some time to prepare. I'll teach you next Wednesday."

"Can you really teach me in one day?"

"We'll see," I answered weakly. She made me shake on it.

Her phone rang. She folded her hands as if in prayer and mouthed "thank you" to me as she returned to her desk. I think she bowed slightly, but it might have been my imagination. Her office was at the end of the hallway, and since it had no door we could see each other constantly. The last hour of work the phone rarely rang, and I sat there trying to write an opening paragraph for a chapter I'd been working on, but my mind was frazzled. I'd been lying my whole life—maybe that was why I was a writer—but it felt like years since it had gotten me into a situation like this.

> Fictional narratives usually include dialogue between characters.

Novel

In this excerpt from a David Yoo novel, the main character remembers his failed attempt to become a popular soccer player.

GIRLS FOR BREAKFAST | David Yoo   57

It was a status symbol to date a soccer player. It was a status symbol to even be seen talking to a soccer player. It was a status symbol to wear a soccer player's varsity jacket. Come to think of it, I didn't really care about playing time or how the team was actually doing.

I did it all for the jacket.

It's silly how excited I was for it. But girls still couldn't care less that I played soccer, because nothing overrode the fact that I was a lowly frosh Asian guy.

In novels, events unfold over an extended period of time.

Autobiography

In this autobiographical essay, Marian Haddad recounts events that shaped her as a writer.

Scheherazade's Legacy includes essays by Marian Haddad and Naomi Shihab Nye. ▶

HADDAD | Marian Haddad   83

I remember being six years old, my mother calling me in Arabic to the living room coffee table. I'd come, sometimes reluctantly, sometimes gladly, to our chocolate brown wooden coffee table, sit on the floor, Indian-style, me and my paper and my pen, there in the early evening light, my mother sitting on the golden green stitched sofa near me, my head near her knees. This was the way we did it. This was the way she spoke to my brother Albert (Abdallah) in Vietnam. All I knew was that he'd gone away to this strange place; I didn't really know when he'd come back, I just assumed he would.

Mother was unable to write in English, and she had not yet taught herself to write in Arabic. So I was her arm, her language. She began dictating her nightly words, and I, barely six years old, began to write them down the best way I knew how.

Some narratives weave together facts to tell about real people and events.

Expository Mode: Inform Your Readers

Expository writing presents information and explains ideas. Most expository writing begins with a strong controlling idea or central thesis. You support the controlling idea with related ideas and details and revisit it in the conclusion.

Some common forms of expository writing are essays, encyclopedia articles, and nonfiction books. Many academic writing forms, such as research papers and literary critiques, are also expository works.

Essay

This essay explains the relationships among plant and animal species on the Galapagos Islands.

Plant Species of the Galapagos

The flora, or plants, on the Galapagos Islands include species that arrived at the islands naturally and species that people brought to the islands. Plants that occur naturally or arrive at a place by natural means are considered native species. For example, migratory birds transported seeds when they flew to the Galapagos. As a result, various plant species developed on the islands. Many of these species are endemic, meaning they aren't found anywhere else. The different species adapted to the islands' environmental conditions over time. Unfortunately, non-native plant species—those that human beings transported to the islands—pose a threat to the native ones.

Expository essays introduce a controlling idea, or thesis, at the beginning.

One of the many varieties of finches found on the Galapagos Islands ▶

Research Paper

In this paper about the two-toed sloth, the writer supports her statements with facts from research.

EFFECTS OF CAPTIVITY ON THE TWO-TOED SLOTH

Experts disagree about whether captivity benefits the two-toed sloth. Zoologist Mark Torres explains that these furry creatures, native to the tropical forests of Central and South America, "have adapted to warm temperatures. Exposure to cold could jeopardize their well-being" (91).

Others argue that zoos can prolong the sloth's lifespan by protecting the animal from harm. Because the sloth moves very slowly, it is vulnerable to predators, such as jaguars, ocelots, and eagles. According to one biologist, "Sloths in captivity survive up to twelve years longer than sloths in the wild" (Durham 67).

Expository writing often makes comparisons or presents causes and effects.

Encyclopedia Article

Nonfiction articles, such as this online encyclopedia article, are written to inform readers about a topic.

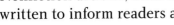

Hermit crabs, worldwide in distribution, occur in sandy- or muddy-bottomed waters and occasionally on land and in trees. The soft abdomen is asymmetrical, usually curling to the right. There are two pairs of antennae and five pairs of legs. The first pair of legs is modified to form *chelae*, or pincers—the right one usually larger—that are shaped  so as to cover the shell entrance when the animal is inside. The crab walks on its second and third pairs of legs and uses its shorter fourth and fifth pairs to grip the central column of the shell.

Abdominal appendages in the female carry the eggs, which are held there until they hatch; the young immediately pass into the water and search for their own shells. As the crab grows, it periodically leaves its shell and finds and moves into a larger one.

The article presents facts about the appearance and behavior of hermit crabs.

Descriptive Mode: Paint a Picture With Words

You can use **descriptive writing** to paint a picture with words. A good description includes plenty of sensory details so the reader knows what something looks, sounds, feels, tastes, or smells like. Vivid word choice, figurative language, and clear organization are key elements of descriptive writing.

Description can appear in many forms of writing, including stories, articles, and poetry. Writers use description to help readers imagine a person, place, or object.

Setting Description

In his memoir *Living Up the Street*, Gary Soto describes the industrial neighborhood in Fresno, California, where he grew up.

82 ᔫ GARY SOTO

Across the street was Coleman Pickles, while on the right of us was a junkyard that dealt in metals—aluminum, iron, sheet metal, and copper stripped from refrigerators. Down the street was Sun-Maid Raisin, where a concrete tower rose above the scraggly sycamores that lined Braly Street. Many of our family worked at Sun-Maid: Grandfather and Grandmother, Father, three uncles, an aunt, and even a dog whose job was to accompany my grandfather, a security guard, on patrol. Then there was Challenge Milk, a printing shop, and the 7-Up Company where we stole sodas. Down the alley was a broom factory and Western Book Distributor, a place where our future step-father worked at packing books into cardboard boxes, something he would do for fifteen years before the company left town for Oregon.

Soto describes the neighborhood stores and factories of his childhood.

Character Sketch

Barbara Kingsolver portrays a fictional couple, Esperanza and Estevan, in her novel *The Bean Trees*.

THE BEAN TREES | Barbara Kingsolver 107

Esperanza and Estevan were their names. It led you to expect twins, not a married couple, and really there was something twinnish about them. They were both small and dark, with the same high-set, watching eyes and strong-boned faces I'd admired in the bars and gas stations and postcards of the Cherokee Nation. Mattie had told me that more than half the people in Guatemala were Indians. I had no idea.

But where Estevan's smallness made him seem compact and springy, as though he might have steel bars inside where most people had flab and sawdust, Esperanza just seemed to have shrunk. Exactly like a wool sweater washed in hot.

> Barbara Kingsolver uses physical details to create a vivid portrait of her characters.

Travel Diary

In this excerpt from *Bill Bryson's African Diary,* the author describes an outdoor market in the city of Kisumu in western Kenya.

AFRICAN DIARY

Jubilee Market is an extraordinary place—crowded, noisy, extremely colorful—with large, open-sided halls specializing in wet fish, dried fish, vegetables, nuts and other farm commodities. I had never seen such luscious produce more beautifully arrayed. Every stall was a picture of abundance and sumptuousness, every peanut and tomato and chili more neatly arranged and more richly colored than any I had seen before anywhere. . . .

Beyond the main food halls was a sort of bazaar of dark alleys containing tiny shops—cubicles really—selling everything from bolts of cloth to small electrical items.

> Precise nouns, verbs, and modifiers help readers picture Jubilee Market vividly.

Expressive Mode: Share Your Feelings

Expressive writing is a powerful tool for saying what you think about the world and your experiences in it. Many expressive writing forms, such as journals, give writers the freedom to choose the style and structure that works best for their purpose. Expressive writing emphasizes the writer's unique voice.

When you are writing in this mode, you express your thoughts and connect intimately with your audience. Common forms for expressive writing include journals and diaries, personal letters, songs, poetry, and blogs.

Journal Entry

Professional and amateur writers often record their daily lives and personal feelings in private journals.

June 16, 2007

    Well, the day has finally come—six hours from now, I'll be a high-school graduate! (I still can't believe I passed my chemistry final after all.)

    The whole house is in an uproar today. Uncle Chuck and Aunt Angelica flew in last night, and Mom just left to pick up Grandma and Grandpa even though the ceremony doesn't start until this afternoon.

    Last night at dinner, Dad told me in front of everyone how proud he was that I'm the first person in our family to be going to college. I felt kind of embarrassed and proud at the same time. It's so weird to think that in a few months I'll be a hundred miles away.

The writer tells how he feels about graduating from high school.

E-mail

People sometimes send e-mail messages to express their thoughts and feelings, or just to stay in touch with friends and family.

Hi, Tony,

How's it going, son? I'm sure you're busy getting settled into your new routine. Hope your first week of college hasn't been too crazy. How are classes? Did you manage to switch out of that 8:00 Psychology section?

Not much exciting news here. Your mom and I have been working out in the yard a lot while the weather's still warm. It feels strange not having you around. We miss you a lot. Drop us a line when you have a chance.

Love,
Dad

The writer uses an informal tone to communicate his feelings to his son.

Poem

The free-verse poem "Greenhouse in the Rain" presents sensory details linked to emotional experience.

Greenhouse in the Rain
Jocelyn Heath

I listen to the rain falling
like fingers drumming the plastic
stretched overhead
in chill gray monotony.
Too cool, unseasonably wet;
my stiffened fingers fumble
along green stalks and stems.
Between the leaves lay dying
buds, half-brown and crumbling
like the melancholy of lost afternoons.
The jaws of my scissors
systematically clip, shrinking
geraniums and squash.
Tomato stalks—Black Krim
and Better Boy—ooze
the smell of steaks from their wounds,
smearing their essence
on my fingertips. Lifting
my hands to my face,
I breathe in the life pouring forth—
free from weighty decay and death;
making room for new growth.

The writer tells what she felt while working in the greenhouse.

Persuasive Mode: Influence Your Readers

You can use **persuasive writing** to present your opinions and try to influence your readers' thinking and actions. Persuasive writing presents an opinion and supports it with reasons and evidence. It includes appeals to the reader's logic, emotions, and sense of right and wrong.

Essays, editorials, letters to the editor, and reviews are common persuasive forms.

Opinion Essay

In an opinion essay, you explain what you think about something and support your opinion with facts and examples.

We Must Face Up to Global Warming

Let's talk about a supposedly trivial topic: the weather. Last week my friends and I strolled through town to the movie theater, enjoying the warm, summery breezes— even though it was the first week of December. Perhaps you've seen the news reports about how the number of Category 4 and Category 5 hurricanes has increased dramatically over the past decade. Maybe you remember the fun of "snow days" when you were a little kid, and you wonder why we never get much snow in the wintertime now. These situations are far from trivial. They're the signs of a major problem: global warming.

The writer gets readers' attention before stating his opinion.

Editorial

In this editorial, the writer talks about an issue her readers are familiar with—then asks readers to take action.

Save Paper Electronically

Everybody talks about the environment, but just talking about it isn't enough. When it comes to recycling and conservation, it's important to remember that even small changes can make a big difference. One change we could make here at Grover High School is to cut back on unnecessary paper use.

Think about it. Every day in class, teachers distribute numerous handouts that end up crumpled and forgotten at the bottom of students' backpacks. Flyers and announcements waste a lot of paper as well. According to school administrative staff, Grover High goes through about 50 reams of paper per week.

Teachers and administrators should cut down on wasted paper by posting announcements and class materials on the Grover High Web site exclusively. In the absence of paper notices, students would learn to check the Web site regularly.

The writer recommends a specific action to solve the problem.

Review

This writer's movie review presents an opinion and supports it with details.

Winged Migration
Directed by Jacques Perrin

You might wonder how an entire movie about birds could possibly be interesting. Surprisingly, director Jacques Perrin has managed to make an everyday experience, watching birds fly, into one that few moviegoers will soon forget. This documentary, which was filmed over a period of four years, forces the viewer to really "see" the beauty of birds in flight. As Perrin followed the migratory paths of various winged creatures on all seven continents, he managed to portray this ritual as a matter of survival. Viewers watch as birds such as Greylag geese, Andean condors, puffins, Eurasian cranes, and white storks make their way to a chosen destination.

The writer supports his opinion with details about the movie.

A Matter of Facts

featuring **Barbara Kingsolver**

"To formulate a new question that hasn't been asked before, and then to set about solving it, to do original research to find the way to an answer—that's what I do when I write a book."

Research and Writing

Think of research as an organized reality check. You find out how things really are in the world—either by observing nature and people directly or by learning about what other observers have found. Once you've gathered the facts (and organized them in your own mind), you can either write *about* your research or *incorporate* your research into your writing.

When you write *about* your research, you simply tell your readers, in a structured, organized way, what you've learned and its significance. This chapter will explain how to pull information together into a research paper, following the process on page 431.

But don't think that research is just for nonfiction. Many fiction authors *incorporate* extensive research into their writing. On pages 427–430, writer Barbara Kingsolver describes how she researched *The Poisonwood Bible*, her novel set in Africa in the late 1950s.

In Love with the Details:
Researching *The Poisonwood Bible*

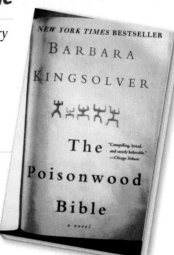

In this best-selling novel, Kingsolver tells the story of an American family's journey to the Congo in Central Africa in 1959. The story is narrated by the wife and four daughters of Nathan Price, a fierce missionary, and unfolds over the course of three decades.

It took me many years to write *The Poisonwood Bible*, most of them spent on research which fell into several categories.

Most obviously, I read a lot of books about
5 the political, social, and natural history of
Africa and the Congo. Some of these are listed in a bibliography at
the end of the novel; dozens more are not. Sometimes, reading a whole
densely written book on, say, the formation and dissolution of indigenous
political parties during the Congolese independence, or an account of
10 the life histories of Central African venomous snakes, would move me
only a sentence or two forward in my understanding of my subject. But
every sentence mattered. I knew it would take years, and tried to be
patient. Some of my sources were famous and well-written, but most were
obscurities, like the quirky self-published memoirs written by missionaries
15 to the Congo in the 50s and 60s, which I'd sometimes find in used
bookstores. These were gems, rendering clear details of missionary life
and attitudes from the era.

Researching *The Poisonwood Bible,* continued

I read, and re-read daily, from the King James Bible. It gave me the rhythm of the Price family's speech, the frame of reference for their beliefs, and
20 countless plot ideas.

Likewise, I began nearly every writing day by perusing a huge old two-volume Kikongo-French dictionary, compiled early in the century (by a missionary, of course). Slowly I began to grasp the music and subtlety of this amazing African language, with its infinite capacity for being misunderstood and mistranslated.

25 One of the novel's challenges was the matter of capturing the language of teenage females from the Southeastern U.S. in the late 1950s. Since I was barely alive then, this was also foreign territory. Teenage speech is stereotyped and notoriously ephemeral; if I'd
30 just guessed, it would have sounded inauthentic. This stumped me, until I hit paydirt in a used bookstore in Boston: 35 pounds (I had to mail them home) of *Life, Look,* and *Saturday Evening Post*
35 magazines from 1958–1961. I spent hours immersed in the news, attitudes, and advertisements of these years. Slowly the voices of my novel began to emerge, and Rachel Price [a teenage
40 daughter of the family portrayed in the novel]—like Athena—was born fully formed, with every hair in place. . . .

The country known today as the Democratic Republic of the Congo was a Belgian colony in the 1950s, the time of Kingsolver's novel.

Another kind of research I did . . . was in the domain of life experience.
I happen to have spent a brief portion of my childhood (1963) in a
45 small village in central Congo, and this undoubtedly gave that place
permanent importance in my mind.

I have strong sensory memories of playing with village children and
exploring the jungle. When I began the novel, my parents shared
photographs and journals from that time, which helped stir my own
50 memories. My parents were not missionaries, but we met several
missionary families in Africa (though none quite like the Prices, I'm
happy to report), so I knew a little of that life. But the bottom line is this:
I was a child, in 1963, and understood only about a thimbleful of what
was happening around me in the Congo. The thematic material of The
55 Poisonwood Bible is serious, adult stuff. I wrote the book, not because
of a brief adventure I had in place of second grade, but because as an
adult I'm interested in cultural imperialism and post-colonial history. I
had to approach the subject in an adult way.

Books can provide only verbally rendered information. I also needed
60 to know things about Africa that must be learned first-hand. I made
research trips into Western and Central Africa (as near as I could get
to Mobutu's Zaire), and kept detailed journals on sounds, smells,
textures, tastes, and the sort of domestic trivia that seldom shows up
in important books.

65 Whenever possible I stayed with residents of the area I was visiting, and
I always volunteered to cook dinner so I could walk to a village market

Researching *The Poisonwood Bible,* continued

with coins in hand and face the daunting, educational experience of
bargaining and bringing home the ingredients of a decent meal. I asked
a lot of questions that many Africans surely found amusing and too

70 personal, but once in a while I struck up a friendship. I'm especially
grateful for these—the Senegalese mother, the University student in
Cotonou, who suffered my curiosity for days on end, frankly giving me
views on religion, history, and family life that would permanently alter my
universe.

75 I spent time in museums, here and abroad, studying exhibits of African
religion and material culture. I lost myself in the amazing Okapi
diorama in the American Museum of Natural History. And I spent one
unforgettable afternoon in the Reptile House of the San Diego Zoo,
watching a green mamba.

80 So there you have it: what I did for many
seasons before publishing my
Poisonwood Bible. If this
laundry list of disparate
observations seems

85 excessive or odd, I
can only say that
this is what it means
to be a novelist. You have
to be madly in love with the details.

The green mamba
is a tree-dwelling
snake of Africa. ▼

The Research Process

Whether you're writing a novel like Barbara Kingsolver or a research paper for history class, the research process is pretty similar. Below is a quick preview. The three parts of this chapter will show you the process in detail with a model research paper on a new medical discovery.

► ## Gather Information

Digging Up the Facts Before you start writing, you need to focus your topic and decide what question or questions you want to explore. Then you gather information from a variety of sources, taking notes to record the most important facts.

► ## Organize and Digest Information

Making Sense of Your Notes Next you need to organize your information and make sure you understand it. You decide which questions you'd like to explore further. Finally, you use your notes to create an outline—a plan for how to present your ideas.

► ## Present Information

Packaging Your Ideas The last step is the most exciting— writing about or with your research findings. If you want to jazz up your presentation, look on pages 486–489 to find tips for creating a multimedia report.

Find out more about Barbara Kingsolver and other authors who rely on research for their writing.

Digging Up the Facts

Your favorite band is in town. How do you find out the date, time, and location of their concert? Maybe you'll dig up the details online, in the newspaper, over the phone—or in all three places! To research any kind of topic, you can gather the information you need from a lot of different sources.

What Do You Look For? Where Do You Look?

For school assignments, you will probably not be entirely free to choose your topic. Your teacher will have an area in mind: the Civil War, let's say, or adaptation of organisms to their surroundings. Still, use what choice you have to suit your research to your interests:

- Focus and narrow your topic to a specific aspect of the general area you have been assigned.

- Write research questions to pinpoint what you want to know about the topic.

Once you have research questions down, check out a variety of different sources to answer them, and keep detailed notes of the information you find. Remember that not all information is found in books.

"**W**e have forgotten what *original source* means. It's not quoting an expert who says a rattlesnake has fangs—technically, it's looking in that snake's mouth yourself. If the snake bites you, you can stop looking."

FOCUS POINT Look at the photo. Choose a research question. Name at least three places you could look for answers. Include at least one "original source."

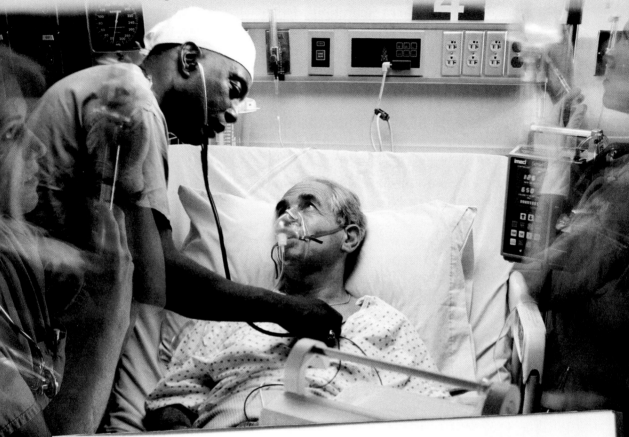

Research Questions

• What kind of training do you need to become a paramedic?

• What's it like to work in the emergency room of a hospital?

• How can research on animals help to save human lives?

• What are the latest advances in the field of organ transplants?

• How are rising medical costs affecting the average person?

Develop a Game Plan

Writing an effective research report takes a lot of thought and preparation. Before you start researching, decide what you want to accomplish with your writing and plan the best way to reach your goal.

Choose Your Form, Audience, and Purpose

Reports aren't the only form of writing that involve research. Writers also research information for articles, biographies, even fiction and poetry.

For this nonfiction essay, Barbara Kingsolver researched information about the scientist Nikolai Vavilov.

Essay

46   A FIST IN THE EYE OF GOD | Barbara Kingsolver

Kingsolver's purpose is to inform. That's why she uses so many facts.

Nikolai Vavilov was an astounding man of science, and probably the greatest plant explorer who has ever lived. He spoke seven languages and could recite books by Pushkin from memory. In his travels through sixty-four countries between 1916 and 1940, he saw more crop diversity than anyone had known existed, and founded the world's largest seed collection.

As he combed continents looking for primitive crop varieties, Vavilov noticed a pattern: Genetic variation was not evenly distributed. In a small region of Ethiopia he found hundreds of kinds of ancient wheat known only to that place. A single New World plateau is astonishingly rich in corn varieties, while another one is rolling in different kinds of potatoes. . . . By looking through his lens of genetics, Vavilov began to pinpoint the places in the world where human agriculture had originated. More modern genetic research has largely borne out his hypothesis that agriculture emerged independently in the places where the most diverse and ancient crop types, known as land races, are to be found: in the Near East, northern China, Mesoamerica, and Ethiopia.

In this short story, Kingsolver relates an incident involving an exotic lizard. Which details do you think the author probably researched?

Short Story

COVERED BRIDGES | BARBARA KINGSOLVER ~ 59

Lena is a specialist in toxicology and operates a poison hotline at the county hospital. People from all over the state call her in desperation when their children have consumed baby aspirin or a houseplant or what have you, and she helps them. It might sound morbid, but no one could be more full of joy of life than Lena, even where her job is concerned. She is magnificent at parties. Her best story is about a Gila monster named Hilda, which served a brief term as the pet of the Norman Clinderback family. Hilda was an illegal gift from an uncle in Tucson, and crossed our nation in a fiberglass container of the type meant for transporting cats. The Gila monster, by all rights a stranger to this part of Indiana, is a highly poisonous lizard, but is thought by most experts to be too lazy to pose a threat to humans. The incident precipitating the call to [Lena] involved a July 4th picnic in which Hilda was teased beyond endurance with a piece of fried chicken. Hilda had a bite of Norm Junior's thumb instead.

Kingsolver's purpose is to entertain. Still she uses **facts** about the Gila monster to help readers better understand the event.

The type of research you do, as well as the research details that you include in your writing, will be determined by your form, audience, and purpose as much as by your topic. It's good to get clear from the beginning not just what you're researching, but how you'll be presenting it, and to whom.

Develop a Game Plan, continued

Choose and Focus Your Topic

You've made the right choice for a research topic if you can answer "yes" to each of these questions:

- Does the topic interest you?

- Will you be able to find enough information about the topic?

- Is your topic focused and specific?

Look at the planning chart that Anita prepared below. How did she narrow her topic?

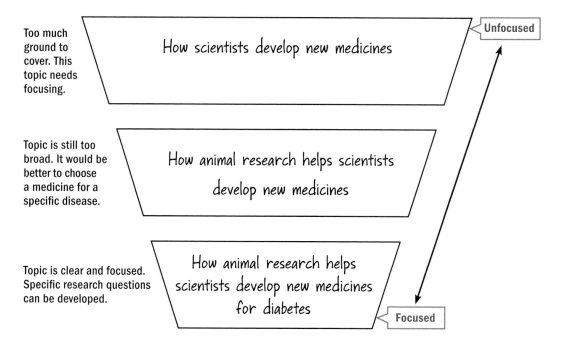

Too much ground to cover. This topic needs focusing.

How scientists develop new medicines

Unfocused

Topic is still too broad. It would be better to choose a medicine for a specific disease.

How animal research helps scientists develop new medicines

Topic is clear and focused. Specific research questions can be developed.

How animal research helps scientists develop new medicines for diabetes

Focused

Presearch and Put Together an FATP Chart

To really nail down your topic, and before diving into in-depth research, it helps to do a little *presearch*—you don't know what's out there until you look around a bit.

The Web is great for presearch. A little time spent Web-surfing at the beginning can help you choose a topic that is interesting, specific and about which there is enough information.

Through her Internet presearch, Anita found out about this new treatment for diabetes using Gila-monster saliva! Now the research project came together in her head and she was able to write her FATP Chart.

FATP Chart

Form: research report

Audience: my teacher and classmates

Topic: how studying the Gila monster helped scientists develop a new treatment for diabetes

Purpose: to inform readers about the new diabetes drug that scientists developed

List Research Questions

Next put together some research questions—these are the questions you want your report to "answer." Start out with a main research question, and then break it down into more-specific subquestions.

Vague

Main Question:
What is the best way to deal with having diabetes?

Sub-Questions:
1. What is diabetes like?
2. What can you do about it?
3. What are some treatments?

Specific

Main Question:
Is the new diabetes drug developed from Gila monster saliva better than traditional treatments?

Sub-Questions:
1. What is it like to live with diabetes?
2. How do doctors treat diabetes?
3. What did scientists discover about Gila monster saliva?

Information Sources

A *source* is a place where you go to get something. Three kinds of sources are:

- the world around you—all you have to do is make a direct observation. This is not always possible (and, if you're researching rattlesnakes, may not be a good idea). But if you're researching the behavior of, say, butterflies in your backyard, open your eyes and look at your backyard!

- experts—people who know a lot about a topic, through study or through experience

- published materials which may be printed, transmitted electronically over the Internet, or captured in media such as films or sound recordings.

Getting Info from Experts

For Anita's paper on the new medicine for diabetes, an expert might be a doctor who specializes in diabetes or someone who has diabetes and has lived with it. Interviews are a great way to get first-hand information and eyewitness accounts of an event. You can interview experts in person, by phone, or through e-mail.

How to Conduct an Interview

1. Explain the purpose of the interview when you contact the person to set up an appointment.

2. Plan your questions in advance. Ask questions that will get more than just a "yes" or "no" response.

3. Always be respectful and courteous to the person you are interviewing.

4. Follow your plan, but be flexible. Your subject might bring up important issues you hadn't thought of before. Ask follow-up questions if you need to know more.

5. Tape-record your subject's responses or take detailed notes.

Getting Info from Published Sources

Most published research resources are available both in print and over the Internet. Different types of sources contain different types of information.

Type of Source	Print	Web	Description and Uses
almanac	√	√	An almanac offers a compact summary of information, such as facts and statistics. Use it to find facts about history, geography, and politics.
encyclopedia	√	√	The most important general information about a topic is in an encyclopedia. Use it to get a broad overview of a topic and verify facts.
magazines and newspapers	√	√	These periodicals contain current news and trends. Use them when you want to learn about recent local, national, and world events.
nonfiction books	√		Books include in-depth information on a topic. Use them to get deep knowledge of a narrow topic.
online database		√	Databases give access to regularly updated facts, statistics, or a bibliography on a topic. Use them to check facts or to locate sources of information on a topic.
primary sources, such as a historical document, diary, letter, speech, etc.	√	√	Primary sources document past events as they were happening. Use them to gain first-hand information about historical or geographically distant people and events.
reference books	√		These books give detailed information on specialized topics. They are useful for gathering and checking facts.
trade journals	√	√	Professional and academic research often appears in journals. These are usually very technical and kind of hard to read, but you can learn what the experts are thinking.
Web sites		√	The Web offers a wide range of information, from general to quite specific. Locate sites that give an overview of your topic and link to other sites with more sources of information.

Get to Know Your Library

Unless you're researching librarians or library design, you won't be doing much direct observation at the library. But libraries have Internet access and tons of print materials, making them very source-rich environments. They also have reference librarians—they may not be expert in the topic you are researching, but they are all-around information experts.

Finding What You're Looking For

Knowing where and how to find materials in the library is key to spending your research time wisely. Here's how research materials are arranged in most libraries:

- **Nonfiction books**—by subject area using call numbers based on the Dewey Decimal System

000–099	General Interest
100–199	Philosophy
200–299	Religion
300–399	Social Sciences
400–499	Language
500–599	Pure Sciences
600–699	Technology
700–799	The Arts
800–899	Literature
900–999	History and Geography

- **Biographies**—grouped with other nonfiction by the last name of the person the book is about

- **Periodicals**—alphabetically by title

- **Reference books**—in their own section or grouped with other nonfiction.

Searching on the Online Catalog

You can use the online catalog to search for print and multimedia resources by title, author, subject, or keyword. With so many sources available, be sure to focus your search to avoid "information overload"!

1 A subject search shows you how many sources are available about your topic. Type in your subject to see what's available, and then choose the ones you want.

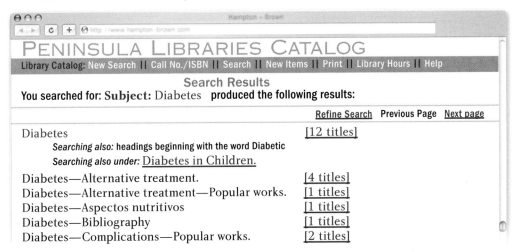

PENINSULA LIBRARIES CATALOG

Library Catalog: New Search || Call No./ISBN || Search || New Items || Print || Library Hours || Help

Search Results

You searched for: **Subject:** Diabetes produced the following results:

Refine Search   Previous Page   Next page

Diabetes	[12 titles]
Searching also: headings beginning with the word Diabetic	
Searching also under: Diabetes in Children.	
Diabetes—Alternative treatment.	[4 titles]
Diabetes—Alternative treatment—Popular works.	[1 titles]
Diabetes—Aspectos nutritivos	[1 titles]
Diabetes—Bibliography	[1 titles]
Diabetes—Complications—Popular works.	[2 titles]

2 Once you've decided which specific subjects to look at, read the titles and locations of sources to find the best ones. The location and call number help to tell you whether the source was written for adults, for teens, or for children.

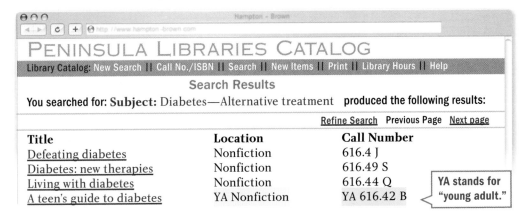

PENINSULA LIBRARIES CATALOG

Library Catalog: New Search || Call No./ISBN || Search || New Items || Print || Library Hours || Help

Search Results

You searched for: **Subject:** Diabetes—Alternative treatment produced the following results:

Refine Search   Previous Page   Next page

Title	Location	Call Number
Defeating diabetes	Nonfiction	616.4 J
Diabetes: new therapies	Nonfiction	616.49 S
Living with diabetes	Nonfiction	616.44 Q
A teen's guide to diabetes	YA Nonfiction	YA 616.42 B

YA stands for "young adult."

Get to Know Your Library, continued

Searching on the Online Catalog, continued

3 Read the **catalog summary** for an overview of the contents. If the source looks promising, check the **status** to see if it's available. Then write down the call number and location or print out the information.

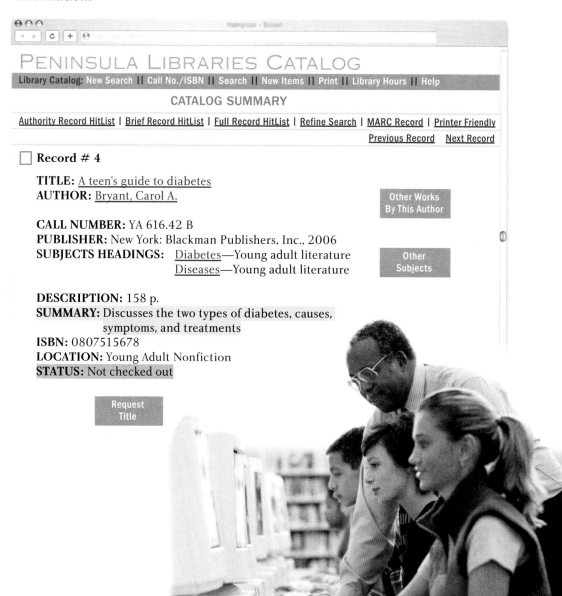

PENINSULA LIBRARIES CATALOG

Library Catalog: New Search || Call No./ISBN || Search || New Items || Print || Library Hours || Help

CATALOG SUMMARY

Authority Record HitList | Brief Record HitList | Full Record HitList | Refine Search | MARC Record | Printer Friendly

Previous Record   Next Record

☐ **Record # 4**

TITLE: A teen's guide to diabetes
AUTHOR: Bryant, Carol A.

Other Works By This Author

CALL NUMBER: YA 616.42 B
PUBLISHER: New York: Blackman Publishers, Inc., 2006
SUBJECTS HEADINGS: Diabetes—Young adult literature
Diseases—Young adult literature

Other Subjects

DESCRIPTION: 158 p.
SUMMARY: Discusses the two types of diabetes, causes, symptoms, and treatments
ISBN: 0807515678
LOCATION: Young Adult Nonfiction
STATUS: Not checked out

Request Title

Selecting Print Sources

Chances are you're going to find more materials than you can possibly read. Just as important as your reading skills will be your "weeding" skills—your ability to sort through piles of materials quickly to zero in on the ones that will be most useful in your research.

Zeroing In: Books

Many of the books you find on your topic won't have the exact information you need. To figure out quickly if the book has what you're looking for:

- Read the library catalog summaries carefully.

- Skim the dust jacket to learn more about a book's contents.

- Read the table of contents to see what topics are covered.

Contents

1 What is Diabetes?	5
2 The History of Diabetes	9
3 Diagnosing Diabetes	16
4 Why Me?	20

The **chapter titles** give a general idea of what the book covers.

- Look up a specific topic in the index at the back of the book.

Index

diabetes
    camps for people with, 124
    causes of, 6, 10, 89
    current research on, 134–135
    diagnosing, 16–19
diet, 13, 14, 15, 26, 27, 28, 31, 32, 38, 39, 65, 66

Topics and **subtopics** are listed in alphabetical order.

Selecting Print Sources, continued

Zeroing In: Articles and Essays

You can also use time-saving tricks to "weed" through articles and essays:

- Look for a summary at the beginning. In scientific journals, the summary is called an **abstract**.

- Skim through the title, headings, and the first sentence in each paragraph to find the main ideas.

- Scan for keywords that relate to your topic.

- Read the conclusion closely. It may sum up the main ideas.

Southern Journal of Medicine, 9.4, April 2004

New Hope for Diabetics
Luis T. Morena, M.D.

Abstract

Type II diabetics have traditionally managed the disease through diet, exercise, and medication. Medication is sometimes ineffective in controlling insulin levels precisely. Clinical studies of the saliva of the Gila monster have found that it contains a hormone which can be used to treat patients with Type II diabetes.

An **abstract** summarizes ideas in a scientific article.

Diabetes in the United States

Look for **headings** and **keywords** that relate to your topic.

Many Americans suffer from Type II diabetes. In fact, so many people in the United States have this disease that it is considered an epidemic. Most Type II diabetics can partially manage their disease through diet. Diabetics are frequently advised to avoid foods that are high in sugar and

---

Beyond Paper: Electronic Sources

Books and periodicals are important in research, but you can get a lot of information without ever opening a book! Just use electronic sources, which store vast amounts of information and include search tools to help you locate information quickly. Electronic sources often include audiovisual information as well.

Some electronic sources are:

- **DVDs** Look for documentaries or educational programs that relate to your topic. Often programs originally on TV are available later on DVDs.

- **CDs** Listen to music, lectures, or books on tape.

- **CD-ROMs** Compact discs aren't just for music and video games. They can also contain information in text or audio format. Because they store a lot of data in one place, CD-ROMs often contain lengthy works, such as encyclopedias.

At the library, the reference librarian can show you how to use these specialized sources.

CyberSources: the World Wide Web

The World Wide Web is your connection to virtually unlimited information on every topic imaginable. And it's not all words, words, words on the Web. Many Web sites feature images, sound files, or video clips.

You can get onto this "information superhighway" from anywhere there is a computer with Internet access—the library, your classroom, your home, or a laptop at the corner coffeehouse.

As with any highway, though, it will only be useful to you if you know how to drive safely in very heavy traffic.

The Web: Time Saver or Time Waster?

The advantage of the World Wide Web is that it has more information than any library could possibly hold. A 10-minute visit to the World Wide Web can let you know what books are available at the public library in the next town, or what research is being conducted halfway across the world.

If you know how to use it, the Web can be a big time saver. Unfortunately, doing research on the Web can also be difficult because there's so much information out there. Finding good sites can be like looking for a needle in a haystack.

If you waste hours online without finding anything useful, you'll end up feeling frustrated. That's why it's important to be a smart searcher.

Results 1–10 out of 9,000,000

"One down, only 8,999,999 to go..."

Keeping Safe While You Search

The Internet makes it easy for people to find and exchange information—and information on the Web is available to anyone, anywhere. That's mostly a good thing, but it's important to be extra careful about protecting your personal information online. Here are some basics:

- **NEVER** give out your personal information to strangers online. Period. People can easily misrepresent themselves on the Internet, so don't take any chances.

- What if you want to make an online purchase or subscribe to a publication? Before you give out contact information and credit card numbers, check with an older relative. Also, check the site's security features.

- Don't give out personal information in chat rooms or on discussion boards, or when posting comments on a blog. These types of sites aren't reliable resources anyway.

- If you do stumble onto a Web site that looks fishy, just click the back button on your Web browser or, if necessary, close the browser window.

Accessing a Database

A database is a huge computer file of information related to a particular subject. Many databases are Web-accessible. Databases also have search tools. You may find information of two types:

1. specific information about a particular topic

This site contains many types of information about Gila monsters.

2. references to other materials with information about a topic

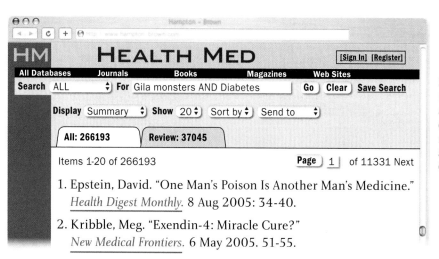

Search results show a bibliography of books and magazine articles about Gila monsters.

Here are some tips for smart searching with databases:

- Before you start, invest a little time in reading the guidelines for using the database.

- Do specific subject and keyword searches.

- If a bibliography-type database includes summaries, read the summaries carefully to see if the article looks promising. Check icons or other indicators to see if the full article is available on the database.

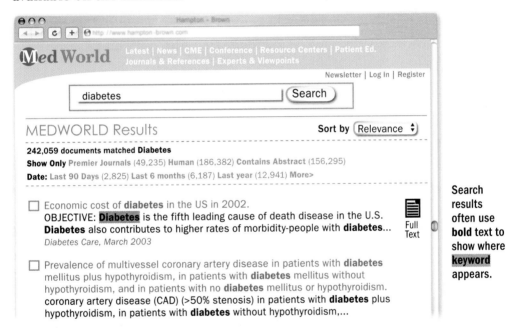

Search results often use **bold** text to show where **keyword** appears.

- Save your searches to a separate document on your computer, so you know which subjects or keywords you have looked for.

- Finally, be sure to save any leads that look promising. You can save them within the database, print out articles or summaries, or e-mail search results to yourself.

Using a Search Engine

A search engine is a powerful computer program capable of "reading" *very* fast through the entire World Wide Web, looking for anything you tell it to.

Usually, the problem with these searches is that they return more information than you know what to do with. To focus your search, try these techniques:

- Make keywords as specific as possible to limit your results.

- When searching for a phrase, like "diabetes symptoms," use quotation marks to group words together. That way you won't get results for Web sites about symptoms for other diseases.

- Don't type in questions. Type in the answer you want to find, such as "Gila monster's habitat."

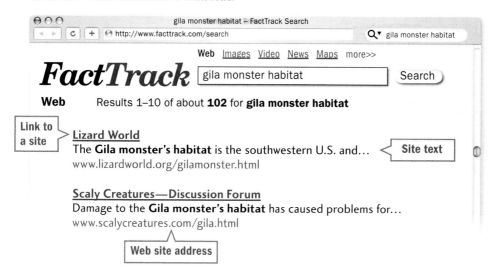

Scan the results and click on a link to go directly to the site.

Saving Search Results

When you find a good Web site, you'll probably want to access it again. Keep track of useful sites using these techniques:

- Use your browser's "Bookmark" or "Favorites" feature to save good links. Organize your links in folders so you can find them easily.

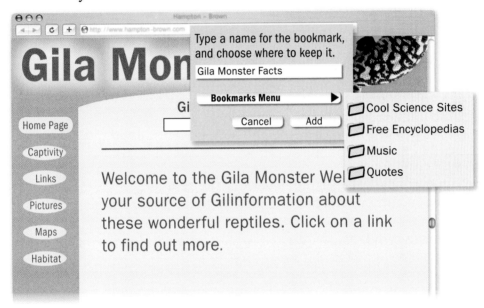

- Copy useful links into a separate document to use as your own handy personal "directory."

- Print out Web pages so you can refer to the paper copies when you're not at your computer.

Evaluating Sources

Part of being a smart searcher is recognizing that not all sources are trustworthy. This is especially true of online sources, because it's fairly easy to put up a Web page. Whatever source you use, always ask yourself how reliable it is.

Evaluating Print Sources

Carefully evaluate print sources by asking these questions:

1. Is it up-to-date?

In many fields, such as science and medicine, information becomes quickly outdated as new discoveries are made. Check the publication date and use the most up-to-date sources to keep your facts accurate.

2. Who wrote it?

Have you ever heard the saying "Consider the source"? Sometimes an author may slant the facts to fit a personal bias or prejudice. Choose sources that are objective and don't have an axe to grind.

You also need to think about whether or not the author is qualified to write about the topic. For example, which would be a more reliable source for an article about a space flight to Mars: an aerospace engineer or a heart surgeon?

3. What's the purpose of the publication?

Was the publication written to entertain or to inform? If you are researching facts about desert reptiles, an entertaining feature about pet lizards is probably not as useful as an encyclopedia article about how lizards survive in the desert.

Evaluating Web Sites

While many Web sites are carefully researched and checked, many others are put up by people without any special knowledge or expertise and contain incorrect information.

When you look at online sources, ask the same questions you ask for print sources, plus a few more:

1. Does it look and sound professional?
   Look for content that is well-written, organized, and free of obvious errors.

2. When was it last updated?
   Many sites include this information on the home page.

3. What kind of site is it?
   The last letters of a site's URL, or Web address, tell what kind of site it is.

If the URL ends in . . .	The site is maintained by . . .
.gov	a federal government organization
.mil	the U.S. military
.edu	a school, college, or university
.org	a professional organization
a state abbreviation (such as CA or TX) followed by .us	a state government
.biz	a business
.com or .net	a business or an individual

Generally, sites maintained by the government, colleges and universities, and professional organizations are more accurate than commercial or personal sites.

4. Is the information confirmed by other Web sites?
   Even when you're using a source that seems very reliable, it's still a good idea to double-check your facts with other sources.

Taking Good Notes

As you gather information from a variety of sources, you're not going to be able to keep it all in your head! So, you'll need a system for recording and organizing what you learn:

- As you come across important facts and ideas in your sources, write them on index cards or in a computer file.

- Keep your notes organized by using a heading for each card or for each group of related notes.

- On each card, or at the end of each note, identify the source (by title or author) and the page where you got the information.

- Separately, also record complete publishing information (title, author, publisher, etc.) for every source you use. You'll need this information for the Works Cited section of your report. (See pages 482–485 for more details.)

Effective note-taking involves a mixture of **paraphrasing**, **summarizing**, and **direct quotation**.

Paraphrasing

When you paraphrase, you use your own words to restate what an author has written. Using your own words is a good way to make sure you understand the ideas. To paraphrase:

1 **Read the source carefully.**

I Am a Gila Monster

Gila monsters are slow moving, non-aggressive lizards. Their venom is quite effective in subduing small prey and is delivered from grooves in the animal's teeth. Gila monsters eat only several times a year. The rest of the time their pancreases are turned off. When they eat, they secrete a hormone that turns their pancreases back on. Unlike poisonous snakes that "inject" their venom, Gilas have to chew on their prey to move the venom into the wound.

2 **Record the important information <u>in your own words</u>.**
Use a heading on the card to help you keep the notes
organized. Make sure each entry relates to the heading.
Use separate cards or headings as needed.

Disorganized

> —Gilas are poisonous.
> —They don't need to eat
>   much.
>
>   I am Gila Monster, 37

Organized

> <u>Gila Monsters—Eating habits</u>   ◁ Heading
> A Gila monster does not eat
> very often. Its digestive system
> processes food very slowly.   Source:
>   book title
>   I am Gila Monster, 37 ◁ and page
>   number

Use your own sentence patterns and vocabulary. Do not use
language that is too close to that of the source unless you
think it's necessary to use a direct quote (see page 458).

Too close to the source

> <u>Gila Monsters—Eating habits</u>
> Gila monsters eat only a few
> times a year. The rest of the
> time, the pancreas is turned
> off.
>   I am Gila Monster, 37

The researcher's own words

> <u>Gila Monsters—Eating habits</u>
> Gila monsters don't eat very
> often. They have a special
> digestive system that is only
> active when they eat.
>   I am Gila Monster, 37

Try to keep your paraphrase about the same
length as the original text or a bit shorter.

Gila monsters live under rocks
and in sandy soils with shrubs. ▼

About the right length

> <u>Gila Monsters—Eating habits</u>
> Gila monsters are poisonous
> lizards that live in the desert.
> They have a digestive system
> that becomes active only after
> they eat.
>   I am Gila Monster, 37

Taking Good Notes, continued

Summarizing

When you summarize an article or passage, you find and condense the most important ideas, leaving out most of the details. To summarize, follow these steps:

❶ Read Your Source Carefully
To locate the most important ideas, look at titles, headings, and key words in *italics* or **bold** type. In an article or a longer passage, determine the main idea of each paragraph.

❷ Keep Track of Important Ideas and Details
You can make notes in a graphic organizer to hold your thinking and then use it as a guide for your summary.

> **Main Idea:** Animal hormones can be used to develop treatments for human diseases.
>
> **Detail:** During the 1980s, Dr. Eng began studying the saliva of Gila monsters.

Or, if you have your own copy of the source, you can highlight ideas. Otherwise, try using sticky notes to mark key points.

The Gila's Healing Hormone
Tricia Fitzpatrick

During the 1980s, Dr. John Eng did extensive research on hormones in a laboratory in the Bronx in New York. Eng hoped to discover how animal hormones could be used to develop treatments for human diseases. Dr. Eng began studying the saliva of the Gila monster, a venomous lizard native to the Southwest, after hearing that people who had been bitten by the monster produced extra insulin. Through his research, Eng discovered that the Gila monster's saliva contains a hormone that is remarkably similar to a human hormone that triggers insulin release. Eng's discovery was used to create a new drug to treat Type II diabetes.

Plagiarism

Plagiarism is the act of passing off someone else's words or ideas as your own. Some writers do this on purpose. At 2 a.m. the night before a paper is due, it can be very tempting to copy something from the Internet and hand it in.

More often, writers plagiarize accidentally. If you haven't taken careful notes, it's easy to forget that you did not in fact come up with that great sentence yourself, but copied it straight out of a book and should have used quotation marks!

Either way, consequences can be harsh. Student writers might fail an assignment or get kicked out of school. Professionals can lose their jobs. Any writer who plagiarizes risks his or her reputation. The bottom line: never plagiarize intentionally, and keep careful notes to avoid doing it accidentally.

The Facts About Plagiarism

FICTION: It's easy to plagiarize without getting caught.
FACT: Teachers get to know different students' writing styles, so they can recognize unoriginal work. They can also use search engines to find writing that's plagiarized from the Internet.

FICTION: It's not plagiarism if you change the author's wording a little bit.
FACT: Any time you use an author's basic wording or ideas, you must credit the author by citing the source.

FICTION: Listing sources on your note cards is a waste of time. You can figure out that stuff later when you're writing your paper.
FACT: Sloppy, incomplete notes can lead to accidental plagiarism. **Always** keep track of sources, use quotation marks when necessary, and separate your own thoughts from the author's.

FICTION: Plagiarism is a great way to cheat the system.
FACT: If you plagiarize, you're cheating yourself. You miss out on the satisfaction that comes from tackling a challenging assignment and doing the best you can.

Plagiarism, continued

What Does Plagiarism Look Like?

Compare the source article below with the student paper based on that article. Notice the too-similar words and phrases.

Source

> When my associates and I studied the chemical structure of exendin-4, we found it to be remarkably similar to that of the naturally occurring glucagon-like-peptide-1, or GLP1. This little-known hormone is produced in the human intestines and can stimulate beta cells in the pancreas to secrete insulin.

Student Paper

> Exendin-4 is remarkably similar to the naturally occurring glucagon-like-peptide-1. This hormone is known as GLP1. It is produced in the human intestines and can stimulate cells in the pancreas to secrete insulin.

How Can You Avoid Plagiarism?

First be sure to use quotation marks when you take word-for-word notes from a source.

Note Card

> The structure of exendin-4 is "remarkably similar to that of the naturally occurring glucagon-like-peptide-1." This hormone, known as GLP1, is "produced in the human intestines and can stimulate beta cells in the pancreas to secrete insulin."

Then when you write your paper, you can credit the source and show the writer's exact words in quotations.

> Researchers have found that the chemical structure of exendin-4 is "remarkably similar to that of the naturally occurring glucagon-like-peptide-1" or GLP1, a hormone found in the human intestines (Hikel 183). GLP1 causes cells in the pancreas to produce insulin

The original writer's words are in **quotations** and the **source** is named.

Or, you can combine the information from the source with other notes and your thoughts to put the information in your own words.

> A research scientist, Frederick Hikel, M.D., has shown an important connection between the structure of exendin-4 and that of a human hormone called GLP1. GLP1 encourages the human pancreas to produce insulin.

Making Sense of Your Notes

When you create a playlist of your favorite tunes, you probably organize the songs by artist or style. That makes it easier to find the one you want to hear. Organizing your research notes is like that, too. Once you get your notes in order, it's easier to find the facts you want to include in your research paper.

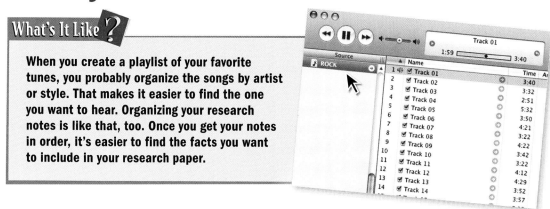

Why Organize Your Notes?

If your notes are organized, your research paper will be, too. Organizing your notes will also help you discover if anything vital is missing, as Barbara Kingsolver once did:

" **S**he pointed out to me a pretty serious flaw in the story I had concocted. . . . The deadline was looming and I was forced to trash about half the book, right then and there. But I was so relieved that I'd found this vital piece of information, because it eventually made everything fall together in that magical way that lets you know, whatever it was, it was right. "

You've taken a lot of notes about your topic. Now you need to

- put together, or synthesize, ideas from different sources
- decide if you have enough information on your topic or need to do more research
- use your notes to create an outline for your paper.

FOCUS POINT Look at the outline below. How did the writer organize the information she gathered?

A Reptile with the Power to Heal

Title ▷

I. Introduction—medicine from a monster
   A. Gila-monster saliva used to create new diabetes drug
   B. More effective in some ways than earlier treatments

Main topic, with roman numeral ▷

II. Description of diabetes
   A. Type I and Type II diabetes
   B. Role of insulin in regulating blood sugar
   C. Living with diabetes

Subtopic, with capital A, B, C, etc. ▷

      1. Daily symptoms and long-term problems
      2. Monitoring and medication

III. Treatments
   A. Restricted diet and increase in exercise
   B. Medication to control blood sugar

IV. Description of Gila monster
   A. Venomous lizard that lives in southwestern U.S. and northwestern Mexico
   B. Side effects of its bite
   C. Probably uses venom as digestive enzyme
   D. Chemical in venom similar to human hormone

V. New medicine based on Gila venom
   A. Dr. Eng's discovery: exendin-4
   B. Advantages over older treatments

Supporting detail, with numeral 1, 2, 3, etc. ▷

      1. Effects last longer than other medicines
      2. Decreased appetite, weight loss

VI. Conclusion
   A. New ways to use plants and animals for medicine
   B. Studying Gilas improved options for diabetics
   C. Davidson example

Synthesizing Ideas

Your research notes may have come from many different sources, but now you have to somehow **synthesize** them, or pull them together, into one paper—the one you're going to write. A great tool for synthesizing ideas is the **Inquiry Chart**. Here's how to build one:

1 **Start with a Chart**

Set up a chart like the one below. Once it's filled in, this chart will help you see how all the information you've gathered fits together and whether you've answered your research questions. Start by filling in the questions.

Research Questions	Source Information	Synthesis
What is it like to live with diabetes?		

Inquiry Chart

2 **Group Note Cards by Related Ideas**

Use the headings and keywords on your note cards to decide which cards should be grouped together.

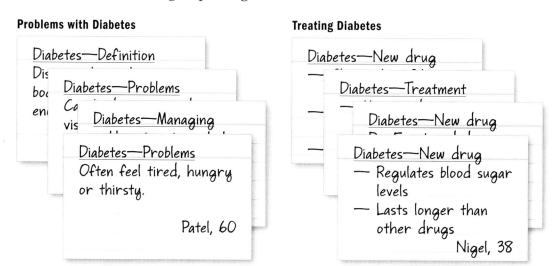

Problems with Diabetes

Diabetes—Definition

Diabetes—Problems

Diabetes—Managing

Diabetes—Problems
Often feel tired, hungry or thirsty.

Patel, 60

Treating Diabetes

Diabetes—New drug

Diabetes—Treatment

Diabetes—New drug

Diabetes—New drug
— Regulates blood sugar levels
— Lasts longer than other drugs

Nigel, 38

❸ Fill In the Chart

Using your grouped note cards, fill in the Inquiry Chart to get an organized overview of what you've learned.

To fill in the **Synthesis** column, review all the notes for a particular research question. What can you conclude from the information? Use your own words to write a statement that synthesizes the ideas.

Research Questions	Source Information	Synthesis
What is it like to live with diabetes?	Diabetics are often hungry or thirsty. (Patel 60) Diabetics have to check their blood sugar often. (Rocker 15) Diabetics live with medical problems like impaired vision, blindness, and kidney damage. (Nigel 35)	Living with diabetes can be difficult because of the daily symptoms, long-term health problems, as well as the need to check insulin levels frequently and to take medication.

Inquiry Chart

If you have trouble synthesizing the ideas, try rereading your notes, or go back to your original sources. Still stumped? You may have to do additional research to get more information about the question that's puzzling you.

Checking for Completeness and Focus

Before you move on to creating a formal outline for your report, take some time to check for

- completeness: Do you have all the information you need?

- focus: Is the information focused on your topic?

Not Enough Information

Take a hard look at your Inquiry Chart. Does it seem complete? Maybe you need to do additional research to answer some of your research questions more fully. Maybe, now that you know more about the topic, you can think of other interesting questions you want to research.

Inquiry Chart

Research Questions	Source Information	Synthesis
What are the treatments for diabetes?	Diabetics follow a special diet. (Patel 60) What is a good diet for diabetics? Can they eat sugar at all? Some diabetics take a daily insulin shot. Others take pills. (Nigel 35) Diabetic patients have mixed feelings about the new Gila monster treatment. (Morena 12) Find articles that include patients' responses.	

Too Much Information

Well, you can never really have too much information, but you want all the information you present to have a focus. Remember that not every note you take has to show up in your paper. Leave out information that

- doesn't relate to your research questions
- is contradicted by several other sources.

Inquiry Chart

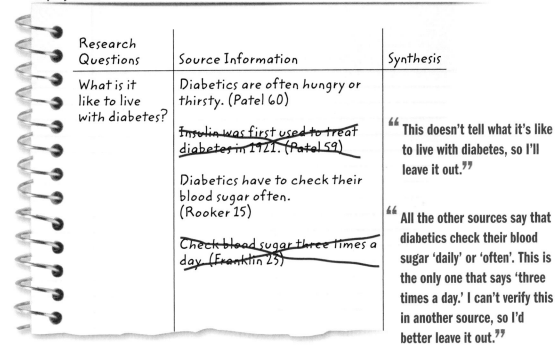

Research Questions	Source Information	Synthesis
What is it like to live with diabetes?	Diabetics are often hungry or thirsty. (Patel 60)	
	~~Insulin was first used to treat diabetes in 1921. (Patel 59)~~	" This doesn't tell what it's like to live with diabetes, so I'll leave it out."
	Diabetics have to check their blood sugar often. (Rooker 15)	
	~~Check blood sugar three times a day (Franklin 25)~~	" All the other sources say that diabetics check their blood sugar 'daily' or 'often'. This is the only one that says 'three times a day.' I can't verify this in another source, so I'd better leave it out."

Good researchers follow their "gut" as they pursue their research. So if you don't have enough information, or if the information isn't focused enough, think of additional questions, head back to the library or into the field.

Interviewing an expert on your topic is a valuable source of information. ▶

Develop an Outline

Now you're ready to develop your outline—a final plan for your paper. Here's how:

1 Start with a Title
Use a title that tells readers what your paper will be about. You can use key words from your research questions or even ask a question.

Outline Title

A Reptile with the Power to Heal

2 Decide On Your Introduction
Your opening paragraphs should introduce your topic. Plan a thesis statement that summarizes your answer to your main research question.

Outline for Part I

A Reptile with the Power to Heal
I. Introduction—medicine from a monster
   A. Gila-monster saliva used to create new diabetes drug
   B. More effective in some ways than earlier treatments

Thesis

Main Research Question
Is the new diabetes drug developed from Gila-monster saliva better than traditional treatments?

3 List Your Main Topics
List them in order, using roman numerals, and see if you like the flow of your ideas.

Main Topics in the Outline

   I. Introduction
  II. Description of diabetes
  III. Treatments
  IV. Description of Gila monster
   V. New medicine based on Gila venom
  VI. Conclusion

These will become the subheads or section heads once you write your paper. Plan on a conclusion, too.

4 Complete Your Outline

Fill in subtopics and supporting details under each main topic, following the model on page 463. Use the information in your completed Inquiry Chart:

- Draw subtopics for your outline from key words in your research questions.

- Your synthesis statements will give you a clue as to which supporting details go under each subtopic.

Inquiry Chart

Research Questions	Source Information	Synthesis
What is it like to live with diabetes?	Diabetics are often hungry or thirsty. (Patel 60) Diabetics have to check their blood sugar often. (Rooker 15) Diabetics live with medical problems like impaired vision, blindness, and kidney damage. (Nigel 35)	Living with diabetes can be difficult because of the daily symptoms, long-term health problems, as well as the need to check insulin levels frequently and to take medication.

Outline for Part II

II. Description of diabetes

    A. Type I and Type II diabetes

    B. Role of insulin in regulating blood sugar

    C. Living with diabetes

        1. Daily symptoms and long-term problems

        2. Monitoring and medication

Armed with your finished outline, you're ready to turn your hard-earned research and thinking into sentences and paragraphs for your research paper.

Packaging Your Ideas

What's It Like ?

Presenting your research is like performing a complicated solo dance after you've finally mastered all the moves. You pull all the different pieces together to create a paper that is unique and all your own.

Make It New

"**W**hen I think about the Library of Congress, I'm inclined to jump in a lake. Who needs another book in the world, even one more sentence? That's how I begin my writing day: by understanding the audacity of what I'm undertaking. I'd better make sure I have something new to say, that's absolutely my own."

For a research report, you have gathered facts from other sources. Now you need to use them as ingredients to cook up something original.

- Use your outline to draft a well-organized report. Integrate the ideas from your sources and your own thinking into a coherent, original work.

- Cite your sources and acknowledge them, but don't let your research facts take over your work.

- Add visuals and sound for a multimedia presentation.

FOCUS POINT Look at the finished report on pages 471–475 to see how Anita integrated her research into an effective, original report. How is it organized? Does it match the outline on page 463?

Research Paper

A Reptile with the Power to Heal
Anita Hernandez

Could doctors use venom from a reptile to help treat a common disease? By studying a venomous lizard known as a Gila monster, researchers have been able to create a new drug to treat diabetes. The drug provides a convenient, effective alternative to traditional treatments for this disease.

Understanding Diabetes

Diabetes is a serious illness. Between 15 and 20 million people in the United States suffer from the disease (Michaels 16). Diabetes comes in two types. People with Type I diabetes (5–10% of sufferers) cannot produce insulin because an autoimmune disorder causes their bodies to destroy insulin-producing cells in the pancreas (Rocker, *Type I Diabetes*, 24–29). People with Type II diabetes cannot produce enough insulin and/or may not respond effectively to the insulin their bodies do produce (Hikel 179).

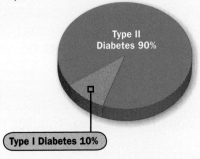

Introduction
A thought-provoking question introduces the topic.

The writer then states the **thesis**.

Body
The writer uses **section headings** to organize the paper.

Research Paper, continued

Each **main idea** is supported by facts and details from the writer's research.

Why is insulin so important? When you eat, your body converts food to glucose, a simple sugar it can use for energy (Michaels 25). Normally, insulin helps cells absorb the glucose from the bloodstream, with the result that blood-sugar levels remain steady (Patel 59). Without insulin, however, or when the body does not respond effectively to insulin, cells cannot absorb glucose properly. The cells can't get the glucose they need from the blood, and blood-sugar levels may become dangerously high, leading to numerous medical problems (Rocker, *Beating Diabetes*, 15).

Since diabetics can't efficiently convert glucose into energy, they often feel fatigued and excessively hungry (Patel 60). More-serious health issues associated with diabetes include poor circulation, vision problems, unexplained weight loss, kidney damage, and increased risk of heart attack and stroke (Nigel 35).

Each section relates to the writer's **thesis**.

Managing Diabetes

Most diabetics need to watch their blood-glucose levels and avoid foods that are high in sugar and fat. Regular exercise can also help, since it forces glucose to move through the body and into muscle cells (Morena 11). In addition, Type I diabetics usually also need daily insulin injections (Patel 65). Type II diabetics may also require medication—either insulin shots or drugs that stimulate increased insulin production in the pancreas (Rocker, *Beating Diabetes*, 20).

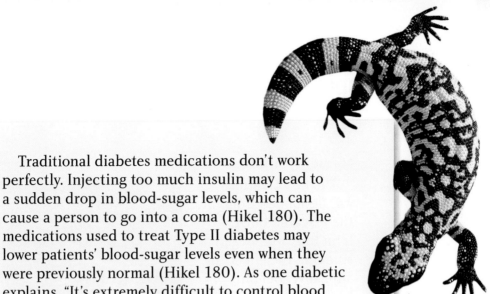

Traditional diabetes medications don't work perfectly. Injecting too much insulin may lead to a sudden drop in blood-sugar levels, which can cause a person to go into a coma (Hikel 180). The medications used to treat Type II diabetes may lower patients' blood-sugar levels even when they were previously normal (Hikel 180). As one diabetic explains, "It's extremely difficult to control blood sugar levels precisely" (Davidson).

Enter the Gila Monster

An unlikely hero, the Gila monster is a poisonous lizard with colorful skin and scales that look like beads. It is found in the southwestern United States and northwestern Mexico, where it hides in burrows for much of its short life (Sampson 23). The Gila monster's bite, while painful, is usually not fatal to humans (Ling 9). Researchers noticed, however, that people bitten by Gila monsters (like those bitten by other venomous reptiles) often developed an inflamed pancreas and—as a side effect—increased production of insulin (Hikel 179-180)!

The Gila monster, a poisonous lizard

Photo adds visual information and enlivens the report.

Research Paper, continued

Medicine from a Monster

The writer cites sources for each fact included.

The new treatment was developed from the research of Dr. John Eng, who began studying the effects of animal venom on humans in the 1980s (Michaels 67). Dr. Eng analyzed Gila-monster venom and discovered that it contains a

Snake venom is extracted in a lab, to be used for scientific research.

previously unidentified hormone he called exendin-4 (Morena 13). Exendin-4 is chemically very similar to a human hormone that triggers insulin release whenever blood-sugar levels get too high (Hikel 185). However, exendin-4 doesn't break down as quickly in the bloodstream as the natural human hormone (Smith et al. 25), making it more useful as a medication. Researchers have synthesized exendin-4 (which means it can be made in the laboratory, without having to use actual Gila monsters) and used it to make a new drug to treat Type II diabetes. The new drug, called exenatide, became available in 2005 (Fitzpatrick 70).

Exenatide has many advantages over older treatments for diabetes. Janet Swanson, a teacher from Ohio, was one of the first people to try out this new treatment. Previously, she had to monitor her blood-glucose levels constantly, which interfered with her work. "Taking exenatide is much more convenient," she says (quoted in Barry 4). The drug remains in the body longer than other medications, so it doesn't have to be taken as often (Nigel 38).

Another advantage of exenatide is that it reduces appetite, often leading to weight loss (Sampson 27). This is helpful for the many diabetics who have difficulty managing their weight. Diabetic John Davidson remarks, "As a chef at a busy restaurant, I found it hard to stay at a healthy weight. But ever since I started taking exenatide, my appetite has been under control. In fact, I've lost 15 pounds."

Thanks to Dr. Eng's work, diabetics now have more options available than ever. Researchers are also looking into new medical treatments that use venom from sea snails and scorpions (Morena 14). Who knows what exciting developments are on the horizon?

Dr. John Eng discovered the Gila monster's power to heal.

How to Get from A to B

The process of creating a report begins with your research questions. As you investigate your topic, you take notes, synthesize your ideas, develop an outline, and use it to write your finished report.

This diagram summarizes the path from "raw research" to finished report.

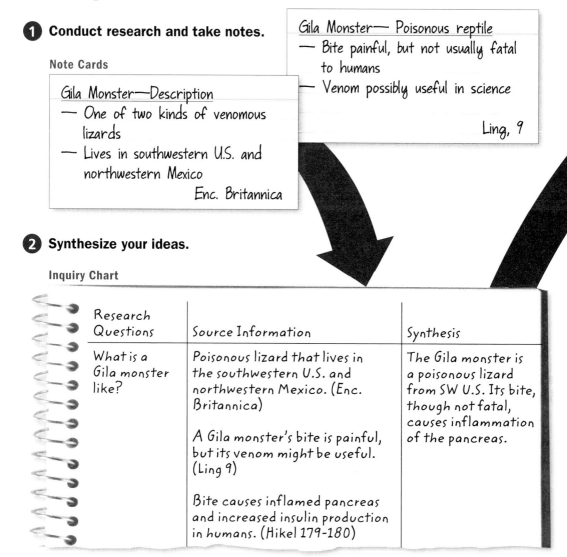

1 **Conduct research and take notes.**

Note Cards

Gila Monster—Description
— One of two kinds of venomous lizards
— Lives in southwestern U.S. and northwestern Mexico
                    Enc. Britannica

Gila Monster— Poisonous reptile
— Bite painful, but not usually fatal to humans
— Venom possibly useful in science
                    Ling, 9

2 **Synthesize your ideas.**

Inquiry Chart

Research Questions	Source Information	Synthesis
What is a Gila monster like?	Poisonous lizard that lives in the southwestern U.S. and northwestern Mexico. (Enc. Britannica) A Gila monster's bite is painful, but its venom might be useful. (Ling 9) Bite causes inflamed pancreas and increased insulin production in humans. (Hikel 179-180)	The Gila monster is a poisonous lizard from SW U.S. Its bite, though not fatal, causes inflammation of the pancreas.

Gila Monsters are one of two species of seriously venomous lizards. ▶

3 **Develop an outline.**

Outline

IV. Description of Gila monster
A. Venomous lizard that lives in southwestern U.S. and northwestern Mexico
B. Side effects of its bite
C. Probably uses venom as digestive enzyme
D. Chemical in venom similar to human hormone

4 **Use the outline to write the research report.**

Research Report

Enter the Gila Monster

An unlikely hero, the Gila monster is a poisonous lizard with colorful skin and scales that look like beads. It is found in the southwestern United States and northwestern Mexico, where it hides in burrows for much of its short life (Sampson 23). The Gila monster's bite, while painful, is usually not fatal to humans (Ling 9). Researchers noticed, however, that people bitten by Gila monsters (like those bitten by other venomous reptiles) often developed an inflamed pancreas and—as a side effect—increased production of insulin (Hikel 179-180)!

Writing Your Report

Work from Your Outline

Your outline shows the framework of your thinking and provides the skeleton of your research paper. As you draft your paper, you'll put some meat on those bare bones. (And, of course, you can change your "skeleton" as you write.) Use your outline to:

1 **Draft the introduction.**

Get your readers interested from the beginning. Try one or more of these techniques:

- Show how your topic relates to your readers' experiences.

- Ask the question you will answer in your paper.

- Present an attention-getting fact, quotation, or anecdote.

Be sure your introduction also includes some background about your topic and a thesis statement that gives the main point of your paper.

2 **Draft the body of your report.**

Look at the sections with roman numerals in your outline. Turn each of those main points into one or more paragraphs.

3 **Sum up your ideas in the conclusion.**

In the final paragraph, relate your ideas to your thesis. Leave your reader with something to remember, such as a solution for a problem, a new question, or an interesting quote.

Revise, Edit, and Polish

Just like other kinds of writing, a research paper will need some revision and editing. Try to plan your schedule so that you can take a break for a day or so before you start revising. Look in the Revising and Editing sections in Chapter 1 (pages 50–77) for tips on how to create a great final draft.

A Reptile with the Power to Heal

I. Introduction—medicine from a monster
   A. Gila-monster saliva used to create new diabetes drug
   B. More effective in some ways than earlier treatments

A Reptile with the Power to Heal

Question

Could doctors use poisonous reptilian venom to help treat common diseases? Scientists are developing new medications based on their study of certain plants and animals. By studying the venom of a reptile called a Gila monster, researchers have created a new drug to treat diabetes. The drug provides a convenient, effective alternative to traditional treatments for this disease.

Thesis statement

Draft of the Introduction

IV. Description of Gila monster
   A. Venomous lizard that lives in southwestern U.S. and northwestern Mexico
   B. Side effects of its bite

The Gila monster is a poisonous lizard found in the Southwest. Its bite is very painful but usually not deadly. However, victims get a swollen pancreas and make more insulin!

Draft of Paragraph in the Body

VI. Conclusion
   A. New ways to use plants and animals for medicine
   B. Studying Gilas improved options for diabetics
   C. Davidson example

Scientists are constantly looking at new ways that plants and animals can be used to cure our problems. Thanks to Dr. Eng's study of Gila-monster poison, diabetics have more options available than ever. John Davidson, who has diabetes, has started a support group to help others learn about the the new drug.

Draft of the Conclusion

Integrating Ideas in Your Research Report

One of the trickiest things to do when you write a report is to make sure your ideas and the information from your research flow together smoothly. As you write and revise your paper, try these techniques for integrating facts and ideas:

1 Support general statements with facts from your research.

Unsupported

> Modern medicine probably uses lots of substances that come from animals and plants. But poison from a reptile? That's hard to believe, yet it's true. A new diabetes drug is based on the Gila monster's venom.

Supported

> Modern medicine is making use of the Gila monster. For over 20 years, Dr. John Eng has been working on a new treatment for diabetes that's based on a chemical found in the Gila monster's saliva (Patel 45).

The writer supports a statement with a **fact**.

2 Stay focused.

Any quoted or paraphrased material within a paragraph should clearly connect to the **main idea**.

Unfocused

> Diabetes interferes with the body's ability to regulate blood sugar. People with Type II diabetes either can't produce enough insulin or can't use the insulin that their body produces (Patel 58). Between 15 and 20 million Americans suffer from diabetes (Michaels 16). Diabetes can also cause vision problems (Nigel 35).

Focused

> Diabetes interferes with the body's ability to regulate blood sugar. People with Type II diabetes may not produce enough insulin and/or may not be able to use effectively the insulin they do produce (Patel 58). If you have ever gone for a long time without eating, you probably noticed that you feel tired and weak. That's because your blood sugar is low.

3 **Use your own ideas as the backbone of your paper.**

As you decide what details to include from your research, think about how you'll "connect the dots" for your readers.

Disconnected Facts/Too Many Citations

Dr. John Eng developed a new diabetes drug from Gila-monster venom (Michaels 67). The Gila monster's venom contains a digestive enzyme (Sampson 24). The Gila "probably uses its digestive enzymes to digest meals over a long period of time" (Sampson 24). The Gila monster only eats a few times in a year (Sampson 24). Its digestive enzyme is similar to a human hormone that triggers insulin release (Sampson 25).

Integrated Ideas and Citations

Scientists have developed a new treatment for diabetics by studying the Gila monster. The Gila monster, which eats only a few times a year, probably uses its venom as an enzyme to digest food (Sampson 24). Researchers have studied the enzyme, which turns out to be similar to a human hormone that triggers insulin release (Sampson 25).

4 **Cue the quotations.**

Pay close attention to how you work direct quotations into your paper. It's usually best not to leave a quotation standing alone; the mix of "voices" can make the writing sound awkward.

Awkward Quotation, Fixed

The drug Dr. Eng developed has many advantages over older treatments for diabetes. John Davidson, a chef from Boston, was one of the first people to try this new treatment. *He explains,* "Being a chef at a busy restaurant, I found it hard to control my cravings for food. But ever since I started taking this new drug, my appetite has been under control. I've lost 15 pounds and I feel great."

The simple addition of transitional words makes for a smooth connection.

Citing Sources

You should briefly identify your source any time you refer to someone else's words or ideas in your paper. That way, you give other writers credit for their work and provide your readers with a way to learn more about your topic. At the end of your paper, provide a full list of your sources.

Keeping Track of Your Sources

If you record your sources right from the start, you won't have to spend hours figuring out where you found each fact.

- As you do research, create a card with bibliographic information for every source, or keep a list of all of your sources. Page 484 tells what information you should record.

- As you take notes, always write down the source's author or title (or both) and the page where you found the information.

Source Card

Source #1
Title: Diabetes
Author: Edward J. Michaels
Publisher: Canton Press
City: Baltimore
Year: 2005

Note Card

Dr. Eng's Research
In the 1980s, Dr. John Eng began to study the effects of animal venom on humans.

Michaels, 67

- Include information about sources in your draft. You don't have to worry about using the perfect format, but do add a note about where you found each fact or idea.

Many diabetics are seeking out new remedies for diabetes. Researchers have recently developed a new drug treatment for people with Type II diabetes. The treatment originated with the work of Dr. John Eng. Eng began studying the effects of Gila-monster venom on humans in the 1980s. (MICHAELS, PAGE 67.)

How to Cite Sources in Your Final Draft

The point of including references in the body of your report is to help your reader find the full bibliographic information that appears at the end (see pages 484–485). The FAQ chart below outlines a system that most teachers will accept.

FAQ	Answer	Example
How do I cite a book or an article?	Give the author's last name and the page number where the information is found.	Dr. Eng began studying venom in the 1980s (Michaels 67).
What if the authors of two or more of my sources have the same last name?	Add an initial or a full first name to the reference.	Dr. Eng began studying venom in the 1980s (R. Michaels 67).
What if my source has more than one author?	If there are two or three authors, list them all. If there are more than three, use the first author's name followed by the abbreviation *et al.,* which means "and others."	Gila monsters spend most of their time in burrows (Anderson and Jones 105). Gila monsters eat very infrequently (Carson et al. 105).
What if I used two different sources by the same author?	Mention the title also, in full or abbreviated.	The symptoms of diabetes can often be partly controlled through diet and exercise (Rocker, *Beating Diabetes* 67).
What if my source has an organization as its author?	Give the name of the organization, in full or abbreviated, just as you would with a person.	Many overweight Americans suffer from diabetes (Diabetes Help Network 12).
How do I cite a Web site?	Use the author's name, if known, or the name of the Web site.	Diabetes affects millions of Americans (Diabetes Information Site).

Do you have a question that's not answered here? Look up a link to more-complete guidelines.

hbgoodwriters.com

Citing Sources, continued

How to Create a List of Works Cited

You won't be finished with your research paper until you create your list of works cited. This is where you give your reader complete bibliographic information for each of the sources mentioned in the body of your report. The rules for putting together this list are many and complicated, so listen up:

1 **List all the publication details about each source you used.**

- For books:

  Michaels, Edward J. *Diabetes*. Baltimore: Canton Press, 2005.

  | Author with last name first | Title, in *italics* | City of publication | Publisher | Year of publication |

- For magazine articles:

  Nigel, Roberto. "Great Gila Monsters." *Nature Weekly*. 2 May 2005: 30–39.

  Article title   Magazine title, in *italics*   Issue date   Page numbers

- For newspaper articles:

  Barry, Todd. "New Hope For Diabetes Sufferers." *Youngstown Times*. 6 April 2003: B4.

  Section and page number

- For articles from academic or professional journals:

  Morena, Luis T. "New Hope for Diabetics." *Southern Journal of Medicine*. 9.4 (2004): 8–14.

  Volume number   Issue number

- For an article in an online magazine:

  Ling, Tara. "Gila Monsters." *Lizard World* 15 Oct. 2005. 26 Aug. 2006. <http://www.lizardworld.org/gila.html>.

  Page URL, underscored   Issue date   Date of access

Head spinning yet? And these are only some of the rules! If you need to know more, you can link to more-complete guidelines through hbgoodwriters.com.

2 **Then list all sources alphabetically. The finished monster should look something like this:**

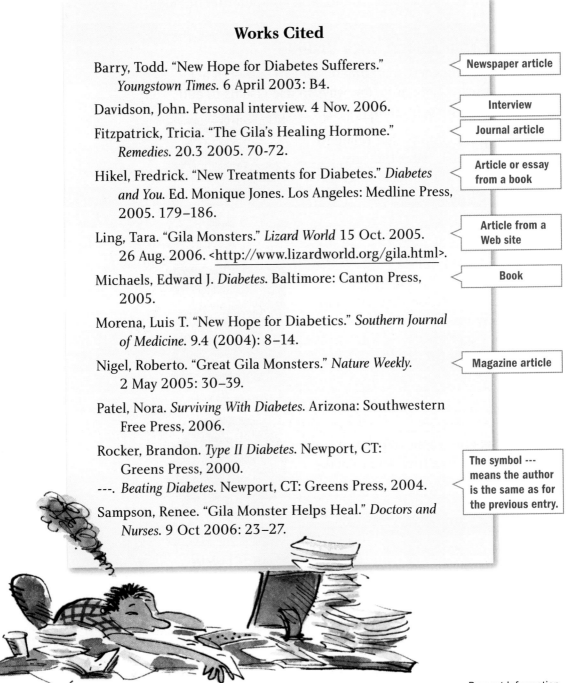

Works Cited

Barry, Todd. "New Hope for Diabetes Sufferers." *Youngstown Times.* 6 April 2003: B4.

> Newspaper article

Davidson, John. Personal interview. 4 Nov. 2006.

> Interview

Fitzpatrick, Tricia. "The Gila's Healing Hormone." *Remedies.* 20.3 2005. 70-72.

> Journal article

Hikel, Fredrick. "New Treatments for Diabetes." *Diabetes and You.* Ed. Monique Jones. Los Angeles: Medline Press, 2005. 179–186.

> Article or essay from a book

Ling, Tara. "Gila Monsters." *Lizard World* 15 Oct. 2005. 26 Aug. 2006. <http://www.lizardworld.org/gila.html>.

> Article from a Web site

Michaels, Edward J. *Diabetes.* Baltimore: Canton Press, 2005.

> Book

Morena, Luis T. "New Hope for Diabetics." *Southern Journal of Medicine.* 9.4 (2004): 8–14.

Nigel, Roberto. "Great Gila Monsters." *Nature Weekly.* 2 May 2005: 30–39.

> Magazine article

Patel, Nora. *Surviving With Diabetes.* Arizona: Southwestern Free Press, 2006.

Rocker, Brandon. *Type II Diabetes.* Newport, CT: Greens Press, 2000.

---. *Beating Diabetes.* Newport, CT: Greens Press, 2004.

> The symbol --- means the author is the same as for the previous entry.

Sampson, Renee. "Gila Monster Helps Heal." *Doctors and Nurses.* 9 Oct 2006: 23–27.

Creating a Multimedia Report

If you're presenting your research to a large audience, make it more impactful with visuals, sound, and computer technology.

Enhance Your Report with Visuals

As the old saying goes, sometimes a picture is worth a thousand words. Here are a few ways to use visuals to add pizzazz to your presentation:

- Display photographs that relate to your topic. Make sure they are eye-catching and large enough to be seen easily.

The Gila Monster

- Show an illustration that will help your audience understand your topic.

A Glucose Molecule

- Use charts or graphs to present a lot of data at one time and to make their relationship clear.

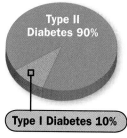

Type II Diabetes 90%

Type I Diabetes 10%

Types of Diabetes

- Does your research involve history or geography? Display a map to help your audience visualize location.

- Present a snippet of video using a DVD player.

Enhance Your Report with Sound

Sound recordings can make your report come alive. Be creative and think of different ways that sound relates to your topic. Try some of these ideas to capture your audience's attention.

- Play a country's national anthem to enhance a report about that country or a recording by a musician of the time period described in your report.

Teen Life in 1957
by Sandra Backer

- Present snippets of a speech by a famous personality, researcher, or politician.

> "Let us all hope that the dark clouds of racial prejudice will soon pass away and the deep fog of misunderstanding will be lifted from our fear-drenched communities."
>
> —*Martin Luther King, Jr.*

- Share parts of a recorded interview or comments by experts who are or were involved in events described in your report.

- Play background sounds relating to the subject of your report.

Remember that the goal of using media is to enhance your report—not to replace it. Use photos, charts, and graphics to convey only information that relates directly to your topic. Use videos and sound recordings sparingly, too. A brief snippet is enough to spark your audience's interest.

Creating a Multimedia Report, continued

Use Presentation Software

There are several software programs available specifically designed for presentations. You can use any of these programs to enhance your oral presentation with images and sound.

- Computer programs can help you create and display time lines, charts, and graphs to present complicated ideas.

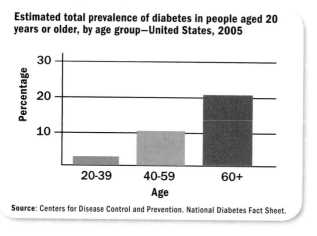

Estimated total prevalence of diabetes in people aged 20 years or older, by age group—United States, 2005

Source: Centers for Disease Control and Prevention. National Diabetes Fact Sheet.

- Create and present a computer "slide show" with images, sound, and text to capture and keep your audience's attention.

The Gila Monster

- ▶ Found in southwestern U.S. and northwestern Mexico
- ▶ Eats only a few times a year
- ▶ Venom was used to develop a new drug to treat diabetes

Remember that the content is what's important in a multimedia report. Visual and sound effects are there to enhance the content.

Use the Internet

Not only is the Internet a great tool for doing research—it can also help you liven up the way you present your findings. Try these ideas:

- Bookmark Web sites with attention-getting images or content. You might find some cool facts that don't quite fit into your paper but can be mentioned in your presentation.

- Download related images, music, or videos.

- Do you have some technical know-how? Create a Web page on your topic with links to other informative sites.

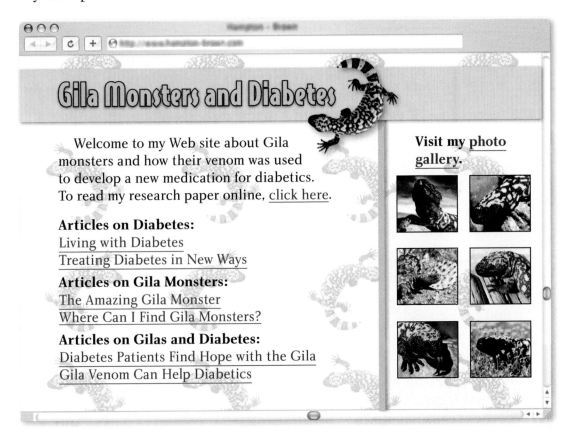

If you plan to use the Internet as part of your presentation, ask your teacher for help in keeping things running smoothly.

Giving an Oral Report

Sometimes you may give a talk to report your research or to share information in your paper. Most people get a little nervous when they have to speak in front of a group. Being well-prepared can go a long way toward helping you feel more confident. After all, you probably know your topic from A to Z by now!

You can share your expertise with others by following these steps:

1 **Plan Your Presentation Carefully**

Let's face it—even if your paper is terrific, reading it aloud is not the best way to get people excited about your topic. Instead, use notes or your outline to plan what main points you'll cover. Think about how to use visuals, recordings, or technology to present your research in a creative way.

2 **Practice, Practice, Practice!**

Practicing your presentation will help you perfect it. You might try practicing in front of a mirror, or tape-recording yourself. Time yourself to see if your presentation needs to be longer or shorter. You might want to practice in front of your family or friends and get their feedback, too.

Feedback Questions and Answers

1. **Was everything that I said loud and clear enough?**

   I could hear you just fine, but you should slow down. Take a deep breath before you start talking. You just need to relax.

2. **Were there any topics you wanted to know more about?**

   I wanted to know more about how many people have tried the new treatment.

3. **Was my presentation interesting and fun?**

   Yes, it was fun, and I also learned a lot! If you added some more pictures and videos, it might be even better.

4. **Do you have any other questions or comments?**

   Just so you know, "Gila" is pronounced "HEE-la."

Finally, if you plan to liven up your presentation with visuals or other media, practice using them ahead of time. Make sure any technological equipment you plan to use is in good working order.

3 Deliver Your Report

As you present your ideas, focus on speaking slowly and clearly. Make eye contact with your audience. Don't be afraid to ask for opinions about your topic—it's a good way to get the audience involved in your presentation. Be sure to allow time for questions at the end.

4 Reflect on Your Work

After you've given your presentation, take some time to reflect on it. What did you do well? What improvements could you make for next time? You might want to use a checklist or journal to help you reflect, or talk with a close friend about how things went.

Hey, Sandra,

Well, I finally gave my presentation today, and guess what—it wasn't nearly as scary as I expected it to be. I know I did a good job of making eye contact with the class and keeping their interest. My voice was a little shaky at first, but once I got into it, I actually felt pretty confident. I knew I was totally prepared.

Thanks so much for showing me how to set up my Web page and helping me practice my presentation. Let me know if there's anything I can do to help you out with yours!

Your friend,
Anita

Handy Handbook of Grammar and Style

Sentences

A **sentence** is a group of words that expresses a complete thought. Every sentence has a subject (a main idea) and a predicate that describes what the main idea is, has, or does. Sentences can be classified according to their function and structure.

Sentence Types	Examples
A **declarative sentence** makes a statement. It ends with a period.	The football game was on Friday. The coach made an important announcement.
An **interrogative sentence** asks a question. It ends with a question mark.	Who heard the announcement? What did the coach say?
An **exclamatory sentence** shows surprise or strong emotion. It ends with an exclamation mark.	That's fantastic news! I can't believe it!
An **imperative sentence** gives a command.	Give the team my congratulations.
• An imperative sentence usually begins with a verb and ends with a period.	**Be** on time.
• If an imperative sentence shows strong emotion, it ends with an exclamation mark.	Beat the opponent!

Negative Sentences	Examples
A **negative sentence** uses a **negative word** to say "no." Here are some negative words: no none no one not never nobody nothing nowhere	The game in Hawaii was **not** boring! **Nobody** in our town missed it on TV. Our team **never** played better.
For school writing, use only one negative word in a sentence. Using two negatives in one sentence is called a **double negative**. Double negatives are not used in modern standard English.	anything The other team could not do ~~nothing~~ right. any Their team never scored ~~no~~ points.

Conditional Sentences	Examples
Conditional sentences tell how one action depends on another. These sentences often use conditional or modal verbs, such as **can**, **will**, **could**, **would**, or **might**.	**If** our team returns today, **then** we will have a party. **Unless** it rains, we **can** have the party outside.

Sentence Structure

Clauses	Examples
A **clause** is a group of words that has both a **subject** and a **predicate**.	California's population / grew during the 1840s. subject predicate
An **independent clause** can stand alone as a complete sentence.	California's population / increased. subject predicate
A **dependent clause** cannot stand alone as a complete sentence because it begins with a subordinating conjunction. A dependent clause can be combined with an independent clause to form a complete sentence.	**because** gold / was found there during that time California's population grew because gold was found. independent clause dependent clause
A **nominalized clause** is a dependent clause that acts as the subject of a sentence.	**That the population grew** is not surprising.
An **adjective clause** gives more details about the noun or pronoun that it describes.	The news **that gold had been found** spread fast.
An **adverb clause** gives more details about the verb, adjective, or adverb that it describes.	**When someone found gold**, people celebrated.

Simple Sentences	Examples
A **simple sentence** is one independent clause with a subject and a predicate. It has no dependent clauses.	Supplies / were scarce. The miners / needed goods and services.

Compound Sentences	Examples
When you join two independent clauses, you make a **compound sentence**. • Use a comma and a **coordinating conjunction** to join independent clauses. • Use a semicolon to join independent clauses that are short and closely related.	People opened stores, **but** supplies were scarce. People went hungry; there was no food.
Joining independent clauses without a conjunction or proper punctuation creates a **run-on sentence**.	**Incorrect:** The miners were hungry supplies were scarce. **Correct:** The miners were hungry, and supplies were scarce.

Sentence Structure, continued

Complex Sentences	Examples
To make a **complex sentence**, join an independent clause with one or more dependent clauses.	Many writers visited camps **where miners worked**. independent dependent
If the dependent clause comes first, put a **comma** after it.	**While the writers were there**, they wrote stories about the miners.

Compound-Complex Sentences	Examples
You can make a **compound-complex sentence** by joining two or more independent clauses and one or more dependent clauses.	Many miners never found gold, **but** they stayed in California **because they found other jobs there**. dependent

Phrases	Examples
A **phrase** is a group of related words that does not have both a subject and a verb. Phrases often function as modifiers.	The team won the game **in overtime**. **With only seconds left**, the quarterback scored.

Properly Placed Modifiers and Clauses	Examples
A **misplaced clause** may make a sentence unclear and accidentally funny.	Unclear: I read that miners traveled by mule **when I studied American history**. (Did the miners travel while you studied?)
When the clause is placed properly, it makes the meaning of the sentence clear.	Clear: **When I studied American history**, I read that miners traveled by mule.
A **misplaced modifier** is a phrase placed too far away from the word or words it describes.	Unclear: The stream rushed past the miners, **splashing wildly**. (Did the miners or the stream splash wildly?)
Correct a misplaced modifier by placing it closer to the word or words it describes.	Clear: **Splashing wildly**, the stream rushed past the miners.
A **dangling modifier** occurs when you accidentally forget to include the word being described.	**Standing in rushing streams**, the search for gold was dangerous. (Was the search standing in the streams?)
Correct a dangling modifier by adding the missing word being described, adding words to the modifier, or rewording the sentence.	The search for gold was dangerous for **miners** standing in rushing streams.

Parenthetical Phrases and Appositives	Examples
A **parenthetical phrase** adds nonessential information to a sentence.	Most miners did not, **in fact**, find gold.
You can leave out a nonessential phrase without changing the meaning of the sentence.	Gold, **every miner's dream**, lay deeply buried.
Use commas to set off a nonessential phrase.	
An **appositive phrase** renames the noun next to it. An appositive phrase usually comes after the noun or pronoun it refers to.	James Marshall, **a mill worker**, started the Gold Rush when he found gold nuggets in 1848.

Clauses with Missing Words	Examples
In an **elliptical clause**, a word or words are left out to shorten a sentence and avoid repetition. You can tell what word is missing by reading the rest of the sentence.	Henry found six nuggets; **James**, **eight**. (You can tell that the missing word is "found.")
Two or more sentences that are similar and include related information may be combined into one sentence. Some words, usually any pronouns that refer back to the subject, can be left out of the combined sentence. This is called **structural omission**.	James counted his gold nuggets. He put them away. He counted them again later.
In this example, the three sentences are combined, using commas and the conjunction *and*. The pronoun *he* is omitted from the final two sentences.	James counted his gold nuggets, put them away, and counted them again later.

Coordination and Subordination	Examples
Use **coordination** to join clauses of equal weight, or importance.	Gold was often found next to streams, **and** it was also found deep beneath the earth.
Use **subordination** to join clauses of unequal weight, or importance.	The miners were called '49ers.
	main idea
Put the main idea in the main clause and the less important detail in the dependent clause.	Many miners arrived in 1849.
	less important detail
	The miners were called '49ers because they arrived in 1849.

Subjects and Predicates

A **subject** tells who or what the sentence is about. A **predicate** tells something about the subject.

Complete and Simple Subjects	Examples
The **complete subject** includes all the words in the subject.	**Many people** visit our national parks. **My favorite parks** are in the West.
The **simple subject** is the most important noun or pronoun in the complete subject.	Many <u>people</u> visit our national parks. My favorite <u>parks</u> are in the West.

Understood Subject	Examples
When you give a command, you do not state the subject. The subject **you** is understood in an imperative sentence.	Watch the geysers erupt. Soak in the hot springs.

It as the Subject	Examples
As the subject of a sentence, the pronoun *it* may refer to a specific noun. Or *it* can be the subject without referring to a specific noun.	See that **stone structure**? **It** is a natural bridge. **It** is amazing to see the natural wonders in these parks.

Complete and Simple Predicate	Examples
The predicate of a sentence tells what the subject is, has, or does. The **complete predicate** includes all the words in the predicate.	Visitors **explore caves in Yellowstone Park**. Some people **climb the unusual rock formations**.
The **simple predicate** is the **verb**. It is the most important word in the predicate.	Visitors <u>explore</u> caves in Yellowstone Park. Some people <u>climb</u> the unusual rock formations.

Compound Subject and Compound Predicate	Examples
A **compound subject** is two or more simple subjects joined by **and** or **or**.	<u>Yosemite</u> and <u>Yellowstone</u> are both in the West. Either <u>spring</u> or <u>fall</u> is a good time to visit.
A **compound predicate** has two or more verbs joined by **and** or **or**.	At Yosemite, some people **fish and swim**. My family **hikes** to the river **or stays** in the cabin. I **have seen** the falls **and have ridden** the trails.

Complete Sentences and Fragments

A **complete sentence** has both a **subject** and a **predicate** and expresses a complete thought. A fragment is written like a sentence but is not a complete thought.

Sentences and Fragments	Examples
Begin a complete sentence with a capital letter, and end it with a period or other end mark.	These parks / have many tourist attractions. *subject* *predicate*
A **fragment** is a sentence part that is incorrectly used as a complete sentence. For example, the fragment may be missing a subject. Add a subject to correct the problem.	**Incorrect:** Fun to visit because they have many attractions. **Correct:** Parks are fun to visit because they have many attractions.
Writers sometimes use fragments on purpose to emphasize an idea or for special effect.	I did not camp in bear country. **No way. Too dangerous**.

Subject-Verb Agreement

The subject and verb of a sentence or clause must agree in number.

Subject-Verb Agreement	Examples
Use a **singular subject** with a **singular verb**.	Another popular **park is** the Grand Canyon.
Use a **plural subject** with a **plural verb**.	We **were amazed** by the colors of its cliffs.
If the simple subjects in a **compound subject** are connected by **and**, use a plural verb. If they are connected by **or**, look at the last simple subject. If it is singular, use a **singular verb**. If it is plural, use a **plural verb**.	**Rafts** and a **boat are** available for a trip down the canyon. These **rafts** or this **boat is** the best way to go down the river. This **boat** or these **rafts are** the best way to go down the river.
The **subject** and **verb** must agree, even when other words come between them.	The **bikers** in the park **are looking** for animals.
The **subject** and **verb** must agree even if the subject comes after the verb.	There **are** other amazing **parks** in Arizona. Here **is** a **list** of them.

Parts of Speech

All the words in the English language can be put into one of eight groups. These groups are the eight **parts of speech**. You can tell a word's part of speech by looking at how it functions, or the way it is used, in a sentence. Knowing about the functions of words can help you become a better writer.

The Eight Parts of Speech	Examples
A **noun** names a person, place, thing, or idea.	**Erik Weihenmayer** climbed the highest **mountain** in the **world**. The **journey** up **Mount Everest** took **courage**.
A **pronoun** takes the place of a noun.	**He** made the journey even though **it** was dangerous.
An **adjective** describes a noun or a pronoun.	Erik is a **confident** climber. He is **strong**, too.
A **verb** can tell what the subject of a sentence does or has.	Erik also **skis** and **rides** a bike. He **has** many hobbies.
A **verb** can also link a noun or an adjective in the predicate to the subject.	Erik **is** an athlete. He **is** also blind.
An **adverb** describes a verb, an adjective, or another adverb.	Illness **slowly** took his eyesight, but it **never** affected his spirit. His accomplishments have made him **very** famous. He has been interviewed **quite** often.
A **preposition** shows how two things or ideas are related. It introduces a prepositional phrase.	Erik speaks **to** people **around** the world. **In** his speeches, he talks **about** his life.
A **conjunction** connects words or groups of words.	Courage **and** skill have carried him far. He has one disability, **but** he has many abilities.
An **interjection** expresses strong feeling.	**Wow**! What an amazing person he is! **Hurray**! He reached the mountaintop.

Nouns

A **noun** names a person, place, thing, or idea. There are different kinds of nouns.

Common and Proper Nouns	Examples
A **common noun** names a general person, place, thing, or idea.	A **teenager** sat by the **ocean** and read a **magazine**.
Capitalize a common noun only when it begins a sentence.	**Magazines** are the perfect thing to read at the beach.
A **proper noun** names a specific person, place, thing, or idea. Always capitalize a proper noun.	**Jessica** sat by the **Pacific Ocean** and read *Teen Talk* magazine.

Count and Noncount Nouns	Examples	
Count nouns name things that you can count. The singular form of a count noun names one thing. The plural form names more than one thing.	**Singular**	**Plural**
	one desk	two desks
	one book	many books
	one teacher	several teachers

Noncount nouns name things that you cannot count. They can be divided into different categories.

Activities and Sports:	baseball, camping, dancing, golf, singing, soccer
Category Nouns:	clothing, equipment, furniture, machinery, mail
Food:	bread, cereal, cheese, lettuce, meat, milk, soup, tea
Ideas and Feelings:	democracy, enthusiasm, freedom, honesty, health
Materials:	air, fuel, gasoline, metal, paper, water, dust, soil
Weather:	fog, hail, heat, rain, smog, snow, humidity, sunshine

Some nouns can be either count or noncount nouns. It depends on how the nouns are used.	Jessica has read the book two **times**. She has plenty of **time** to read.

Nouns, continued

Plural Nouns	Examples
Plural nouns name more than one person, place, thing, or idea. Add **–s** to most count nouns to make them plural.	My favorite **guitar** was made in Spain, but I also like my two American **guitars**.

Other count nouns follow different rules to form the plural.

Forming Noun Plurals

When a Noun Ends in:	Form the Plural by:	Examples
ch, **sh**, **s**, **x**, or **z**	adding -**es**	box—box**es** brush—brush**es**
a consonant + **y**	changing the **y** to **i** and adding -**es**	story—stor**ies**
a vowel + **y**	just adding -**s**	boy—boy**s**
f or **fe**	changing the **f** to **v** and adding -**es**, in most cases for some nouns that end in **f** or **fe**, just add -**s**	leaf—lea**ves** knife—kni**ves** cliff—cliff**s** safe—safe**s**
a vowel + **o**	adding -**s**	radio—radio**s** kangaroo—kangaroo**s**
a consonant + **o**	adding -**s**, in most cases; other times adding -**es**	ego—ego**s** potato—potato**es**

A few count nouns are **irregular**. These nouns do not follow the rules to form the plural.

Forming Plurals of Irregular Count Nouns

For some irregular count nouns, change the spelling to form the plural.	one child many **children** one foot many **feet**	one man several **men** one ox ten **oxen**	one mouse a few **mice** one woman most **women**
For other irregular count nouns, keep the same form for the singular and the plural.	one deer two **deer**	one fish many **fish**	one sheep twelve **sheep**

Possessive Nouns	Examples
Possessive nouns show ownership or relationship of persons, places, or things.	**Ted's** daughter made the guitar. The **guitar's** tone is beautiful.
Follow these rules to make a noun possessive: • Add **'s** to a singular noun or a plural noun that does not end in **s**. • Add an apostrophe after the final **s** in a plural noun that ends in **s**.	When she plays the piano, it attracts **the children's** attention. Three **musicians'** instruments were left on the bus.

Noun Phrases	Examples
A **noun phrase** is made up of a noun and its modifiers. Modifiers are words that describe, such as adjectives.	**The flying frog** does not actually fly. It glides on **special skin flaps**. Thailand is a **frog-friendly habitat**.

Articles

An **article** is a word that helps identify a noun.

Articles	Examples
A, an, and **the** are **articles**. An article often comes before a count noun. Do not use the articles **a** or **an** before a noncount noun.	It is **an** amazing event when **a** flying frog glides in **the** forest.
A and **an** are **indefinite articles**. Use **a** or **an** before a noun that names a nonspecific thing.	**A flying frog** stretched its webbed feet. **An owl** watched from a nearby tree.
• Use **a** before a word that starts with a consonant sound.	a **f**oot a **r**ainforest a **p**ool a **u**nion (*u* is pronounced like *y*, a **n**est a consonant)
• Use **an** before a word that starts with a vowel sound.	an **e**gg an **a**nimal an **a**dult an **i**dea an **o**cean an **h**our (The *h* is silent.)
The is a **definite article**. Use **the** before a noun that names a specific thing.	Leiopelmids are **the** oldest kind of frog in **the** world. They are survivors of **the** Jurassic period.

Pronouns

A **pronoun** is a word that takes the place of a noun. A pronoun often changes its form depending on how it is used in a sentence.

Subject Pronouns	Examples
Use a **subject pronoun** as the subject of a sentence.	**Antonio** is looking forward to the homecoming dance. **He** is trying to decide what to wear.

Singular	Plural
I	we
you	you
he, she, it	they

The pronoun **it** can be used as a **subject** to refer to a noun.

But: The pronoun **it** can be the subject without referring to a specific noun.

The **dance** starts at 7:00. **It** ends at 10:00.

It is important to arrive on time.

It is fun to see your friends in formal clothes.

Object Pronouns	Examples
Use an **object pronoun** after an **action verb**.	Tickets are on sale, so buy **them** now.

Singular	Plural
me	us
you	you
him, her, it	them

Also use an **object pronoun** after a **preposition**.

Antonio invited Caryn. He ordered flowers for **her**.

Possessive Pronouns	Examples
A **possessive pronoun** tells who or what owns something or belongs with something.	**His** photograph of a tree won an award. The digital camera is **mine**.
Some forms of possessive pronouns are always used before a noun.	Aleina's photographs are beautiful because of **her** eye for detail.

Forms Used with Nouns

Singular	Plural
my	our
your	your
his, her, its	their

Possessive Pronouns	Examples
Other forms of possesive pronouns are used alone, without a noun.	Which camera is Aleina's? The expensive camera is **hers**. **Mine** is a single-use, disposable camera.

Forms Used without a Noun

Singular	Plural
mine	ours
yours	yours
his, hers, its	theirs

Demonstrative Pronouns	Examples
A **demonstrative pronoun** points out a specific person, place, thing, or idea.	**That** phone takes great photographs. I've never seen **those** before.

Singular	Plural
this	these
that	those

Demonstrative Pronouns	Examples
Like possessive pronouns, demonstrative pronouns can be used with a noun or by themselves. The same form is used n both cases.	**These** photographs are of my grandparents as children. A life of hard work from morning till night—I can't even imagine **that**!

Pronouns, continued

Indefinite Pronouns	Examples
Use an **indefinite pronoun** when you are not talking about a specific person, place, or thing.	**Someone** has to lose the game. **Nobody** knows who the winner will be.

Some Indefinite Pronouns

These **indefinite pronouns** are always singular and need a **singular verb**.	
anybody either neither one anyone everybody nobody somebody anything everyone no one someone each everything nothing nothing	**Something is** happening on the playing field. We hope that **everything goes** well for our team.
These **indefinite pronouns** are always plural and need a **plural verb**.	
both few many several	**Many** of us **are** hopeful.
These **indefinite pronouns** can be singular or plural.	
all any most none some Look at the phrase that follows the indefinite pronoun. If the noun or pronoun in the phrase is plural, use a **plural verb**. If it is singular, use a **singular verb**.	**Most** of the players **are** tired. **Most** of the game **is** over.

Relative Pronouns	Examples
A **relative pronoun** introduces **a relative clause**. It connects, or relates, the clause to a word in the sentence.	**Relative Pronouns** who what which whom whoever whatever whose whomever whichever
Use **who**, **whom**, or **whose** for people. The pronouns **whoever** and **whomever**, also refer to people.	The student **who** was injured is Joe. We play **whomever** we are scheduled to play.
Use **which**, **whichever**, **what**, and **whatever** for things.	Joe's wrist, **which** is sprained, will heal.
Use **that** for people or things.	The trainer **that** examined Joe's wrist is sure. The injury **that** Joe received is minor.

Reflexive and Intensive Pronouns	Examples
Reflexive and **intensive pronouns** refer to nouns or other pronouns in a sentence. These pronouns end with –**self** or –**selves**.	I will go to the store by **myself**.

Singular	Plural
myself	ourselves
yourself	yourselves
himself, herself, itself	themselves

Use a **reflexive pronoun** when the object **refers back to the subject**.	To surprise her technology teacher, **Kim** taught **herself** how to create a Web site on the computer.
Use an **intensive pronoun** when you want **to emphasize a noun or a pronoun** in a sentence.	The technology **teacher himself** learned some interesting techniques from Kim.

Agreement and Reference	Examples
When nouns and pronouns **agree**, they both refer to the same person, place, or thing. The **noun** is the **antecedent**, and the **pronoun** refers to it.	**Rafael and Felicia** visited a local college. **They** toured the campus. *antecedent* *pronoun*
A pronoun must agree (match) in **number** with the noun it refers to. • **Singular pronouns** refer to one person. • **Plural pronouns** refer to more than one person.	**Rafael** plays violin. **He** enjoyed the music school. **The teenagers** were impressed. **They** liked this college.
Pronouns must agree in **gender** with the nouns they refer to. Use **she, her**, and **hers** to refer to females. Use **he, him**, and **his** to refer to males.	Felicia told **her** uncle about the college visit. **Her** uncle told **her** that **he** received **his** graduate degree from that school.

Adjectives

An **adjective** describes or modifies a noun or a pronoun. It can tell what kind, which one, how many, or how much.

Adjectives	Examples
Adjectives provide more detailed information about a noun. Usually, an adjective comes before the noun it describes.	Deserts have a **dry** climate.
But an adjective can also come after the noun.	The climate is also **hot**.
Number words are often used as adjectives.	While I was out in the desert I saw one road runner, two Gila monsters, and six cacti.
Sometimes the number word tells the **order** that things are in.	The **first** day, I just saw some lizards. The **third** day, I got to see a coyote!

Coordinate Adjectives	Examples
When two or more adjectives come before a noun, they are called **coordinate adjectives**. A **comma** normally separates coordinate adjectives.	The world of science has rarely seen a more **devoted, caring** professional than desertologist John Wallach.
But, if the second adjective is so closely linked with the noun that together they form a noun phrase, then a comma should **not** be used. A useful test is to try inserting *and* between the two adjectives. If *and* changes the meaning, then don't use a comma.	He was without a doubt one of the most **brilliant scientific** minds of the 20th century.

Proper Adjectives	Examples
A proper adjective is formed from a proper noun. It always begins with a capital letter.	Major deserts are found in Africa, Asia, and the Americas.
	The largest **African** desert is the Sahara.

Adjectives That Compare	Examples
Comparative adjectives help show the similarities or differences between two nouns.	Deserts are **more fun** to study than forests.
To form the comparative of most adjectives, add -**er**, and use **than**. Use **more ... than** if the adjective has three or more syllables.	The Sechura Desert in South America is small**er than** the Kalahari Desert in Africa. Is that desert **more interesting than** this one?
Superlative adjectives help show how three or more nouns are alike or different.	Of the Sechura, Kalahari, and Sahara, which is the **largest**?
To form the superlative of most adjectives, add -**est**. Use **most** if the adjective has three or more syllables.	Which of the three deserts is the **smallest**? I think the Sahara is the **most beautiful**.
Irregular adjectives form the comparative and superlative differently. good better best bad worse worst some more most little less least	I had the **best** time ever visiting the desert. But the desert heat is **worse** than city heat.
Some two-syllable adjectives form the comparative with either -**er** or **more** and the superlative with either -**est** or **most**. **Do not form a double comparison by using both.**	Desert animals are usually **more lively** at night than during the day. Desert animals are usually **livelier** at night than during the day.

Adjective Phrases and Clauses	Examples
An **adjective phrase** is a group of words that work together to modify a noun or a pronoun. A phrase has no verb.	Plants **in the desert** have developed adaptations.
An **adjective clause** also works to modify a noun or a pronoun. Unlike an adjective phrase, an adjective clause has a subject and a verb.	The saguaro, **whose flowers bloom at night**, soaks up surface water after it rains. Desert plants **that have long roots** tap into water deep in the earth.

Verbs

Every complete sentence has two parts: a subject and a predicate. The subject tells what or whom the sentence is about. The predicate tells something about the subject. For example:

The dancers / **performed** on stage.

The **verb** is the key word in the predicate because it tells what the subject does or has. Verbs can also link together words in the subject and the predicate.

Action Verbs	Examples
An **action verb** tells what the subject of a sentence does. Most verbs are action verbs.	Dancers **practice** for many hours. They **stretch** their muscles and **lift** weights.
Some **action verbs** tell about an action that you cannot see.	The dancers **recognize** the rewards that come from their hard work.

Linking Verbs	Examples
A **linking verb** connects, or links, the subject of a sentence to a word in the predicate. Forms of the verb *be* are most commonly used, but other verbs are used as well.	

Forms of the Verb *Be*

am	are	were
is	was	

Other Linking Verbs

appear	seem	become
feel	smell	taste
look		

The word in the predicate can describe the subject.

Their feet **are** calloused.

Or the word in the predicate can rename the subject.

These dancers **are** athletes.

Helping Verbs	Examples
Some verbs are made up of more than one word. They need help to show exactly what is happening.	Ballet **is considered** a dramatic art form. helping verb · main verb
The action word is called the **main verb**. It shows what the subject does, has, or is.	This dance form **has been evolving** over the years. helping verbs · main verb
Any verbs that come before the **main** verb are the **helping verbs**.	Ballet **must have been** very different in the 1500s. helping verbs · main verb

Helping Verbs

Forms of the Verb *Be*	Forms of the Verb *Do*	Forms of the Verb *Have*
am are were is was	do did does	have had has

Other Helping Verbs

To express ability:
  can, **could**

I **can** dance.

To express possibility:
  may, **might**, **could**

I **might** dance tonight.

To express necessity or desire:
  must, **would**

I **must** dance more often.
I **would** like to dance more often.

To express certainty:
  will, **shall**

I **will** dance more often.

To express obligation:
  should, **ought**

I **should** practice more often.
I **ought** to practice more often.

Helping verbs agree with the subject.	Baryshnikov **has performed** around the world. Many people **have praised** this famous dancer.
In negative sentences, the adverb "*not*" always comes between the **helping verb** and the main verb.	If you **have** not **heard** of him, you can watch the film *Dancers* to see him perform.
In questions, the subject comes between the **helping verb** and the **main verb**.	**Have** you **heard** of Mikhail Baryshnikov?

Verb Tense: Past, Present, Future

The **tense** of a verb shows when an action happens.

Present Tense Verbs	Examples
The **present tense** of a verb tells about an action that is happening now.	Greg **checks** his watch to see if it is time to leave. He **starts** work at 5:00 today.

Habitual Present Tense Verbs	Examples
The **habitual present tense** of a verb tells about an action that happens regularly or all the time.	Greg **works** at a pizza shop. He **makes** pizzas and **washes** dishes.

Past Tense Verbs (Regular and Irregular)	Examples
The **past tense** of a verb tells about an action that happened earlier, or in the past. • The past tense form of **regular verbs** ends with -**ed**. • **Irregular verbs** have **special forms** to show the past tense. Here are some examples of irregular verbs:	Yesterday, Greg **worked** until the shop closed. He **made** 50 pizzas. He **learned** how to make a stuffed-crust pizza. Then Greg **chopped** onions and peppers. Greg **cut** the pizza. It **was** delicious. We **ate** all of it!

Present Tense	Past Tense
cut	cut
is	was
eat	ate

Future Tense Verbs	Examples
The **future tense** of a verb tells about an action that will happen later, or in the future. To show future tense, use: • the helping verb **will** plus a main verb • the phrase **am going to**, **is going to**, or **are going to** plus a verb.	Greg **will ride** the bus home after work tonight. Greg's mother **will drive** him to work tomorrow. On Friday, he **will get** his first paycheck. He **is going to** take a pizza home to his family. They **are going to** eat the pizza for dinner.

Verb Tense: Perfect Tenses

All verbs in the **perfect tenses—present perfect, past perfect**, and **future perfect**—have a helping verb and a form of the main verb that is called the **past participle**.

Present Perfect Tense Verbs	Examples
The **present perfect tense** of a verb uses the helping verb **has** or **have** plus the past participle.	
Use the present perfect tense to tell about something that happened at an unknown time in the past.	I **have looked** things up on the Internet.
You can also use the present perfect tense to tell about something that happened in the past and may still be going on.	The public **has used** the Internet since the 1980s.
For **regular verbs**, past participle ends in -**ed**. **Present Tense** like **Past Participle** liked	I like the Internet. I **have** always **liked** the Internet.
Irregular verbs have **special forms** for the past participle. See pages 517–518. **Present Tense** know **Past Participle** known	I know a lot about the Internet. I **have known** about it for a long time.

Past Perfect Tense Verbs	Examples
The **past perfect tense** of a verb tells about an action that was completed before some other action in the past. It uses the helping verb **had**.	My grandmother **had graduated** from high school before computers were even invented!

Future Perfect Tense Verbs	Examples
The **future perfect tense** of a verb tells about an action that will be completed at a specific time in the future. It uses the helping verbs **will have**.	By the end of next year, 100,000 people **will have visited** our Web site.

Verb Forms

The **form** a verb takes changes depending on how it is used in a sentence, phrase, or clause.

Progressive Verbs	Examples
The **progressive** verb forms tell about an action that occurs over a period of time.	
The **present progressive** form of a verb tells about an action as it is happening.	They **are expecting** a big crowd for the fireworks show this evening.
• It uses the helping verb **am**, **is**, or **are**. The main verb ends in -**ing**.	**Are** you **expecting** the rain to end before the show starts?
The **past progressive** form of a verb tells about an action that was happening over a period of time in the past.	They **were thinking** of canceling the fireworks.
• It uses the helping verb **was** or **were** and a main verb. The main verb ends in -**ing**.	A tornado **was heading** in this direction.
The **future progressive** form of a verb tells about an action that will be happening over a period of time in the future.	The weather forecasters **will be watching** for tornados.
• It uses the helping verbs **will be** plus a main verb. The main verb ends in -**ing**.	I hope that they **will** not **be canceling** the show.

Transitive and Intransitive Verbs	Examples
Action verbs can be transitive or intransitive. A **transitive verb** needs an **object** to complete its meaning and to receive the action of the verb.	**Not complete:** **Complete:** Many cities **use** Many cities **use** fireworks.
The object can be a **direct object**. A direct object answers the question *Whom*? or *What*?	**Whom:** The noise **surprises** the audience. **What:** The people in the audience **cover** their ears.
An **intransitive verb** does not need an object to complete its meaning.	**Complete:** The people in our neighborhood **clap**. They **shout**. They **laugh**.
An **intransitive verb** may end the sentence, or it may be followed by other words that tell how, where, or when. These words are not objects since they do not receive the action of the verb.	The fireworks **glow** brightly. Then, slowly, they **disappear** in the sky. The show **ends** by midnight.

Active and Passive Voice	Examples
A verb is in **active voice** if the **subject** is doing the action.	Many cities **hold** fireworks displays for the Fourth of July.
A verb is in **passive voice** if the **subject** is not doing the action.	Fireworks displays **are held** by many cities for the Fourth of July.

Two-Word Verbs

A **two-word verb** is a verb followed by a preposition. The meaning of the two-word verb is different from the meaning of the verb by itself.

Some Two-Word Verbs

Verb	Meaning	Example
break	to split into pieces	I didn't **break** the window with the ball.
break down	to stop working	Did the car **break down** again?
break up	to end	The party will **break up** before midnight.
	to come apart	The ice on the lake will **break up** in the spring.
check	to make sure you are right	We can **check** our answers at the back of the book.
check in	to stay in touch with someone	I **check in** with my mom at work.
check up	to see if everything is okay	The nurse **checks up** on the patient every hour.
check off	to mark off a list	Look at your list and **check off** the girls' names.
check out	to look at something carefully	Hey, Marisa, **check out** my new bike!
fill	to place as much as can be held	**Fill** the pail with water.
fill in	to color or shade in a space	Please **fill in** the circle.
fill out	to complete	Marcos **fills out** a form to order a book.
get	to receive	I often **get** letters from my pen pal.
get ahead	to go beyond what is expected	She worked hard to **get ahead** in math class.
get along	to be on good terms with	Do you **get along** with your sister?
get out	to leave	Let's **get out** of the kitchen.
get over	to feel better	I hope you'll **get over** the flu soon.
get through	to finish	I can **get through** this book tonight.

Verb Forms, continued

Verb	Meaning	Example
give	to hand something to someone	We **give** presents to the children.
give out	to stop working	If she runs ten miles, her energy will **give out**.
give up	to quit	I'm going to **give up** eating candy.
go	to move from place to place	Did you **go** to the mall on Saturday?
go on	to continue	Why do the boys **go on** playing after the bell rings?
go out	to go someplace special	Let's **go out** to lunch on Saturday.
look	to see or watch	Don't **look** directly at the sun.
look forward	to be excited about something	My brothers **look forward** to summer vacation.
look over	to review	She **looks over** her test before finishing.
look up	to hunt for and find	We **look up** information on the Internet.
pick	to choose	I'd **pick** Lin for class president.
pick on	to bother or tease	My older brothers always **pick on** me.
pick up	to increase	Business **picks up** in the summer.
	to gather or collect	**Pick up** your clothes!
run	to move quickly	Juan will **run** in a marathon.
run into	to unexpectedly see someone	Did you **run into** Chris at the store?
run out	to suddenly have nothing left	The cafeteria always **runs out** of nachos.
stand	to be on your feet	I have to **stand** in line to buy tickets.
stand for	to represent	A heart **stands for** love.
stand out	to be easier to see	You'll **stand out** with that orange cap.
turn	to change direction	We **turn** right at the next corner.
turn up	to appear	Clean your closet and your belt will **turn up**.
	to raise the volume	Please **turn up** the radio.
turn in	to go to bed	On school nights I **turn in** at 9:30.
	to present or submit	You didn't **turn in** the homework yesterday.
turn off	to make something stop	Please **turn off** the radio.

Forms of Irregular Verbs

Irregular verbs do not follow the same rules of conjugation as the "regular" verbs do. These verb forms have to be memorized. Here are some irregular verbs.

Irregular Verb	Past Tense	Past Participle	Irregular Verb	Past Tense	Past Participle
be: am, is, are	was, were	been	eat	ate	eaten
beat	beat	beaten	fall	fell	fallen
become	became	become	feed	fed	fed
begin	began	begun	feel	felt	felt
bend	bent	bent	fight	fought	fought
bind	bound	bound	find	found	found
bite	bit	bitten	fly	flew	flown
blow	blew	blown	forget	forgot	forgotten
break	broke	broken	forgive	forgave	forgiven
bring	brought	brought	freeze	froze	frozen
build	built	built	get	got	gotten
burst	burst	burst	give	gave	given
buy	bought	bought	go	went	gone
catch	caught	caught	grow	grew	grown
choose	chose	chosen	have	had	had
come	came	come	hear	heard	heard
cost	cost	cost	hide	hid	hidden
creep	crept	crept	hit	hit	hit
cut	cut	cut	hold	held	held
dig	dug	dug	hurt	hurt	hurt
do	did	done	keep	kept	kept
draw	drew	drawn	know	knew	known
drink	drank	drunk	lead	led	led
drive	drove	driven	leave	left	left

Verb Forms, continued

Forms of Irregular Verbs

Irregular Verb	Past Tense	Past Participle	Irregular Verb	Past Tense	Past Participle
let	let	let	sink	sank	sunk
light	lit	lit	sit	sat	sat
lose	lost	lost	sleep	slept	slept
make	made	made	slide	slid	slid
mean	meant	meant	speak	spoke	spoken
meet	met	met	spend	spent	spent
pay	paid	paid	stand	stood	stood
prove	proved	proved, proven	steal	stole	stolen
put	put	put	stick	stuck	stuck
read	read	read	sting	stung	stung
ride	rode	ridden	strike	struck	struck
ring	rang	rung	swear	swore	sworn
rise	rose	risen	swim	swam	swum
run	ran	run	swing	swung	swung
say	said	said	take	took	taken
see	saw	seen	teach	taught	taught
seek	sought	sought	tear	tore	torn
sell	sold	sold	tell	told	told
send	sent	sent	think	thought	thought
set	set	set	throw	threw	thrown
shake	shook	shaken	wake	woke, waked	woken, waked
show	showed	shown	wear	wore	worn
shrink	shrank	shrunk	win	won	won
sing	sang	sung	write	wrote	written

Verbals

A **verbal** is a word made from a verb but used as another part of speech.

Gerunds	Examples
A **gerund** is a verb form that ends in -**ing** and that is used as a noun. Like all nouns, a gerund can be the subject of a sentence or an object.	**Cooking** is Mr. Jiménez's favorite hobby. *subject* Mr. Jiménez truly enjoys **cooking**. *direct object* Mr. Jiménez is very talented at **cooking**. *object of preposition*

Infinitives	Examples
An **infinitive** is a verb form that begins with **to**. It can be used as a noun, an adjective, or an adverb.	Mr. Jiménez likes **to cook**. *noun* Mr. Jiménez's beef tamales are a sight **to see**. *adjective* Mr. Jiménez cooks **to relax**. *adverb*

Participial Phrases	Examples
A **participle** is a verb form that is used as an adjective. For regular verbs, it ends in -**ing** or -**ed**. Irregular verbs take the past participle form. See pages 517–518.	His **sizzling** fajitas taste delicious. Mr. Jiménez also makes tasty **frozen** desserts.
A **participial phrase** begins with a participle. Place the phrase next to the noun it describes.	**Standing by the grill**, he soon had the hamburgers cooked to perfection. **Not:** He soon had the hamburgers cooked to perfection standing by the grill.

A phrase that utilizes a gerund, an infinitive, or a participle is known as a **verbal phrase**.

Contractions

A **contraction** is a shortened form of a verb plus the word *not,* or of a verb-and-pronoun combination.

Contractions	Examples
Use an **apostrophe** to show which letters have been left out of the contraction.	is net = isn't I would = I'd can net = can't They are = They're
In contractions made up of a verb and the word **not**, the word **not** is usually shortened to **n't**.	I **can't** stop eating these cookies!

Adverbs

An **adverb** describes a verb, an adjective, or another adverb.

Adverbs	Examples
Adverbs answer one of the following questions: • How? • Where? • When? • How much? or How often?	**Carefully** aim the ball. Kick the ball **here**. Try again **later** to make a goal. Cathy **usually** scores.
An adverb can come before or after a **verb**.	Our team **always wins**. The whole team **plays well**.
An adverb can modify the meaning of an **adjective** or another **adverb**.	Gina is **really good** at soccer. She plays **very well**.

Adverbs That Compare	Examples
Some **adverbs** compare actions. Add -**er** to compare the actions of two people. Add -**est** to compare the actions of three or more people.	Gina runs **fast**. Gina runs **faster** than Maria. Gina runs **the fastest** of all the players.
If the adverb ends in -**ly**, use **more** or **less** to compare two actions.	Gina aims **more carefully** than Jen. Jen aims **less carefully** than Gina.
Use **the most** or **the least** to compare three or more actions.	Gina aims **the most carefully** of all the players. Jen aims **the least carefully** of all the players.

Prepositions

A **preposition** comes at the beginning of a prepositional phrase. **Prepositional phrases** add details to sentences.

Uses of Prepositions				Examples
Some prepositions show **location**.				The Chávez Community Center is **by my house**.
behind	between	inside	outside	The pool is **behind the building**.
below	by	near	over	
beside	in	on	under	
Some prepositions show **time**.				The Teen Club's party will start **after lunch**.
after	before	during	until	
Some prepositions show **direction**.				Go **through the building** and **around the fountain** to get **to the pool**.
across	down	out of	toward	The snack bar is **down the hall**.
around	into	through	up	
Some prepositions have **multiple uses**.				We might see Joshua **at the party**.
about	among	for	to	Meet me **at my house**.
against	as	from	with	Come **at noon**.
along	at	of	without	

Prepositional Phrases	Examples
A **prepositional phrase** starts with a preposition and ends with a noun or a pronoun. It includes all the words in between. The noun or pronoun is the **object of the preposition**.	I live **near the Chávez Community Center**. *object of preposition* Tom wants to walk there **with you and me**. *objects of preposition*
Prepositional phrases can function either as **adjectives** or as **adverbs**. • They function as **adjectives** when they serve to modify a noun or pronoun. • They function as **adverbs** when they serve to modify a verb, an adjective, or another adverb.	The **guy in the yellow shirt and khaki pants** is my friend Joel. He is **excited about the new Chávez Center**. He wants to **come with us**.

Conjunctions

A **conjunction** connects words or groups of words.

Conjunctions	Examples
A **coordinating conjunction** connects words, phrases, or clauses.	
To show similarity: **and**	Irena **and** Irving are twins.
To show difference: **but**, **yet**	I know Irena, **but** I do not know Irving.
To show choice: **or**	They will celebrate their birthday Friday **or** Saturday night.
To show cause/effect: **so**, **for**	I have a cold, **so** I cannot go to the party.
To put negative ideas together: **nor**	My mother will not let me go, **nor** will my father.
Correlative conjunctions are used in pairs. The pair connects phrases or words.	**Some Correlative Conjunctions** both … and — not only … but also either … or — whether … or neither … nor
A **subordinating conjunction** introduces a **dependent clause** in a complex sentence. It connects the **dependent clause** to the main clause.	**Some Subordinating Conjunctions** after — before — till although — if — until as — in order that — when as if — since — where as long as — so that — while because — though
A **conjunctive adverb** joins two independent clauses. Use a semicolon before the conjunction and a comma after it.	**Some Conjunctive Adverbs** besides — meanwhile — then consequently — moreover — therefore however — nevertheless — thus

Interjections

An **interjection** expresses strong feeling or emotion.

Interjections	Examples
An **interjection** shows emotion. If an interjection stands alone, follow it with an exclamation point.	**Help!** **Oops!** **Oh boy!**
An interjection used in a sentence can be followed by a comma or an exclamation mark. Use a comma after a weak interjection. Use an exclamation mark after a strong interjection.	**Oh**, it's a baby panda! **Hooray**! The baby panda has survived!

Capitalization

Knowing when to use capital letters is an important part of clear writing.

First Word in a Sentence	Examples
Capitalize the first word in a sentence.	**W**e are studying the Lewis and Clark expedition.

In Direct Quotations	Examples
Capitalize the first word in a **direct quotation**.	Clark said, "**There is great joy in camp**." "**We are in view of the ocean**," he said. "**It's the Pacific Ocean**," he added.

In Letters	Examples
Capitalize the first word used in the **greeting** or in the **closing** of a letter.	**D**ear Kim, **Y**our friend,

In Titles of Works	Examples
All important words in a **title** begin with a capital letter. Short words like *a, an, the, in, at, of,* and *for* are not capitalized unless they are the first or last word in the title.	**book:** *The Longest Journey* **poem:** "Leaves of Grass" **magazine:** *Flora and Fauna of Arizona* **newspaper:** *The Denver Post* **song:** "The Star-Spangled Banner" **game:** Exploration! **TV series:** "The Gilmore Girls" **movie:** *The Lion King*

Pronoun *I*	Examples
Capitalize the pronoun *I* no matter where it is located in a sentence.	**I** was amazed when **I** learned that Lewis and Clark's expedition was over 8,000 miles.

Proper Nouns and Adjectives	Examples
Common nouns name a general person, place, thing, or idea. Proper nouns name a particular person, place, thing, or idea. All the important words in a **proper noun** start with a capital letter.	**Common Noun:** team **Proper Noun:** **C**orps of **D**estiny
Proper nouns include the following: • names of people and their titles Do not capitalize a title if it is used without a name. • family titles like *Mom* and *Dad* when they are used as names.	**S**tephanie **E**ddins **C**aptain **M**eriwether **L**ewis The **captain's** co-leader on the expedition was William Clark. "William Clark is one of our ancestors," **Mom** said. I asked my **mom** whose side of the family he was on, hers or my **dad's**.
• names of organizations	United Nations History Club Wildlife Society
• names of languages and religions	Spanish Christianity
• months, days, special days, and holidays	April Sunday Thanksgiving
Names of geographic places are proper nouns. Capitalize street, city, and state names in mailing addresses.	**Cities and States:** Dallas, Texas **Streets and Roads:** Main Avenue **Bodies of Water:** Pacific Ocean **Countries:** Ecuador **Landforms:** Sahara Desert **Continents:** North America **Public Spaces:** Muir Camp **Buildings, Ships, and Monuments:** *Titanic* **Planets and Heavenly Bodies:** Neptune
A **proper adjective** is formed from a **proper noun**. Capitalize proper adjectives.	Napoleon Bonaparte was from **Europe**. He was a **European** leader in the 1800s.

Capitalization, continued

Abbreviations of Proper Nouns

Abbreviations of geographic places are also capitalized.

Words Used in Addresses

Avenue	Ave.	Drive	Dr.	North	N.	Suite	Ste.
Apartment	Apt.	East	E.	Place	Pl.	West	W.
Boulevard	Blvd.	Highway	Hwy.	South	S.		
Court	Ct.	Lane	Ln.	Street	St.		

State Names

Alabama	AL	Indiana	IN	Nebraska	NE	South Carolina	SC
Alaska	AK	Iowa	IA	Nevada	NV	South Dakota	SD
Arizona	AZ	Kansas	KS	New Hampshire	NH	Tennessee	TN
Arkansas	AR	Kentucky	KY	New Jersey	NJ	Texas	TX
California	CA	Louisiana	LA	New Mexico	NM	Utah	UT
Colorado	CO	Maine	ME	New York	NY	Vermont	VT
Connecticut	CT	Maryland	MD	North Carolina	NC	Virginia	VA
Delaware	DE	Massachusetts	MA	North Dakota	ND	Washington	WA
Florida	FL	Michigan	MI	Ohio	OH	West Virginia	WV
Georgia	GA	Minnesota	MN	Oklahoma	OK	Wisconsin	WI
Hawaii	HI	Mississippi	MS	Oregon	OR	Wyoming	WY
Idaho	ID	Missouri	MO	Pennsylvania	PA		
Illinois	IL	Montana	MT	Rhode Island	RI		

Abbreviations of Personal Titles

Capitalize abbreviations for a personal title. Follow the same rules for capitalizing a personal title.

Mr. . . . . Mister	**Mrs.** . . . . . . Missus	**Dr.** . . . . Doctor
Jr. . . . . Junior	**Capt.** . . . . . Captain	**Sen.** . . . . . . Senator

Punctuation

Punctuation marks are used to emphasize or clarify meanings.

Apostrophe	Examples
Use an **apostrophe** to punctuate a **possessive noun**.	
If there is one owner, add **'s** to the owner's name, even if the owner's name ends in **s**.	Mrs. Ramos**'s** sons live in New Mexico.
If there is more than one owner, add **'** if the plural noun ends in **s**. Add **'s** if it does not end in **s**.	Her sons**'** birthdays are both in January. My children**'s** birthdays are in March.
Use an **apostrophe** to replace the letters left out of a contraction.	could n~~ot~~ = couldn**'t** he w~~oul~~d = he**'d**

End Marks	Examples
Use a **period** at the end of a statement or a polite command.	Georgia read the paper to her mom**.** Tell me if there are any interesting articles**.**
Or use a period after an indirect question. An indirect question tells about a question you asked.	She asked if there were any articles about the new restaurant on Stone Street near their house**.**
Use a **question mark** at the end of a question. Or use a question mark after a question that comes at the end of a statement.	What kind of food do they serve**?** The food is good, isn't it**?**
Use an **exclamation mark** after an interjection. Or use an exclamation mark at the end of a sentence to show you feel strongly about something.	Wow**!** The chicken parmesan is delicious**!**

Colon	Examples
Use a **colon**:	
• after the greeting in a business letter	Dear Sir or Madam**:**
• to separate hours and minutes	The restaurant is open until 11**:**30 p.m.
• to start a list	If you decide to hold your banquet here, we can**:** 1. Provide a private room 2. Offer a special menu 3. Supply free coffee and lemonade.

Punctuation, continued

Comma	Examples
Use a **comma**:	
• before the **coordinating conjunction** in a compound sentence	Soccer is a relatively new sport in the United States, **but** it has been popular in England for a long time.
• to set off words that interrupt a sentence, such as an **appositive phrase** that is not needed to identify the word it describes	Mr. Okada, **the soccer coach,** had the team practice skills like passing, **for example,** for the first hour.
• to separate three or more items in a **series**	Shooting, passing, and dribbling are important skills.
• between two or more adjectives that tell about the same noun	The midfielder's quick, unpredictable passes made him the team's star player.
• after an **introductory phrase or clause**	**In the last game,** he made several goals.
• before someone's exact words and after them if the sentence continues	Mr. Okada said, "Meet the ball after it bounces," as we practiced our half-volleys.
• before and after a **clause** if the clause is not necessary for understanding the sentence	At the end of practice, **before anyone left,** Mr. Okada handed out revised game schedules.
• before a question at the end of a statement	You talked to Mr. Okada, **didn't you?**
• to set off the name of a person someone is talking to	Mr. Okada said, "That's not how you do it, **Jimmy.**"
Use a comma in these places in a letter:	
• between the city and the state	Milpas, AK
• between the date and the year	July 3, 2008
• after the greeting of a personal letter	Dear Mr. Okada,
• after the closing of a letter	Sincerely,

Dash	Examples
Use a **dash** to show a break in an idea or the tone in a sentence.	Water—a valuable resource—is often taken for granted.
Or use a dash to emphasize a word, a series of words, a phrase, or a clause.	It is easy to conserve water—wash full loads of laundry, use water-saving devices, fix leaky faucets.

Ellipsis	Examples
Use an **ellipsis** to show that you have left out words.	A recent survey documented **...** water usage.
Or use an ellipsis to show an idea that trails off.	I don't know **...** so much waste **...**

Hyphen	Examples
Use a **hyphen** to:	
• connect words in a number and in a fraction	**One-third** of the people surveyed used at least **thirty-two** gallons of water every day.
• join some words to make a compound word	A **15-year-old** boy and his **great-grandmother** have started an awareness campaign.
• connect a letter to a word	They designed a **T-shirt** for their campaign.
• divide words at the end of a line. Always divide the word between two syllables.	Please join us today in our awareness **campaign**. It's for the good of the planet.

Italics and Underlining	Examples
When you are using a computer, use **italics** for the names of:	
• magazines and newspapers	I like to read *Time* magazine and the *Daily News*.
• books	They help me understand our history book, *The U.S. Story*.
• plays	Did you see the play *Abraham Lincoln in Illinois*?
• movies	It was made into the movie *Young Abe*.
• musicals	The musical *Oklahoma!* is about Southwest pioneers.
• music albums	*Greatest Hits from Musicals* is my favorite album.
• TV series	Do you like the singers on the TV show *American Idol*?
If you are using handwriting, underline.	

Parentheses	Examples
Use **parentheses** around extra information in a sentence.	The new story (in the evening paper) is very interesting.

Punctuation, continued

Quotation Marks	Examples
Use **quotation marks** to show:	
• a speaker's exact words	"Listen to this!" Jim said.
• the exact words quoted from a book or other printed material	The announcement in the paper was: "The writer Josie Ramón will be at Milpas Library on Friday."
• the title of a song, poem, short story, magazine article, or newspaper article	Her famous poem "Speaking" appeared in the magazine article "How to Talk to Your Teen."
• the title of a chapter from a book	She'll be reading "Getting Along," a chapter from her new book.
• words used in a special way	We will be "all ears" at the reading.

Semicolon	Examples
Use a **semicolon**:	
• to separate two simple sentences used together without a conjunction	A group of Jim's classmates plan to attend the reading; he hopes to join them.
• before a conjunctive adverb that joins two simple sentences. Use a comma after the adverb.	Jim wanted to finish reading Josie Ramón's book this evening; however, he forgot it at school.
• to separate a group of words in a series if the words in the series already have commas	After school, Jim has to study French, health, and math; walk, feed, and brush the dog; and eat dinner.

Spelling

Correct spelling is important for clarity.

How to Learn a New Word	
1. Study the word and look up its meaning. 2. Say the word aloud. Listen as you repeat it. 3. Picture how the word looks. 4. Spell the word aloud several times. 5. Write the word several times for practice.	6. Use the word often in writing until you are sure of its spelling. 7. Keep a notebook of words that are hard for you to spell. 8. Use a dictionary to check your spelling.

Knowing spelling rules can help you when you get confused. Use the rules shown in the boxes to help improve your spelling.

Memorize Reliable Generalizations	Examples
Always put a **u** after a **q**.	The **qu**ick but **qu**iet **qu**arterback asked **qu**antities of **qu**estions. *Exceptions:* Iraq Iraqi
Use **i** before **e** except after **c**.	The f**ie**rce rec**ei**ver was ready to catch the ball. *Exceptions:* • **ei**ther, h**ei**ght, th**ei**r, w**ei**rd, s**ei**ze • w**ei**gh, n**ei**ghbor (and other words where **ei** has the long **a** sound)

Spell Correctly	Examples
If a word ends in a consonant plus **y**, change the **y** to **i** before you add -**es**, -**ed**, -**er**, or -**est**.	The coach was the happ**iest** when his players tried their best.
For words that end in a vowel plus **y**, just add -**s** or -**ed**.	For five days before the game, the team sta**yed** at practice an extra 30 minutes.
If you add -**ing** to a verb that ends in -**y**, do not change the **y** to **i**.	The players learned a lot from stud**ying** the videos of their games.
When a one-syllable word ends in one vowel and one consonant, double the final consonant before you add an ending.	Then they **planned** some new plays for the game. They were ready for their **biggest** challenge.

Using Words Correctly

This section will help you to choose between words that are often confused or misused.

a lot • allot

A lot means "many" and is always written as two words, never as one word. *Allot* means "to assign" or "to give out."

> I have **a lot** of friends who like to eat.

> We **allot** one hour for lunch.

a while • awhile

The two-word form *a while* is often preceded by the prepositions *after*, *for*, or *in*. The one-word form *awhile* is used without a preposition.

> Let's stop here for **a while**.

> Let's stop here **awhile**.

accept • except

Accept is a verb that means "to receive." *Except* can be a verb meaning "to leave out" or a preposition meaning "excluding."

> She would not **accept** any gifts, **except** the gifts that Joe sent.

advice • advise

Advice is a noun that means "ideas about how to solve a problem." *Advise* is a verb and means "to give advice."

> I will give you **advice** about your problem today, but do not ask me to **advise** you again tomorrow.

affect • effect

Affect as a verb means "to cause a change in" or "to influence." *Effect* as a verb means "to bring about." As a noun, *effect* means "result."

> Sunshine will **affect** my plants positively.

> The governor is working to **effect** change.

> The rain had no **effect** on our spirits.

ain't

Ain't is not used in formal English. Use the correct form of the verb *be* with the word *not*: *is not*, *isn't*; *are not*, or *aren't*.

> We **are not going** to sing in front of you.

> I **am not going** to practice today.

all ready • already

Use the two-word form, *all ready*, to mean "completely finished." Use the one-word form, *already*, to mean "previously."

> We waited an hour for dinner to be **all ready**.

> It is a good thing I have **already** eaten today.

alright • all right

The expression *all right* means "OK" and should be written as two words. The one-word form, *alright*, is not used in formal writing.

> I hope it is **all right** that I am early.

all together • altogether

The two-word form, *all together*, means "in a group." The one-word form, *altogether*, means "completely."

> It is **altogether** wrong that we will not be **all together** this holiday.

among • between

Use *among* when comparing more than two people or things. Use *between* when comparing a person or thing with one other person, thing, or group.

> You are **among** friends.

> We will split the money **between** Sal and Jess.

amount of • number of

Amount of is used with nouns that cannot be counted. *Number of* is used with nouns that can be counted.

> The **amount of** pollution in the air is increasing.

> A record **number of** people attended the game.

assure • ensure • insure

Assure means "to make certain." *Ensure* means "to guarantee." *Insure* means "to cover financially."

> I **assure** you that he is OK.

> I will personally **ensure** his safety.

> If the car is **insured**, the insurance company will pay to fix the damage.

being as • being that

Neither of these is used in formal English. Use *because* or *since* instead.

> I went home early **because** I was sick.

beside • besides

Beside means "next to." *Besides* means "plus" or "in addition to."

> Located **beside** the cafeteria is a vending machine.

> **Besides** being the fastest runner, she is also the nicest team member.

bring • take

Use *bring* to speak of transporting something to where you are now. Use *take* to speak of transporting something to a place where you're not now.

> **Bring** the snacks here to my house, and then we'll **take** them to the party at Ann's.

bust • busted

Neither of these is used in formal English. Use *broke* or *broken* instead.

> I **broke** the vase by accident.

> The **broken** vase cannot be fixed.

Using Words Correctly, continued

can't • hardly • scarcely

Do not use *can't* with *hardly* or *scarcely*. That would be a double negative. Use only *can't*, or use *can* plus a negative word.

> I **can't** get my work done in time.

> I **can scarcely** get my work done in time.

capital • capitol

A *capital* is a place where a government is located. A *capitol* is the actual building the government meets in.

> The **capital** of the U.S. is Washington, D.C.

> The senate met at the **capitol** to vote.

cite • site • sight

To *cite* means "to quote a source." A *site* is "a place." *Sight* can mean "the ability to see" or it can mean "something that can be seen."

> Be sure to **cite** all your sources.

> My brother works on a construction **site**.

> Dan went to the eye doctor to have his **sight** checked.

> The sunset last night was a beautiful **sight**.

complement • compliment

Complement means "something that completes" or "to complete." *Compliment* means "something nice someone says about another person" or "to praise."

> The colors you picked really **complement** each other.

> I would like to **compliment** you on your new shoes.

could have • should have • would have • might have

Be sure to use "have," not "of," with words like *could*, *should*, *would*, and *might*.

> I **would have** gone, but I didn't feel well last night.

council • counsel

A *council* is a group organized to study and plan something. To *counsel* is to give advice to someone.

> The city **council** met to discuss traffic issues.

> Mom, please **counsel** me on how to handle this situation.

different from • different than

Different from is preferred in formal English and is used with nouns and noun clauses and phrases. *Different than*, when used, is used with adverbial clauses.

> My interest in music is **different from** my friends'.

> Movies today are **different than** they used to be in the 1950s.

farther • further

Farther refers to a physical distance. *Further* refers to time or amount.

> If you go down the road a little **farther**, you will see the sign.

> We will discuss this **further** at lunch.

fewer • less

Fewer refers to things that can be counted individually. *Less* refers to things that cannot be counted individually.

> The farm had **fewer** animals than the zoo, so it was **less** fun to visit.

good • well

The adjective *good* means "pleasing," "kind," or "healthy." The adverb *well* means: "ably."

> She is a **good** person.

> I am glad to see that you are **well** again after that illness.

> You have performed **well**.

immigrate to • emigrate from

Immigrate to means "to move to a country." *Emigrate from* means "to leave a country."

> I **immigrated to** America in 2001 from Panama.

> I **emigrated from** El Salvador because of the war.

it's • its

It's is a contraction of *it is*. *Its* is a possessive word meaning "belonging to it."

> **It's** going to be a hot day.

> The dog drank all of **its** water already.

kind of • sort of

These words mean "a type of." In formal English, do not use them to mean "partly." Use *somewhat* or *rather* instead.

> The peanut is actually a **kind of** bean.

> I feel **rather** silly in this outfit.

lay • lie

Lay means "to put in a place." It is used to describe what people do with objects. *Lie* means "to recline." People can *lie* down, but they *lay* down objects. Do not confuse this use of *lie* with the verb that means "to tell an untruth."

> I will **lay** the book on this desk for you.

> I'm tired and am going to **lie** on the couch.

> If you **lie** in court, you will be punished.

learn • teach

To *learn* is "to receive information." To *teach* is "to give information."

> If we want to **learn**, we have to listen.

> She will **teach** us how to drive.

leave • let

Leave means "to go away." *Let* means "to allow."

> He will **leave** the house at noon.

> I will **let** you borrow my pen.

Using Words Correctly, continued

like • as

Like can be used either as a preposition or as a verb meaning "to care about something." *As* is a conjunction and should be used to introduce a dependent clause.

> She sometimes acts **like** a princess. But I still **like** her.

> She acts **as** if she owns the school.

loose • lose

Loose can be used as an adverb or adjective meaning "free" or "not securely attached." The verb *lose* means "to misplace" or "to be defeated."

> I let the dog **loose** and he is missing.

> Did you **lose** your homework?

> Did they **lose** the game by many points?

passed • past

Passed is a verb that means "to have moved ahead of." *Past* is a noun that means "the time before the present."

> I **passed** my English test.

> Poor grades are in the **past** now.

precede • proceed

Precede means "to come before." *Proceed* means "to go forward."

> Prewriting **precedes** drafting in the writing process.

> Turn left; then **proceed** down the next street.

principal • principle

A *principal* is "a person of authority." Principal can also mean "main." A *principle* is "a general truth or belief."

> The **principal** of our school makes an announcement every morning.

> The **principal** ingredient in baking is flour.

> The essay was based on the **principles** of effective persuasion.

raise • rise

The verb *raise* always takes an object. The verb *rise* does not take an object.

> **Raise** the curtain for the play.

> The curtain **rises**.

> I **rise** from bed every morning at six.

real • really

Real means "actual." It is an adjective used to describe nouns. *Really* means "actually" or "truly." It is an adverb used to describe verbs, adjectives, or other adverbs.

> The diamond was **real**.

> The diamond was **really** beautiful.

set • sit

The verb *set* usually means "to put something down." The verb *sit* means "to go into a seated position."

> I **set** the box on the ground.

> Please **sit** while we talk.

than • then

Than is used to compare things. *Then* means "next" and is used to tell when something took place.

> She likes fiction more **than** nonfiction.

> First, we will go to the bookstore; **then** we will go home.

they're • their • there

They're is the contraction of *they are*. *Their* is the possessive form of the pronoun *they*. *There* is used to indicate location.

> **They're** all on vacation this week.

> I want to use **their** office.

> The library is right over **there**.

> **There** are several books I want to read.

this • these • that • those

This indicates something specific that is near you. *These* is the plural form of *this*. *That* indicates something specific that is farther from you. *Those* is the plural form of *that*.

> **This** book in my hand belongs to me. **These** pens are also mine.

> **That** book over there is his. **Those** notes are his, too.

where

It is not necessary to use *at* or *to* with *where*.

> **Where** are you going?

> **Where** is Ernesto?

who • whom

Who is a subject. *Whom* is an object. If you can replace *who* or *whom* with *he*, *she*, *they*, or *it*, use *who*. If you can replace the word with *him*, *her*, or *them*, use *whom*.

> **Who** is going to finish first?

> My grandmother is a woman to **whom** I owe many thanks.

who's • whose

Who's is a contraction of *who is*. *Whose* is the possessive form of *who*.

> **Who's** coming to our dinner party?

> **Whose** car is parked in the garage?

you're • your

You're is a contraction of *you are*. *Your* is a possessive pronoun meaning "belonging to you."

> **You're** going to be late if you don't hurry.

> Is **your** backpack too heavy?

Index of Skills and Strategies

O

Observation report 384

Online catalog 441–442

Opening 107, 150–151, 282, 285, 290, 298, 306, 311, 316–317, 319, 335, 358, 360, 362, 364, 399, 478

Opinion 304–313, 314–321, 355, 362–363, 374–375, 376, 382, 399

Oral report 490–491

Organization

cause and effect in paragraphs 27, 34, 126

chronological order in paragraphs 27, 32, 112, 125

comparison and contrast in paragraphs 27, 35, 128

flow in paragraphs 55, 60, 110–111, 113, 118–121, 131

in published models 112–117

in writing for tests 118–121

logical order in paragraphs 27, 30–31, 113, 124

main idea and details in paragraphs 122–123

opinion and support in paragraphs 27, 37, 130

paragraph order in longer works 50–51, 110–111, 116–121, 132–133

problem and solution in paragraphs 27, 36, 129, 291

rubric 111

spatial order in paragraphs 27, 33, 127

topic sentence 110, 122–123

transitions 62–63, 110–111, 114–121, 134–139, 234–239, 286, 361

Organize and digest information (Research Process)

check for completeness and focus 466–467

develop an outline 468–469

synthesize ideas 464–465

Organizing your writing

during prewriting 16, 27–37, 46, 222–225, 252–253, 285, 292–293, 300, 311, 318–319, 326, 327, 335, 462–469

idea organizers 222–225

text structures 27–37

with headings 95, 378, 379, 396

Outlining 463, 468–469, 476–477

P

Paragraph

cause-and-effect 126

chronological order 125

comparison-contrast 128

logical order 124

opinion-and-support 130

problem-and-solution 129

spatial order 127

Paragraphs

flow 55, 60, 110–111, 113, 118–121, 131

focus and unity 106

main idea and details 94, 96–99, 101, 104, 106–107, 113, 122–123, 311

order in a longer work 50–51, 107, 110–111, 116–121, 132–133

organization 122–130

transitions between 62–63, 114, 116–121, 238–239

Paraphrasing 453–454

Parentheses 203, 529

Parody 385

Participles and participial phrases 200, 211, 268–269, 513, 519

Parts of speech

adjectives 266–267, 508–509

adverbs 520

conjunctions 522

interjections 523

nouns 501–502

prepositions 521

pronouns 504–507

verbs 510–519

passed / past 536

Past participle 513, 517–518

Past tense 512–513

Peer conferencing 52–54, 490

Period 203, 527

Personal narrative 48–49, 55, 82, 245, 247, 253

Persuasive appeals 308–309, 312, 348, 349, 400–401

Persuasive writing 422–423

addressing objections 307, 312, 365

ads 25, 348, 349

appeals to emotion 309, 312, 348, 349, 400–401

appeals to logic 308, 312

editorial 25, 382, 423

opinion essay 362–363, 422

persuasive essay 231, 304–313, 364–365

stating a position 27, 37, 306, 310, 313, 364

supporting arguments and opinions 37, 130, 306–312, 316–320, 362–363, 364–365, 422

Phrases 496, 497, 503, 509, 519

Plagiarism 459–461

Forms at a Glance

Student Contributors

Our thanks to the following 11th-grade students of Sandra Day O'Connor High School, in San Antonio, Texas, who contributed pieces of writing for consideration.

Zachry Addison	Sarah Chu	Bernice Garza
Hector Aguilar	Halim Chtata	Justin Garza
Louis Alvarado	Chris Clay	Stephanie Garza
Dustin Anastas	Tara Coleman	Michele Giese
Justin Apodaca	Corey Collier	Michael D. Gonzalez
Stacey Arias	Brianna Cook	Kimberly Goss
Margo Ascencio	Destiny Costley	Bernard Gottschalk
Tricia Asher	Sarah Crickmore	Clayton Graham
Laquette Barksdale	Stephen Crisp	Gerald Granato
Armando Barrera	Dash Dalrymple	Seth Greco
Joshua Bellows	Robert Degollado	Lebert Grinan
Asia Bliss	Diana Diaz	Amanda Grosch
Alexander Blue	Samantha Dralle	Chelsea Grubbs
Cristina Brantley	Rebecca Dschduden	Alyssa Hacker
Arturo Briceño	David Duggan	Abdalla Harhara
Ashley Brzostowski	Marisa Farias	Robert Harmon
Michael Bozarth	Alyssa Flores	Nathan Hay
Alexander Burke	Eric Flores	Greg Herbst
Matthew Cadena	Tabitha Flores	Gabriel Hernandez
Adam Carrillo	Elyssa Galvan	Leanna Hernandez
Ofelia Carrillo	Carmen Garcia	Adam Hinds
Anissa Castaneda	Marcus Garcia	Christopher Hooks
Jennifer Cervantes	Amanda Garza	Cary Inzerello

Nicholas Johnson

Stephen Kennick

Brenda Kibler

Joseph Kidder

Kristy Kubes

Marissa LaRochelle

Julie Lanum

Jessica Lemon

Casey Lewis

Remy Locascio

Rebekah Long

Chris Lopez

Tim Lovell

Curtis Lyon

Kelsey Mahan

Tyler Maltsberger

Adrian J. Martinez

Artemis Martinez

Nathaniel McCann

Jessica McFarlin

Casey Miles

Abraham Moreno

Charlynn Mueller

Christopher Naranjo

Gisela Navarro

Giovanni Ocasio

Carrie Olvera

J. Ouellette

Rafael Pacheco

Jeremy Parras

Molly Pierce

Carly Pratchett

Wesley Pruitt

Jessica Quiroz

Celeste Ramirez

Matthew Randel

Aaron Rickert

Laura E. Rodriguez

Samantha Ross

Samantha Runnels

Adam Saenz

Israel Saenz

Carlos Samaniego

Dominique Sanders

Alison Scollard

Ryan Sessums

Ryan Shappell

Sarah Sinclair

Michelle Skipper

Bryan Slayden

Shawn St. Hilaire

Gregory Stark

Kenzie Timmins

Casey Towle

Krizia Towler

Cassandra Trevino

Michael Trevino

Jessie Tubbs

Sky Verkaik-Bushby

Marco Vidaurri

Amanda Walker

Adria Warner

Whitney Wastel

Trenton Weaver

James Wells

Matthew Wickern

Amber Wojtek

Amanda Yanez

Steven Young

Acknowledgments and Credits

Grateful acknowledgment is given to the authors, artists, photographers, museums, publishers, and agents for permission to reprint copyrighted material. Every effort has been made to secure the appropriate permission, but if any omissions have been made, please contact the Publisher.

Page 17 "Waterwheel" from NEW AND SELECTED POEMS © 1995 by Gary Soto. Used with permission of Chronicle Books LLC, San Francisco. Visit ChronicleBooks.com

Page 51 Excerpt from TAKING SIDES, copyright © 1991 by Gary Soto, reprinted by permission of Harcourt, Inc.

Page 65 From OXFORD AMERICAN WRITER'S THESAURUS. Christine A. Lundberg. By permission of Oxford University Press, Inc.

Page 72 By permission. From MERRIAM-WEBSTER'S SCHOOL DICTIONARY ©2004 by Merriam-Webster Inc.(www.Merriam-Webster.com).

Page 79 "Little League Try-Out" by Gary Soto. Used by permission of the author.

Page 92 From ON WRITING FOR CHILDREN AND OTHER PEOPLE by Julius Lester, copyright © 2004 by Julius Lester. Used by permission of Dial Books for Young Readers, A Division of Penguin Young Readers Group, A Member of Penguin Group (USA) Inc., 345 Hudson Street, New York, NY 10014. All rights reserved.

Page 94 "How Jim Crow Travels in South" by Claude Sitton. Copyright © 1961 by The New York Times Co. Reprinted with permission.

Page 105 "Going for Water" by Robert Frost from A BOY'S WILL by Robert Frost. New York: Henry Holt Company, 1915.

Page 112 From ON WRITING FOR CHILDREN AND OTHER PEOPLE by Julius Lester. Copyright © 2004 by Julius Lester. Used by permission of Dial Books for Young Readers, A Division of Penguin Young Readers Group, A Member of Penguin Group (USA) Inc., 345 Hudson Street, New York, NY 10014. All rights reserved.

Page 142 "Why Men Have to Work" from BLACK FOLKTALES by Julius Lester, copyright © 1969 by Julius Lester. Reprinted by permission.

Page 144 Reprinted, with permission, from WHAT COLOR IS YOUR PARACHUTE? 2004 by Richard Nelson Bolles. Copyright © 2004 by Richard Nelson Bolles, Ten Speed Press, Berkeley, CA, www.tenspeed.com Subsequent editions of the book were published after 2004.

Page 160 Text from "Brer Rabbit Finally Gets Beaten," from THE TALES OF UNCLE REMUS as told by Julius Lester, copyright © 1987 by Julius Lester. Illustration from THE TALES OF UNCLE REMUS as told by Julius Lester, illustrated by Jerry Pinkney, copyright © 1987 by Jerry Pinkney. Both used by permission of Dial Books for Young Readers, A Division of Penguin Young Readers Group, A Member of Penguin Group (USA) Inc., 345 Hudson Street, New York, NY 10014. All rights reserved.

Page 163 Excerpts from FOOTSTEPS' May/June 2006 issue: TELL ME A STORY: FOLKTALES THEN AND NOW, © 2006, Carus Publishing Company, published by Cobblestone Publishing, 30 Grove Street, Suite C, Peterborough, NH 03458. All rights reserved. Used by permission of the publisher.

Page 174 From OXFORD AMERICAN WRITER'S THESAURUS. Christine A. Lundberg. By permission of Oxford University Press, Inc.

Page 184 Excerpt from DOMITILA: A CINDERELLA TALE FROM THE MEXICAN TRADITION by Jewel Reinhart Coburn © Shen's Books. Reprinted by permission.

Page 185 Text from YEH-SHEN: A CINDERELLA STORY FROM CHINA retold by Ai-Ling Louie, copyright © 1982 by Ai-Ling Louie. Illustrations from YEH-SHEN: A CINDERELLA STORY FROM CHINA retold by Ai-Ling Louie, illustrated by Ed Young, copyright © 1982 by Ed Young, illustrations. Both used by permission of

Page 390 "Stopping by Woods on a Snowy Evening" in THE POETRY OF ROBERT FROST edited by Edward Connery Lathem. Copyright 1923, 1969 by Henry Holt and Company, Copyright 1951 by Robert Frost. Reprinted by permission of Henry Holt and Company, LLC.

Page 391 "Elevator Music" by Henry Taylor. Reprinted by permission of Louisiana State University press from UNDERSTANDING FICTION: POEMS, 1956-1996 by Henry Taylor. Copyright © 1996 by Henry Taylor.

Page 392 From MOTHER by Maya Angelou, copyright © 2006 by Maya Angelou. Used by permission of Random House, Inc.

Page 393 From HAIKU. Selected and edited by Peter Washington. NY: Random House (Knopf), 2003. Originally published in Nicholas Virgilio, *Selected Haiku*, co-published by Burnt Lake Press and Black Moss Press, copyright © 1988 Nicholas A. Virgilio. Reprinted by permission.

Page 393 "A bitter morning" by James W. Hackett from hacketthaiku.com. Reprinted by permission.

Page 393 Reprinted by permission from BASHO'S HAIKU: SELECTED POEMS OF MATSUO BASHO by Matsuo Basho, translated by David Landis Barnhill. the State University of New York Press © 2004, State University of New York. All rights reserved.

Page 394 "Jenny." Words and music by Matt Brown © 2000. Used by permission.

Page 398 Sample resume adapted from CREATING YOUR HIGH SCHOOL RESUME: A STEP-BY-STEP GUIDE TO PREPARING AN EFFECTIVE RESUME FOR JOBS, COLLEGE AND TRAINING PROGRAMS (2nd Edition) by Kathryn Kraemer Troutman. Used with permission of the JIST Publishing, Inc., a Division of EMC/Paradigm Publishing, St. Paul, Minnesota.

Page 400 Excerpt from Keynote Address at the 2004 Democratic National Convention by Barack Obama. Copyright © 2004 by Barack Obama.

Page 402 "The Censors" by Luisa Valenzuela in SHORT SHORTS: AN ANTHOLOGY OF THE SHORTEST STORIES edited by Irving Howe and Ilana Wiener Howe. NY: Random House (Bantam), 1982.

Page 406 Reprinted from RESISTANCE by Janet Graber with permission of Marshall Cavendish.

Page 408 Excerpt from AMERICAN GOVERNMENT: PRINCIPLES AND PRACTICES copyright © 1991 by Glencore/McGraw Hill. Reprinted by permission.

Page 415 Excerpt from GIRLS FOR BREAKFAST by David Yoo. NY: Random House (Delacorte Press), © 2005.

Page 415 Excerpt from "For My Mother Who Gave Me the Words, and My Father Who Gave Me the Sound" by Marian Haddad in SCHEHERAZADE'S LEGACY: ARAB AND ARAB AMERICAN WOMEN ON WRITING edited by Susan Muaddi Darraj. Westport, CT: Greenwood Publishing Group, Inc. Copyright © 2004.

Page 417 Excerpt from "Hermit crab." Reprinted with permission from ENCYCLOPÆDIA BRITANNICA, © 2007 by Encyclopædia Britannica, Inc.

Page 418 Excerpt from BILL BRYSON'S AFRICAN DIARY copyright © 2002 by Bill Bryson. NY: Random House (Broadway Books). First hardcover edition published in 2002 by Doubleday UK.

Page 418 Excerpt from "Being Mean" by Gary Soto from LIVING UP THE STREET (Dell, 1990) © 1985 by Gary Soto. Used by permission of the author.

Page 419 Excerpt from THE BEAN TREES by Barbara Kingsolver. NY: Harper Collins (HarperTorch), © 1988.

Page 419 Excerpt from "Turning Japanese" by David Yoo. Copyright © 2005 by David Yoo. Reprinted with permission of the author.

Page 421 "Greenhouse in the Rain" by Jocelyn Heath. Copyright © Jocelyn Heath, 2007.

Page 426 Excerpt from "Poisonwood Bible Questions and Answers" from www.kingsolver.com. Copyright © by Barbara Kingsolver. Reprinted by permission of the Frances Goldin Literary Agency.

Page 434 Excerpt from "Fist in the Eye of God" in SMALL WONDER: ESSAYS by BARBARA KINGSOLVER. Copyright © 2002 by Barbara Kingsolver. Reprinted by permission of HarperCollins Publishers.

Page 435 Excerpt from "Covered Bridges" in HOMELAND AND OTHER STORIES by BARBARA KINGSOLVER. Copyright © 1989 by Barbara Kingsolver. Reprinted by permission of HarperCollins Publishers.

Page 443 Excerpt from COPING WITH DIABETES by Pat Kelly. First published by the Rosen Publishing Group Inc., 29 East 21st Street, New York, NY 10010. Copyright © 1998, 2000, 2003 by Pat Kelly. Reprinted by permission.

Page 454 Excerpt from "I Am a Gila Monster." The Native Conservatory website. Copyright © 2007 The Nature Conservancy.

Photographs

Advertising Archives: p348 ("Whistle" © Image courtesy of The Advertising Archives).

AGE Fotostock: p125 (pencil © Photospin); p295 (© Douglas Williams).

Alamy: p253 (© Mark J. Barrett); p310 (© Corbis Collection); p323 (application © Cn Boon); p337 (© Mike Goldwater); p358 (three boys eating ©BananaStock).

Animals Animals: p430 (© Lynn Stone).

Associated Press: p364 (© Associated Press); p401 (Barack Obama © Associated Press); p475 (© Associated Press).

Art Resource: p132 (© Schomburg Center).

Artville: p346 (Mexican money © Artville); p346 (sheet music © Artville); p346 (pen © Artville); p346 (candy © Artville); p361 (spaghetti © Artville).

BigStock: p346 (stamps © Tupungato); p346 (car © Debbie Kay); p346 (tickets © siamimages); p399(© siamimages).

Bill Smith Studio: p17 (shell © Bill Smith Studio).

Corbis: p18 (fishing trip © Larry Hirshowitz); p20 (two boys © Jose Luis Pelaez, Inc.); p29 (boys at computer © Jose Luis Pelaez, Inc.); p38 (diver © Royalty-Free/Corbis); p41 (girl long hair © Royalty-Free/Corbis); p41 (boy red shirt © Royalty-Free/Corbis); p41 (boy red and white shirt © Royalty-Free/Corbis); p41 (girl with books © Paul Barton); p43 (girl purple shirt © Michael Keller); p43 (girl with books © Royalty-Free/Corbis); p45 (boy striped shirt © Simon Marcus); p45 (girl leaning on tree © Paul Barton); p50 (girl in mirror © Ariel Skelley); p60 (© Jose Luiz Pelaez, Inc.); p61 (© Jose Luiz Pelaez, Inc.); p82 (© Jose Luiz Pelaez, Inc.); p92 (© Bettmann); p95 (man drinking © Bettmann); p96 (© Buddy Mays); p125 (contact sheet © Ansel Adams Publishing Rights Trust); p163 (© Catherine Karnow); p164 (Indian Storyteller © Catherine Karnow); p164

(campfire © Royalty-Free/Corbis); p186 (© Blue Lantern Studio); p220 (chess © Tom & Dee Ann McCarthy); p221 (moon © Corbis); p221 (boys building © Ariel Skelley); p232 (sandals © Tim McGuire); p297(thinking © Michael Prince); p303 (© Royalty-Free/Corbis); p318(© Royalty Free/Corbis); p324(© Royalty-Free/Corbis); p325(© Joseph Sohm/Visions of America); p330 (Fargo © Lake County Museum); p330(South Carolina © Lake County Museum); p330 (Palm Springs © Lake County Museum); p345 (© Jed Share and Kaoru); p350 (coins © Royalty-Free/Corbis); p346 (vote button © William Whitehurst); p354 (© Royalty-Free/Corbis); p356 (© Todd Gipstein); p360 (© Atlantide Phototravel); p361 (ravioli © Royalty-Free/Corbis); p366-367 (© Christies Images/Corbis); p368 (tomatoes © S. Kirchner/photocuisine); p374-375 (background © Royalty-Free/Corbis); p376 (© Tom Bean); p377 (Bronx © Royalty-Free/Corbis); p379(© Royalty-Free/Corbis); p381 (© John Arsenault/zefa); p382 (face © Royalty-Free/Corbis); p383 (sign © Franz Marc Frei); p383 (sattelite © Reuters); p384 (Lightbulb © Tetra Images); p387 (© Royalty-Free/Corbis); p391 (buttons © Bill Varie); p392 (© Royalty-Free/Corbis); p394-395 (background © Royalty-Free/Corbis); p396-397 (© Linda/zefa); p398 (© Royalty-Free/Corbis); p399 (red carpet © Lew Robertson); p400-401 (background © Peter Turnley); p404-405 (© B. Warnecke/plainpicture);

p406(© Hulton-Deutsch Collection); p407 (L'arc de Triomphe © Bettman); p407(Eiffel Tower © Hulton-Deutsch Collection); p409 (© Royalty-Free/Corbis); p412 (Toco Toucan © Kevin Schfer); p413 (beads © Carl & Ann Purcell); p432 (boy © Jim Craigmyle); p461 (© Royalty-Free/Corbis).

Dinodia Photo Library: p109 (© Sanjay Shah).

Fotosearch: p334 (© Fotosearch).

Getty Images: p20 (teens sitting © Arthur Tilley); p20 (teens with basketball © Arthur Tilley); p45 (girl with books © Digital Vision); p54 (© Holly Harris); p66 (© Sean Justice); p79 (baseball © Orlando/Hutton Archive); p93 (young girl © Hulton Archive); p93 (bus terminal © Ted Russell/Time Life Pictures); p95 (man pointing © William Lovelace/Express); p95 (segregated bus © Tan Wayman/Time Life Pictures/); p101 (© John-Francis Burke); p117 (© PhotoDisc); p118 (© Digital Vision); p129 (© Mike Hewitt); p135 (© Eliot Elisofon/Time Life Pictures); p146 (© Marc Romanelli/Photographer's Choice); p154 (© SW Productions); p166 (© SW Productions); p196 (© Gustavo Di Mario); p221 (couple shopping © Lee Page); p235(© Ryan McVay); p236(© altrendo images); p241(© Steve Allen); p243(© Car Culture); p257 (© PhotoDisc); p261(© Ryan McVay); p266 (Ryan McVay); p267 (© Donn Thompson); p284 (© Philip Nealey);

p288 (© Blasius Erlinger); p292 (© Javier Pierini); p297 (background © Ryan McVay); p299(© StockDisc); p307(© Donovan Reese); p314(© Jamie Squire); p322(© SW Productions); p338 (pink glasses © Mike Goldwater); p338 (black glasses © Vicky Kasala); p338 (blue glasses © Image Source Black) p340 (© Stockbyte); p341 (© Image Source); p 346 (cat © image100); p346 (chocolate © PhotoDisc); p347 (keyboard © PhotoDisc); p350 (lunch © Yellow Dog Productions); p358-359 (© Still Images); p363 (corsage © Stockbyte); p386 (actor © Emmanuel Faure); p388-389 (© Rod Morata); p390 (© Bruce Dale); p393 (© Christie's Images); p412 (Autumn leaves © Getty Images); p421 (© Martin Barraud/Photographer's Choice); p433 (© Richard Price); p440 (© Anderson Ross); p442 (© F64); p445 (© Kevin Cooley); p448 (© Tim Flach); 451 (© Tim Flach); p470 (dancing © Ron Krisel); p473 (Gila Monster body © Tim Flach); p477 (Gila Monster looking up © Tim Flach); p486 (Gila Monster © Tim Fladh); p487 (Buddy Holly © CBS Photo Archive); p488 (© Tim Flach); p489 (top Gila Monsnter © Tim Flach); p489 (top left Gila Monster © Tim Flach); p489 (center right Gila Monster © Walter Meayers Edwards); p492 (men and women reaching upwards © White Packert/Stone).

The Granger Collection: p353 (pioneers © The Granger Collection, New York); p353 (Laura Ingalls Wilder © The Granger Collection, New York).

iStock Photo: p410 (drums © Anthony J Hall).

The Image Works: p165 (Griot © Syracuse Newspapers); p333 (© Elizabeth Crews).

Julius Lester: p113 (photo courtesy of Julius Lester).

Jupiter Images: p125 (photographer © Comstock); p140 (pizza © FoodPix); p153 (studying © Thinkstock Images); p158 (© PYMCA); p221 (girls staring © StockImage); p315 (teens © Jean-Louis Bellurget); p343 (© Comstock Images); p351 (© Dynamic Graphics); p357 (newspaper © Corbis Images); p359 (boy eating © Image100); p363 (boy © BananaStock); p412 (necklace © Technnologies/PhotoObjects.net).

The Kobal Collection/Picture Desk: p32 (© 20TH CENTURY FOX).

Masterfile: p24 (boys © Masterfile); p25 (girl © Masterfile); p295 (© Garry Black); p296 (©Aluma Images); p338 (yellow glasses © Masterfile Royalty Free); p338 (two girls © Royalty Free Masterfile); p338 (blue glasses © Royalty Free Masterfile); p338 (black and white glasses © Royalty Free Masterfile); p355 (© Russell Monk); p391 (elevator passengers © Masterfile Royalty Free); p452 (© Masterfile Royalty Free); p487 (desert © Bill Frymire); p487 (jungle © Ed Gifford).

MetaPhotos: p346 (flowers © Metaphotos); p347 (bee © Metaphotos); p412 (butterfly © Metaphotos).

Minden Pictures: p416 (© Tui De Roy); p417 (© Ingrid Visser/Foto Natura); p455 (© Patricio Robles Gil/Sierra Madre), p473 (Gila Monster face © ZSSD); p477 (Gila Monster face © ZSSD); p489 (bottom left Gila Monster © ZSSD).

Moore Photography: p282 (© Shannon D. Moore).

National Geographic Image Collection: p19 (elephant © Michael Lewis).

National Geographic: p19 (Tattooed Mummy and Strange Terrain Courtesy of the publisher).

Nature Picture Library: p384 (© Kim Taylor); p423 (© Rolf Nussbaumer); p474 (© Tony Phelps); p489 (bottom right Gila Monster © John Cancalosi).

Newscom: p130 (© Alfred Eisenstadt/The National Archives/REUTERS); p347 (bottle caps © Anthony Nex); p348 (bottle caps © Anthony Nex); p372 (© REUTERS/Larry Downing).

New York Stock Photo: p173 (© Joseph A. Rosen).

Aicha Nystrom: p352 (Firoozeh Dumas © Aicha Nystrom).

PhotoDisc: p126 (flower pot © PhotoDisc); p165 (leprechaun © PhotoDisc); p170 (PhotoDisc); p315 (film © PhotoDisc);

PhotoEdit, Inc.: p131 (© Jeff Greenberg); p153 (working © Michael Newman); p156 (© Jeff Greenberg); p205 (© Michael Newman); p265 (© Kayte M. Deioma); p313 (© Tony Freeman); p323 (girls © David Young Wolfe); p329 (© Susan Van Etten); p332 (© Michael Newman); p362 (prom king © Tom Carter); p368 (young chef © Jeff Greenberg); p378 (© Spencer Grant); p438 (© Michael Newman); p467 (© Bonnie Kamin).

PhotoFest: p33 (© MGM).

Photo Researchers, Inc.: p165 (storytellers © Lawrence Migdale); p369 (moon © Frank Zullo); p489 (top right Gila Monster © Tom McHugh); p489 (center left Gila Monster © Gerald C. Kelley).

Photos.com: p17 (bamboo © photos.com); p17 (water beads © photos.com); p103 (© photos.com); p145 (© photos.com); p161 (path © photos.com); p143 (clouds © photos.com); p219 (© photos.com), p227 (© photos.com); p228 (© photos.com); p229 (© photos.com); p249 (© photos.com); p255 (© photos.com); p271(© photos.com); p281(© photos.com); p283 (© photos.com); p287 (© photos.com); p289 (© photos.com); p305 (speech © photos.com) p321(© photos.com); p336(© photos.com); p363 (the dance © photos.com); p382 (tanning © photos.com); p403 (© photos.com); p408 (© photos.com); p422 (© photos.com).

Science Photo Library: p349 (crushed cans © Damien Lovegrove); p486 (glucose molecule © Andrew Lambert Photography).

Scott B. Rosen: p244 (© Scott B. Rosen); p245 (headshot © Scott B. Rosen); p245 (climber © Scott B. Rosen).

Scott B. Rosen/Bill Smith Studio: p16 (girl tries on hats © Scott B. Rosen); p25 (camera © Scott B. Rosen); p70 (girl and dog © Scott B. Rosen); p76 (hands © Scott B. Rosen); p78 (frame © Scott B. Rosen); p83 (portfolio © Scott B. Rosen); p90 (spraying water © Scott B. Rosen); p123 (crayons © Scott B. Rosen); p126 (oil pastels © Scott B. Rosen); p115 (binder © Scott B. Rosen); p116 (binder © Scott B. Rosen); p290 (sandal © Scott B. Rosen); p331 (index cards © Scott B. Rosen); p339 (magnets © Scott B. Rosen); p349 (folder © Scott B. Rosen).

Superstock: p43 (boy gray sweatshirt © Comstock); p59 (© Comstock); p108 (© Blend Images); p232 (eyes © Comstock).

Terra Galleria: p105 (© QT Luong).

Veer: p45 (boy plaid shirt © Alloy Photography); p48 (girl pink dress © Blend Images Photography); p192 (guitar player © Stockbyte Photography); p272 (© image100 Photography).

Author Photos

p12, 16, 38, 43, 50, 70, 78 (Gary Soto Courtesy of the Author); p86, p90, 110, 113, 140, 158, 192 (Julius Lester Courtesy of the Author); p214, 218, p226, 240 (Marian Haddad Courtesy of the Author); p234, 248, 254, 260

(Marian Haddad © J. Scott Schraeder); p276, 278, 281, 289, 297, 305, 315, 323, 331, 339 (David Yoo Courtesy of the Author); p426, 432, 462, 470 (Barbara Kingsolver ©Steven L. Hopp).

Book Covers

Farrar, Straus, and Giroux Publisher: p86 "Time's Memory," by Julius Lester. Copyright © 2006. Cover used by permission of the publisher.

Greenwood Publishing Group, Inc.: p415 "Scheherazade's Legacy" Edited by Susan Muaddi Darraj. Copyright © 2004. Cover reprinted by permission of the publisher.

Grove/Atlantic, Inc.: p86, 194 "Black Folktales" by Julius Lester. Copyright © 1969. Cover used by permission of Grove/Atlantic, Inc.

Harcourt, Inc.: p13 "Mercy on These Teenage Chimps". Courtesy Harcourt, Inc.

Harper Collins Publishers: p86, p194 "Pharoh's Daughter" by Julius Lester. Copyright © 2000. Cover used by permission of the publisher. p375, p419 "The Bean Trees," Copyright © 1988. Cover used by permission of the publisher.

Harper Perennial Modern Classics: p427 "The Poisonwood Bible", Copyright © 2005. Cover used by permission of the publisher.

Pelican Grove Press: p215, 216 "Somewhere Between Mexico and a River Called Home" by Marian Haddad. Copyright © 2004. Cover reprinted by permission of Pelican Grove Press.

Penguin Books: p185 "Yeh-Shen": A Cinderella Story From China, text © Ai-Ling Louie, illustrations © Ed Young. Used by permission of Penguin. http://www.penguin.com.

Random House: p377 "When I Was Puerto Rican" by Esmeralda Santiago. Copyright © 1993. Jacket cover used by permission of Vintage Books, a division of Random House, Inc.

Shen's Books: p184 "Domitila" by Jewell Reinhart Coburn. Copyright © 2000. Cover used by permission of Shen's Books.

Fine Art

p110 *Window Looking to Panarea,* 2000 (oil on canvas) by Morrocco, Leon (b.1942)/© Private Collection. p112 *Aaron Douglas,* 1953 by Betsy Graves Reyneau (1888-1964). Oil on canvas. Gift of the Harmon Foundation. Location: National Portrait Gallery, Smithsonian Institution, Washington, DC, U.S.A. p124 *NUMBER 22,* 1949 by Jackson Pollock, © Christie's Images/CORBIS Artwork: © Pollock-Krasner Foundation/Artists Rights Society (ARS), New York. p127 *Man Loaded with Lilies,* 1950 by Diego Rivera, © Christie's Images/The Bridgeman Art Library. p133 *Aspects of Negro Life: An Idyll of the Deep South,* 1934 by Aaron Douglas

(1899-1979) © Copyright 1934. Oil on canvas, 5' x 11'7". Photo: Manu Sassoonian. Location: Schomburg Center for Research in Black Culture, The New York Public Library, New York, NY, U.S.A, Photo Credit: SCHOMBURG CENTER/Art Resource, NY. p137 M.C. Escher's "Hand with Reflecting Sphere," © 2006 The M.C. Escher Company-Holland. All Rights Reserved. p139 *Self Portrait,* 1889 by Vincent Van Gogh. © Gianni Dagli Orti/CORBIS. p195 *Maestro's Tunes,* 2003 by Nenad Mirkovich. p280 *Le Café des Artistes,* 1994 © Faith Ringgold.

Art/Illustrations

Norm Bendell: p176, p180, p182, p188, p189, p191.

Steve Bjorkman: p22, p26, p40, p47, p56, p63, p69, p77, p80, p83, p122, p150, p171, p172, p177, p178, p179, p200, p201, p204, p218, p222, p224, p226, p230 (angry teen), p234, p239, p240, p248, p254, p256, p260, p263, p269, p291, p385, p435, p437, p443, p446, p447, p465, p485, p490, p532, p533, p534, p537.

Rudy Gutierrez: p10, p84, p212, p274, p424.

Grizelda Holderness: p143.

Samuel A. Minik: p228, p229, p230 (object icons).

Wendy Wax: p304, 395.

Winson Trang: p317.